The
South
Atlantic
Quarterly
Fall 1996
Volume 95
Number 4

Dear Bruce

This to the recollection of an enjoyable conversation — you, Alison, me — driving back from Rutgers to NYC, sometime in April 1995.

As ever
Ian.

The *South Atlantic Quarterly* (ISSN 0038-2876) is published quarterly, at $75.00 for libraries and institutions and $28.00 for individuals, by Duke University Press, 905 W. Main St., 18-B, Durham, NC 27701. Periodicals postage paid at Durham, NC. POSTMASTER: Send address changes to *South Atlantic Quarterly*, Box 90660, Duke University, Durham, NC 27708-0660.

Photocopying. Photocopies for course or research use that are supplied to the end-user at no cost may be made without need for explicit permission or fee. Photocopies that are to be provided to their end-users for some photocopying fee may not be made without payment of permissions fees to Duke University Press, at $1.50 per copy for each article copied.

Permissions. Requests for permission to republish copyrighted material from this journal should be addressed to Permissions Editor, Duke University Press, Box 90660, Durham, NC 27708-0660.

Library exchanges and orders for them should be sent to Duke University Library, Gift and Exchange Department, Durham, NC 27708.

The *South Atlantic Quarterly* is indexed in *Abstracts of English Studies, Academic Abstracts, Academic Index, America: History and Life, American Bibliography of Slavic & East European Studies, American Humanities Index, Arts & Humanities Citation Index, Book Review Index, CERDIC, Children's Book Review Index (1965–), Current Contents, Historical Abstracts, Humanities Index, Index to Book Reviews in the Humanities, LCR, Middle East: Abstract & Index, MLA Bibliography, PAIS,* and *Social Science Source.* This journal is a member of the Council of Editors of Learned Journals.

ISSN 0038-2876

ISBN for this issue: 0-8223-6440-9

Ethical Politics

SPECIAL ISSUE EDITOR: VASSILIS LAMBROPOULOS

Introduction: Approaches to Ethical
Politics   849
VASSILIS LAMBROPOULOS

Nomoscopic Analysis   855
VASSILIS LAMBROPOULOS

When There Are Gray Skies: Aristophanes'
Clouds and the Political Education of
Democratic Citizens   881
J. PETER EUBEN

The Case of the Resistant Captive   919
LEONARD TENNENHOUSE

The Ethical Reaches of Authorship   947
PETER JASZI AND MARTHA WOODMANSEE

From Exegesis to Ethics: Recognition and Its
Vicissitudes in Saul Bellow and Chester Himes
979
ADAM ZACHARY NEWTON

Sade: The Boudoir and the City   1009
CLAUDE LEFORT

The Text as Legislator: *Devoir* and the
Millennial Stendhal   1029
RICHARD H. WEISBERG

The
South
Atlantic
Quarterly
Fall 1996
Volume 95
Number 4

We Endure, Therefore We Are: Survival,
Governance, and Zhang Yimou's *To Live*   1039
REY CHOW

Political Theology and Reason of State
in *Samson Agonistes*   1065
VICTORIA KAHN

Literary Theory in Civil Life   1099
IAN HUNTER

Notes on Contributors   1135

Index to Volume 95   1137

STATEMENT OF OWNERSHIP AND MANAGEMENT. *The South Atlantic Quarterly* (ISSN 0038-2876) is published four times a year in Winter, Spring, Summer, and Fall by Duke University Press. The Office of Publication and General Business Office are located at 905 W. Main St., 18-B, Durham, NC 27701. The editor is Fredric Jameson at 115 Art Museum, Duke University, Durham, NC 27708-0676. The owner is Duke University Press, Durham, NC 27708-0660. There are no bondholders, mortgagees, or other security holders. EXTENT AND NATURE OF CIRCULATION. *Average number of copies of each issue published during the preceding twelve months*: (A) total number of copies printed, 2369; (B.1) sales through dealers and carriers, street vendors and counter sales, 277; (B.2) paid mail subscriptions, 1140; (C) total paid circulation, 1417; (D) samples, complimentary, and other free copies, 115; (E) free distribution outside the mail (carriers or other means), 0; (F) total free distribution (sum of D & E), 115; (G) total distribution (sum of C & F) 1532; (H.1) office use, left over, unaccounted, spoiled after printing, 837; (H.2) returns from news agents, 0; (I) total, 2369. *Actual number of copies of single issue published nearest to filing date*: (A) total number of copies printed, 2489; (B.1) sales through dealers and carriers, street vendors and counter sales, 275; (B.2) paid mail subscriptions, 1135; (C) total paid circulation, 1410; (D) samples, complimentary, and other free copies, 112; (E) free distribution outside the mail (carriers or other means), 0; (F) total free distribution (sum of D & E) 112; (G) total distribution (sum of C & F), 1522; (H.1) office use, left over, unaccounted, spoiled after printing, 967; (H.2) returns from news agents, 0; (I) total, 2489.

Vassilis Lambropoulos

Introduction: Approaches to Ethical Politics

Ethical politics is neither a field nor a trend within scholarship. It is, rather, a focal point around which diverse modes of inquiry that are breaking with poststructuralism and cultural studies now tend to coalesce. It is the point where republicanism, socialism, communitarianism, feminism, and multiculturalism, as well as theories of the polis, civil society, public virtue, and the law, converge when they abandon negative hermeneutics and its denunciation of secularism, to take a worldly interest in ethical questions of justice and governance. What is ethical about these questions is precisely their constructive emphasis on *ethos*—the autonomous and collective constitution of a polity based on local, shared, and negotiable democratic values and practices. Viewed in this light, the most comprehensive expression of ethical conduct in a republic is citizenship.

Given this grid of ethico-political directions, when the editor of *SAQ* read my "Nomoscopic Analysis" (included here) and invited me to guest-edit a special issue based on its main ideas, I had a much better sense of the audience for such an issue than of its pool of prospective

The *South Atlantic Quarterly* 95:4, Fall 1996.
Copyright © 1996 by Duke University Press.

writers. Thus I could not set out to cover an existing domain by including representative voices. Instead, I had to seek contributors whose work, regardless of period and provenance, exemplifies the best and most wide-ranging possibilities for this kind of inquiry. I began approaching colleagues in late 1994 with the following statement of purpose.

Over the last few years it has been increasingly acknowledged that identity politics has led interpretative research in the human and social sciences (not to mention debates in the public domain) to a dead end. The hope that the turn from an analysis of texts, events, lives, and facts to the study of culture would revitalize fields such as language and literature, history, sociology, or anthropology was only partially fulfilled. In the end, cultural studies, with its exclusive focus on identity and its representations, created a widespread sense of weariness or fatigue as a new generation of scholars specialized in competing narratives of suffering and resistance.

One reaction to the impasse of this particularism is the segregationist stance, determined to protect the interests of its own minority at all costs. Another is the postmodern emphasis on multiple identities—developed at the crosscurrents of oceans and the crossing posts of borders—that refuse singular categorization. However, in both cases the primary concern is still with subject positions and identity formation as well as their accompanying themes of oppression and redemption.

It seems that in order to overcome the monotony of cultural politics we need not a different approach to identity, be it essentialist or interstitial, but a historicist comprehension of its institutional, especially its legal, logic. Interest in identity has long been motivated by a strong attachment to group rights. The poststructuralist thematization of activism is predicated on the hypostatization of otherness and the pursuit of warrants for collective identity. The sense of exhaustion has been caused by the fragmentation of mass alliances and the proliferation of collectivities insisting on ever-expanding lists of rights for marginalized texts, canons, voices, diets, bodies, faiths, languages, practices, or communities. The current pursuit of social empowerment through judicial avenues is based on a formalist view more dedicated to compensatory benefits and advantages than to civil and political rights, the public good, or civic virtue.

It is conceivable, though, that the best interests (in fairness, equality, power, or ethics) of the recent ethnographic turn of theory to the study of minority cultures can be combined in a different configuration. The principle that cuts across these interests and gives them their ethical force is the latent idea of political justice. If we take identity and the narratives of victimization away from their engagement with discrimination and compensatory natural rights, we see that the ultimate commitment of theory belongs to the idea of justice as the reinstitution of proportional reciprocity when there are demands for representative apportioning.

In a remarkable convergence, many strands of recent European and American philosophy and political theory (the late Foucault, Derrida, Castoriadis, Lyotard, Habermas, Heller, MacIntyre, Rawls, Williams, Walzer, Mouffe, Nussbaum, Benhabib) seem to pursue an ethical inquiry into politics. Parallel trends can also be noticed in other areas, such as legal feminism and development economics. Cultural studies has not become interested in these rich investigations yet, but can orient itself toward ethical politics by adding to its ethnographic pursuits a topic which literary humanities has neglected for a very long time: the issue of governance.

Because of its fascination with the resistance practices of the new social movements and cultural communities, theory has basked in its ascetic morals and utopian projects while exhibiting a marked aversion toward questions of authority. However, an affirmative politics of citizenship and engagement requires a return to the oldest philosophical question, that of the openly self-governed community: How should we run our society? What values should we share, and what laws should we make? And how should we adjudicate among the competing principles of legitimacy, freedom, and conduct? Thus the commitment of theory to justice and civil rights can be extended to the ethical foundations of constitutional thought and public life. Literature of any period, place, or language is a vast repository of human experience which deserves intense exploration as we begin a new search for these foundations.

For a special issue of the *South Atlantic Quarterly* on ethical politics, we are interested in papers exploring the potential contribution of literary studies to a constructive analysis of political organization—papers which promote ethical values in a citizens' state through the analysis of poetry, fiction, theater, and related genres. We are not looking for deconstructions of representation or critiques of domination but for proposals of new laws, procedures, principles, or charters which can make for a more accountable conduct of rule and a more equitable order of law. We are seeking literary scholarship which, drawing on criteria of virtue, purpose, and merit, deploys political ethics to examine how law and governance can serve justice. Such an approach could ultimately help to dissolve the most fateful differentiation of modernity, the separation of the just and the good. It could also give back to literary study the academic centrality and public relevance it has lost since the bankruptcy of the aesthetic ideology.

The essays collected here take up this challenge in a great variety of interesting, learned, productive, and sometimes complementary ways. They all have a basic starting or reference point in literature (e.g., lyric poetry, novel or novella, tragedy or comedy), but each expands into a broader domain, such as ethics, aesthetics, hermeneutics, law, statecraft, or warfare. They deal with political regimes as diverse as ancient and modern democracy, monarchy, communism, and the republic. They examine such constitutional matters as sovereignty, reason of state, the people, citizenship, freedom, violence, and revolution. Finally, they investigate the private and public morality of character, virtue, survival, resistance, recognition, and discourse, with questions of moral value and political autonomy looming large everywhere.

Had contributions been solicited from philosophers and political theorists, the task of putting together this issue would have been much easier. For some time now, tremendous work of great variety and high quality has been produced within the broader areas of ethics and politics beyond academic disciplines and specialized journals. My primary goal, however, was to find literary scholars who were also interested in moral theory and autonomy projects. I proposed that contributors establish an explicit, though quite flexible, literary starting point, if not a frame of reference, in order to counter the overwhelming enchantment of cultural studies with paraliterary forms of low culture from soaps to advertising. At the same time, I encouraged them to attempt the most demanding task, especially for literary scholars, of putting aside aesthetic understanding, that is, close, intrinsically interpretative readings. I made a point to exclude protest writing which substitutes experience for argument and draws its moral strength from other people's immoral actions. Thus the essays included here look

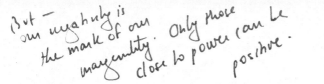

But — our unsteadiness is the mark of our marginality. Only those close to power can be positive.

at the ethico-political work, rather than the artistic nature or cultural production, of what is commonly understood as literary writing.

Another task that these essays fulfill in many promising ways is to provide representative examples of analysis and indicate avenues of inquiry.
Instead of creating a self-contained method or offering a model for instant
adoption, they outline and exemplify a set of questions that may be raised
in a study of ethical politics. Thus the issue as a whole does not constitute
a survey of a given field or a manifesto for a new trend. It is much more
tentative and provisional, content to express a strong discomfort with the
present state of humanistic scholarship, sometimes examining its sources
but more often providing glimpses of an entirely different agenda. The
consensus seems to be that this is all that can be done for now. There is
indeed a limit on this inquiry which all the contributors, more or less re-
luctantly, seem to acknowledge. I am referring to a kind of scholarship that
would be directly and explicitly edifying, in that it would offer practical
suggestions about the constitution, principles, values, rules, and institutions of a democratic ethical politics. Such suggestions about the regimes
we should build and the laws we should make emanate these days from
both conservative and progressive academic factions (such as the law and
economics movement, on the one hand, and critical race studies, on the
other). Literary and cultural studies, however, together with all the other
interpretive and historicist disciplines, still find it quite impossible (and
almost unconscionable) to engage actively with issues of governance. In
these Hellenistic times, one might say, academic intellectuals—whether of
a Cynic, Epicurean, or Stoic disposition—are still devoted to the practices
of critique that condemn the decline of political culture but at the same
time keep these intellectuals outside of the life of the polis, thus further
contributing to the erosion of its values and institutions.

Nevertheless, it seems clear in the 1990s that ethical politics is going to
continue exerting a strong influence on several disciplines and fields. In an
era when the party politics of the 1950s is not just corrupt but bankrupt,
when the social politics of the 1960s has become fragmented in separatist
communities of interest and advocacy, and when the cultural politics of
the 1980s has witnessed the collapse of both the Communist empire and
the welfare state without giving rise to any alternatives, a politics endeav-
oring to integrate the achievements of emancipatory radicalism into a civic

ethics that has shed its antinomian legacy may represent the best democratic option for the future of public engagement. To that end, ethics can contribute a renewed sense of merit, virtue, and responsibility driven by the ideals of self-governance in a citizens' polity.

Acknowledgments. In addition to the people acknowledged at the end of "Nomoscopic Analysis," I would also like to thank Nancy Armstrong, John Chioles, David Ames Curtis, John King, Satya Mohanty, Alexander Nehamas, Martha Nussbaum, Elaine Scarry, Khachig Tölölyan, Candice Ward, Luke Wilson, and especially all the contributors to this issue, for their ideas and support.

Vassilis Lambropoulos

Nomoscopic Analysis

Since the late 1980s, a growing anxiety has been evident within American (and much of European) literary studies and in the humanities more generally. This anxiety is quite different from the turmoil these fields experienced in the early 1970s with the emergence of poststructuralist theory. Even though poststructuralism often had a divisive effect, forcing scholars to side with either traditional humanism or its philosophical and ideological critique, several academic disciplines were swept by enthusiasm for the new venture—the availability of alternative methods, the possibility of interdisciplinary work, the (re)discovery of long-neglected material, the revision of the canon, and the promise of reflexivity offered by Continental thought.

The present situation is characterized less by excitement than by ennui, more a sense of boredom and exhaustion with current professional practices and scholarly ideals than a view of Theory as resting too comfortably on the laurels of its unquestionable success or as having been reduced to a spiritless exercise of interpretative virtuosity. Neither should we blame this situation on a lack of intellectual leadership,

The *South Atlantic Quarterly* 95:4, Fall 1996.

although several of the figures who pioneered the turn to Theory have since withdrawn into different, mostly private, pursuits (often of an auto-biographical nature), while their successors have been unable to sustain the intensity of their inquiry or the breadth of their analysis. The ever-increasing number of articles, books, journals, conferences, and centers in literary, cultural, and other humanistic studies does not suggest a dearth of productivity, movement, exchange, or debate. It is rather the uniform and predictable results of this extensive, polyphonic enterprise which seem to bother or bore growing numbers of scholars—the sense that more and more people are saying (albeit with increasing sophistication) fewer and fewer things of broad relevance or lasting significance.

Is this a correct assessment of large areas which are still undergoing so much reevaluation, continuing to create space for forgotten works, ex-ploited groups, marginalized approaches, outlawed experiences? Yes, if we take into account the sprawling fragmentation to which the growth of canons and interests has led. Despite the tremendous demands made on them for retraining in a variety of fields far beyond their graduate educa-tion, many people found the first wave of theoretical expansion, the move toward multi-methodological and cross-disciplinary work, challenging and exhilarating. They felt that new avenues of inquiry had burst wide open. The fragmentation came in on the second wave, however, with Theory's ethnographic turn to the study of particular cultures, habitats, and identi-ties. Having cleared an inhospitable terrain of brazenly antagonistic mar-gins, borders, and peripheries, its explorers were expected to make pledges of allegiance to specific positions and places.

This recent phenomenon has become known as identity politics on the Left and as victim politics on the Right. Both sides agree that it is the out-come of the politicization of Theory in the mid-1980s. Both labels have some validity, one articulating the essentialist thrust of the trend, the other its preference for narratives of collective suffering. But if we want to grasp its ideological bent, we need to examine closely the historical moment when Theory began to thematize political activism, namely, the transfor-mation of Theory into cultural politics.

The idea in Continental philosophy that American literary theory found most congenial to its concerns was that of negativity, especially in its articulations as otherness and difference. In many respects, this problematic was an unlikely source of illumination and incentive since its philosophical trajectory (through Nietzsche, Bergson, Heidegger, Adorno, and Deleuze) was quite alien to the influence of Hegelian and Marxist thought—not to mention analytic philosophy per se—in American intellectual circles and universities. But with the populist mediation of thinkers like Reich, Marcuse, Paul Goodman, and Norman O. Brown in the 1960s, notions of negation began to appear as countercultural principles of resistance—as criteria for a negative politics the revolutionary agenda of which stemmed from an ecstatic defiance of all authority.

In the heyday of structuralism and stylistics, the exemplary locus of this resistance had been the radical modernist text (Khlebnikov for Jakobson, Faulkner for Brooks, Proust for Genette, Lawrence for Lodge, Joyce for Eco); its self-sufficient, unyielding complexity withstood all exegetical invasion and institutional appropriation. This reconceptualization of engagement on the basis of absolute aesthetic autonomy gave the disciplines of interpretation a triumphant eminence, elevating literary criticism to model status among the human and social sciences. If the integrity of self-reflexive style could successfully repel the marketing devices of bourgeois ideology, then the comparable task for the guardians of writing and its culture was to mobilize their interpretative resistance against the forces of managerial and monological capitalism.

Following the post-1970s demise of revolutionary politics, however, the exploration of the distinct, writerly features that made the text such a vigilant voice of doubt and defiance veered off in an existential direction, which neither Marxism, psychoanalysis, phenomenology, nor critical theory had predicted—launching an effort to include in the work's intrinsic qualities the group identity (preferably racial and/or sexual) of its author, who became less important as a creator than as a representative of a particular collective orientation and tradition. Authorial intention returned with a vengeance not as personal story (of a biography) but as shared style (of a life). Furthermore, several critics (Sontag, Barthes, Harold Bloom, Lentricchia, Fish, West, Paglia) could not resist turning themselves into art by adopting the traits of a literary character. Thus revolution as self-expression was succeeded by self-expression as revolution.

Although modernist philosophers like Bloch, Wittgenstein, Ingarden, or Sartre, who fervently believed in the moral superiority of literature to the products of the media and mass culture, often saw the creator as a martyr to his vocation, they never thought that there might be any inherent heroism in the way that literature reflected the struggles of a particular group to find its identity and true voice. Even Lukács, despite his devotion to realism, would have denounced such a view as crudely mimetic. But after negativity had been literalized as aesthetic resistance, otherness was hypostatized by concrete groups of oppressed others—namely, those who had been marginalized because they were or appeared to be different. In their study of Kafka, for example, Deleuze and Guattari capitalized on the heroic aura of avant-gardism and perverted the old slogan "every writer is a Jew" to say that every minority person is a writer. Negativity was not a mere mode of aesthetic integrity, of artistic defense against alienation and assimilation; rather, it articulated the history of an oppressed collectivity as a minority's cultural experience of difference. Thus the countercultural principles of resistance were fused with both the intellectual archetype of the Jew as outcast and certain tactical lessons of the civil rights movement to produce a new, postrevolutionary paradigm of otherness—minority discourse—and its respective social technology—multiculturalism—or the managing of lifestyle diversity.

As a result, the grand philosophical narrative of identity and difference collapsed into innumerable tales of brutal discrimination and local resilience. The ensuing atmosphere of openness created an invigorating sense of liberation where the silence of exclusion was broken by cries of long suffering, demands for equality, and hopes of restitution. Testimonies of prejudice and inequity began pouring in from all corners of private and public life as individuals and groups kept coming out of confinement, exclusion, or isolation, seeking new definitions of legitimacy and practices of tolerance. But after several minorities won recognition and support, an uneasy feeling of sectarianism and balkanization settled in and is still very much with us today, since, as has been bitterly acknowledged, no public declaration or even recognition could ever turn the personal into the political. One reason is that too many stories of nativism sound the same and too many minority identities look alike for people to notice them individually, let alone be moved by each instance. After all, whether grand or small, these narratives still observe the same generic rules of suffering and redemption. Another reason is that the reigning spirit of separatism often prevails when groups fight over dwindling resources, with collectivities tending to emphasize what makes them completely distinct and unlike any other—in other words, not their need for solidarity but their superiority. In addition, acrimonious tribal antagonisms have contributed to a loss of credibility on the part of the humanities within the university as the broader intellectual community and the public at large have reacted with suspicion, if not hostility, to a situation resembling civil strife. Most importantly, it appears that the protesting minorities have learned how to denounce their opponents, but have given little thought to the kind of regime with which they would replace the present one.

Thorough and eloquent critiques of domination still offer remarkably few concrete suggestions regarding the society they implicitly envision. As a result, even though many adjustments have been made to accommodate minority demands, especially through the distribution of reparative privileges, the fundamental structures of production, administration, and management have not changed even within the university. The reason is simple: the politics of resistance may be well versed in issues of "hegemony," but it shows no understanding of authority—for example, of Gramsci's own meditations on governance. After all, without its minority status resistance would be obsolete.

Literary criticism and cultural studies have in general insisted on treating questions of power in a Manichean way that precludes any consideration of authority whatsoever. In effect, their practitioners have resigned themselves to the self-absolving idea that their fate is sealed by the overwhelming socioeconomic forces of our time—that they will always belong to the opposition and therefore need not concern themselves with governance, the effective exercise of public power. There is obviously a certain age-old allure to this moralist minimalism—the belief that the hands of the intelligentsia will never be dirtied by the concessions and compromises of government, but will remain clean as they wield the holy sword of the pen and cut a swath through the corruption of the age. It is worth remembering that this was a cardinal point of agreement between F. R. Leavis and Raymond Williams.

Take the idea of representation, with its pervasive popularity. Exegetical skills of great subtlety have been employed to posit the manipulative ways in which various groups, Western and non-Western, have been portrayed in "high" or "low" culture. The uniform goal of such approaches is to show how the very act of talking about others, let alone speaking out on their behalf, is one of violence and exclusion which colludes in silencing those who cannot participate in hegemonic games. Thus representation is denounced as exploitation, sometimes even as extermination, while this kind of study stakes its own claim to the higher moral ground of authenticity and inclusion. Ultimately, though, the issue that is elided in such an otherwise worthy unmasking of re/presentation is not presentation (i.e., how the group could faithfully present itself to others) but presence (i.e., how the group should be present to itself). If a collectivity wants to resist appropriation, then it certainly must find ways of presenting itself to those who would exploit it for their own purposes. But the means of effective resistance cannot be devised before the collectivity engages in becoming fully present, manifest, and real to itself—before establishing, instituting, and practicing its distinct character in ways that can lead to a comprehensive, meaningful, strong, and, yes, representational self-understanding. This first step requires, indeed mandates, systematic engagement in the practices of collective self-governance.

Discussions of outward representation and resistance to the imperial or panoptic gaze obscure the primary ideal of autonomy, which is not authenticity but independent, internal rule. As recent history reminds us, a day always comes when Somalis, say, or South Africans or Palestinians or Bosnians, are called upon (never without foreign intervention, of course) to run their own affairs. While years of endurance and resolve certainly prepare people for this glorious day, nothing can compare with the ultimate responsibility of internally handling and equitably distributing authority. Critiques of representation have little, if anything, to contribute to this task since the study of texts and other aspects of culture has abdicated its position to exercise political power. The same can be said about postcolonial studies, which concerns itself with the competing loyalties of the displaced intellectual and extols the advantages of hybridity and border-crossing, but has no patience with questions of state sovereignty. Intellectuals who thrive on the rites-of-passage of exile find it hard to understand why people might want a home, an identity, and a collective sense of shared space, history, and rule.

It is this self-defeating narcissism of resistance that has led the politicization of Theory to its present dead end of intensifying friction and fatigue.

As scholars and other intellectuals become aware of the growing fragmentation and isolation of innumerable research projects, each of which is focused on the invention and violation of still another (ethnic, national, linguistic, religious, sexual) identity, how can they help but despair of ever seeing such studies either combine forces in broader explorations or transcend the discursive and generic limitations of politicized Theory, specifically, the ethnography of discrimination? Furthermore, they are witnessing a disturbing parallel fragmentation of partnerships and coalitions among their own ranks as ceremonies of experience effectively turn alliances into subcultures of martyrdom while meticulously screening their membership. Personal politics promised to support small cultures of style in order to reconstitute civil society, thus enabling the anonymous shopper at the postmodern mall to safeguard an intractably idiosyncratic taste which could not be reduced to a demographic feature. The hope was that a new public sphere of shared sentiments and beliefs, of criticism and conversation, could emerge to replace the salon of the early Romantics with the support group, thus encouraging alternative modes of grassroots cooperation in community affairs. This noble hope did not take into account a major historical change since the second half of the eighteenth century — the fact that in our time culture does not constitute a separate domain, with its own independence and energy, and therefore cannot play a compensatory role. Instead, culture is now everywhere, permeating all aspects and corners of social life, and has therefore lost its distinct critical potential. Ironically, this makes cultural politics less of a bold diagnostic tool than a dominant marketing approach ("niche" culture). To admit this is not to discredit culture entirely as a major autonomous sphere of modernity but simply to place it in its present socioeconomic context.

The failure of personal politics to help bring about a new civil society, centered on the canons and institutions of culture, and its present collapse into identity politics should be attributed not only to the complete aestheticization of the public sphere in postmodernity but also to the essentialist dilemmas in which so many intellectuals are now entangled. While poststructuralism once vigorously proclaimed the provisional and positional character of its critique, it gradually began seeking some ideological indemnity for its lost philosophical legitimacy — a casualty of the deconstructivist and historicist attacks on metaphysics. Thus the face of the subject, which the high tides of Foucaldian archaeology had erased from the sands of existentialism, reappeared on the holy shroud of agency, and the enticing voices of ontology were heard again in debates on essentialism. The idea of "strategic essentialism" offered a historical compromise between skepticism and universalism for a while, giving positional understanding the advantage of a rhetoric of transcendence. But this compromise could not withstand the pressure from demands for categorical articulations of agency that would enable people to get jobs, contracts, and fellowships. (No one would settle for a provisional *academic* position.) As a result, agency and essentialism converged into a new naturalism and *professional* activism—the cultural politics of unitary group identity. In the mid-1980s, theory discussion groups were rapidly succeeded by proliferating communities of gender, race, and lifestyle whose clashing claims for givenness (nature), priority (origin), superiority (moral worth), power (entitlement), and compensation (suffering) have developed histories of collective difference and discrimination into the most valuable form of transnational cultural capital.

If we use identity politics to define the thematization of resistance in Theory, we can see that the poststructuralist concern with otherness was self-avowedly limited to a dialectical understanding of difference, an aesthetic view of negativity. To the extent that difference could never be radically disassociated from the one and the same, from its idealist heritage of antithetical thinking and conciliation, otherness remained within the synthetic horizon of identity—an interest in the spiritual ordeal of assimilation rather than in the legal trials of, say, the immigrant, the refugee, the foreigner, or the alien, let alone the disenfranchised citizen. To put it crudely, in this view the "other" was always the new resident in the suburbs, not the inhabitant of the inner city.

Ultimately, though, references to identity, useful as they often are, obscure the most important dimension of the ethnography of discrimination and the communities of culture whose special interests it promotes: a strong attachment to group rights. The goal of those who seek representation and reparation through the recognition of a unique collective identity is not merely to win acknowledgment of their distinctiveness or to preserve a tradition. Their goal is to obtain and safeguard rights on the legal basis afforded by civil society and the liberal state (which is by definition the state of right). If remarks on entitlement stress privileges, they should be balanced by an appropriate recognition of the major juridical dimension of this entire campaign. Identity politics is the strategy of "weak" (to use Vattimo's term) autonomy in an era marked by the decline of engaged citizenship and the rise of individual rights.

———

What is sometimes referred to as the rights revolution began after World War II, but probably found its most eloquent and influential American expression in the 1960s with the civil rights movement. At one crucial point in the next decade, however, and especially following the expiration of the revolutionary project, other social groups which took this movement as a model decided that the courts, rather than the backrooms or the streets, provided the best means to empowerment. Equality was to be advanced by gaining rights through legal decisions—not through legislation via administrative arrangements—with tactics shifting accordingly from regulation to litigation. As a formalist view of liberty reduced legitimacy to legality, mass politics yielded to the local politics of the critical social movements.

As I have shown in *The Rise of Eurocentrism,* the modern rule of autonomy is the regime of immanence, the formalist rule of immanent law which derives its legitimacy from its own rationality. The precondition of this autonomy was the civil liberation of (biblical) interpretation from the heteronomous law (of church/theology, tradition, and court) by the Protestant reformers and its promotion to the new supreme law, the immanent (secular) rule of the textual revelation of full, divine meaning. Thus religious autonomy, with its inherent emancipatory promise, advanced the independence of reading and its transformation into the model technology of freely chosen self-regulation. But the covenant of modern autonomy eventually led to the aesthetic nomocracy of interpretation—the absolute faith in the validity intrinsic to the form of the text or work—which culminated in the explicit aestheticization of autonomy by Kant, in his effort to reconcile freedom/morality and necessity/law, and to the further aestheticization of politics by Schiller. Critical philosophy could conceive of only the form of freedom.

Driven by the rule of autonomy, modern societies are not stratified but polycentric, not governed by an all-encompassing system but differentiated into several functional systems, into separate sub-regimes of immanence. In a society differentiated by function, systems are controlled and directed internally on the basis of their own rationality (according to the circularity of modern theoretical reasoning). Functional systems (e.g., morality, politics, law, religion, or education) operate on the assumption that they are self-organizing, self-regulating, self-producing, closed autopoietic structures. Therefore, they are endowed with the self-referential qualities of the organic artwork, drawing their justification exclusively from their own resources. Autopoiesis and validity are identical. Each separate system validates its own operations, so its validity is by definition beyond the reach of any outside normativity. Within each specialized system, everything is meaningful, purposeful, and valid. This conception eliminates questions of authority, renders the morality of social criticism impossible, and makes legitimacy a formal (i.e., interpretative and aesthetic) issue.

The values of functional systems are not moral ones. In fact, moral values are superfluous (what Luhmann, from his nihilist perspective, has called the "higher amorality of the functional code"). Morality has given up all control over the coding of systems in exchange for its own functionalization. By relinquishing its interventionist responsibilities, it has effectively withdrawn from public relevance into the security of a closed system, where it concentrates on judging only itself in moral terms. In a functionally differentiated society, the scope of ethics is limited to the justification of moral judgments. Kant's moral autonomy is formal.

The same formalism can be observed in the operationally closed legal system: on the one hand, there is no law outside it; on the other, the evaluation of its operations is possible only from within and is therefore just another of its functions. The only reality the system accepts (and for which it may thus feel responsible) is the one that it constructs. Legal formalism isolates the law from the continuum of politics, ethics, and history, endowing it with its own values. The political question of justice, the question of establishing institutions of authority which are compatible with the rule of law, lost its basic ethical dimension when politics and morals were integrated into different spheres in the eighteenth century. The separation of law from politics renders the latter inferior because, as critical legal studies has argued, legalism despises negotiation and arbitration, considering all purposive social action expedient bargaining that serves vulgar interests. In this view, all politics must be modeled on the impartial judicial process which, untainted by any ideology, serves the objective requirements of pure justice. The complementary separation of law from morals strengthens formalism in the name of reasoned agreement *my worldliness — dirty hands!*

and social cohesion. Questions of character, virtue, or responsibility are considered too arbitrary to be incorporated into the due-process system.

Western liberal theory has programmatically ignored the ethical dimension of the political question of justice by arguing that legitimacy and legality are identical. The legitimacy of modern political systems is based upon a belief in the legality of their exercise of power—in other words, it is secured by faith in the rationality intrinsic to the form of law. As a result, the bourgeois liberal state simply consists of its laws and bureaucratic regulations. The legal code is a closed system with its own distinct normativity, independent of all other spheres of thought, activity, and study. The legal system is a configuration of valid legal norms, excluding, as Kelsen demanded, propositions of law and their ethico-political value. These norms are an intrinsically valid and mutually compatible set of *legal* propositions. Modern law legitimates, makes legal, the exercise of power through its own formal properties and dispenses with the external support of morality. As Weber argued, the intrinsic justification of modern "domination" is the formal independent rationality of the law, which is able to resist ethical demands for "substantive" justice because it is morally neutral. Thus law provides positive legitimation for domination through established legal procedure. The rationality of law is exclusively a matter of law, a matter of its procedural–rational characteristics. Legal operations determine everything that pertains to law. The generality and autonomy of law supports this formal concept of justice which neutralizes the political through the general legalization of social relations: everything is juridically formalized, rationalized into a matter of law. The same constructivist (as opposed to transcendent) a priori that turns law into a fully normative closed system also makes justice immanent to the system and identifies it with positive law.

The study of law was reduced to legalism and reconstructed from a civil science to a self-conscious science of social control in the nineteenth century. The basic differentiation of the social from the political (on which the de-moralization of jurisprudence was later predicated) put legalism in charge of the former and political economy in charge of the latter. When the ethical concept of justice was transformed into a social one, the political question of justice was relegated to a new area of inquiry, the positivistic study of society. This kind of study was interested in the best possible social world, conceived as one of (individual) freedom and (public) order.

The concept of social justice was understood in terms of ideal conditions of control that enabled everyone to determine, and to exercise without outside interference, personal moral, political, or other choices. These conditions, these basic freedoms, were considered human rights. Thus the quest for the best social world shunned ethical issues and focused on problems of just procedure. The procedural view of justice sought the legitimacy of processes and the impartiality of legislative and judicial procedures.

But today we are witnessing the dissolution of the immanent rule of law because legality no longer offers an adequate basis for legitimacy. Instead it has been succeeded by the instrumentalization of basic human rights— their strategic use to achieve favorable treatment. The understanding of rights as universal, inalienable, and inviolable has been a cornerstone of modernity. But a legalistic view, extending their importance by making them natural, intrinsic, and absolute, endows them not with content but with depth—enabling them also to function as (counter-)claims before the court of a law now conceived of as a discrete entity. Indeed, because legalism holds moral conduct to be a matter of rule-following, it normativizes human relations as a matter of clashing claims adjudicated under established rules. Taking the court of law as its social paradigm, legalism concentrates on specific cases and regulations, thereby becoming a social policy for the classification of identities and the adjudication of complaints. The result is a judicialization of public life—the resolving of conflicts by judicial means and courtlike procedures.

Individual rights, which were first promoted negatively as limitations on aristocratic, court, and church authority, have become positive, processual claims on the liberal state. Now rights are no longer seen as part of the law, but rather as its very essence. These individual or group rights are all dedicated to the pursuit of private happiness, as circumscribed by experiences of cultural identity. The identity politics of the new cultural communities has entailed countering social engineering by pushing legalism to its formalist limits: since culture is now everywhere, the aesthetic presuppositions of legalism can be exploited by making interpretative (i.e., "deep") claims based on cultural identity and organic affiliation. Dreams of great social hope have been superseded by exhibitions of personal preference and group performance in the museum of racial and cultural genocide. Furthermore, this view quantifies rights and demands their detailed enumeration. In addition to traditional civil and political rights, the list of human rights now appears to include social, economic, and cultural ones. Thus it has turned into a list of birthrights and titles that individuals and groups *possess*, connoting acquisitions and advantages. These rights license behavior and authorize compensatory benefits: they are something to claim more than to practice; instead of enabling one to act, they qualify one to receive.

According to the formalist view, individual rights, whether personal or collective, are self-sufficient and therefore separate. They are something people own and bear rather than share and exercise. Rights-bearers enjoy liberty as separation, freedom as privacy. It is this legalistic discourse of rights that encourages the formation of identity as self-expression, of history as purgatorial experience. If an appeal to rights requires reference to organic and self-regulating characteristics, then a set of unique aesthetic qualities must be constructed to isolate a person or group from all others and to endow them with the formal entitlements of difference. Our political predicament today is caused not by the politics of cultural identity but by the formalism of legal rights. Cultural identity has become the postmodern expression of global citizenship, but this egalitarianism of authenticity is grounded on a segregationist essentialism. The emphasis on difference has led to nativism (territorialization of identity), while demands for recognition have produced reparationist claims for distributive justice and invocations of diversity have resulted in celebrations of autochthony. It is fair to conclude that identity politics, with its commercialization of pluralism as commodified difference, signals the end of culture as we have known it in modernity (including its critical and emancipatory potential) under disorganized corporatism. Paradoxically, we have come full circle, in a reversal of Schiller's assurances, having witnessed the politicization of aesthetics in the name of interpretative resistance.

Steering clear of identity politics, Habermas's "theory of communicative action" is based on a formal principle of right as the consensual regulation of social interaction. He believes that, given the axiological pluralism of modern societies, the ethical must be excluded from the sphere of justice. Therefore, normative rightness must reside not in shared ethical values but only in the rational structure of communication. He calls his model of practical argumentation and validity claims "discourse ethics" since it emphasizes the just normative requirements of a procedure rather than any "value ethics" (i.e., substantive ethical principles of justice). This emphasis mandates in turn a sharp differentiation (on the basis of the legality/legitimacy distinction) between universal justification (the realm of the social/moral) and situated application (the realm of the political/evaluative), thus splitting the overarching question of validity in a political society between two separate domains of inquiry. In seeking to provide a universal foundation of morality in the Kantian tradition, this theory limits itself to a formalist understanding of morality and justice; it is unable to accept ethics as the ethos of a citizens' state and as therefore embodied in specific actualizations of the political. Habermas appears to have sensed this severe limitation recently when he called for a renewal of the sentiments and values of social solidarity, warning against an exclusive emphasis on rights and visions of emancipation. However, the formal priority he continues to attribute to the defense of rational autonomy does not allow him to transcend his proceduralist paradigm. Interestingly enough, if we see the current battles among cultural minorities over group rights as a diversion from administrative and mass power to judicial and social entitlement, we can perceive in the history of rights their close connection with ideas of correctness. What is "right" is what is decreed as straight, the direct line of the ruler and the regime from above, the regal control, the reign of the supreme *directorate*. Rights constitute a protest against tyranny, setting limits to what hierarchical authority can do to people but not stipulating what people can do once they have gained access to authority. The language of rights applies to subjects, to people who are subject to rule and seek power in terms of entitlements or concessions. The search for rights and remedies, for the rectitude of judgment, is the search for valid reasons, for grounds of subjection. Thus rights are by etymology politically correct in that they are correctively political. One corollary is the increased policy-making role played by the judiciary over the course of this decade in a variety of U.S., French, Italian, and Greek cases (to limit ourselves to Western countries). Today, individual rights do not so much right a wrong as generate more rights, more specifically enumerated minor rights, more strictly defined identities based on narrower differences, more minorities vying over remedial powers and competing for accreditation.

This situation has driven federalism into a centrifugal spin of separatism while reducing citizenship to a single sanction, the right to have (multiplying) rights, with no consideration given to citizenship as a set of franchises:

the right to assume responsibilities. This consideration is political rather than moral. It has nothing to do with commandments and duties, rules of conduct and belief; it refers to the ideal of a political society consisting of free and equal citizens who can all respond, who are together responsible for the welfare of their state—for how their institutions and governance stand. The right to practice one's citizenship—to be able to meet one's responsibilities by presenting oneself publicly, in an open assembly, to be accountable (i.e., to give a public account of one's actions)—is the political enfranchisement that gives the collectivity its presence, making it fully present to itself, hence making participatory governance possible.

Since the interest in individual rights has eclipsed any consideration of authority or engagement in responsibility (i.e., any interest in the practices of democratic governance), the poststructuralist thematization of political activism has led to the hypostatization of otherness and the cultural politics of minority privilege, namely, to the pursuit of warrants for group identity. The pervasive sense of ennui and exhaustion affecting the present decade has been caused by the fragmentation of alliances and the proliferation of identities demanding an ever-extending list of rights for all sorts of entities—texts, canons, voices, diets, bodies, faiths, languages, communities, or cultures. With monotonous predictability each new set of disagreements is sanctioned as a domain of difference, which then gels into another negative essentialism and, using the dominant rhetoric of resistance, indignantly announces its own list of claims. Since this strategy often meets with institutional success, it remains an attractive proposition for many who do not notice how quickly this success dissolves the victorious group into several factions. It is therefore hardly surprising that the recent extensive critiques of rights mounted from outside literary and cultural studies (such as those of critical legal studies, feminism, and communitarianism) have not affected the political aspirations of Theory. Meanwhile, the importance of literature has diminished, the centrality of the humanities has been questioned, and scholars have had to look for counter-hegemonic protests in trivial areas of popular culture. At the same time, the first denunciations (including those by minority intellectuals who until recently advocated large-scale multicultural policies without any reservations) of cultural politics as anomie have been heard. For all these reasons, this is the most opportune moment to search for a way out of the present impasse. The fundamental question of autonomy is once again wide open. What justifies its auto-claim? How do we ground its nomos?

One way might be to abandon the discourse of rights altogether and to engineer a new social contract based on mutually agreed moral duties. Communitarians, for example, seeking an alternative to the principle of legality, find it in the ideal of a community bound together by a shared tradition and committed to its just self-institution. The insurmountable problem with this model is how to secure Rawls's "original position," which would enable the citizens of a society to negotiate such a contract of peaceful cooperation. Another way might be to return to the universal principles of the enlightened civil society, which addresses citizens as rational people with needs rather than interests.

It seems, however, that the most productive advance toward a new paradigm would not reject the ethnographic turn of Theory as another fraud of modernity, but would attempt to combine its best interests (in equality, power, resistance, distribution, and social movements) in a different configuration. The principle that cuts across these interests and gives them their ethical force is the latent idea of political justice. If we disassociate identity and the narratives of victimization from their engagement with discrimination and rights, we see that the ultimate commitment of Theory belongs to an ideal of justice for all. The aggressive rhetoric of grievance and indictment is inspired by an indignant sense of injustice over the oppression and exploitation that so many groups of people have endured at the hands of victors and colonizers, the rich and the powerful. The moral urgency of this indignation should not be underestimated. On the contrary, it could be the starting point for an alternative project, a constructive involvement with public values—an ethical politics.

Furthermore, the Herodotean analysis present in much of today's inquiry could serve as another enabling condition for such a project. It has gone unnoticed that Theory's ethnographic turn has brought it into a surprising alignment with Herodotus: his interest in the plurality of indigenous "histories" (the very title of his work), in local custom as knowledge, in storytelling, in the experience of otherness, in a radical understanding of representation, in cultural geography, and in the ways that traditions are constructed. Several writers today (Vidal-Naquet, Todorov, Said, Jameson,

Clifford, Spivak, Pratt, Franco, Appiah, Chatterjee, Chow) seem to be using the "mirror of Herodotus" to examine both their subject matter and their own social positions.

Contemporary Herodotean analysis is, of course, much more related to broad developments in the geopolitical world than to any explicit reapplication of the ancient historian. However, a comparison with Herodotus's project also reveals that a major dimension of ethnography is lacking in contemporary explorations, which have focused so far on custom and culture. The word used for both of these (by Herodotus and many other authors) is *nomos*. This same word, however, also has a third important meaning, "law as solemn usage," which brings it very close to "type of government" and "constitution." Political law (as opposed to cultural custom) is a matter not merely of local tradition but of conscious design, founded on agoric scrutiny and agonistic debate. Although it often studies nomos as *allotment* (the setting of lots), especially an unfair and discriminatory one, ethnographic Theory lacks any interest in nomos as *constitution*, as the political conduct of authority—in short, politics—the realm of *governance*. The course of ethnography today does not lead into the polis because the exploration of habitats stops with the study of nomos as cultural life alone. Humanist thought currently identifies itself with cultural studies because it is still committed to the view of culture advocated by critical thought, that is, culture as critique, as emancipatory practice, and therefore as counter-politics. Considerations of governance are thus inadmissible, and justice is invariably reduced to a question of rights.

A nomoscopic analysis that included the dimension of law/constitution along with those of culture and custom would direct the Herodotean thrust of Theory toward ethical politics by placing governance among the central topics of ethnography. We know how this nomological integration operates in the *Histories*. Herodotus is not telling stories. He is giving public, edifying accounts/*logoi* about different peoples and their traditions, which include substantive consideration of the ways in which people institute explicit power and exercise authority. In his work, *logos* still retains its pre-Platonic meaning, local knowledge. Furthermore, for our purposes, it can make its modern borrowing, "law," resonate with the meaning of their common root **leg-*, to gather, to set in order. Law is logos/account laid down.

In order to benefit from the lessons of constructivism (with its emphases on contingency, production, analysis, and institution), but also to avoid the traps of deontology and conventionalism, this project ought to abandon the dialectical quest for aesthetic transcendence, interpretative emancipation, and utopian politics to find the code and the courage to propose new principles and criteria for a just shared life. At the moment this may seem impossible, if not downright ridiculous: self-respecting intellectuals today are sufficiently schooled in the subversive techniques of unmasking to be able, on short notice, to prove their fellow travelers hopelessly metaphysical, idealistic, xenophobic, Eurocentric, sexist, and in general blinded by essentialist assumptions. Who would risk discrediting their de Manian awareness of Teiresian insight by articulating some positive values that can be collectively debated and embraced? Even those few who feel challenged to take up this task can propose only emaciated ("thin," "weak," or "minimal") descriptions and values. Still, it is a step forward that needs to be taken, and the humanities is probably the most appropriate site for it. Specifically, literary and cultural studies, which have felt the poststructuralist impasse most acutely, could again play a leading role in charting future directions. Philosophically, this would entail complementary moves from individual to civic rights and from identity to ethical politics. The two paths would converge in a new composition of citizenship based not on membership and entitlement but on responsibility and engagement. Epistemologically, this reorientation would require a different approach to the products of communal life, one focusing not on culture but on governance.

═══════

I have proposed such a reorientation of the humanities under the name of "nomoscopy" (from the noun *nomos*, customary practice, and the verb *scopein*, to examine closely). Nomoscopy is the scrutiny of governance, an ethical inquiry into political organization. This kind of analysis retains the moral urgency of politicized Theory, with its desire to redress long-neglected inequities; but it also goes one step further by shedding the resentful tone of Theory to address questions of law and sovereignty directly. Thus authority is restored as a cardinal interest of the humanities, and justice is understood in a positive manner that makes it relevant to the conduct of rule and the distribution of order.

Nomoscopy adopts an ethical standpoint to adjudicate among competing principles of discourses and institutions regarding legitimacy, power, freedom, and authority. Acknowledging the agonistic contention of forces in the polis (i.e., the inherently polemical nature of politics), it defends the ethical as what is common, or collectively deliberated, distributed, and instituted. It examines politics from the standpoint of the citizens' state, of the self-instituted, self-governed, historically situated equitable society. Since its true scope is polity, this approach operates as a kind of constitutional thought comparable to the Herodotean study of societies. Above all, it constitutes not an antilogic critique but an elenchic yet interested analysis. Its topic is the distribution of justice and the administration of equality—the tentative and incomplete harmonizing of freedom and authority, of *polemos* and *polis*.

The specific focus of nomoscopy is the antinomies of governance, the tragic conflict between law and authority over the apportioning of justice. What makes this conflict tragic is that, in a political society, there can be no higher level of appeal, no outside point of reference, beyond what is internally discussed and determined among the citizens. When law and authority clash over the meaning of the constitution, and they have no supreme divine, monarchic, or bureaucratic ruler to resolve their differences or to arbitrate their claims, then these must be adjudicated and ordered (which does not mean resolved or reconciled) according to principles and procedures intrinsic to the particular political organization of that constitutional government. This is the lesson of all tragic drama, from ancient times to the present. It is worth emphasizing that this lesson does not apply to every society but only to those which are consciously political ones, that is, societies with an explicit awareness of the historical, constructive, and eristic character of self-rule.

What could be a viable and flexible criterion for this kind of adjudication and ordering? Tragedy itself points to justice as the answer—justice understood not as a moral imperative or metaphysical principle but as a cosmic view of what is right in a particular polemical situation. This is not a value-neutral conception of justice by which the same rule would be legalistically applied to every occasion. It is a conception that takes such ideas as measure, limit, responsibility, and proportionality into serious consideration, and, without accepting the cultural-relativist view that, in some way, all positions are right, it grants that they can indeed all be meaningful. Justice is defined not as an eternal truth to be revealed but as a valid account to be rendered. It is associated with notions of requital and return, of restoring a balanced order. It is a constitutional rendition of a conflict and therefore must show respect for the complexity of that conflict, as well as sensitivity to what is due to whom. Justice is the re-institution of proportional (as opposed to Hegel's symmetrical) reciprocity where an inequitable and unrepresentative apportioning has occurred.

It follows that nomoscopic judgment can ensure that the conduct of government and the administration of the law observe the principle of right/order, of proportional reciprocity, by adjudicating the tragic confrontation between the two major forces in political society, law and authority, by rendering a just account of constitutional rule, by defining the common measure of ethical citizenship, and by guarding against the excesses of hubris. The humanities, in taking a nomoscopic turn, would consolidate the shared concerns of various approaches about politics, power, and justice, and would reorient them toward the pressing issues of sovereignty by treating justice as the limit of autonomy, the aporia of immanence. At the same time, it would restore to humanistic research, and in an appropriately ethical context, the interconnected questions of law and authority which were abandoned to the legal and political sciences about a century ago. As a result, issues such as righteousness, goodness, excellence, and happiness would no longer be banished from considerations of power and justice. Thus nomoscopy would enable Theory to move on from cultural to ethical politics and to join forces with political philosophy at large—to become not political theory but political ethics. It would also enable Theory to accommodate the political thought of Arendt, Castoriadis, Habermas, Laclau, or Unger, and the philosophical work of Heller, MacIntyre, Rawls, Williams, Nussbaum, Taylor, Benhabib, Walzer, or Fraser.

We can get a better sense of the concrete tasks of nomoscopy by exploring what it could do for literary study in particular. Our starting point should be an extraordinary silence that has gone unnoticed even by those immersed in interdisciplinary work: the total absence of theater from the major theoretical (including philosophical) considerations of literature and of aesthetics in general. Since the time of Russian Formalism, if not earlier, all major twentieth-century theories of the text have drawn their inspiration from and applied their methods to poetry and fiction, but they have never learned from drama. If we take a look in any anthology of modern criticism, we shall find no major theoretical statement about drama of any period that has had a significant influence. (Even Bakhtin, with his interest in carnival and the dialogical approach, drew all his examples from novels. Similarly, Lyotard's early idea of a "theatrics," which he soon abandoned, was itself predicated on a denunciation of all theater. As for theories inspired by Oedipus, Hamlet, or Faust, they always de-dramatize these figures, ignoring not only the play's performance but its entire theatrical condition. Unfortunately, Kenneth Burke's "dramatism" has had no impact on criticism.) A parallel observation can be made about playwrights. In sharp contrast to the continuing popularity of criticism generated by poets and novelists, and with the possible exceptions of Artaud and Brecht (whose seminal contribution has been buried under Adorno's successful canonization of Benjamin), no dramatist since Schiller has produced any influential statement that reached beyond his own craft to touch on the meaning of literature in general. Not since Nietzsche's shattering explorations of tragedy has theater been an important locus for critical reflection, philosophical or methodological.

While this may not be the place to explain that broad phenomenon, it is certainly time to call for a renewed interest in the genre that enabled philosophers from Plato to Kierkegaard to raise crucial issues of ethics and politics as well as aesthetics. It is also time to challenge literary criticism to change its model text from the novel to the play. This is not to say that it should study drama exclusively, but that the conflict of drama rather than the friction of the novel should be its focus. The novel—Hegel's "bourgeois epic"—dissects manners and accommodates the postmodern interest in representation, or the requisite cultural conditions for modernity. Drama, by enacting strife on a public stage, brings civics center stage and so encourages reflection on the political organization of society. Indeed, it is hardly a historical accident that theater has flourished only in political societies. For our purposes, its decisive feature is the release of the open space, the unfolding of the agora, the gathering of the assembly, the display of public deliberation, which exposes governance to the common light of day. In this sense, drama is an eminent example of nomoscopic inquiry in its own right, for it stages the complex operations of power and justice and holds them up to the scrutiny of citizens.

Taking its cue from drama, nomoscopy should cultivate ethical politics by rehearsing public debates over the legitimacy of authority and adjudicating the validity of contending claims. The goal here would be a drama criticism that could stage and judge civic conflicts within and outside its texts, particularly conflicts pertaining to the constitution of rule and the distribution of justice in society. Thus might literary studies maintain its current heartfelt commitment to politics by engaging directly with civic problems while playing an explicitly didactic role. In contrast to an interpretative project (explicating aesthetic works) or a pedagogical mission (disciplining atomized individualities), the didactic role is oriented more toward message than toward beauty or training, and its addressees are not an audience of disinterested spectators but a public responsive enough to reconsider values in terms of the sociopolitical contingencies of strategic position and common interest.

A didactic literary criticism that took a nomoscopic approach to texts would dramatize—bring into the light of the open space—civic conflicts which also inhere in its own practice (hence its interested standpoint). The goal would be a public education in the art and science of responsible citizenship. Instruction in the pleasures of identity, the tactics of resistance, and the evils of representation is no longer enough; it is often not even interesting. We have spent too much time admiring Antigone's spirit of resistance, forgetting that, with her single-minded devotion to bloodline and birthright, Antigone faces no dilemma. Her determination to follow the aristocratic tradition by symbolically burying her brother never wavers, and nothing can shake her rigid refusal to see the other side, much less to change her mind. The tragic option is decidedly Creon's, the king who is caught between the tasks of sovereignty and the mandates of law, and who suffers while groping for (and erring on) the criterion of political justice. His agonized reflections on the meaning of the constitution are what take center stage and win our attention.

It is therefore time to address ourselves again to the oldest philosophical inquiry, the questions intrinsic to the openly self-governed community: How should we run our society? What values should we share, and what laws should we make? Consequently, it is also time to acknowledge again that some values, criteria, and achievements are more important than others. Literary studies lost its direction and credibility when it elevated identity and experience over their creations—membership over excellence, validation over value. Its future depends on its willingness to provide viable answers to ethical questions by defending such values as worth and strength over expression and advantage. In addition to nomoscopic readings of drama, nomoscopy could be applied to the organization of political authority in such fiction as *Gulliver's Travels, A Sentimental Education*, or *War and Peace*; the rule of law in *Billy Budd, The Red and the Black*, or *The Trial*; and the constitution of public space in *A Tale of Two Cities, Buddenbrooks*, or *Invisible Cities*. It could also pursue similar issues in feminist science fiction, slave narratives, prison memoirs, post-Independence writing, or the literature of emergent nations. The ultimate goal would be to draw lessons, as well as practical suggestions about the ways in which a political society could better govern itself, from such literature.

Of course, the study of governance would not be limited to the operations of government, any more than the scopesis of law is limited to bills before the Senate or Parliament. Governance encompasses the complex and open network of authorities by which the life of society—its institutions, bodies, souls, money, canons, knowledge, news—is monitored and managed. Laws are the rules, regulations, measures, and procedures, the decrees, charters, and orders, which organize, direct, and coordinate human interaction. What makes nomoscopy different from and richer than prevailing modes of inquiry is not just its lack of aversion toward such mechanisms and operations (because of their presumed oppressive character) but its voluntary, active, and constructive engagement with them, especially to ensure that the exercise of authority conforms substantively to the values of self-rule and the principles of justice. The goals of nomoscopic reading would be interventionist and affirmative, above all: to dramatize the conflict of opinions about the compatibility of law and governance, to support the cause of justice as agonistic reciprocity, to draw useful lessons regarding the constitution of political society, and to educate in the rights and responsibilities of citizenship. Nomoscopy scrutinizes diverse principles, stakes out consistent ethical positions, and endorses a systematic view, based on historical perspectivism, of how a free society should be put together—how its values, laws, institutions, procedures, spaces, and alliances should be constituted.

Nomoscopy does not, however, advocate a utilitarian view of literature, but rather an instrumentalist one based on the model of drama—an idea that may sound hopelessly humanistic and terribly old-fashioned. Have we come to just that—to literature as Burke's "equipment for living"? Not quite. This would probably apply if nomoscopy were invoking liberal

Vassilis Lambropoulos

for GWU ?
achvism as
an interpretive
paradigm !

principles of tolerance, pluralism, diversity, individual freedom, and equal rights. The idea of justice as agonistic reciprocity, however, does not assume any rationality or require consensus, but aims to desegregate and reintegrate ethics and governance by applying austere, rigorous, exacting criteria of goodness, purpose, and merit. The instrumentalist view conceives of literature as one among many experimental public sites for rehearsing a good society. The drama model shifts moral determinations from the courts and back to the domain of governance. It also balances the law's prohibitive function (protecting natural rights) with its affirmative one (enabling the exercise of human capabilities). The ultimate goal is not to establish formally, judicially, or procedurally whose individual rights (to do with life, death, preference, health, privacy, work, or faith) have been violated, but to suggest how a political society could be structured to assure a good and dignified life for all its citizens—and ideally to dissolve that most fateful differentiation of modernity, the separation of the just and the good.

Only

Regardless of their specific positions, interventionist legal scholars like Catharine MacKinnon and Lani Guinier offer a good, if too obvious, example of nomoscopic activism when they put their ideas into practice by proposing and working for legislative reform. In contrast, literary scholars today would consider such a direct intervention on their part presumptuous, arrogant, and of course futile—but not primarily because they lack the expertise to write legislation or lobby for it. Instead, they fear the impression of pretentiousness and smugness that an ethical stance and an engaged interest in authority might convey within their profession. Everybody these days is adept at taking superstructures apart, deconstructing millennia of logocentric tyranny, explaining how a particular community has been "imagined," "invented," or "orientalized." At the same time, with the exception of separatists, no one can muster the determination and fortitude to advocate a vision of how such a community should be democratically assembled, organized, and run—here and now. Ever since intellectuals acknowledged that they could be neither "legislators" nor "interpreters," they have been trying to give legislative force to their own interpretations exclusively. Their current thematization of politics in Theory is but the latest phase in this endeavor. The project of nomoscopy would challenge them to cease their moralistic denunciations of all forms of power and to become constructive legislators again (following the example of Leibniz, Vico, Montaigne, Rousseau, Humboldt, Paine, Bentham, Gramsci, Dewey, or Schmitt); to participate voluntarily in governance by contributing an upright and proper perspective on justice; to identify those ethical principles, rules, and structures, those strategic formations of authority and positions of effective administration, that are appropriate for their society at this particular historical moment.

What may seem like a very old memory now has actually been an important concern for poets from Dante to Pound, from Milton to Heaney. For example, the poetry of Cavafy is variously populated by rulers, politicians, orators, sophists, and laymen who, in the midst of intensely dramatic situations, raise questions regarding the nature of authority, the administration of public affairs, lawmaking, the structure of the polity, the definition of citizenship, the requirements of virtue, and the like. By working in a similar direction, analysis can leave behind the negative dialectic of master-slave narratives and the decadent thematization of activism (in which engagement yields to the politics of not-yet, of whatever is always already beyond politics) and can turn to that most basic dimension of collective life and creativity—the ever-unfolding agoric space of daylight, appearance, presence, voice, argument, and action, the theater of the gathered assembly, the secular civic association of contentious solidarities—to the political itself.

This change of direction could have a number of beneficial effects on the study of literature and culture, on the reflective production of intellectual life, and even on the rest of society. It could give positive content to rights, based not on erecting boundaries but on confederating responsibilities. It could reorient the drive for justice from utopianism and protest toward an affirmative engagement with law, power, greatness, virtue, and self-rule. It could bring this kind of research into the contested areas of public service and political duty. It could reinforce the ethical character of analysis and, emphasizing its didactic role in the training of responsible citizenship, endow the study of texts with recognition and honor. It could finally lend literature a new importance within the university by setting a trend toward constructive involvement not only with questions of method but primarily with issues of ethics and governance, with the creation of a more just democratic society and a richer, better life.

Note

For their generous and helpful comments, I am grateful to Jon Erickson, Kermit Hall, Eugene Holland, Fredric Jameson, Gregory Jusdanis, P. John Kozyris, Artemis Leontis, Stephen Melville, Peter Murphy, James Phelan, Bruce Robbins, and Beth Sullivan.

J. Peter Euben

When There Are Gray Skies: Aristophanes' Clouds and the Political Education of Democratic Citizens

Is there anyone here I haven't offended?
—Lenny Bruce

Lord, heap miseries upon us yet entwine our arts with laughter's low. . . . In the name of the former and of the latter and of their holocaust, All men.
—James Joyce

In this essay, I want to retrieve classical texts from their use by conservatives to legitimate a political and educational agenda as well as to defend their generative power against detractors who regard them as constituting a canon allegedly hostile to democracy and plurality. Such "dead White texts" can be crucial in reconstituting an ethos of democratic citizenship alert to, but also critical of, identity politics. Moreover, Athenian practices developed in the fifth century B.C. constituted a culture of self-scrutiny that exemplifies democracy's distinctive capacity to revise and reform itself, to think about what it was doing and, in that way, to suspend its

The *South Atlantic Quarterly* 95:4, Fall 1996.
Excerpt from *Corrupting Youth: Socratic Political Education and Democratic Politics* by J. Peter Euben © Princeton University Press (forthcoming). Reproduced by permission of Princeton University Press.

own ideological hegemony.[1] One central aspect of this culture was the demand for accountability, itself part of the democratization of political power and responsibility that occurred during this period. All magistrates, whether chosen by lot or elected (in effect, all adult male citizens), had to undergo *dokimasia*, a preliminary scrutiny, and, as they left office, *euthūnai*, in which they were asked to give an "account" (in all senses) of their actions. It was this demand for accountability that Socrates built on when he insisted that all men, but especially those of his compatriots who claimed a political and cultural position of power/knowledge, render an account of their claims, actions, and lives. In this way Socratic political philosophy elaborated and extended democratic practices that it was also subjecting to critique.[2]

There was, however, another dimension of this culture of self-scrutiny that pluralized accounts and accountability: Greek drama, more specifically Old or Aristophanic Comedy.[3] In the most general terms, Aristophanic comedy detached its audience from the charms and chains of national narcissism, defusing patriotic tirades and puncturing official ideology. While Pericles called upon his compatriots to fall in love with their city (in the Funeral Oration in Thucydides), Aristophanes warned them to guard against the seduction of self-love and the self-aggrandizement such love encourages. "One must make the Athenians laugh at the praise that they are so happy to address to the city and to the democratic system," Nicole Loraux writes, "both on the tragic stage and on the speaker's platform of the dēmosion sēma."[4] Comedy also raised the question of the limits of human power and the possibly "constructed" nature of "nature." Thus, in the *Ecclesiazusae* (Women in the Assembly), the question was whether Athenian women could be constituted male if the Assembly voted for it. After all, if the *dēmos* could constitute political realities by legal enactment, and if human intelligence were powerful enough to tame the sea (as the chorale ode in "praise" of man in *Antigone* and Pericles' boast in the Funeral Oration assert), then why couldn't men reconstruct nature so that women could be rulers of the city?[5] Other comedies raised similar questions about war and peace, wealth and poverty, Athenian litigiousness, public poetry, demagoguery, and the possibly corrosive effects of new philosophical teachings (and teachers).

The latter, dramatized in *The Clouds* as part of the contemporary contest between Old and New Education, has a startling resonance with current debates over the canon. Moreover, the play is useful for our purposes because its critique of Socrates questions the relationship between democracy and philosophy, its enactment of the social tensions and contradictions of Athenian society does not try to rationalize them,[6] and its author claims an ethical and political importance for comedy rivaling that of tragedy. Aristophanes' extraordinary suggestion here is that mockery, irreverence, ridicule, parody, scatology—in other words, everything that is low—is an essential ground for ethical and political critique. As one recent critic put it, the *"Clouds'* skōmmata [joking mockery] aim at ethical criticism and pointedly hold disgraceful behavior up to public scrutiny through humiliating ridicule, much as Aristophanes claims to do through his comedies to his city's benefit."[7] The fact that Socrates also saw himself (at least in Plato's *Apology*) as a political educator of his fellow citizens makes him all the more provocative as a target of *The Clouds*. Both Plato and Xenophon attest to the efficacy, though not to the accuracy, of the weapon and the aim.[8]

In what sense can we speak of comedy as a mode of democratic political education? What is the connection between comedy and democracy, and how did comedy educate its citizen audience? These questions are parasitic upon another: Did comedy challenge powerful figures, policies, and cultural norms, or were its anarchic, transgressive, and radical impulses generally domesticated by the desire of the playwright to please the audience and judges of the plays, by the need to "reassert and reaffirm" the "traditional norms of society [that] tragedy put at risk," and by the "controlled environment" of "state sponsored religious rituals . . . within the civic festival calendar and communal civic space"?[9]

It is certainly true that the Greeks regarded laughter as ambiguous and volatile. The word *skōptein* and its cognates mean both to joke, with connotations of play, fun, and humor, and to mock or deride in ways that dishonor. So there *was* a need for social practices to contain the antagonism that ridicule created in a society with so strong a sense of shame and to keep it from exploding the social fabric entirely.[10] As a civic institution assigned a specific place and time, comedy helped to do this. Yet I suspect that the attempt to contain laughter and ridicule was at best imperfect and that a continual tension remained between the spirit of celebratory, playful release and the force of divisive antagonism; between circumscribing what could be said where and the constant possibility that laughter would transgress whatever rules and boundaries had been set up to contain it.[11] Moreover, the quarantining of comedic effects would seem to vitiate the explicit claim Aristophanes makes for his significance as a political educator. Plato and Xenophon certainly thought *The Clouds* had consequences outside the theater and the confines of ritual.[12] Finally, if comedy was indeed part of a radically democratic culture of self-scrutiny and self-critique, the fact that Aristophanes challenged certain aspects of that democracy is hardly proof of a conservative reluctance to transgress accepted norms.

There are other considerations specific to *The Clouds* that should make us wary of accepting the domestication-of-comedy argument. For one thing, the play lacks the joyous celebratory ending posited by virtually all critics as essential to resolving the tensions generated in and by comic dramas. Whatever inversions and transgressions take place in *The Clouds* remain in place, or at least unresolved. For another thing, since *The Clouds* is a hybrid of tragedy and comedy, it cannot simply reinforce the norms that tragedy puts at risk.

At bottom, I think the domestication argument rests on the assumption that juries of ordinary men chosen by lot to judge the plays could not have honored works which mocked their own leaders and political commitments. If they did, however, it must have been because they were too unsophisticated to discern the nuanced mockery. They were either suffering from a version of working-class Toryism, victims of the irresistible power of an aristocratic value system,[13] or were seduced by the crude buffoonery and obscenity of comedy. But in any case they were oblivious to anything intellectual in the play or didactic about it. In effect, then, this argument divides the Athenian audience into the sophisticated, knowing few and the crude, manipulated many. Thus one of the most perceptive commentators on *The Clouds* argues that when Aristophanes complains in the parabasis about being forced to rely on theatrical tricks in the second version to make it more appealing, but then shifts back and forth between references to each version so as to leave us uncertain which version is being discussed at any point, he is "deliberately playing with the audience, winking at its more perceptive members while deliberately confusing the majority."[14] And it is pretty clear who these "more perceptive members" are—people like "us."

But it may be that the play warns against just such an interpretative strategy insofar as it mocks the pretensions of intellectuals and philosophers. Indeed, it seems to display each character projecting himself onto the clouds according to his own half-sublimated desires and half-acknowledged ambitions, as if to warn interpreters that they are in danger of doing the same thing to *The Clouds*. For both characters and philosophical readers, the clouds are ciphers: goddesses for atheists, nature for conventionalists, and foundations for antifoundationalists. Both the clouds and the poets use their powers of mimetic illusion to engage and mirror men's fantasies and follies—at least until the end, when both turn moralistic, or so it seems.

What has this to do with our initial set of questions concerning comedy as a mode of democratic political education? Simon Goldhill expresses the current consensus when he argues that "democracy is the very condition of possibility for Aristophanic comedy."[15] But Nicole Loraux suggests that the converse is also true, that comedy was essential to democracy because, in my terms, it helped to constitute a tradition of self-critique. Loraux's remarks also point to both the differences between and the complementarity of comedy and tragedy as modes of political education.[16]

———————

Unlike tragedy, comedy was brought in from the periphery and below, from the countryside to the center of the polis, as a supplement and perhaps an alternative to tragedy.[17] What makes this history particularly relevant to *The Clouds* is that Strepsiades, the old man whose oppressive debts lead him to study the new learning and then to insist that his son do so when he fails, has the same history. He is a farmer and rustic brought into the city and a way of life he finds confusing and uncongenial. But comedy also had a different sense of time, space, and event than tragedy, which relocated contemporary events and pressing issues, as well as certain characters, to a remote mythical past. Comedy, by contrast, was firmly anchored to the moment of performance, openly topical, and unequivocal about its objects of ridicule—Pericles, Cleon, the war with Sparta, the sophists, and Socrates in the case of *The Clouds*. And unlike tragedy, comedy's treatment of such issues as sexuality, war and peace, the relationship between mind and body, right and wrong, or education and nurture was embedded in the concrete, particular world of ordinary people.[18] While comedy sometimes "gestured toward the universal," it was pulled down and back, as tragedy and intellectuals were not, by the need to cope with the specific exigencies of everyday life.[19] Comedy's sense of time could also be suggested by far more radical shifts of language, plot, character, and action than even a tragedy such as *Oedipus Tyrannos*, with its roller coaster of emotions before the king learns the truth about himself, could sustain.[20] Moreover, comedy used language and engaged topics in ways that were permissible in no other venue. In this regard, it was perhaps a unique expression of *parrhēsia*, the right to speak freely to power, to say almost anything to anybody.[21] Comedy could ridicule gods and politicians, generals and intellectuals, mocking the favorites and the critics of the dēmos, resorting to violence and verbal abuse, thriving on uninhibited sexuality and scatology, and always exulting in the pleasures of general vulgarity.

Finally, comedy could transgress "the fourth wall," eliminating the distance between stage and audience as tragedy never could. Indeed, the emotional intensity of the spectator's reaction to tragedy depended on enhancing the power of the fiction that what was taking place on stage was "real." The chorus in tragedy did not call attention to the play's being a play, but masked the fictional action, providing spatial and emotional mediation between the protagonists and the audience as the audience in the seats watched another audience (the chorus) on stage accept the play's reality and its emotional logic. But comedy broke the spell and the audience's concentration, calling attention to the fictive character of the (often absurd) actions on stage. Actors, speaking of themselves as performers rather than characters, would refer to the stage and scenery rather than to the dramatic setting and thereby make not only spectators but a spectacle of the audience.[22] Thus when New Education invited Old Education to look at "the flaming homosexuals" in the audience, the spectators would become a self-conscious assembly of citizens—an especially active one, in fact, laughing and applauding, hissing and booing, drumming the wooden benches when the spirit moved them or calling out as the fancy took them.[23]

This interaction between play and audience became institutionalized in the parabasis, a midway point when the chorus directly addresses the audience in its own name and that of the playwright. But if the comedy's self-awareness is to this extent generic, and Aristophanes "the most metatheatrical playwright before Pirandello,"[24] then *The Clouds* is his most self-aware and most metatheatrical play. For the play we have is a revision in which Aristophanes himself talks to his projected audience about the inadequacies of the original *Clouds*, which had left him humiliated with its third-place award. By virtue of the playwright's talking about that audience, about the nature and status of comedy in a democracy, and about his own talents as a dramatist, *The Clouds* becomes a narrative in which the history of its performance intersects with its thematic preoccupations. One might even say that *The Clouds* is Aristophanes' most Socratic and sophisticated play. (Of course, *you* could say that, but *I* couldn't possibly comment.) One might also say that the playwright becomes as much spectacle as spectator, as much a creature caught up—seemingly unaware— in the inescapable web of comic discourse as he is the omniscient author of it. Thus he becomes implicated in the human condition that he shares with his fellow citizens on stage and in the audience.[25]

The Clouds is different in one other way: it blurs the lines between comedy and tragedy. Not only is the opening song of the chorus formally closer to tragedy than to comedy,[26] but there is no sympathetic comic hero, and the violent, unforeseen, and discordant ending obviously does not bring the action to a harmonious conclusion. Indeed, the closing mood suggests the "ironic gloom of intellectual despair," not joy. Appropriately enough, then, given its characters and themes, *The Clouds* is a dramatic hybrid.[27]

═══════

The Clouds focuses on the sophistic challenge to traditional education. What is so disconcerting about the tone and substance of the contest between that tradition and this New Education is how exactly it anticipates the issues and polemics of our own culture's war over curriculum, cultural power, educational reform, and American political identity.[28] Old Education's aggressive traditionalism—his insistence that existing practices are natural, present identities are fixed, and established hierarchies are necessary, its apocalyptic prophecies and ranting against promiscuous sex, self-indulgent youth, wayward teachers, the decline of standards, and disrespect for authority—is summed up in a call for "Decorum, Discipline and Duty"[29] reminiscent of a National Association of Scholars pamphlet. But the play is not much more sympathetic to either the romanticizing of multiple identities, moral libertinism, transgressive politics, and polymorphous perversity or the denigrating of hierarchy, authority, and traditions, let alone to the deconstruction of the natural, that mark some forms of postmodernism.

Socrates' airiness suggests another central theme of the play (and a concern of this essay): the relationship between political theory or philosophy and democratic culture. Scholars have been sharply divided over the meaning of this vision of Socrates. Some have read it as malicious anti-intellectualism, and the identification of Socrates with his sophistic opponents as sheer perverseness, the dire consequences of which are alluded to in Plato's *Apology*. But others, with the *Symposium* in mind, have seen nonobvious but nonetheless profound affinities between the two men, reading *The Clouds'* Socrates as distancing himself from sophistic teachings and Aristophanes as committed to the kind of self-awareness that is typically Socratic. Yet neither view quite confronts perhaps the most radical implication of Socrates' portrait: that what intellectuals, theorists, and philosophers regard as disagreements of substantial import are, with some justice, regarded by the ordinary citizen as the narcissism of petty differences. As Gerald Graff reminds us, for our students "a Roland Barthes and an Allan Bloom would seem far more similar to one another than to people like themselves, their parents and friends. In their eyes a Barthes and a Bloom would be just a couple of intellectuals speaking a very different language from their own about problems they have a hard time recognizing as problems."[30] Perhaps academic culture is so tightly enclosed, the language of its sensibilities and problems so remote from that of ordinary citizens, that the differences between Rawlsians, Arendtians, Straussians, and Habermassians seem casuistic at best.[31]

But this is all too serious and somber, too cerebral and philosophical, which is to say that it misses half the point and all the fun. In the *Symposium* the long night is almost over, but Socrates is still talking. Near the end of his speech and the dialogue, when he suggests that comedy and tragedy spring from the same roots, his audience is "constrained to assent, being drowsy, and not quite following the argument. And first of all Aristophanes drop[s] off to sleep."[32] So fascinating was the first theory of comedy that the most eminent comic poet of his time, perhaps of any time, was put to sleep by a philosopher's lecture on the comic spirit.[33]

Undaunted, I propose that we look at the opening scene of *The Clouds*, with its portrait of Strepsiades, and contrast it with our initial impression of Socrates; then, carrying this contrast through to the *agōn* between Old and New Education,[34] look at how *The Clouds* negotiates the oppositions it constructs, as a way of returning to our principal concern, the education of democratic citizens.

The play opens with Strepsiades tossing and turning in his sleep, restlessly awaiting the dawn. He is driven to distraction by his son's debts and by nostalgia for his own rustic past. Those were the good old days before the Peloponnesian War and Pericles' policy which had forced farmers to abandon their land and take shelter behind the city walls. For Strepsiades this meant removal from the rhythms of nature and rural life that had given the shape of purpose to his existence. In Thucydides the Corinthians characterize the Athenians as a people who came into the world to give no rest to themselves or anyone else, a sentiment echoed by Pericles when he boasts that his compatriots have made every sea and land the highway of their daring.[35] Both suggest that Athens deliberately turned its back on the agricultural traditions in which it was "grounded" and declared itself free of the cycle of nature and inherited cultural forms.[36] Strepsiades is the product of that attitude and policy, and *The Clouds* an ironic commentary on it. For the restlessness that the Corinthians define as a cultural trait we see played out on the smaller stage of everyday life in the twitching bodily movements of Strepsiades. No grandiloquent phrases here, no exultation in imperialist ventures, no mesmerizing visions of collective power—just a man who can't sleep well seemingly because he has been removed from his former life. (I say "seemingly" because the self-destructive nostalgia of Old Education later in the play puts us on guard against nostalgia of any kind.)

Strepsiades lives the philosophical opposition between nature and convention posited by the sophists and by Platonic characters like Callicles, whose epistemological, moral, and political challenges to conventional beliefs are, in the first instance, physical, sensual, and geographic. Their rejection of a natural (ontological, theological, or metaphysical) grounding for political and moral life, or their appeal to nature as a way of rejecting conventions deemed natural, has confounded Strepsiades' life. When Thrasymachus, in *The Republic*, and Callicles, in *The Gorgias*, look to nature to justify aggressive behavior—the opposite of what is commonly regarded as the conduct mandated by nature and the gods[37]—or claim that "nature" is socially constructed either by the strong to legitimize their domination or by the weak to prevent such domination, it has consequences for the way in which fathers and sons act toward each other. As the newly educated Pheidippides later asks, if laws are man-made, then why should beating your father be less privileged than its opposite? This is a question of some force in a culture where Zeus had murdered Kronos for his power, and Oedipus (albeit unknowingly) had killed *his* father and, coincidentally, replaced him in public and in bed.

Strepsiades has been not only literally forced off the land, but also figuratively uprooted and socially displaced by his marriage to an aristocratic city girl with corresponding tastes. Unsurprisingly, these two fight over what to name their son:

> She, of course, wanted something fancy, some upper class high-horse handle with hippos in it. While I naturally wanted to give him the fine old name of Pheidonides in honor of his thrifty grandfather. We, we haggled and at last agreed on a compromise name: Pheidippides. She gushed over the baby: "Just imagine. Some day he'll be an important man, just like his Uncle Megakles, and drive in his purple robes up to the Akropolis." And I'd put in, "Ha, drive his goats from the hills, you mean, dressed like his dad in a filthy smock."[38]

Given the Greek belief that the validity and efficacy of language is guaranteed by its "magical, homeopathic relationship to the things of the world," words possess their own nature and structure, unmediated by any artificial grammar, syntax, or rhetoric.[39] This gives an "ontological" dimension to the couple's debate over what sort of life their boy will lead—his class affiliation and political alliances, his dress and deportment, his friends and their values. The parents eventually compromise on "Pheidippides" ("cheap aristocrat"), an oxymoron that combines the worst of both worlds and fails to reconcile them.[40] But the name does indicate a new conception of language introduced or elaborated by the sophists. If words can be made up, then so can things, such that rhetorical skill becomes the ultimate power in the world, as Gorgias claims in asserting that he could convince an assembly of a medical diagnosis against the most expert doctors. But even more troubling is the prospect that words and things have no direct or singular connection, that the world is unanchored, leaving us up in the air with Socrates, self-indulgently and condescendingly looking down on others.

The circumstances of Strepsiades, his wife (who has obviously married beneath her station), and especially their son indicate that the older world of fixed identities and places romanticized by the old man no longer exists—and that democracy is largely responsible for its disappearance.

Democratic culture blurs the lines between classes and places, making boundaries permeable and identities unstable. Democracy, together with the new, sophistic view of language, has consequences for comedy as an institution and a genre. It is not simply that comedy, like all drama and public life, relies on language, but that the idea of speech as a form of power and the relationship of that power to violence is the play's subject.[41] When language becomes an extension of violence, as New Education argues and demonstrates, the celebration of civilization as the triumph of persuasion over force becomes problematic. More than that, insofar as all arguments—just and unjust alike—rely on the capacity to speak, the position taken by New Education is not only self-defeating but, more pointedly, makes comedy impossible. For comedy plays on words which play on words, and at least part of its role in the education of democratic citizens is to rhetorically counter the narcissism Loraux laments and to play out, in the confines of stage and theater, potentially destructive impulses toward violence and revenge.

In any case, Strepsiades is a man preoccupied with his body, or at least with the lowest parts of it: stomach, anus, and phallus. The lofty sentiments of the Funeral Oration have no more meaning to him than the scientific claptrap Socrates pronounces. They are equally irrelevant to his life, which is preoccupied with getting rid of his goddamned debts and keeping his horsy son from bankrupting him. Strepsiades is relentlessly literal-minded, bringing every thought down to earth with a resounding thud,[42] as if his body and his worries weigh upon him with such force that he cannot raise his sights or his mind. Socrates seems to be everything that Strepsiades is not. Whereas the latter is all body, Socrates is all mind; while Strepsiades has no lofty thoughts, Socrates seems to have nothing but; whereas Strepsiades seems stupid and gullible, Socrates seems sophisticated and smart.

We first hear about Socrates not by name but by vague reputation, as one of those philosophers who lives in a dirty little hovel called the Thinkery (*phrontistērion*).[43] What Strepsiades knows about the Thinkery is that the intellectuals and professors who live in it can prove anything to anyone. He has heard that they teach something called just, philosophical, or moral logic, which he does not pretend to understand or care about. What does interest Strepsiades is the other, immoral Socratic/sophistic logic that will enable him to escape his debts. While the father knows only this about the Thinkery, the son knows more—the names of those ashen-faced, flabby, barefoot pedants, those disgustingly miserable, utterly fraudulent charlatans (*aiboi, ponēri, alazonas, ōchriōntas, anupoldētous*) who run the place, Socrates and Chaerephon—and he wants nothing to do with them. So Strepsiades has no choice. He will become a student and save himself, although he knows going in that he lacks the talent for it.

Strepsiades' kick at the Thinkery door disrupts a delicate experiment aimed at discovering how many flea-feet a flea can broad-jump. Not only has Socrates already solved this problem, but he has gone on to resolve the age-old metaphysical conundrum of whether gnats fart through their mouths or behinds.[44] But best of all, Socrates has demonstrated how food can be miraculously manufactured out of nothing by distracting some gullible student with a pretentious experiment, deftly stealing his cloak, and selling it to buy food. Strepsiades is not merely impressed, he is over-whelmed. Anyone who has closely studied the asses of gnats can certainly vanquish the asses in the law courts; anyone who can manufacture some-thing out of nothing by chicanery and stealth is his kind of professor: "Why Thales was an amateur compared to this! Throw open the Thinkery. Unbolt the door and let me see this wizard Socrates in person. Open up. I'm mad for education."[45]

We are less so. It is not merely that these pompous professors waste their time on utterly trivial matters they take to be of great moment or that they are too clever for their own good and so far removed from life that they look dead, but that, as the cloak-stealing episode suggests, their lofty ideas and high-minded studies are a spectacular cover for their petty manipula-tions of others. Their motives are no different from those of Strepsiades; they only disguise them better, and so cheat more successfully. If we think of cloaks metaphorically—it is the first thing Strepsiades has to give up on entering the Thinkery—as man-made garments that shield us from the elements and cover our nakedness, Socrates' stealing of them represents a stripping away of convention and tradition.

When we first meet this wondrous figure, he is suspended in the air, his head in the clouds, looking down from his lofty perch on his students, who, with their noses to the ground and asses in the air, are double majors in geology and astronomy. When Socrates is asked why he has his head in the clouds, he pompously replies, "I walk on air and look down upon the sun from a superior standpoint . . . [because] only by dangling my mind in the heavens and mingling my rare thought with the ethereal air could I achieve exact knowledge in a survey of all that is highest."[46] Although bewildered by all of Socrates' mumbo-jumbo, Strepsiades asks him to teach him sophistic logic so that he can evade his debts—for which he promises, with his own peculiar logic, to pay anything. As surety, he swears by the gods. That turns out to be a mistake, since, as Socrates informs him, belief in the old gods is merely vulgar prejudice.[47] The real gods, or goddesses rather, of philosophers (as of all quacks, prophets, charlatans, poets, dandies, astrologers, and men of leisure who have their heads in the air or somewhere darker) are the clouds.[48] It is to these goddesses that intellectuals owe their skill at fraud and casuistry, and their prodigious vocabularies (not to mention their postmodern Rawlsian–Foucaldian–Habermassian refinements). And the clouds are unusually useful goddesses since their formlessness allows each of us to comprehend them after our own fashion and in our own image. We see in them the shape of our ambitions, while others see a caricature of those ambitions. Just as we project our pursuits and desires onto the world and see the world as legitimating them and reflecting us as we would like to be seen, what others see is the shape of our real motives, unrecognized or denied. That is what happens with the clouds and in *The Clouds*.

If you are looking for female (or male) "companionship" (read: horny), then you appear to others as a centaur; if you are respectful of lobbyists (read: those who defraud the government), you appear as a wolf; and if you are an academic dedicated to truth and reason (read: to maximizing your institutional power and imposing your views on your field), you will appear as a snake. Because the play ends with the clouds mouthing Aeschylean pieties, commentators have concluded that Aristophanes wants to show Strepsiades and the audience that crime does not pay.[49] But I read the play's conclusion as inconclusive, and so this interpretation as problematic. Better to say that *The Clouds*, like the clouds, can assume many shapes, all of which mirror the follies of the human imagination. Better to conclude that the play plays with the audience, leaving it open to their own political and interpretative projections,[50] though they had best be prepared to have them thrown back in their faces, caricatured and unmasked. Better still, we might regard these goddesses not as Aeschylean surrogates but as deities of comedy.

"Naturally," these puffed-up, chameleonesque windbags prefer Socrates to any other theorist or educator. For he is the most superannuated of philosophers, the great bird dog of culture, the most incorrigible purveyor of bullshit and consummate flapper of tongues. Yet the clouds also present themselves as fertility spirits, associated with the rustic life for which Strepsiades longs, and as teachers of the audience (*didaomen*), like the comic poet himself. Here, as in the naming of Pheidippides and the battle between Old and New Education that follows, the terms and boundaries of life—body, mind, spirit, animal, human, and divine—are, quite literally, up for grabs.

Socrates and Strepsiades are both very funny: this boorish old farmer with his gastronomical vision, two-digit IQ, and desperation for an easy way out of his worldly problems; and the otherworldly, pretentiously prattling intellectual who thinks he is superior to everyone. Yet they are not as different from one another as each supposes. Socrates pulls off the business with the cloak, and there is a certain gift in Strepsiades' ability to find concrete reference and to recognize the airy nonsense that Socrates spouts. But neither knows himself or the other well enough, and their putative opposition is itself a danger, as we shall see.

Strepsiades turns out to be a hopeless student, and Socrates' promise that he will be "reborn" goes for naught.[51] He cannot follow what Socrates says or do what Socrates says he must do to master the logic that will save his ass.[52] His memory is so bad that he only recalls those situations in which someone owes him money. He has no talent for speaking or patience with learning meter and no desire to learn rhythm, since he has no interest in entering polite society, for which such learning would qualify him. Furthermore, he is totally befuddled by the analytic word games Socrates plays. (This Socrates is less a gadfly than a bedbug, like those in the Thinkery mattress Strepsiades is forced to lie on and which make a meal of him.) He concretizes to absurdity every concept, idea, and argument that Socrates presents to him. He reduces philosophical speculations about measurement into a worry about whether the flour man's scales are honest; he thinks Socrates' pontification on how to keep time by tapping one's fingers means giving someone the finger; and he cannot see why the female duck is a duchess or "baskette" is feminine. Since Strepsiades cannot think for himself or decide what to think about, this Socrates, like the one of the early dialogues, cannot help him.

Having failed to become a philosopher himself, Strepsiades has only one recourse: convince his son to take up philosophy. Pheidippides thinks his dad is off his rocker, but finally agrees out of (what will be his last act of) filial piety. Strepsiades wants his son tutored in both logics, though of course his primary interest is in having Pheidippides learn the immoral one. Socrates calls on the two logics to come forward and compete for Strepsiades, a contest that parallels the struggle over the boy's name and the debate between Socrates and Strepsiades over the meaning of the clouds. Socrates himself leaves the stage, which suggests that the initial opposition between him and Strepsiades is not identical with the agōn between the two kinds of education.

≡≡≡≡

As the play makes clear, the competition is not merely for this particular son but for the city's sons, and so for the future of Athens. It is a struggle over how the past will be remembered and constructed, and so how the present is to be understood. It is over what vision of the city and what concept of democratic culture, moral imagination, and political education will prevail, and so over what elements of a tradition are renewable and what can be clung to only at the cost of repression and disaster. In times of crisis the question is not simply who will define what is right or wrong, but who will define the discourse in which such claims are recognized as being either right or wrong. Whose statements or arguments will be heard and taken seriously, even if ultimately rejected as wrong, and whose will not be given a hearing because they are construed as insane, immature, perverse, or otherwise beyond the pale?

   The crisis in education and political identity has implications for comedy as well. For the license of Old Comedy presupposed a climate in which the city could accept mockery of almost everything it took seriously. Comedy "tested the limits of festivity—and thus the limits of the experience of laughter as a force for communal release and play—by constantly and irreverently toying with subjects on which life outside the festival depended."[53] But radical questioning (with its affinities to Socratic elenchus) has always been risky, even in a democracy which recognizes its significance as a form of self-education.

   Whatever the stakes, the competition itself is great fun. At first the antagonists jab wildly at each other. Right (Moral, Old) Education and Logic calls his opponent a swaggering peacock, precious pederast, and cheap stunted runt, as moronic as the audience of citizens who, having made him so popular and powerful, have left the schools of Athens deserted. The young wander the streets trying to "find themselves," moving from one New Age religion to another or into the numbing world of corporate law and international finance. They take their moral cues from Bart Simpson, Beavis and Butthead, or Howard Stern, from *Hard Copy*, the *National Inquirer, Barron's Weekly*, or the *Wall Street Journal*, rather than from the great books and accumulated wisdom of the past. Wrong (Immoral, New) Logic and Education promises to deflate Old Education's hot-air balloon with a post-postmodern ultra-unorthodoxy.[54] He will do so before an audience of what *he* calls "sophisticated gentlemen."[55] The truth is, there is no naturally sanctioned, divinely prescribed justice. (How *did* Zeus become powerful? Just answer that. Go ahead.) He will prove that dishonor is honorable, abuse is welcome, and everything once thought wise is merely the fossilized ranting of Dead White Males. "Times change. The vices of your age are stylish now."[56] And style is everything.

The battle rages only a little less wildly after the chorus leader intervenes to formalize this spontaneous aggressiveness as a debate. Old Education speaks first, as befits his age (and irrelevance). He extols the good old days of family values, traditional discipline, and docile students. In those days, children learned the three R's, read great books, and respected the authority of parents and political leaders (just like in the 1950s). They knew their place and their duty. Students kept their hair short and one color, and listened to Mozart or Bach rather than to the Stones, hip-hop, blues, or rap; young women were virgins when they married, so were protected and respected by men. Those were the ways and the values of the generation that had defeated the Persians at Marathon. Not one of them was a cheap shyster lawyer or a prestige-seeking, status-conscious, who's-the-smartest-of-them-all disputatious academic. They were men of vigor and physique, of courage and honor, of moral discernment and virtue. If Pheidippides follows Old Education, he will be a credit to his family and his city (not to mention to his race).

Behind this caricature is a version of the education that most of the Athenian audience had experienced, one in which the young learned the time-honored ways of their ancestors through imitating the models and absorbing the myths drawn from the great body of lyric and epic poetry. Grounded in custom and experience, it provided a venerable ideal of character and action. But this same audience would also have experienced the erosion of this education and of the world from which it had emerged—the world upon which its intelligibility depended. Old Education thinks a mere description of the traditional ways will suffice, just as Strepsiades will later think that the mere fact of his son's beating him is enough to condemn Pheidippides.[57] Both are wrong. The world has changed. The old ways must be defended by arguments, which leaves the old men vulnerable, if not helpless, since (as Burke and Oakeshott could have told them) by being forced to make an "argument," Old Education and Strepsiades have lost before they begin. It is a predicament that Old Education implicitly acknowledges when he speaks in the past tense. Worse than that, his revealingly detailed warning about the impression of young boys' buttocks being left in the sand not only implicates him in the promiscuity he excoriates, but raises questions about the status of the ancestral ways he celebrates.

It is this hopelessness that drives Old Education to adopt an aggressive sentimentality which is useless in convincing Pheidippides to adopt the way of life being endorsed; it all sounds like reactionary propaganda and for the same reasons that the shriller pamphlets of the National Association of Scholars do in the current debate over multiculturalism. But nothing puts the dilemma Old Education faces more starkly than his injunction to Pheidippides to honor his parents. What can that mean to a son whose parents come from different classes and ways of life? Honoring one entails dishonoring the other. (Of course, Pheidippides will eliminate this "cognitive dissonance" by *dishonoring* both.) He cannot follow the admonition to honor his parents because to do so presumes what does not exist: social stability, singular identities, and cultural homogeneity. In these terms the ease with which Pheidippides is transformed from a self-indulgent young aristocrat into an ascetic sophist who can make "the worse argument" appear "the better" and "twist" the truth for selfish ends suggests not so much the power of the new education as the weakness of what opposes it.

Sophistry (or Philosophy or New Education) can barely restrain himself not because he has an alternative vision of life to offer, but because he is anxious to demolish the one just presented (such as it is).[58] Consistent with his view that moral judgments are arbitrary human constructions, he is unembarrassed about being known as the immoral logic—a reputation due to his being the first to devise "A Method for the Subversion of Established Social Beliefs and the Undermining of Morality." Moreover, what he calls "these little inventions of mine, this knack of taking what might appear the worse argument and making it the better," have proved to be extremely lucrative.[59] Nihilism is profitable. Attacking "The Moral Argument," he shows the contradictory nature of its precepts. Old Education had dismissed baths as a sign of softness, for example, yet Heracles, the greatest of all Greek heroes, is the namesake of hot baths. Old Education had been likewise contemptuous of the Athenian preoccupation with politics and had extolled the greatness of Homer, yet it was Homer who praised the passion for politics displayed by Nestor. The most glaring contradiction, however, especially given the themes of this play, is the example of Kronos and Zeus. Although New Education is accused of threatening traditional Athenian education—as dramatized by Pheidippides' beating his father and promising to do the same to his mother—the old order was itself founded on patricide, so an "Athenian father who played Kronos to his son's Zeus was merely playing a traditional role."[60]

Old Education rambles on and on about moderation, yet he cannot produce anyone who has ever profited from it. How could Pheidippides be expected to emulate a life so filled with contradictions? Why would he *want* to, given what he would have to give up—the pleasure of satisfying his natural desires unstintingly and without fear of reprisal. In *The Republic*, the shepherd Gyges finds a magic ring that makes him invisible. Armed with the ring he does what any red-blooded man would do: seduces the queen, kills the king, and gets all the money, sex, and power he wants. (He is right in valuing two of the three.) Sophistry is the magic ring in *The Clouds*, where it creates a verbal fog around human actions, rendering the characters immune to retribution and punishment. This is accomplished by "proving" that "natural" distinctions among realms, activities, and persons are conventional, if not arbitrary. The most explosive and impressive example of sophistry's ability to destabilize (or reveal already destabilized) moral discourse is its strategy of making the worse, weaker, or inferior (*hēttōn*) argument appear the better, stronger, or superior (*kreittōn*) one.

These Greek words have a physical as well as a moral sense and were, among aristocratic circles in Athens, virtually indistinguishable. Given a heroic ideal that honored physical and martial excellence above all things, to be stronger was to be better, and vice versa, an identity that grounded *nomos* (law, custom, convention) in nature (*phusis*). Although the phrase "law of nature" was probably first coined by Callicles in Plato's *Gorgias* as an attack on democratic equality, something like it had been taken for granted until the sophists made explicit a separation between nature and convention that emerged (albeit only half-articulated) with the increased politicizing and democratizing of Athenian life.[61] As what had been the private prerogatives of kings and priests were brought out into the open and before the public, what had been "the way things are and must be" became subject to debate and interrogation. Before the sophists the implications of broadening what could be debated—and by whom—remained unspoken. Although men might make laws and societal arrangements, these were seen as divinely inspired. But this could no longer hold if the gods themselves were human inventions. Then laws and societal arrangements had to be justified in human terms, such as those used by Protagoras in his Great Speech in Plato's dialogue of that name.

Part of this democratizing process involved the increasing significance of speech. For one thing, the power of speech was regarded as independent of social class, which physical prowess was not. For another, persuasion and deliberation became, as I indicated earlier, recognized alternatives to violence and were viewed as the special achievements of democracy. But when, as in this play and its debate, words become weapons rather than an alternative to them, or they work like drugs in leaving their listeners powerless to resist them,[62] then everything associated with the triumph of speech, including the polis, democracy, and comedy itself, becomes deeply problematic. Consequently, the violent ending of the play, in which the outraged Strepsiades burns down the Thinkery, is a logical as well as a dramatic extension of New Education's use of language.[63] To the degree that speech is nothing but deception and a strategy for domination, comedy itself cannot possibly perform its institutional role as an educator of the audience. It is not just that the ideal of a democratic citizenry making independent judgments as part of a process of deliberation becomes utterly impossible to realize, but also that comedy's playing on and with words, like its social and cultural radicalism, is only possible if there are some stable meanings and cultural continuities—and if persuasion and deliberation remain civilized alternatives to violence and war.

No one wins the debate between Old and New Education. Neither side can win if political life and comedy are to persist. One can no more go back to the old ways than one can restore one's virginity or, in our time, speak of "nature" naively. Things are too politicized. Yet the new way in which everything is politicized is no way at all. "What," to quote Lenin, "is to be done?"

—————

The battle between philosophy/sophistry, or Immoral Argument/New Education, and Old Education ends when the latter, convinced that the punishment for adultery (reaming a radish up the offender's rectum) is meaningless since everyone—including the great tragic poets, the city's most respected statesmen, and the entire audience—practices buggery, has no choice but to throw in the towel and run into the Thinkery. As for Strepsiades, his son unfortunately proves a far more adept pupil than he was. Pheidippides emerges from his studies so white-faced and smart-assed that his proud father feels safe in ridiculing the audience as well as his creditors. Sure that his son is invincible, he is unaware of how vulnerable that invincibility leaves him.

Initially, everything goes according to plan, although we know from the chorus's moralizing that "this poor man's Socrates" will soon learn that crime does not pay, that you reap what you sow, that no man is an island, that there are no atheists in foxholes or when a father is being beaten by his son. And sure enough, the celebratory speeches of the graduation dinner break down into mutual insults whose tone and substance recall the equally rancorous confrontation between New and Old Education. And, as with that earlier contest, the chorus intervenes to set up a more formal agōn, now between father and son, to be judged by the audience in the theater.[64] During dinner Strepsiades asks his son to sing songs from the works of the great poet-educators of Greece, as is customary. But Pheidippides will have nothing to do with these boring, bombastic bullshitters and instead recites a passage from one of what his father calls "Euripides' slimy tragedies where a brother screws his sister."[65] Furious, the father berates the son, and the son returns the compliment in spades *and* justifies the outrage as natural and necessary after first extolling the virtues of his new education, which gives him the power to destroy the moral order, as a preface to doing so.

Pheidippides never dreamed how sensual the sound of words could be, never imagined the rapturous pleasure he would get from hearing himself talk, never once anticipated the thrill of sabotaging the established order.[66]

He owes everything to Socrates, who transformed him from a stuttering horse lover into a man of such consummate philosophical subtlety and profundity that he can easily prove why beating one's father is justified. Did not his father beat him for his own good? So Pheidippides beats his father for Strepsiades' good. Is there not a saying that old men are boys writ large? Then it follows that old men deserve to be beaten more, since at their age they have less of an excuse for the mischief they commit. When Strepsiades invokes all that he has so far disparaged—Zeus, nature, and law—his son responds as did New Education: law is man-made, the product of powerful words, revocable and reversible by any eloquent man who can convince the assembly that sons should have the right to administer corporeal punishment to their wayward fathers. Nor will appeals to nature help Strepsiades: just look at the permanent state of open warfare between rooster fathers and sons, as between those of other animal species. And as for Zeus, remember Kronos.

Strepsiades has no choice but to admit defeat on behalf of the older generation, thereby echoing the capitulation of Old Education in the earlier debate. At first, he blames his troubles on the chorus of clouds. Why did they mislead him, or at least not warn him? The clouds insist that the guilt is his since they but tempt men to give in to their dishonest dreams, drawing forth their illicit desires so that, like Aeschylean protagonists, men can become wise through suffering. At last, Strepsiades realizes that he could only have evaded his obligations to his creditors by destroying the very social fabric that guaranteed Pheidippides' filial obligations to him. Rebuffed by a son who revels in his new self and worships Socrates rather than Zeus, and who infuriates the old man beyond words by threatening to beat his mother, Strepsiades doesn't withdraw into the Thinkery as defeated Old Education did. He burns it down. There are, after all, some brute facts in the world, some things that words cannot extinguish, and fire is one of them. Standing on top of the Thinkery, torch and axe in hand, Strepsiades first chops down the house of the logic-choppers, then sets it ablaze. Now it is he who "walks on air and looks down upon the sun from a superior standpoint."

≡≡≡≡

Where is Aristophanes in the play? With whom, for what, and where does he stand in the opposition between Strepsiades and Socrates and the agōn between Old and New Education? Surely not with the narrow materialism, dumb immoralism, and gullible rusticism of the farting, finger-giving, crotch-grabbing, phallus-waving country bumpkin, Strepsiades. Here, surely, is a dramatic invention created merely for ridicule, obscene in our legal sense of being "without redeeming social value." Of course, he is a caricature—not an ordinary Athenian, as some commentators have argued in order to show Aristophanes' contempt for democracy and affinities with Socrates—at whose bodily fixation we are intended to laugh. But we can also laugh with him and at those who laugh at him.

After all, compared to the airy pomposities of the philosophers, there is a certain integrity to Strepsiades' boorish grounding of concepts in the everyday world: his supposition that students with their noses to the ground are looking for truffles, that geometry is good for surveying lots, and that the map he sees cannot be one of Athens since there are no law courts visible; his desire, upon viewing the map, to have Sparta moved further away from Athens; and his repeated attempts to find (usually gastronomical) meaning in astronomical and philosophical speculations. Many of us have such thoughts, though we are wise or cautious enough not to speak them.

Moreover, comedy and Strepsiades share a history. Both have moved from the country to the city,[67] so comedy may understand and represent predicaments like his with particular insight. If it does, it may be able to help him (and others in similar straits) understand the contradictions of his life, perhaps even to help him laugh at them and so give rise to second thoughts about resorting to violence to end them. Strepsiades, "at a loss" in every sense of that phrase, is thus susceptible to the crackpot schemes of intellectuals and the pretentious prattle of philosophers or anyone else who promises to save him from the hybrid world in which he owes money and to which he owes his confusion. Surely, this is not an unfamiliar situation. To the degree that comedy can save people from themselves and this manipulation by making them more attentive to the seductions around them, it can help sustain the vitality of a democratic citizenry. Political education is not a matter of foisting a particular agenda on an audience, but of helping them think about what they are doing, and what others are trying to do to them, sometimes in their name, often for their unrecognized benefit. Just like Socrates of the *Apology*.

But what about Socrates? I want to largely bypass the extensive scholarly debate over how much the character Socrates is like the historical Socrates—whether what we hear him saying represents his own views or an amalgam of often contradictory philosophical positions; whether one can reconcile the animus Aristophanes seems to display toward Socrates in *The Clouds* with his seeming affection for him depicted in Plato's *Symposium*; and whether Aristophanes can be blamed for creating the atmosphere of suspicion that led to Socrates' death—to assert that "Socrates" is, like Strepsiades, a caricature of the self-important, superior intellectual who looks down on the people.[68] As such, however, he can no more be dismissed than Strepsiades can because he, too, shares something with the comic poet.[69] To the degree that one can call the Athenians as a whole an "intellectual" people, then, what is caricatured and mocked in Socrates is a shared cultural trait that is exaggerated in, but not unique to, one particular man.[70]

The Clouds presents philosophers and intellectuals as pretentious quibblers, destroyers of people's beliefs and lives, and self-aggrandizing purveyors of esoteric knowledge which they only teach to initiates who can afford the fee and who actually learn how to steal people blind through the power of words. They are dramatized as impatient and imperious, constantly alert to everyone's assumptions but their own, and, with their heads in the clouds, oblivious to what is obvious. Their logic-chopping is useless, and their interpretations—theological, political, and literary—merely project themselves onto the world even as they proclaim their neutrality, objectivity, and impartiality. Philosophy is autobiographical in ways that become clear only when caricatured by an Aristophanes or a Nietzsche.

Perhaps worst of all, these intellectuals and philosophers try to exempt themselves from the ignorance they are so ready to attribute to others. To object that this cannot be true of anyone who, like Socrates, claims to know that he does not know is to ignore how this becomes yet another, more mystifying ploy by which philosophers claim the superior ground they seem to be giving up. But comedy, or at least this one, permits no such claims and allows no such mystification, and in this, as in other ways, it is antihierarchic and egalitarian. In a statement that might be a commentary on the role of the cloak in *The Clouds*, James Redfield argues that the "great instruments" of Old Comedy "are obscenity and scatology, which remind us that we are all naked under our clothes." Individuals are deprived of their dignity, but in the process "mankind in general," embodied in the audience, recovers a sense of power and liberty.[71] When cultural forms or great political and intellectual leaders are ridiculed, we are reminded that neither culture nor those leaders are anything but our creation and that both can be recreated.[72]

But I am not sure Redfield is entirely right about *The Clouds* because here everyone becomes a spectacle before everyone else: the chorus and characters on stage; the characters who, stepping out of their roles, talk directly to the audience about themselves as actors and refer to the theater in Athens;[73] Aristophanes, when he comes forward to address the audience in the parabasis, and the spectators when he looks out at them; New Education and these spectators, when he invites his opponent to tell him what kind of men he sees in the audience. No one escapes being part of the spectacle—as if Aristophanes were imitating the rotation in office that was so central to Athenian democracy—and so no one escapes the mocking that accompanies the ignorance of being human. Each moment of superiority, of laughing at others and ridiculing their foibles, is imperceptibly reversed. This includes the city as well as the comic poet who is its educator. For the vices ridiculed in Aristophanes' comedies and laughed at by his audience "are in fact the vices of the audience." In the parabasis the audience of citizens is berated for its political ineptitude and its failure to give Aristophanes his due. Yet this spectator of society/audience becomes a spectacle himself when his "personal hopes, ambitions, feelings, and disappointments are witnessed and laughed at by the audience."[74] So everyone becomes a member of the comic event, sharing in the fallibility, vulnerability, and imperfect self-knowledge it reveals.

There is one more thing about the democratic community that comedy creates in the theater and presumably helps to constitute outside it. Comedy assumes that the people are capable of self-awareness and self-critique, that thinking can and perhaps must be an aspect of democratic citizenship. All this points to the affinities between Socrates and Aristophanes. Most generally, comedy helped to constitute a tradition of democratic self-awareness and self-critique that may well have inspired Socrates' political philosophy. It certainly grounds the exaggerated intellectualism contained in Socrates' injunction against the unexamined life as not worth living, a proposition that would have been laughed out of court instead of taken seriously by a people who did not already see themselves as in some sense "intellectuals."

Thus it is not surprising that Aristophanes had some sympathy with Socratic intellectualism, nor that one could say about Socratic questioning what has been said about *The Clouds*: "It transfers the last word to the audience," who are left to enact their own part but a little more reflectively than before.[75] One could also show how the play evinces "Socratic" irony, how the shared risks of dialogue unite the interlocutors in a recognition of their mortality much as the comic event does, and suggest that Socrates shared the risks of dialogue as Aristophanes did the risk of laughter and ridicule. Moreover, Aristophanes and Socrates both saw themselves as political educators of a democratic polity. Each was concerned with the corruption of language and sought to teach their compatriots how to judge speech and speakers.[76] Both show why it was necessary to move beyond a narrow self-interest, although they certainly differed about what was worth a citizen's attention and care. By precept and example, both sought to provide a more comprehensive framework within which their fellow citizens could understand what they were doing to others and themselves. And both could be caustic critics of the dēmos—knowing well enough that ordinary people could be anti-intellectual, intolerant of difference, and irrational—but neither concluded that the dēmos required institutional limits on their power or rule by "responsible elites" to save them from their excesses.[77] What they did conclude was that a democratic polity had need, most of all, of political education.

The problem for Aristophanes was to find a mode of speech that was tied to but not weighed down by physical desire, a way of thinking that was sensual and concepts that remained connected to their physical grounding in place and body. In terms of intellectuals, it means their owning up to their worldliness and anchoring their free-floating ideas, which would otherwise spin off into absurdity. In Aristotelian terms, it means carving out a political language that mediates our being both beasts and gods, at once natural and cultural. In terms of *The Clouds*, it means connecting Socrates and Strepsiades in a way that they are not connected in the play. (I think Aristophanes regarded his revised version of *The Clouds* as doing something like this, or at the very least as dramatizing why such an alliance was essential to a democratic citizenry. I also think he believed that, by educating the Athenian audience to judge the rhetoric of comedy, he would be assisting his fellow citizens in judging the rhetoric of demagogues, orators, and philosophers.) This mode of speech would be one that recognized the power of language to change character and the world, but that used such power responsibly in terms of the traditions sustaining a democratic culture. The sense of possibility that attends the recognition of the world as open to the shaping hand of human power can too easily initiate a dialectic capable of destroying the culture that made such power possible in the first place. One can see this in Thucydides' *History*, as words lose their meaning, and in the counsel of New Education in *The Clouds*. If the medium of both politics and comedy is speech, then the comic poet is necessarily committed to maintaining its "integrity." He seeks to keep it connected to things in the world, but free to confront (and mock) the categories by which we make such connections and construct that world, and to ridicule and provoke without turning language exclusively into a weapon that bludgeons rather than persuades or convinces. After all, if speech is simply war by other means, what is to stop someone from burning down the theater along with the Thinkery?

This mode of speech would also be a form of political knowledge—not just knowledge about politics, but knowledge that is political in origin and texture.[78] Let me use Machiavelli by way of illustration. In *The Prince*, the political theorist is likened to a landscape painter. Unlike the Prince and the people, who are frozen in their positions, the theorist is able to stand on the mountain with the Prince to see the people below and to stand with the people in the valley to see how the Prince appears on high. This double perspective is the theorist's special claim to knowledge and power. Unlike in Plato, where the "ground" of politics is only on high *(The Republic* is a path upward), the high and the low in Machiavelli are equally valid sources of political knowledge. It is this double perspective that makes the theorist valuable to the Prince and allows him to mediate between the Prince and the people, showing both the need each has for the other and thereby constituting them as a whole. I want to suggest that Aristophanes is making a similar claim, that *The Clouds* as a form of speech mediates between classes and between the double capacity—let us call it Socratism and Strepsiadism—of the citizenry as a whole and perhaps singly.

This view is at odds with the still dominant one on *The Clouds*. Responding to that view will allow me to return to questions broached in the opening section and to comment on the play, and comedy, as a mode of democratic speech and education.

The prevailing view of *The Clouds* is that it sides with Old Education because, as a conservative by class, choice, and institutional position, Aristophanes thought (or could not help believing) that the sophists were corrupting Athenian education and politics.[79] From this point of view, the play endorses the burning down of the Thinkery and oppressive legislation against intellectuals generally, seeks to convince the dēmos to accept the guidance of the rich and wellborn, and shows a "love of simple virtues" and of "the good old times."[80] Indeed, even if this love were not Aristophanes' personal predilection, it would have been imposed on him by his social role because being "commissioned to speak for the solidarity of the audience" rendered him necessarily "hostile to all innovations, including those that might improve society."[81] Although Aristophanes might complain about the current state of things, his most intense ridicule was reserved for those intellectual and political leaders who would ameliorate it. Thus he was a critic of critics, a celebrator of the grotesque only against a background of commonsense normality, which he does everything he can to reinforce. The final scene, in which the clouds reveal themselves as traditional deities who punish wrongdoing, clinches the argument. As Strepsiades takes full revenge on those who have outraged the gods (urged on by the Koryphaios), both the cosmic and the political order are reestablished. Justice triumphs, morality rules, and the old farmer, "put in touch with the rustic energy of his background," is "restored to himself."[82]

As I have already argued, there are good reasons to be suspicious of this reading and the political portrait of the playwright on which it rests. These have to do with the clouds being goddesses of poets as well as philosophers, Old Education's rejection of comedy, Aristophanes' boasts (in the parabasis), and the utter impotence of Old Education, who winds up throwing himself into the arms of his enemy for dumb reasons. But there are other, perhaps more powerful reasons to reject what might be called the "Platonic" Aristophanes.[83] The first arises from a general consideration of the connection between elite and popular culture, the second from Aristophanes' identifying himself with what he supposedly repudiated, and the third from the play's ending.

A major assumption of those who believe Aristophanes to be a conservative, and *The Clouds* an endorsement of Old Education, is that Athenian democracy was controlled by elite families and elite culture. It is an argument made by both "conservatives," who wish to explain how the marvelous artistic achievements of the Athenians could coexist with a mobocracy, and "leftists," who find in Aristophanes little criticism of oligarchs but much of the dēmos.[84] As Josiah Ober has argued (using a particularly apt image, given the previous discussion), however, the discursive basis of Athenian society "was not given on high and was not a unique product of elite culture, but rather was established and constantly revised in the prac- tice of public debate."[85] Ober is specifically referring to public oratory, but I think his point can be extended to include Old Comedy, which was in its own way part of that oratory. What he says about a juryman deciding a case of hubris—that he had no juridically given external model of ap- propriate behavior but had to judge within and through a regime of social knowledge and truth—is also true of a juryman deciding on the prizes to be awarded to comedies. For both were part of a regime in which their decisions participated by being articulated, whether to reinforce existing assumptions about social categories and behavior or to revise them. Given such power, the central political and cultural ideals of the aristocracy are at once transformed, co-opted by, and delimited within a public environment of democratic politics. When Aristophanes turns our gaze to Socrates and the new aristocratic elite formed by sophistic education, he is turning the power of the people on targets that embody the continuing threat by aris- tocratic pretensions to superiority, including any new elite tied to wealth rather than heredity.

Second, the play is replete with *sophos* and its cognates, especially in the parabasis. There, Aristophanes insists that he speaks truth without limit or restraint, that *The Clouds* is the wisest of all his plays, and that he has writ- ten it for the *sophoi*, who appreciate its clever new ideas. He seems to ally himself, at least here, with the new ideas that the rest of the play ridicules. This is not to deny a conservative element or sympathies, but to insist that these are not the play's only sympathies and that, to put it anachronistically, we may need to be conservative in education so as to be radical in politics.

In an essay entitled "The Crisis in Education," Hannah Arendt argues that a crisis means we lose "the answers on which we ordinarily rely with- out even realizing that they were originally answers to questions."[86] Being forced back to the questions themselves is a "disaster only when we re- spond to it with preformed judgments," as Old Education does. Such an attitude not only deepens the crisis, but makes us forfeit the opportunity for reflection that a crisis provides. While democratic politics entails "join- ing with one's equals in assuming the effort at persuasion and running the risk of failure," any intervention based upon the absolute superiority of the adult, with its associated attempt to produce the new as a fait accompli, "is dictatorial," since it supposes that the new already exists.[87] Educators (and all adults) "must assume responsibility for the world even if they themselves did not make it and even though they may, secretly or openly, wish it were other than it is." In education we must conserve, cherish, and protect the child against the world and the world against the child, the new against the old and the old against the new. But in politics this *conservative* attitude—striving to preserve the status quo—"can only lead to destruction because the world in gross and in detail, is irrevocably delivered up to the ruin of time, unless human beings are determined to intervene, to alter, to create what is new."[88]

If it is legitimate to appropriate Ober's view of oratory for mine of comedy, then the ending of *The Clouds* upon which the conservative view rests can be read differently. And if I am right to see Aristophanes' understanding of himself as that of a political educator in Arendt's terms, then it must be read differently. For one thing, Pheidippides is left unregenerate and pointedly absent from the ending. If all is supposed to return to normal and order to be restored, then something is rotten in the city-state of Athens. Moreover, given that the clouds have continually changed their shape and that *The Clouds* has relied on verbal equivocation and unexpected turns in action, plot, and character, one should be careful about accepting the ending as any permanent shape or form. And while it is true that the "ceremonial aspect of the festival, the highly articulated structure of the plays themselves, provided a frame of containment for comedy's challenge,"[89] so that whatever destabilizing surprises posed in and by the play are circumscribed by ritual stage and theater, *The Clouds* stretches the form to the limit and challenges the frame itself. This is not only because the caricature of Old Education, who represents "the good old times," "simple virtues," and "normality," is too powerful to be put to rest outside the theater (as Plato's *Apology* suggests)—and not only because the play itself is so innovative—but because its ending is virtually unique in its uncomic aspects and absolutely unique in its self-consciousness about its own form and purposes.

I do not want to deny how much fun it is to watch (or even to be) Strepsiades taking his revenge by turning the kiln-shaped Thinkery into a real oven while parodying Socrates' pretentiousness. (It is a little like seeing a snob sitting in a proctologist's waiting room.) But the ending is not the festive celebration and joyous ordering of what has gone before that is typical of final scenes in comedy. It is, rather, as abrupt as it is violent, and the burning is as much an act of futility as of defiance and revenge. Indeed, as I have noted, the ending resembles that of a tragedy, which makes this play, like its characters and Athens, a hybrid.[90] Nor would I deny that the play is condescendingly critical of the glib, aggressive immoralism of New Education or that it dramatizes the cost of denaturing practices and relationships and the myopia of New Education in encouraging conditions that make its own existence problematic. But, as I have tried to suggest, the play does not endorse either form of education; instead, it provides a stage on which the absurdity of both positions and the partisans of each in the audience are ridiculed. By caricaturing each side, the play provides a middle ground and an occasion for laughter so as to free its audience not only from a fascination with their city but from a more particular fascination with party and class. For what *The Clouds* dramatizes is the dangerous political dynamic among sophistic intellectuals, their students—who form a new class of revolutionary aristocratic-elite youth united in elite clubs opportunistically using democratic rhetoric to assume power—and their fathers, whose reaction is sometimes violent.

═══

On the other hand, I do not want to claim too little for comedy by claiming too much for it. Comedy is not philosophy or theory. It is far funnier and can do things that philosophy and theory cannot. But while it can dramatize the predicament of its characters, and thus help its citizen audience recognize and live with their own hybrid identities, it offers no solutions and prescribes no cures, though whether or how that is a deficiency is much debated these days.

Nor do I want to ignore what the Greeks never did: the moral ambivalence of comedy. Humor and laughter can be playful and infectious and can defuse potentially explosive situations. But it can also be derisive and caustic, creating tension and animus or being used to shame miscreants. We have all been in situations where a joke breaks the ice or tension, where self-mockery is charming, gentle ridicule amusing, and we couldn't help laughing even when we were angry or resentful. But we have also been with couples whose bantering had a disquieting edge to it, or in situations where a joke seemed inappropriate or "bombed," or where self-mockery revealed much more than intended.

Nor, finally, can I point to any comic work and say with certainty that it led to a specifiable change in policy attitude or mood. I do not know for sure that Aristophanes' comedies had any effect on the political fate of Cleon, the standing of Euripides, the relationship between men and women or fathers and sons, or even the fate of Socrates (where we have a claim that it did), any more than I can say what effect, if any, Michael Moore's *TV Nation* has had on attitudes toward corporate executives, the Gulf War, health care, or a dirt-poor Texas town being inundated with New York's excrement. But I am willing to bet (though not too much) that *Roseanne* has done more to change popular attitudes toward same-sex relationships, family values, class, and being overweight than most arguments, books, or government policies. (How can one be condescending toward her working-class life when she makes better jokes about her family, food, and home furnishings than we could?) These shows are funny, and they make us think by grounding abstract debates and pontifications about "family values" or corporate "relocations" in the "real" lives of everyday people. They also remind us of the enormous gap between our own comedic conditions of performance and those of fifth-century B.C. Athens, and perhaps of certain parallels as well: that irreverence and mockery may provide a basis for political critique, while effrontery and excess can be an impulse toward ethical insight.

In some striking ways our ethical situation is, as Bernard Williams has written, "more like human beings in antiquity than any Western people have been in the meantime. More particularly, we are like those who from the fifth century and earlier have left us traces of a consciousness that had not yet been touched by Plato's and Aristotle's attempts to make our ethical relations to the world fully intelligible."[91] Aristophanic comedy, like the dung of Strepsiades' rustic beginnings, is such a trace, at one and the same time rude and offensive *and* fertile and productive.[92]

Notes

1 See Josiah Ober, "How to Criticize Democracy in Late Fifth- and Fourth-Century Athens," in *Athenian Political Thought and the Reconstruction of American Democracy*, ed. J. Peter Euben, John R. Wallach, and Josiah Ober (Ithaca, 1994), 149–71; and "Civil Ideology and Counterhegemonic Discourse: Thucydides on the Sicilian Debate," in *Athe-*

nian Identity and Civic Ideology, ed. Alan L. Boegehold and Adele C. Scafuro (Baltimore, 1994), 102–26; see also Sheldon Wolin, "Norm and Form: The Constitutionalizing of Democracy," in Euben, Wallach, and Ober, eds., *Athenian Political Thought*, 29–58.

2   As G. E. R. Lloyd notes, "The fundamental point remains that much Greek philosophy and science presupposes an audience that prides itself on its ability in the evaluation of evidence and arguments; and if we ask where that ability came from, the experience in law courts and political assemblies provides at least part of the likely answer"; see his "Greek Democracy, Philosophy, and Science," in *Democracy, the Unfinished Journey 508 BC to AD 1993*, ed. John Dunn (New York, 1992), 41–56; quotation from 47. And no citizens spent more time in law courts and assemblies than did these Athenians.

3   On the senses in which Greek tragedy can be regarded as a "theoretical" institution, see the introduction to J. Peter Euben, *Greek Tragedy and Political Theory* (Berkeley, 1986); and *The Tragedy of Political Theory* (Princeton, 1990), chap. 2.

4   Nicole Loraux, *The Invention of Athens* (Cambridge, MA, 1986), 304–11; quotation from 306.

5   See the discussion in Josiah Ober, "Power and Oratory in Democratic Athens: Demosthenes 21, Against Meidia," in *Persuasion: Greek Rhetoric in Action*, ed. Ian Worthington (London, 1994), 85–108.

6   See the discussion in the introduction to David Konstan, *Greek Comedy and Ideology* (New York, 1995).

7   Anthony T. Edwards, "Aristophanes' Comic Poetics: TRUX Scatology, SKŌMMA," *Transactions of the American Philological Association* 121 (1991): 157–79; quotation from 171. Edwards argues that the ethical ground for Aristophanes lies in the sentiment of *aidōs*, "the impulse to avoid public humiliation affronts to one's honor and self-esteem resulting either from an objective failure to satisfy accepted public standards or from criticism that one has fallen short of such expectations" (174).

8   See Terence Irwin's excellent discussion of Plato's and Xenophon's understanding of *The Clouds* as initiating the criticism of Socrates, in "Socrates and Athenian Democracy," *Philosophy and Public Affairs* 18 (1989): 184–205. The version of *The Clouds* we have is a revised one from 418/17; the original (which won third prize) was produced in 423. This, of course, makes the play an atypical comedy, in that it was (probably) circulated without being performed, but its atypicality highlights some crucial qualities of Aristophanic comedy in general.

9   Paul Cartledge, *Aristophanes and His Theatre of the Absurd* (Bristol, 1990). See also note 80.

10 See Stephen Halliwell, "The Uses of Laughter in Greek Culture," *Classical Quarterly* 41 (1991): 279–96; A. M. Bowie, *Aristophanes: Myth, Ritual and Comedy* (Cambridge, 1993), chaps. 1 and 5; Simon Goldhill, "Comic Inversion and Inverted Commas: Aristophanes and Parody," in *Poet's Voice: Essays on Poetics and Greek Literature* (New York, 1991), 167–222; and Thomas K. Hubbard, *The Mask of Comedy* (Ithaca, 1992).

11 In many respects this tension recapitulates a more general one between a highly agonal politics and the processes of collective deliberation that require some mediation of such agonism. For a general discussion, see Dana R. Villa, *Arendt and Heidegger* (Princeton, 1995).

12 Plato *Apology* 18a–19c. Malcolm Heath, in *Political Comedy in Aristophanes* (Göttingen, 1987), reads Socrates' insinuation that the charges against him were based on comedy as meant "to discredit the prosecutors' case" (9–10); Arthur Kingman Rogers, in *The Socratic Problem* (New York, 1971), sees Socrates as implying that Aristophanes was merely trading on a calumny that had been current for some time (86).

13 Cf. Loraux's argument on this issue in *Invention of Athens* with the work of Josiah Ober—for instance, "Power and Oratory in Democratic Athens."

14 Hubbard, *Mask of Comedy*, 101.

15 Goldhill, "Comic Inversion and Inverted Commas," 183.

16 Loraux, *Invention of Athens*.

17 I am referring, of course, to Old Comedy. On the differences between Old Comedy and New Comedy, see E. W. Handley's discussion in "Comedy," in *The Cambridge History of Classical Literature*, ed. P. E. Easterling and B. M. W. Knox (New York, 1989), chap. 3, pts. 10, 11. On the recognition and place of comedy, see Dora C. Pozzi, "The Polis in Crisis," in *Myth and the Polis*, ed. Dora C. Pozzi and John M. Wichersham (Ithaca, 1991), 126–63; and Jeffrey Henderson, "The Demos and the Comic Competition," in *Nothing to Do with Dionysos?* ed. John J. Winkler and Froma Zeitlin (Princeton, 1990), 271–313, esp. 313.

18 But these "ordinary" people are caricatured every bit as much as Socrates is, which means that their ordinariness is as generic and exaggerated as his extraordinariness. Interestingly, those critics who think Socrates is caricatured and Aristophanes is grossly unfair to him do not make the same point about the dēmos.

19 See O. P. Taplin, "Fifth Century Tragedy and Comedy: A Synkrisis," *Journal of Hellenic Studies* 106 (1986): 163–74, esp. 173.

20 There is, by the same token, a compelling logic and air of inevitability to Oedipus's self-discovery that is absent from *The Clouds*.

21 On "parrhēsia," see Sara Monoson, "Frank Speech, Democracy, and Philosophy: Plato's Debt to a Democratic Strategy of Civic Discourse," in Euben, Wallach, and Ober, eds., *Athenian Political Thought*, 172–97.

22 When Strepsiades farts in imitation of a clap of thunder, Socrates tells him to leave that filth for the comic stage. (Mark Twain called flatulence a "fundamental sigh.") With the arrival of the clouds, Socrates tells Strepsiades to look at them over the theater of Dionysus, and when Strepsiades complains that he can't see them, Socrates instructs him to look along the entryway onto the stage. See James Redfield, "Drama and Community: Aristophanes and Some of His Rivals," in Winkler and Zeitlin, eds., *Nothing to Do*, 314–35. On the complex ways in which seeing and being seen work in *The Clouds* and in Greek theater generally, see Hubbard, *Mask of Comedy*, chap. 1; and Bowie, *Aristophanes*, chaps. 1 and 5.

23 See Cartledge, *Aristophanes and His Theatre*, 9.

24 Taplin, "Fifth Century Tragedy and Comedy," 164.

25 Ibid., 164–65.

26 But given the way the chorus reflects what is projected onto it, I am not sure how "seriously" to take this song.

27 Hubbard, *Mask of Comedy*, 112. He goes on to suggest that the ending reveals the comic poet's uncertainty about his role as intellectual mentor.

28 J. Peter Euben, "The Debate over the Canon," *The Civic Arts Review* 7 (1994): 3–15.

29 This is William Arrowsmith's (condensed) translation of lines 960–62 of *The Clouds* (New York, 1962), 86. Arrowsmith takes considerable liberties with the text, but they almost always work. I have taken some liberties myself by trying to make his modernization even more contemporary. Unfortunately, the Arrowsmith edition has no line numbers, so I refer to pages in citing quotations.

30 As quoted in Catherine R. Stimpson, "On Differences: Modern Language Association Presidential Address 1990," in *Debating PC*, ed. Paul Berman (New York, 1992), 40–60; quotation from 54.

31 That such language remains remote even when it warns about the "systems world" invading "the life world" suggests a dissonance between text and subtext. (The phrases are Jürgen Habermas's.)

32 Plato *Symposium* 223d. Taplin reminds us that "though we know of well over 100 fifth century playwrights, we do not know of a single one who produced both tragedy and comedy" ("Fifth Century Tragedy and Comedy," 163).

33 See Robert W. Corrigan, "Comedy and the Comic Spirit," in *Comedy: An Anthology*, ed. Robert W. Corrigan (Boston, 1971), x.

34 I follow Arrowsmith in using these terms to describe the opposition, but other ways of formulating it include philosophy versus sophistry, the just or stronger argument versus the unjust or weaker one, and the moral argument versus the immoral one. These ways of putting it seem to me, however, to beg the questions that the play is trying to raise.

35 Thucydides *History of the Peloponnesian War* 1.70–72. See William Arrowsmith, "Aristophanes' Birds: The Fantasy Politics of Eros," *Arion N.S.* 1 (1993–94): 116–67.

36 This is an exaggeration dictated by the occasions: the Corinthians are trying to convince the Spartans to fight; Pericles is deflecting the pain of loss. In fact, these older values remained a part of Athenian life, reasserting themselves with particular force in times of crisis. Nevertheless, compared with Archaic Athens and the rest of Greece, these traits were more characteristic of fifth-century Athenians.

37 The moral history of this period and the role of the sophists in it has been told by A. W. H. Adkins, F. Heinimann, W. K. C. Guthrie, Mario Untersteiner, G. B. Kerferd, F. Solmsen, and Eric Havelock. Nietzsche spawned a quite different tradition from both the moral-decline and the moral-improvement/Greek Enlightenment arguments, one which has, through the influence of Foucault, Derrida, and Lyotard, led to a spate of recent studies of the sophists and their rhetoric—mainly by professors of literature.

38 Arrowsmith, trans., *The Clouds*, 21.

39 See George B. Walsh, *The Varieties of Enchantment* (Chapel Hill, 1984), 80; see also chap. 5.

40 Only at the end of the play are the parents united—as victims of their son's new education.

41 This issue is discussed at length by Daphne Elizabeth O'Regan in *Rhetoric, Comedy, and the Violence: Language in Aristophanes' Clouds* (New York, 1992).

42 Perhaps "thud" is the wrong word, given the way that Strepsiades understands Zeus's thunder; see Arrowsmith, trans., *The Clouds*, 45.

43 The fact that Socrates is introduced so indirectly may be evidence that Aristophanes is

less concerned with the specific person than with the generic intellectual/philosopher. Of course, some of the character's traits must have been specific to Socrates for the joke to have worked, but it was his identification as an Athenian that would have been crucial for an Athenian audience.

44 This question is dramatically connected with the discussion of Zeus's thunder and sophistic speech in ways that link the purest thought (*nŏema*) to the lowest bodily functions, the gods' power, and the new education.

45 Arrowsmith, trans., *The Clouds*, 29.

46 Ibid., 33.

47 The Greek word here (related to *nomos*) means both "currency" and "custom," so Socrates is saying here that belief in Zeus is not current coin or custom.

48 Note that poets and philosophers have the same gods (or goddesses).

49 The most persuasive case for this conclusion is made by Charles Segal in "Aristophanes' Cloud-Chorus," *Arethusa* 2 (1969): 143–61.

50 See the discussion in Hubbard, *Mask of Comedy*, 89.

51 There is a sense in which Strepsiades is reborn as father becomes child of the son. Sophistry seems powerful enough to change the "natural" sequence of things—at least for the moment.

52 Compare Strepsiades' "I admire you but I don't follow you" with Crito's similar confusion (Arrowsmith, trans., *The Clouds*, 44).

53 Halliwell, "Uses of Laughter," 296.

54 The Greek suggests something contrived or newly invented (like the word "thinkery").

55 This is, of course, an example of the flattery with which the New Logic gained such power. It is the subject of Plato's *Gorgias*.

56 Arrowsmith, trans., *The Clouds*, 83.

57 See C. T. Murphy, "Aristophanes and the Art of Rhetoric," *Harvard Studies in Classical Philology* 49 (1938): 52–67.

58 See the discussion by Martha Nussbaum, "Aristophanes and Socrates on Learning Practical Wisdom," *Yale Classical Studies* 26 (1980): 43–97.

59 Arrowsmith, trans., *The Clouds*, 93.

60 Barry Strauss, *Fathers and Sons in Athens: Ideology and Society in the Era of the Peloponnesian War* (Princeton, 1993), 160.

61 On the one hand, the declaration that phusis is distinct from nomos entails either a denigration of the latter, since it still distinguishes us from animals, or the conclusion that all laws are morally equal (or outside morality) because they are all conventional. On the other hand, eliminating nature as the ground and sanction for belief and action does and did leave nomos vulnerable to sophistic attack.

62 In the debate over the fate of the rebellious Mytileneans (Thucydides 3.37–48), Cleon accuses his fellow citizens of being so in love with verbal displays, and more susceptible to the aesthetics than the substance of an argument, that they are unable to adhere to a settled policy. The irony is that Cleon, the most violent man of his time, is here defending the death penalty for all of the Mytileneans, no matter what their politics, and is using speech to persuade his own people not to be so enamored of speech; see O'Regan, *Rhetoric, Comedy, and the Violence* (esp. chap. 6), on how this plays out in *The Clouds*.

63   It is worth remembering that Strepsiades got himself into this predicament, so his violence is the result of his own greed and lack of moral principles. It was because of such a possibly violent reaction that both Gorgias and Protagoras (in the Platonic dialogues named after them) take such pains to proclaim their innocence (as when Gorgias declares rhetoric a neutral instrument) or to disguise what they are doing (as Protagoras does at precisely the point when he insists that he is being honest).

64   Throughout *The Clouds*, the audience is appealed to and asked "to judge" what is happening before them (e.g., by Amynias, one of Strepsiades' creditors, who asks them to be witnesses and by Strepsiades himself, who appeals to the audience when his son is hitting him). Of course, plays themselves were judged, and Athenian citizens spent considerable time in various courts, as suggested above.

65   Arrowsmith, trans., *The Clouds*, 120.

66   Like Socrates earlier and Strepsiades later (as he stands on top of the Thinkery with axe and torch in hand), Pheidippides too talks of being able to look down on others and their common, conventional ways (*tōn kathestōtōn nomōn*).

67   See the discussion in Pozzi, "Polis in Crisis."

68   See Plato's discussion of laughter (in *Philebus* 48c–d) as the opposite of the Delphic "know thyself." I am making something close to the opposite case. It will not do to say simply that Socrates was a real person and Strepsiades a character invented by Aristophanes, since "Socrates" is also a character and Strepsiades a caricature of (some) "real" people. On the Aristophanic Socrates as an accurate portrait of Socrates' "first sailing," see Paul A. Vander Waerdt, "Socrates in the Clouds," in *The Socratic Movement*, ed. Paul A. Vander Waerdt (Ithaca, 1994), 48–86.

69   See Edwards, "Aristophanes' Comic Poetics," for an excellent discussion of Socrates' warning to Strepsiades not to do the sort of things comic poets do (line 296), since that will disrupt his teaching and their speech.

70   Pericles talks about the Athenians as a school of or paradigm for Hellas; he also claims and exemplifies a kind of intellectual power for the city that distinguishes it from all others, as I argue in *Tragedy of Political Theory*, chap. 6.

71   Redfield, "Drama and Community," 328.

72   Perhaps such vilification by Old Comedy served as a kind of cathartic ostracism, marking the danger to the city of the overly powerful man without actually leading to his exile.

73   Of course, insofar as this is mandated or expected by the audience, it becomes part of the dramatic illusion rather than a violation of it.

74   Hubbard, *Mask of Comedy*, 14, 14–15.

75   O'Regan, *Rhetoric, Comedy, and the Violence*, 132. But see Nussbaum's criticism of this view, and of a "democratic" Aristophanes, in "Aristophanes and Socrates."

76   The preoccupations of *The Clouds* and *The Gorgias* are remarkably similar.

77   As asserted in a report to the Trilateral Commission entitled *The Crisis of Democracy* (New York, 1975). I have made this admittedly counterintuitive argument in "Democracy and Political Theory: A Reading of Plato's *Gorgias*," in Euben, Wallach, and Ober, eds., *Athenian Political Thought*, 198–226.

78   *Sophia* is a dominant theme throughout the play, but especially in the parabasis. For a

general discussion of how Aristophanes uses it, and of how the use of *sophos* in regard to *both* forms of education plays upon the ambiguity of a word which designated both cleverness in the narrow sense of technical skill and worldly knowledge, see Hubbard, *Mask of Comedy*, 94–96.

79 See A. W. Gomme, "Aristophanes and Politics," *Classical Review* 52 (1938): 9–109. For a very different view that is explicitly critical of Gomme, and implicitly so of my argument here, see G. E. M. de Ste. Croix, "The Political Outlook of Aristophanes" (Appendix 30), in *The Origins of the Peloponnesian War* (Ithaca, 1972). He argues that Aristophanes "had an essentially *paternalistic* attitude toward them (the *dēmos*)," that he "resented" their political power and thought it "intolerable when ignorant and ill-educated men demanded a share in the delicate art of government" (357; his emphasis). Ste. Croix draws on all of the plays, taking various passages to be propositions representing Aristophanes' views. His strongly political reading is a useful challenge to the kind of position I take here, but I think his reading of the various texts unpersuasive. The specific argument that I refer to here as the "prevailing view" is Redfield's, in "Drama and Community," 331.

80 Redfield, "Drama and Community," 331. There is a lively controversy about whether Bakhtin's notion of Carnival (see especially *Rabelais and His World*, trans. H. Iswolsky [Cambridge, 1968]) illuminates or obscures the function of comedy in fifth-century Athens. Bakhtin argues that during Carnival the norms of the everyday world were suspended, with polarities, hierarchies, and oppositions based on power, status, and sex inverted, and that traditionally subordinate groups got to exercise a ritualized authority over their superiors. During such times limits were suspended and the forbidden practiced, as men and women were released from the obligations that otherwise circumscribed their lives and sustained the established order. But the festival at Athens entailed institutionalized competitive displays; it was not an occasion for revolt by the oppressed or the repressed, but an opportunity for the citizens of a radical democracy to confront and perhaps rethink their decisions and loyalties. Bakhtin thought Carnival liberating, but his critics (such as Balandier and Gluckman) have argued for Carnival, as Redfield does for Comedy, as a ritual release of protest that allowed power to consolidate itself even more effectively. For obvious reasons, I think this is overstated, though not entirely mistaken.

81 Redfield, "Drama and Community," 331.

82 The language is Charles Segal's, in "Aristophanes' Cloud-Chorus," 157.

83 See Nussbaum's argument that Aristophanes and Plato are both critical of Socrates for the same reasons: his neglect of the importance of habituation, his intellectualism in denying the reality of *akrasia* (weakness of will, incontinence, without power over oneself), his not restricting questions to those who would not be corrupted by them. "Plato and Aristophanes," she concludes, "believe that for the ordinary man questioning is destructive without being therapeutic" ("Aristophanes and Socrates," 88).

84 See the discussion in Ste. Croix, *Origins of the Peloponnesian War*; and Kenneth Dover, *Aristophic Comedy* (London, 1972), both of whom make this argument about his politics. Cf. Henderson, "Demos and Comic Competition," 306.

85 Ober, "Power and Oratory in Democratic Athens," 102–4.

86 Hannah Arendt, "The Crisis in Education," in *Between Past and Future: Eight Exercises in Political Thought* (New York, 1977), 173–96; quotation from 174.

87 Ibid., 176–77.

88 Ibid., 189, 192.

89 Pozzi, "Polis in Crisis," 148.

90 Kenneth J. Reckford argues in *Aristophanes' Old-and-New Comedy* (Chapel Hill, 1985), that Aristophanes combined Old and New Comedy as he did tragedy and comedy in *The Clouds*. Old Comedy "he thought was what his precursors had performed and what his rivals, had they known better, could have outgrown" (338).

91 Bernard Williams, *Shame and Necessity* (Berkeley, 1993), 166.

92 Again, see Edwards's discussion in *Aristophanes' Comic Poetics*, 179.

Leonard Tennenhouse

The Case of the Resistant Captive

Consider this all too familiar scenario: members of a survivalist family, an urban commune, or a religious community do something that makes it possible for some U.S. government agency to represent them as a threat to other Americans. Perhaps the family lives in Ruby Ridge, Idaho, and the father sells sawed-off shotguns to undercover federal agents; the commune could be located in Philadelphia, say, where it bombards its neighbors with music and is rumored to sell illegal substances; the community could be Christian fundamentalists stockpiling guns at a farm near Waco, Texas, in preparation for some sort of Armageddon. Out of concern for the children living within these estranged communities, as well as for the safety of neighbors and passersby, we all agree that the group must be put under surveillance. But although the government has convinced itself that the group is a threat to the larger community of Americans, members of the group feel that they are under assault rather than surveillance. They may kill a U.S. Marshal, threaten a policeman, or take a shot at Alcohol, Tobacco and Firearms officers. Such an act provokes an immediate and

The *South Atlantic Quarterly* 95:4, Fall 1996.
Copyright © 1996 by Duke University Press.

forceful response: the FBI opens fire on Randy Weaver's farmhouse, killing his wife, with infant in arms, and his fourteen-year-old son; a police helicopter drops a satchel of explosives on the multiunit dwelling that houses MOVE, and six city blocks are destroyed in the ensuing fire; federal agents attack the Branch Davidians' compound, which triggers a suicidal conflagration. The conflict between what may be provisionally termed legitimate authority and a dissident group does not arise from the same cause in any two of these cases. Yet the cultural logic with which the nation grasps, addresses, and interprets such events boils down to a rather simple story, a major feature of which is our astonishment when peacekeeping measures are met with violence that provokes extreme forms of violence from "us" in return.

This astonishment substantiates the fable of American innocence by demonstrating our capacity to lose it over and over again. As Henry James was not the first to notice, the innocence to which we ascribe our characteristic befuddlement is nothing more nor less than faith in the ideology of the European Enlightenment, as perhaps most fully elaborated in the contractual theories of government associated with Locke and Rousseau. Under the sway of the logic of the social contract, we assume that individuals are inherently rational—which means they will not only think and act in their own best interests as individuals, but will also identify those interests with the survival of their bodies, the autonomy of their households, and the security of their property. On the other hand, whosoever acts on this logic invariably discovers what eighteenth-century Europe knew full well: (1) that the world—including much of Western Europe—is not actually populated by rational individuals who perceive their own interests in Lockean–Rousseauian terms; (2) that parties rarely enter into mediation on an equal footing; and (3) that any agreement they may reach is embarrassingly ineffectual without some means of enforcement. Thus we found at Ruby Ridge, in downtown Philadelphia, and on a farm outside of Waco that the government had no authority to mediate on behalf of the peace-loving citizens of the United States because the "other" party in each of these conflicts resented the intervention. For them, the agents of the government were in effect agents of the enemy. Indeed, the officials who are delegated to represent the government in such situations are generally subject to attack and prepared to meet that attack with superior force. All pretense to rational discourse dissolves, and violence is met with greater violence.

According to contractual thinking, such an ending to this story is simply a mistake; it does not follow logically from Enlightenment premises. Moreover, even the more heavy-handed critics of Enlightenment thinking ignore the fact that attempts to combat violence with discourse consistently lead to further violence. Althusser argues that the Ideological State Apparatus (e.g., education) replaces the Repressive State Apparatus (e.g., the military) in modern states. Foucault, following in the footsteps of his teacher, argues that at some point in the nineteenth century, the state's monopoly on violence gave way to a monopoly on the technologies of spatial positioning and surveillance, with a corresponding shift to domination by discourse. What the contemporary moral investment in an inevitable failure of mediation suggests to me, however, is that—despite all the genuine astonishment at such an outcome—any purely disciplinary apparatus is designed to fail, for only such failure can legitimate the exercise of violence by the modern state against dissident groups.

What happens to our examples once we entertain the possibility that its failure to displace violence is built into the discourse on violence? We have to consider the first half of the story—in which mediation and/or surveillance is instituted—as leading necessarily to the second—in which violence is exercised in defense of the larger community of potential victims, namely, the rest of America. Moreover, the two halves of the narrative are linked not only by the dictates of the plot, but also by nearly three centuries of subtle collusion between Enlightenment thinking, with its imperative to render state violence obsolete, and an earlier conception of the state as an entity that openly and avowedly required violence to maintain its authority. Perhaps it is neither the degree nor the importance of violence that changes as we move into the modern period, however, but simply the way in which violence tends to be interpreted when a modern culture takes a stance against it: violence then becomes something that other people do, people who are either naturally savage or culturally backward. Somewhere in that interlude between the elaborate display of violence in aristocratic dress and the modern reduction of violence to the essence of savagery presumably lies the reason why the resurgence of massive violence is a regular event in late modernity and startles us—as if we believed ourselves no longer capable of such violence, at least not against our own people. The logic of the social contract apparently dictates its failure insofar as the contract itself—the foundation of a truly ethical government—depends on

force, even though it is from government by force that contractual government distinguishes itself on ethical grounds.

When Foucault opposes the spectacle on the scaffold to the disciplinary
procedures of the modern penal institution, in theory he bids an entic-
ingly gruesome farewell to the culture of violence, abandoning the tech-
nicolor world of corporal punishment for the present world of discourse,
shot in drab documentary style. The historical presuppositions that shape
the magnificent opening to *Discipline and Punish* are as misleading as they
are compelling, however.[1] Foucault's opposition between government by
discourse and government by force is surely a hallmark of modern (i.e.,
Enlightenment) discourse. Indeed, this opposition, which undergirds the
very progressive narrative of modernity that Foucault was debunking, is
clearly not between present and past governments, but is rather a strictly
modern opposition. For what else but this opposition, which allows us to
relegate certain cultural behaviors to the status of the primitive and the
obsolete, gives them the power to surprise us and gives us, in turn, the
authority to put them down? If the opposition between discourse and violence has been part of the conceptual architecture of modern culture since
the Enlightenment, then it is no wonder that violence has blossomed in
such strange new forms under our watchful noses, for our sense of who
we are as a modern nation depends on it. The story of how we came to de-
pend on violence begins in the early modern period, when the difference
between statecraft by force and principled rule by means of ethics and
argumentation first became central to Western theories of government.

After years alone on his island, Robinson Crusoe encounters a footprint in
the sand—which sends him running for home in terror. He takes neither
comfort in the prospect of human company nor reassurance from the fact
that God has always come to his rescue thus far. (Defoe spends a number
of pages and much rhetorical work on implanting the violence that has
controlled the hero's destiny up to this point, describing his dreams, his
behavior, indeed every aspect of the culture he reproduces on an utterly
compliant island.) Crusoe first regards the single footprint as Satan's trace,
an interpretation that Defoe almost immediately revises as Crusoe begins
to speculate that it is the footprint of a savage, who by his very nature

would be bent on Crusoe's destruction, whether aiming to devour his body or to destroy his enclosure, crops, and flock, condemning him to "perish for meer want."[2] When weeks pass and nothing happens to validate this interpretation, Crusoe confronts a problem which must be resolved before he can budge from his enclosure—namely, the problem of difference. Being who he is—a man of piety and practicality as well as of property—how can Crusoe exist in a society with men who do not share these virtues? The answer Defoe gives is clear: he can't. Stuck with the stubborn fact of difference and his own intolerance of it, Crusoe returns to the site of this dilemma, determined that something must give. If the footprint is no longer there, he can revert to his supernatural explanation; if it is still there, perhaps it will prove to be his own. The trace proving to be that of someone other than himself, however, Crusoe proceeds to refortify his home. Again, Defoe allows self-doubt to flower as Crusoe waits in vain during the next two years for the trespasser to return, time enough to begin wondering all over again if the savage man were not of his own conjuring. Just when the world seems free of danger, Defoe supplies some body parts, the gruesome leftovers of cannibalistic rites, to reestablish the one truth with which his hero, significantly, seems unable to deal.

The problem is obviously not one of survival since Crusoe got along quite well sharing the island with savages, as long as he did not know they were there. Upon encountering the remains of their rites, however, he immediately begins to consider "how I might destroy some of these Monsters." His first impulse is to blow them up with five or six pounds of gunpowder, but he eventually comes to favor the efficiency of ambushing them: "I should be sure to kill or wound perhaps two or three at every shoot; and then falling upon them with my three Pistols and my Sword, I made no doubt, but that if there was twenty I should kill them all."[3] Up to this point, such ferocity has been perfectly compatible with—indeed necessary to—establishing Crusoe's character as what might be called a modern individual. With his rescue and socialization of Friday, however, this is no longer true. When it comes to establishing a community, Crusoe's signature tactics of isolation, enclosure, and expulsion of others will not do. Thus the scene in which Friday puts Crusoe in charge can be read as Defoe's refiguration of early modern monarchy in Enlightenment terms. Rather than forming such a community through conquest or marriage,

Crusoe does so by rescuing the savage from his own culture, if such it can be called given its inherent violence. Seeing one savage, Friday, in flight from would-be captors, Crusoe makes a snap decision that, along with the rest of the novel, will turn cultural history on its ear: "Now was my Time to get me a Servant, and perhaps a Companion, or Assistant. . . . I was call'd plainly to save this poor Creature's life."[4]

This displacement of violence from the European to the savage, and thus to a primitive past, is overdetermined, as Crusoe himself knocks down one of the cannibals in self-defense and leaves Friday the task of executing another. Next, Defoe has Friday twice stage an elaborate ritual—strictly of his own devising—to express his debt to Crusoe. This is a performance in which the savage body "talks" while the civilized European interprets: "He kneeled down . . . kiss'd the Ground, and laid his Head upon the Ground, and taking me by the Foot, set my Foot upon his head; this it seems was in token of swearing to be my Slave for ever."[5] By so acknowledging that his body now belongs to Crusoe, who is thereby granted the power to dispose of it as he will, Friday demonstrates that he knows the early modern rules of warfare regarding the taking of captives. Having rebelled against his former captors, he now enters into essentially the same master–slave relationship with Crusoe. What makes this scene important enough to be staged twice within two pages, however, is that *Friday subordinates himself,* thus transforming the antithetical relationship of slave to master into the more reciprocal one of vassal to lord. A small distinction in modern parlance, perhaps, but a radical shift in early modern terms, for Friday is no longer property under these conditions but a party to a contract, however lopsided. To enslave or abuse him would be entirely within Crusoe's power, perhaps even within the law, but absolutely contrary to the ethical obligation created when Friday willingly submits to Crusoe's authority. From the moment he first casts eyes on Friday, however, Crusoe imagines him not as a vassal but "as a Servant, and perhaps a Companion." The difference between "servant" and "companion," as Crusoe implies, constitutes a difference in degree rather than in kind. One's status must be this carefully defined, in a modern reading of the contractual gesture, before one can be a party to a contract in the first place.[6] Thus the logic of the contract unravels as Defoe stretches it across the abyss separating Friday's voluntary vassalage from Crusoe's still private wish for a companion as well as for a servant, thereby separating the early modern from the modern subject.

Scholars habitually look to either the wars and revolutions of seventeenth-century Europe or the debate over "economy" to explain those curious moments in early modern literature when the text must coax and nudge the available cultural material into accommodating a recognizably modern subject. Curiously enough, however, we do not have any satisfactory answer to the question of why Defoe would go to such lengths to maroon Crusoe on a deserted island only to torment him with unwanted visitors. More often, scholars have tended to read Crusoe's overdetermined reaction to the footprint and Friday's equally overdetermined submission to Crusoe's foot in terms of theological doctrine or proto-psychological realism.[7] To understand these moments that define the hero's ethical character in relation to other men rather than to God or nature, however, we might better turn to what was not only a body of rules developed over centuries to deal with the problem of difference but an international paradigm undergoing subtle and irreversible changes during the seventeenth century. I have in mind the rules governing the treatment of men under conditions of war.

From about the twelfth through the fourteenth century, canon lawyers and civil legal authorities debated the legal bases for war. By the mid-fourteenth century, "a set of rules had been evolved that could guide in the trial of disputes arising out of war no matter where they were tried or by whom."[8] This body of law was, as Peter Haggenmacher notes, relatively unified because "it governed the activity of a fairly distinct, though quite heterogeneous class of men, that is, those following the profession of arms."[9] From the fourteenth to the sixteenth century, the debate took the form of cataloguing various causes and examples of war in hopes of pinning down what constituted a just war. The appearance of Grotius's treatise *De Jure Belli ac Pacis* in 1625 and the subsequent revised versions published during his lifetime could be said to have ushered in a new epoch in this long-standing debate, for Grotius shifted its focus from what constituted a just war to what constituted a just cause for war: "No other just cause for undertaking war can there be excepting injury received [*Causa iusta belli suscipiendi nulla esse alia potest, nisi injuria*]."[10] Having used the first book of his treatise to detach this issue from the tangle of canon and civil juridical opinion, Grotius devoted the second book to the concept of *injuria*, defining not only its unlawful and unjust aspects but also who could receive such an injury and under what conditions. By so reshaping the debate, then, Grotius turned a question of canon law into a purely secular question of property rights.

Scholarly discussions of *De Jure Belli ac Pacis* invariably stress book 2, where Grotius develops his concept of "injury," long considered one of the major sources for the discourse of natural rights that emerged during the seventeenth and eighteenth centuries. But if book 2 established Grotius's work as a precursor to modern theories of international law, book 3 has been a source of bafflement. What exactly was Grotius up to here? Why did he merely urge restraint in the exercise of war rather than going on to lay down legal interdictions? Indeed, why was he so concerned with the aftermath of war at all? Perhaps he simply digressed from his initial purpose of sorting out the legal issues of war, as some scholars have surmised, and got caught up in appealing for the humane treatment of prisoners because history had positioned him "so close to the rape and pillaging that characterized the Thirty Years War."[11] Contrary to this view, however, the third book of *De Jure Belli ac Pacis* can be read as the logical extension of the second. It is here that Grotius arguably completed his swerve away from the whole project of justifying war and toward a new project devoted to a question with which international law is still struggling: What principles constrain the captors in their treatment of a captive nation?

Although I do not think of Grotius as an early architect of what we now call "the rights-bearing subject," without his fastidious attention to rules by which certain individuals could maintain their status as subjects even after they had been taken captive, I cannot imagine Locke's concluding that the son could occupy a position comparable to that of the father once he had developed the intellectual faculties to understand the law.[12] Nor can I imagine Defoe's feeling compelled to have Friday express his relationship to Crusoe in such a bizarre yet precise fashion. By focusing on the constraints that govern those who govern a captive population, Grotius attached ethics to property, asking to what extent the property of a nation belongs to the victor. Is the conqueror entitled to dispose of it in any way whatsoever? Grotius takes every opportunity to warn against the unnecessary destruction of town and countryside, a warning that initially appears to be motivated by a utilitarian principle.[13] Given his argument that a just war is a fundamentally *defensive* action, we have to entertain the possibility that something of greater historical significance is actually at stake in his intrusive admonitions to avoid unnecessary violence: if a captive nation becomes the agent rather than the recipient of "injury," then the ethical ascendancy shifts to its enemy—once the aggressor but now the victim of violence.

Indeed, it can be argued that when Grotius redefined the just war in terms of property rights, he stirred up long-stagnant ethical waters and rendered them permanently muddy. The relationship between victim and aggressor, never morally simple or clear, was now vexed by reversibility as well, namely, when the injured party proved to be the victor in a just war. Once an injured party had triumphed over its former oppressor, it could no longer occupy the ethically secure position of the victim. It had to be careful not to injure the now-vanquished party and thereby become injurious in turn, or so Grotius implies. While establishing the rights of the captor over prisoners of war, for example, in the seventh chapter of book 3, Grotius reminds early-seventeenth-century legal scholars and jurists of the medieval commonplace that although no holds are barred in the treatment of heathen peoples, Christian nations warring among themselves should not practice the enslavement of prisoners. Each subsequent chapter further circumscribes the permissible violence of war and expands the class of people who should be treated with moderation. Chapter 8 details the limits on the right to rule conquered nations; chapter 10 cautions against actually doing everything the law permits; and chapter 11 argues that not only should the lives of women, children, and innocent bystanders be spared, but so should those of farmers, merchants, scholars, the clergy, and prisoners of war. Grotius mounts this argument for moderate treatment of a defeated people on the same basis that he argued against laying waste to countryside or town. The unnecessary destruction of life and property alike is "ordinarily committed from motives of hatred rather than from consideration of prudence" and therefore does not reflect well upon the leadership responsible for such injurious behavior.[14]

The reversibility of justice and injustice that results when "justice" depends on "injuria" is further problematized in situations where people are treated in contradistinction to property, and Grotius frequently encounters just such situations among the examples he culls from biblical and classical texts. As a result, chapters 7 through 15, if not the entire third book, turns into an argument for the immutability of the individual subject over and above the radical mutability of his social status and national identity under wartime conditions. For the introduction of this inherently modern basis of identity—let us call it "humanity"—is surely what separates the fate of captives from that of any other booty of war.

Drawing a line where his culture has failed to distinguish between people and things appears to be the whole point of book 3, as Grotius moves from the way that captives trouble this line to the more difficult problem of slavery. Here, if anywhere, legal tradition proved to be contradictory and imprecise. He begins by moving the basis for slavery across the nature–culture line: "By nature . . . apart from a human act, or in the primitive condition of nature, no human beings are slaves."[15] He then concedes that enslaving captives is and always has been perfectly legal, whether they "surrender themselves" or are "captured in a formal public war." Having come down on the side of legal tradition on this issue, however, Grotius immediately raises the thornier question of whether it is legal for such captives to flee their captors. Here, on what may appear a relatively minor point, he takes issue with canon law by distinguishing between *slaves* who flee "after peace has been made," and "must be given up to the master who claims them," and *captives* who have escaped "to their own people while the war is still in progress, [and] attain their freedom by right of postliminy."[16]

Having established an instance where a slave is not by nature property, because he can cross back over the line distinguishing property from people, Grotius returns to the situation of the captive and applies the principle there: even "if men are taken in a past war" and reclassified as slaves, "it does not follow as a consequence that a bond of conscience is laid also upon [such] captives." It is important to note that Grotius does not reject the logical possibility that by taking possession of their bodies the conquering nation may acquire captive spirits as well. But he does not regard such captives as just so much property. On what grounds could the seventeenth-century Dutch jurist have made this distinction? Neither Roman law nor canon law apparently providing any precedent, Grotius turns again to natural law to support his innovative notion of humanity. Captives from a just war do not belong to their captors in the same way that property does because forms of ownership vary over time and from culture to culture, especially where captives and slaves are concerned. He even returns to the famous example of Deuteronomy (23:15), often cited by those who wish to show that the Old Testament did not authorize the absolute ownership of such captives.[17]

Why does Grotius devote so much attention to questions of slavery in a treatise that wants to limit the authority of the victor in a just war? The first and most obvious response to this question is that Grotius was in fact what historians understand him to have been—a man committed to systematizing the existing body of law on warfare. As such, he was concerned with elaborating the logic of that tradition, especially where it seemed to stop short or to waver. The legal ambiguity of the captive was an obvious target for such systematization. Captivity offered the possibility that a free man could become someone else's property, a slave. Even if it were not natural, slavery was legal; indeed, it was the prerogative of the victor of a just war. But what would happen to a man's nature—his humanity—once he had crossed that line and was held for ransom or enslaved? Grotius could not let such a man become an object. The very possibility apparently struck him as an inconsistency in an argument that goes back to antiquity. Clearly bothered, he devoted a whole book of his treatise to resolving this one little glitch in that great body of legal opinion. The result of this epic attempt to tidy up the tradition of law on slavery was to render that tradition problematic, though hardly obsolete.[18] When Grotius shifted the status of the slave to the culture side of the nature–culture divide, he slid another concept of human nature into place, one defined by virtue of its distinction from property: a nation might own the bodies of those it took captive, but it could not own their minds ("conscience"). Even when stripped of all his rights and property, a captive would still retain the potential to have rights and to own property, thus making him fundamentally different from property.

In revising the nature of people subject to a conquering nation, Grotius inadvertently transformed the very nature of those who were subject to any form of state authority. The subject subjected to another nation implicitly becomes a subject in a double sense, whether he tries to escape from captivity or elects to submit, as Friday does. In redefining the slave, Grotius also transformed the master. Repeating an earlier quotation from Seneca, Grotius declares: "Although against a slave all things are permissible, there are some things which the common law of living things forbids to be done against a human being."[19] This quotation initiates a sequence of examples from both classical and Christian sources that allows Grotius to place slaves in the category of the human alongside their masters. Having cited another passage from Seneca to this effect, he then quotes Philemon: "He, Master, who is born a man, though he may serve / In slavery, still ceases not to be a human being." Using such examples and citations, he moves from descriptions of slaves as servants to accounts of slaves as companions, concluding by quoting the sage who advised the owner of a slave to "treat him as a brother, for he is such as you are."[20] This particular display of erudition gradually but inextricably links the natures of slave and master, transforming their defining relationship from that of difference to that of identification. In an early rendering of the master–slave dialectic, then, Grotius cancels out both categories in order to formulate the one that we now consider the foundation of humanity.

It is surely no coincidence that when Milton chose to write a drama about a great warrior who was captured and made a slave, he found himself working within the same problematic and trying to clarify that same vague area of jus gentium dealing with captives. Both Grotius and Milton took on the task of explicating the conduct of victorious European armies during or immediately after particularly brutal internecine wars. Whereas Grotius had done so from the perspective of the victor, explaining why his power should be curtailed and urging him toward moderation in his treatment of prisoners, Milton used the story of Samson as a way of considering this situation from the position of the vanquished and thereby revealed the rhetorical advantage that might inhere in that position under contemporary cultural conditions. As the author of any of a number of puritan captivity narratives could have told him, the individual who was taken captive by a heathen people had a unique opportunity to demonstrate his faith in God. Such stories not only circulated orally from the 1630s onward, but also began to appear in printed sermons, in histories, and later in captivity narratives. Moreover, under international law, the captive could easily become the injured party, in which case violence on his part would be justified so long as he remained a captive.

The account in Judges renders Samson a warrior hero pure and simple, one who lost and then regained his identity as God's champion. Milton alters this account in *Samson Agonistes* so as to convert the debilitated Samson into a new kind of hero. As a captive, Samson holds the moral advantage over his captors, with Milton thereby throwing the traditional alignment between might and right into question, much as Grotius did by interrogating the status of the captive who becomes a slave. To work this

Restoration change upon the biblical story, Milton invents four visitors—
Manoa, Dalila, Harapha, and the Philistine officer—each of whom offers
Samson a way out of captivity. In their respective dialogues with him, these
interlocutors take different positions on the question of Samson's status
as a captive and how to change it. Only by rejecting all of these historical
alternatives, however, can Samson hang onto his moral advantage and still
crush the Philistines.

The process begins when Samson's father, Manoa, tries to ransom his
son. As Milton well knew from Roman law and medieval chivalric practice,
a prisoner who could be ransomed was not considered property, as a slave
was. Either that prisoner or his people could gain his release by paying a
percentage of the value of his lands or a portion of his revenues, but whatever the ransom, the mere fact that such a captive could regain his social
position through the payment of money or goods meant that he was not a
slave by nature. To enter into such an exchange, he must have owned or
stood to inherit property; without property, he would have lacked the legal
standing to recuse himself from battle following his release. Even when
captured in a just war, furthermore, such a man would retain some property and hence some rights. For, as Grotius argues concerning the status of
a prisoner who can be ransomed, "it follows that there is no room for the
complete acquisition [of his property] which, as we have said elsewhere, is
the essential condition of ownership over the person."[21] These are the same
suppositions on which Manoa proceeds in planning his son's release, but
Samson cannot accept what makes perfect sense to his father, as presumably it would to those familiar with the international rules of warfare.[22]

In refusing to let Manoa ransom him, Samson makes it clear that the
loss of neither his eyesight, his social position, nor his physical freedom
and prowess causes him nearly so much remorse as his having fallen from
favor with God. The cause of his captivity, then, lies not with his captors but
with his own act of abandoning the Israelite God for a Philistine woman.
While scholars have speculated as to why Milton changed the biblical story
to make Dalila Samson's wife,[23] surely the most obvious reason must be
the one that shaped almost every puritan captivity story that crossed the
Atlantic from British America. The possibility of precisely such a marriage
haunts the accounts of puritans taken captive by Indians.[24] The real threat
to the English community was the captive's incorporation into native culture through marriage, which effectively cut all his or her ties to the En-

glish community through language, membership in the reformed church, and national identity. Accordingly, captivity narratives demonstrate a faith capable of resisting the most subtle inducements and tortuous persuasions of the flesh, with captives often feeling compelled to declare their preference for death over conversion. Casting his lot with his New World counterparts, Milton's Samson counters his father's ransom plot with one that will bring on "speedy Death, / The close of all my miseries, and the balm."[25] In other words, Samson regards his spiritual exile from the community of the righteous, not his enslavement, as the cause of social death.

Dalila offers Samson another way of removing himself from the category of "slave." Instead of ransoming him, she would reclaim him from her countrymen as something that belongs to her—as if he were her property. Claiming that he would simply be exchanging one term of captivity for another, Samson responds with something less than gratitude:

> How wouldst thou insult
> When I must live uxorious to thy will
> In perfet thraldom, how again betray me,
> Bearing my words and doings to the Lords
> To gloss upon, and censuring, frown or smile?[26]

His refusal to occupy the position of Dalila's spouse has several implications. First, the scene recalls the circumstances under which Samson had succumbed to her blandishments. As he has already explained to his father, Samson has no one to blame but himself for his captivity:

> I yielded, and unlock'd her all my heart,
> Who with a grain of manhood well resolved
> Might easily have shook off all her snares:
> But foul effeminacy held me yoked
> Her bondslave.[27]

His downfall has no more to do with his lack of physical strength than with the Philistines' superior force. On the contrary, Samson insists that he renounced his position as a national hero when he chose to become a domestic man: "I was no private but a person raised / With strength sufficient and command from Heav'n / To free my country."[28]

Poised as he was on the fault line between an early modern and a modern culture, Milton undoubtedly felt the contradiction between their respective forms of government—one based on the ability to maintain and strategically deploy a monopoly on violence, the other based on subject formation or what Foucault calls "discipline." But why would Milton transform his warrior into a slave by that hero's own consent? Having done so, moreover, why give him a chance to repeat his fatal error, to refuse the offer of release this time around, only to show us how little difference it would have made anyway? This repetition seems at least as curious as the one that Defoe puts Friday through, for when Samson rejects Dalila's offer to reclaim him as her husband, he rejects domestic thralldom to reclaim his masculinity. A curious double bind it is in which a hero must remain a captive in order to retain his masculinity, but such indeed is the dilemma that Milton has gone out of his way to concoct for Samson.

With the entrance of Harapha, the Philistine giant who has come to taunt the Israelite champion in his state of decrepitude, Milton abandons the logic of jus gentium and demonstrates instead—as Grotius did—that it is necessary to reclassify the captive as a human being. Moreover, he has Samson declare his humanity, much as Defoe would later have Friday do, by resisting any other classification, even risking his neck to challenge the churlish Philistine to test his strength against him in mortal combat. If he accepted this challenge, Harapha would effectively acknowledge Samson as his social and legal equal, and the Philistines would implicitly honor Samson as the champion of the Israelites. Understandably, then, Harapha feels compelled to decline, claiming that the Israelite god would not allow a captive and a criminal to act as his champion. Loathe to kill him in a way that would lend Samson full human status, the giant leaves him "a Man condemn'd, a Slave enroll'd, / Due by the Law to capital punishment. / To fight with thee no man of arms will deign."[29]

The first three dialogues establish Samson's inability to change his status as a slave. By allowing either Manoa to ransom him or Dalila to claim him, he would be exchanging one state of captivity for another, while Harapha's refusal to fight him denies Samson the one way out of his dilemma that early modern culture offered such a champion. With the appearance of a fourth interlocutor, however, Milton creates a situation that will allow Samson to wiggle out of the category of slave. In the biblical rendition of this crucial scene, the Philistines simply "called for Samson out of the prison house; and he made them sport" (Judges 16:25). But Milton does not present the summoning of Samson from the perspective of those doing the summoning, as the biblical account does. Instead, he shifts the agency to Samson by conjuring up a Philistine officer who orders Samson to appear along with sundry "Gymnic Artists, Wrestlers, Riders, Runners, / Jugglers and Dancers," all to perform in honor of Dagon, the Philistine god.[30] Where the biblical narrator saw only a foregone conclusion—that Samson did go to the temple—Milton builds in an option, a forking of the narrative path and an outcome that, by implication, Samson must have already plotted out for himself.

By inserting a dramatic occasion when Samson can refuse to go to the temple, Milton creates a split between the self as subject and the self as object that doubles the subject and places the two in potential conflict: "Can they think me so broken, so debased / With corporal servitude, that my mind ever / Will condescend to such absurd commands?" Milton installs the rudiments of a modern individual in what is clearly an archaic hero simply by having Samson refuse the officer's summons to the temple. However extraneous it may be in narrative terms, this gesture ripples back to suggest that Samson has been laboring for his captors by his own design and not because they own that labor; his work in their mill has not been "Idol-worship," Samson claims, "but by labour / Honest and lawful to deserve my food / Of those who have me in their civil power."[31] This sudden refiguring of his situation as that of a party to contractual exchange conforms to both Locke's theory of property and Grotius's argument for considering the captive a subject because he works in exchange for his food.

Once endowed with the ability and an occasion to make the choices that distinguish a modern subject, Samson can choose to go to the temple of Dagon. As he contends, "Commands are no constraints. If I obey them, / I do it freely; venturing to displease / God for the fear of Man." When Milton lets Samson go to the temple under his own steam rather than being dragged there "like a wild Beast," he tells us that Samson's mind is not constrained by his body, even in its most abject state, that he cannot do anything "scandalous or forbidden in our Law." Indeed, it is to the Philistine misreading of Samson as a hero taken captive in accordance with early modern rules of war that their downfall can be attributed in Milton's version of the story—a downfall that consequently spells the obsolescence of the rules governing the taking of captives as well. The Philistines see nothing more in Samson than a spectacle of their own authority. They have no idea that he has become a kind of Trojan horse: a subject (to Philistine power) that contains a second (irreducibly other) subject. The officer reveals the double irony of Samson's doubled nature and the Philistines' blindness to it when he commends Samson for his submissive behavior: "By this compliance thou wilt win the Lords / To favour, and perhaps to set thee free."[32] Of course, Samson's behavior is neither new, in the sense of a change of attitude, nor submissive, but simply proceeds from another set of cultural assumptions.[33] By resisting domination, it is fair to say, he destroys much more than Philistine power.

Until the seventeenth century, legal thinking was constrained by the assumption that the only just war was implicitly or explicitly a holy war. Since the losers in such a war were presumably infidels, the laws governing warfare placed few, if any, limitations on the conduct of the winners. Grotius selected the specific body of opinions from classical and Christian sources that would allow him to produce a set of ethical injunctions against mindless brutality in the conduct of warfare in general. The principle of injuria obliges the injured party to acknowledge the humanity he shares with those he has conquered in a just war: if the positions of victor and victim are reversible, so are the ethical imperatives attached to each position. Milton evidently decided to explore the possibility of reversing the ethics of holy war by updating the biblical story of Samson, hence the hero's choosing to go to the temple. Indeed, the four dialogues that transform the biblical story into a Restoration drama display a growing sense of identity on Samson's part that strikes most contemporary readers as modern. Had Milton simply aimed to demonstrate the Lockean proposition that a man can have no master but himself once he has achieved self-mastery, however, there would have been no need for the Philistine genocide.

What, then, do we make of the fact that Milton modified the story from Judges in an apparently modern direction only to have Samson's achievement of self-mastery culminate in the kind of violence condoned by holy war—namely, the annihilation of the infidel?[34] The messenger describes the carnage wreaked by Samson when,

> those two massy Pillars
> With horrible convulsion to and fro
> He tugg'd, he shook, till down they came, and drew
> The whole roof after them with burst of thunder
> Upon the heads of all who sat beneath,

> Lords, Ladies, Captains, Counsellors, or Priests,
> Thir choice nobility and flower . . .
> *Samson* with these immixt, inevitably
> Pull'd down the same destruction on himself.[35]

In representing Samson's final, suicidal act, Milton makes a point of telling us that, though blind and degraded, he slew "foes in number more / Than all [his] life had slain before."[36] Reconceptualized as the captive, Samson becomes the bearer of a humanity that his captors lack the cultural equipment to recognize. That he brings the temple down upon the Philistines cannot signal the reappearance of the warrior, regardless of how much the new Samson may resemble the former one. In an effort to produce another basis for identity, one unencumbered by patrilineage of any kind, Milton refigures the warrior's brutality as a form of violence that is not violence in comparison to the superior and therefore "bad violence" of Samson's captors. Today, we like to characterize such "good violence" as "resistance."

Writing about fifty years after the publication of *Samson Agonistes*, Defoe could not allow the categories of good and bad violence to slide into one another so imperceptibly. Thus he went to enormous lengths to convince his readers that Friday *chose* to work for Crusoe, and it took at least as much convincing before Friday would believe that Crusoe intended him to be a servant and companion rather than a slave. In this regard, Defoe's narrative is absolutely consistent with Grotius's position that enemies, once taken captive, should be viewed as fellow human beings lest we injure them and legitimate their resistance in turn. Accordingly, in elaborating Crusoe's relationship to European intruders on the island, Defoe attempts to avoid the problem of reversibility (i.e., the victor's authority becoming unjust the moment he ceases to identify with his captives) by imagining how a community composed of potentially violent groups might be ruled by other than violent means. In contrast to Friday, these intruders can neither be construed as culturally lacking nor figured as an underdeveloped Crusoe. The contractual gambit may work with a noble savage such as Friday, but it will not help Crusoe solve the problem of difference and get along with the other Europeans, who greatly outnumber him.

To purge Crusoe's island of violence, and purge it he must, Defoe first rules out the possibility that paternal authority will inspire filial duty. The

Europeans happen to be mutineers, thus men predisposed to overthrow their government. Crusoe must therefore convince them that any such revolt against him will be bound to fail because he embodies superior force; whatever social contract he may make with them will thus be predicated on the early modern notion of power. Outnumbered many times over and lacking the technological means to compensate for this imbalance, Crusoe must nevertheless maintain a monopoly on violence. Lacking any superior force of arms or men, however, Crusoe must instead (and with the cooperation of the captain against whom the crew had mutinied) deploy the force of discourse. Stealing upon the mutineers in the dark, Crusoe and the captain convince the sailors they are surrounded. Once it has been conjured up in the dark out of thin air, then, this discourse must produce a body, a sign of power that will be received as power itself, at once a reproduction and a violent displacement of (early modern) government: "The Captain told [a mutineer to] lay down his Arms at Discretion, and trust to the Governour's Mercy, by which he meant me; for they all call'd me Governour."[37] As it turns out, though, this simple ruse will not sustain governmental power where material force is lacking, for Crusoe's first fabrication initiates a sequence of displacements that simultaneously calls power into being and locates it somewhere else.

The governor's force does not originate on the island or in his men, but in England. Nevertheless, the captain informs this still-volatile population that "the Governour was an *English* Man; that he might hang them all there, if he pleased: but as he had given them all Quarter, he supposed he would send them to *England* to be dealt with there, as Justice requir'd." Various members of the mutinous crew are selected from the mob, sequestered in a cave, and convinced that "if they were sent to *England*, they would all be hang'd in Chains."[38] This discourse proves miraculously self-substantiating, as Crusoe demonstrates by means of one of those lists that have come to be associated with his role as the modern acquisitive individual:

> Our strength was now thus ordered for the Expedition: 1. The Captain, his Mate and Passenger. 2. Then the two Prisoners of the first Gang, to whom having their Characters from the Captain, I had given their Liberty, and trusted them with Arms. 3. The other two who I had

kept till now, in my Bower, pinion'd but upon the Captain's Motion, had not releas'd. 4. These five releas'd at last: So that they were twelve in all, besides five we kept Prisoners in the Cave, for Hostages.[39]

Thus has a web of fictions multiplied two good guys into twelve and miraculously halved the number of their opponents.

As the embodiment of English power, it is apparently necessary for Crusoe to withhold himself from the skirmish in which the boat is recaptured and its wayward crew intimidated. Sometimes he even finds it effective to masquerade as an emissary of his own representation of English power: "The Captain . . . told them, I was the Person the Governour had order'd to look after them." When Crusoe finally dresses up as an English governor, Defoe makes it clear that the power is invested in the role, not in the man who plays it. At least, such may be inferred from Crusoe's confession that "never was anything in the World of that Kind so unpleasant, awkward, and uneasy, as it was to me to wear such cloaths at their first putting on."[40] Why does Defoe go to such lengths to distinguish the man from his role, the body as a limited physical force from the body as a sign of an immense colonial power? By putting himself in the position of a mediator, Crusoe can fabricate the first party to the social contract (the governor), and this role can in turn empower him to initiate the social contract. This governor figure is, in other words, the *enforcer* of the law that Crusoe makes. His double embodiment of force and discourse enables their mutual authorization, without which the one would collapse into the other and risk the mediator's being mistaken for the opponent in a holy war — as was indeed the case at Ruby Ridge, Philadelphia, and Waco.

Since the double embodiment in question is nothing more nor less than a doubling of discursive functions, it is not only impossible to display both bodies simultaneously, but also necessary for the nonviolent state to display a great capacity for violence from time to time. How else will potential mutineers come to believe themselves at the mercy of the state? The contradictory imperatives of the modern state just as surely control Crusoe and with the same quality of force that they exercise on others: "I came thither dress'd in my new Habit, and now I was call'd Governour again; being all met, and the Captain with me, I caused the men to be brought before me."[41] After assuming this role, he must stay out of sight or run the risk of revealing the disparity between sign and substance — the power he claims to embody and the limitations of one unexceptionally human body. No matter how cleverly Defoe manages to avoid violence in populating this island, then, he is finally unable to imagine how its government will achieve lasting stability, for the moment the sign of law's coercive force disappears, discourse collapses into action. Unless a mediator is capable of enforcing contractual relations, mediation will fail and the two parties will fall on one another, tooth and claw, thus validating the Hobbesian view of human nature.

═════

As we follow this shifting relationship between force and discourse into the modern period, it is instructive to see what happens to their coupling. How does the concept of humanity change as it is taken up by nations dedicated to preserving the rights of individuated subjects? Writing at the end of the eighteenth century, Kant would scoff at the early modern idea of a just war. In doing so, more surprisingly, he would also challenge what we still regard with some affection as the modern idea of government rule by law alone:

> When we consider the perverseness of human nature, which shews itself unveiled and unrestrained in the relations of nations with each other, where it is not checked, as in a state of civilization, by the co-ercive power of the law, one may well be astonished that the word right has not yet been totally abolished from war-politics as a pedan-tic word, and that a state has not yet been found bold enough openly to profess this doctrine. For hitherto Grotius, Puffendorf, Wattel, and other useless and impotent defenders of the rights of nations, have been constantly cited in justification of war; though their code, pure philosophic or diplomatic, has never had the force of law, and cannot obtain it; states not being as yet subjected to any coercive power.[42]

Against the rights of individual and nation, Kant posits a universal principle of right. On which side of the opposition does the early modern concept of "humanity" belong? "Humanity" appears in distinctly modern dress, as "the perverseness of human nature," and since nothing but this perverseness causes war, there can be no just wars—war is by definition bad.

At the heart of his argument against his early modern predecessors lies Kant's insistence that nature works according to the principle of difference, which likewise operates between individuals and among groups within a nation, as well as among the nations themselves. To be civilized, a nation must enact laws that will force such individuals and groups to tolerate difference in one another. If they are to enjoy peace on an international scale, then, nations must not only have the legal mechanisms to keep their populations in line, but must also employ similar mechanisms at the international level. They have to create laws forbidding all violent conflict; these laws, however, are ineffective without "coercive power." If war is necessarily imagined as the violation of the universal power of "right," Kant reasons, then "the coercive power of law" necessarily acts on the side of "right" when it opposes war. Therefore, such coercive power is by definition good. Thus Kant appears to have solved the problem that plagued our early modern authors, namely, the reversibility of victor and victim, or how to keep justified violence from becoming injurious. Grotius tried to solve this problem by urging combatants to establish a basis for identification with their former enemies once they had subdued them; Kant, in contrast, asks lawmakers to see themselves as part of a vast differential system of individuals, groups, and nations who are by nature hostile to the differences that would bar such identification. Thus he confronts as well the problem faced by the modern author, as represented by Defoe—namely, the problem of difference.

To solve the problem of ethical reversibility (whereby the victor becomes the victimizer in waging a just war), Kant reverses the problem and the solution. The problem is not for Kant, as it was for Grotius, that humanity has been torn asunder by war and must be reunited according to the principle of identification (whereby the slave becomes the master's companion). On the contrary, Kant locates the problem of war in a humanity shot through with differences, albeit partly as the result of a history of continuous warfare among the nations. Given this reconception of the problem, there is only one way to end the violence: nations must develop laws that force men to tolerate, even to grow respectful of, their differences. Kant would, in other words, have no truck with the principle of identification. In its place, he put his own carefully restricted concept of involuntary "hospitality," which would prohibit the members of a nation from harming anyone who happened to cross their boundary; the host nation would thus be forced to tolerate the presence of foreigners. Given "the perverseness of human nature" (i.e., its intolerance of difference in favor of sameness), ethical appeals based on the common humanity of conquerors and their captives are destined to fail, in Kant's account.[43] But this introduces a logical dilemma: How to establish and empower laws to enforce hospitality, thus making war obsolete? By implication, Kant's model requires a war to end all wars, a war against war. Such a war would, of course, be the last and only justifiable form of violence.

Let us return to the fortress on Ruby Ridge, the commune in Philadelphia, or the compound outside of Waco, where we arrive with the baggage of several centuries' long, hard thinking on the ethical use of violence. Whether it is the Weavers, the members of MOVE, or the Branch Davidians who have captured national attention and drawn us here, these groups are all of a piece in one respect: they have set themselves outside the purview of the law by rejecting the principle of difference. This statement may sound counterintuitive; after all, don't such groups characteristically wrap themselves in the Bill of Rights and insist on their own right to be different? In doing so, Kant would contend, they are in fact violating the law of hospitality that guarantees tolerance for difference; their acts — forming an enclave, fixing rigid boundaries, righteously annihilating intruders — are performed in anticipation of the end of difference and are therefore *acts of war*. For the end of difference will occur on that day when the island of sameness within the nation of difference becomes the nation itself. Traditional appeals to our common humanity will always prove completely powerless to moderate the behavior of either side in such a conflict, if we think in Kantian terms, unless and until these appeals have become a matter of law and this law has acquired "coercive power."

Tired by now of playing the object of Kantian contempt, the shade of Grotius might well rise up and point to a gaping hole that opens in thinking that is too quick, as perhaps Kant's is, to brush off the problem of reversibility. While it may be true that, for lack of laws capable of enforcing sociability, humanity will revert to practices that observe the logic of identification, it is also true that some individuals, groups, and even nations will stick to the principle of identification despite our best attempts to make them tolerate differences. In that case, the logic of Grotius prompts us to ask whether some violence isn't justified. Neither the fact of law nor the mere threat of violence can enforce hospitality, which alone will ensure that differences peacefully coexist. Although we may never have dreamed such an occasion would come about, there invariably arises yet another instance when we must wage war against war for the sake of peace.

According to the historical problematic within which Grotius, Milton, and Defoe worked, discourse proves a rather unreliable weapon against war—except in the hands of those already in power. Discourse has to be backed up by force. Whenever discourse collapses into violent action, it is fair to say, the entire charade of the "Governour" necessarily disintegrates. Whatever has placed itself rhetorically above the fray—the law, the mediator, the apparatus of the social contract, the universal principle of "right" (they are all pretty much the same thing under such conditions)— descends in a wink to the level of the combatants and generally proves to be of the party with superior force. This alliance between force and law invariably creates the situation where, according to Milton and Defoe as well as Grotius, ethical reversibility is most likely to set in, shifting the rhetorical advantage to the victim's position.

To the question of why any attempt to master violence with discourse is destined to fail, the answer I draw from early modern literature is this: because the opposition between discourse and violence tends to collapse, making it possible to read either one as the other, depending on the position from which one proceeds to do so. But to answer the question of why we are so surprised by eruptions of violence, especially those that we ourselves may have caused, we must look to a more modern theory, such as Kant's influential essay on "perpetual peace." The principle of difference, as he articulates it, is not all tolerance and light. Unbeknownst to itself, this principle harbors an exclusionary principle: it cannot tolerate those who cannot tolerate difference. Indeed, such were the people who troubled Grotius because they had no qualms and expressed no reservations about their use of violence. They felt perfectly righteous in laying waste to an enemy—leveling cities, killing women and children, and destroying the food supplies of civilian populations. Where Grotius coaxed victorious warriors to acknowledge the humanity they shared with those whom they had conquered, Kant virtually excluded from his model those people who could not see the need for peace. They did not meet his standard of "civilization."

Thinking in terms rather like Kant's, our own government officials and policy makers flounder in precisely those cultural confrontations where the other guy has no interest in getting along. Tolerance of difference is out of the question for such a person (or group); what he wants is not only an honorable death for himself but the annihilation of his enemies. Modern cultures imagine that they have outgrown such an attitude. Meanwhile, the fallibility of a political ethic that depends on this assumption of tolerance becomes increasingly evident with the growth of domestic fundamentalisms, which produce a variety of nations within the nation. As the Weaver family, the MOVE commune, and the Branch Davidians come to seem less exceptions than the rule, we can observe the exclusionary operations of the difference model returning to haunt the claims to inclusion and heterogeneity that authorize governments based on that model: we simply cannot tolerate those who cannot tolerate difference.

—————

I began by asserting that the model of difference is actually designed to fail, and such an apparently paranoid explanation for our perpetual surprise in the face of violence could certainly follow from and complete this genealogy. It is entirely possible to say of the relationship between our discursive opposition to violence and the forms of physical violence that have flourished in the present century what Judith Butler says of Robert Mapplethorpe and Jesse Helms, namely, that neither one makes sense without the other.[44] Each calls the other into being as a threat to our American identity. This is simply to point out the logical limitations of any difference model: it cannot tolerate intolerance, or the will to sameness, which it conceptualizes in terms that hark back to the notion of the holy war.[45] Mapplethorpe, of course, understands Helms in just such terms, as the will to universalize bourgeois heterosexuality; in opposing the principle of sameness, the photographer defines himself as the champion of inclusion and heterogeneity. Most of us buy into this avant-garde fantasy.[46] In doing so, we fail to consider whether its way of opposing difference to sameness might not work the other way around as well—whether, that is, Helms might not think of Mapplethorpe as the agent of an aggressive bohemianism, a latter-day version of the contagious degeneration that Max Nordau deplored a century ago. From such a perspective, Mapplethorpe's art would seem to violate our personal beliefs and community values. In opposing Mapplethorpe, then, Helms similarly establishes himself as the representative of a minority resistant to the menace of encroaching sameness.

Since any individual or group whose very existence depends on maintaining, if not extending, the regime of sameness has implicitly declared itself the mortal foe of difference, we are obliged, in the name of difference, to exclude and even to crush that individual or group; this alone distinguishes the violence that would put an end to violence. My readings of Grotius's argument with his predecessors and of Kant's subsequent argument with Grotius suggest that both repeat this typically Western move. Each legitimates secular government by opposing it to the practices associated with holy war. Does our own demonstrable propensity for violence arise, then, from elements of early modern culture that are still with us and could, in theory, be excised—or is there something in the very culture of modernity that requires us to oppose with such violence what we perceive as sameness?

Notes

1   Michel Foucault, *Discipline and Punish: The Birth of the Prison*, trans. Alan Sheridan (New York, 1979 [1975]).

2   Daniel Defoe, *Robinson Crusoe*, ed. Michael Shinagel (New York and London, 1975 [1719]), 122.

3   Ibid., 132.

4   Ibid., 158.

5   Ibid., 159.

6   I am relying here on the critique of the contractual model by Louis Althusser, "Rousseau: The Social Contract," in *Montesquieu, Rousseau, Marx: Politics and History*, trans. Ben Brewster (London, 1982), 111–60.

7   See, for example, the fine readings by George Starr, *Defoe and Spiritual Autobiography* (Princeton, 1965); J. Paul Hunter, *The Reluctant Pilgrim: Defoe's Emblematic Method and Quest for Form in Robinson Crusoe* (Baltimore, 1966); Patricia Meyer Spacks, *Imagining a Self: Autobiography and Novel in Eighteenth-Century England* (Cambridge, 1976), 28–40; Leopold Damrosch, Jr., *God's Plot and Man's Stories: Studies in the Fictional Imagination from Milton to Fielding* (Chicago, 1985), 187–212; and Michael McKeon, *The Origins of the English Novel, 1600–1740* (Baltimore, 1987), 316–37.

8   M. H. Keen, *The Laws of War in the Late Middle Ages* (London, 1965), 22.

9   Peter Haggenmacher, "Grotius and Gentili: A Reassessment of Thomas E. Holland's Inaugural Lecture," in *Hugo Grotius and International Relations*, ed. Hedley Bull, Benedict Kingsbury, and Adam Roberts (Oxford, 1990), 133–76; quotation from 159.

10 Hugo Grotius, *The Law of War and Peace*, trans. Francis W. Kelsey (Indianapolis and New York, 1925), 170–71 (II.I.i.4).

11 G. I. A. D. Draper, "Grotius' Place in the Development of Legal Ideas about War," in Bull, Kingsbury, and Roberts, eds., *Grotius and International Relations*, 177–208; quotation from 198. Draper also asks if Grotius's plea for leniency were "an implicit concession that contemporary cruelties were permitted by the Law of Nations?"

12 See John Locke, *Two Treatises of Government*, ed. Peter Laslett (Cambridge, 1988 [1690]), 306–7 (II.vi.58).

13 Advising moderation in laying waste, for example, Grotius notes that even with a legal basis for destroying another's property, "it would be foolish to injure another without securing any good for oneself. Those, therefore, that are wise are usually influenced by considerations of utility" (*Law of War and Peace*, 745 [III.XII.i.2]).

14 Ibid., 746 (III.XII.i.3).

15 Ibid., 690 (III.VII.i.1). Grotius has already made this point in the second book, when qualifying Aristotle's claim that some men are born slaves (551 [II.XXII.xi]), but he raises it again in book 3 to bring it to bear on war-related captivity, a context in which it will do entirely new things in ideological terms.

16 Ibid., 693 (III.VII.vi.1).

17 "Thus among the Jews, who by their institutions were separated from the common practice of other peoples, there was an asylum for slaves" (ibid., 695 [III.VIII.viii]).

18 Grotius's position tends to be understood as the opposite of the so-called school of Realpolitik that can be traced to Machiavelli and Hobbes. It should not, however, be seen as the antecedent to the idealism commonly identified with Kant. I prefer to see Grotius in much the same way that Thomas S. Kuhn taught us to view Copernicus in *The Copernican Revolution: Planetary Astronomy in the Development of Western Thought* (Cambridge, 1957), which is to say that Copernicus was not self-consciously fashioning a scientific revolution when he set out to tighten a few screws in a paradigm that was already weak and shaky. In retrospect, of course, we can see that, in trying to tidy up that model, he discovered the entire paradigm to be erected on a contradiction. So, too, with Grotius, who sought to reconcile conflicts between the great legal traditions he inherited. In the process, he set the concept of humanity against the legality of unconstrained war, the seizure of slaves, and the utter devastation of an enemy's cities, crops, and people.

19 Grotius, *Law of War and Peace*, 762 (III.XIV.ii.3).

20 Ibid.

21 Ibid., 843 (III.XXI.xxviii).

22 On the Law of Ransom, see Keen, *Laws of War*, 156–85.

23 Mary Ann Radzinowicz discusses various reasons why Milton might have chosen to make Dalila a wife, rather than the harlot of Judges, in *Toward Samson Agonistes: The Growth of Milton's Mind* (Princeton, 1978), 36–50.

24 This point is discussed at length in Nancy Armstrong and Leonard Tennenhouse, *The Imaginary Puritan: Literature, Intellectual Labor and the Origins of Personal Life* (Berkeley, 1992), 196–216.

25 John Milton, *Samson Agonistes*, ed. F. T. Prince (Oxford, 1957 [1671]), 41 (lines 650–51).

26 Ibid., 57–58 (lines 944–48).

27 Ibid., 38 (lines 407–11).

28 Ibid., 67 (lines 1211–13).

29 Ibid., 68 (lines 1224–26).

30 Ibid., 71 (lines 1324–25).

31 Ibid., 72 (lines 1345–47), 73 (lines 1365–67).

32 Ibid., 74 (lines 1372–74), 38 (lines 403–9), 75 (lines 1411–12).

33 One might think here of the account of Damien's torture at the opening of Foucault's *Discipline and Punish*, 3–6. It is a sign of the power of the prince that he can bring such violence down upon the body of the criminal. As Foucault goes on to argue, "The tortured body is first inscribed in the legal ceremonial that must produce, open for all to see, the truth of the crime" (35). Samson, alternatively, maintains control over his body, especially the circumstances of its destruction, and thereby takes back from the Philistines the authority to determine the fate of his body.

34 In an important departure from much of the criticism that reads the conclusion of the drama as affirming Samson's salvation, Stanley Fish has argued that nothing in the poem indicates God's having taken charge of Samson; see "Spectacle and Evidence in *Samson Agonistes*," *Critical Inquiry* 15 (1989): 556–86; and "Question and Answer in *Samson Agonistes*," *Critical Quarterly* 11 (1969): 237–64. See also Joseph Wittreich, *Interpreting Samson Agonistes* (Princeton, 1986).

35 Milton, *Samson Agonistes*, 83 (lines 1649–58).

36 Ibid., 84 (lines 1667–68).

37 Defoe, *Robinson Crusoe*, 208.

38 Ibid., 208, 209; his emphases.

39 Ibid., 210.

40 Ibid., 210, 213.

41 Ibid., 213.

42 Immanuel Kant, *Perpetual Peace*, ed. Nicholas Murray Buter (Los Angeles, 1932), 31. This is a reprint of the first, 1796 English translation.

43 See Pierre Saint-Amand's discussion of Kant's notion of sociable unsociability in *Les lois de l'hostilité* (Paris, 1992), 162–68; Saint-Amand's discussion of the problematic of hospitality in Diderot (195–96) also bears directly on my thinking.

44 Judith Butler, "The Force of Fantasy: Feminism, Mapplethorpe, and Discursive Excess," *differences* 2 (1990): 105–25.

45 Ellen Rooney identifies this same intolerance as the concealed principle of exclusion in American pluralism; see *Seductive Reasoning: Pluralism as the Problematic of Contemporary Literary Theory* (Ithaca, 1989).

46 As Vassilis Lambropoulos puts it, "Humanist thought . . . is still committed to the view of culture advocated by critical thought, that is, culture as critique, as emancipatory practice, and therefore as counter-politics"; see "The Rule of Justice," *Thesis Eleven*, No. 40 (1995): 1–24; quotation from 17.

Peter Jaszi and Martha Woodmansee

The Ethical Reaches of Authorship

An "author" in the modern sense is the sole creator of unique literary and artistic "works," the originality of which warrants their protection under laws of intellectual property known as "copyright" and "authors' rights." This notion is so firmly established that it persists and flourishes even in the face of contrary experience. Experience suggests that our creative practices are largely derivative, generally collective, and increasingly corporate or collaborative. Yet we continue to think of *genuine* authorship as solitary and originary.

This individualistic notion of authorship is a relatively recent invention, the product of a radical reconceptualization of the creative process that culminated less than two centuries ago in the heroic self-presentation of Romantic poets. In the view of poets from Herder and Goethe to Wordsworth and Coleridge, genuine authorship is *originary* in the sense that it results not in a variation, an imitation, or an adaptation, and certainly not in a mere reproduction, but in an utterly new, unique—in a word, "original"—work which, accordingly, may be said to be the property of its creator and to merit the law's protection as such.

The *South Atlantic Quarterly* 95:4, Fall 1996.
Copyright © 1996 by Duke University Press.

With its emphasis on originality and self-declaring creative genius, this notion of authorship has functioned to marginalize or deny the work of many creative people: women, non-Europeans, artists working in traditional forms and genres, and individuals engaged in group or collaborative projects, to name but a few. Exposure of these exclusions—the recovery of marginalized creators and underappreciated forms of creative production—has been a central occupation of literary studies for several decades. But the same cannot be said for the law.

Our intellectual property law evolved alongside of and to a surprising degree in conversation with Romantic literary theory. At the center—indeed, the linchpin—of Anglo-American copyright as well as of Continental "authors' rights" is a thoroughly Romantic conception of authorship. So it should not surprise us to learn that this body of law tends to reward certain producers and their creative products while devaluing others: no copyright can exist in a work produced as a true collective enterprise (rather than by one or more identifiable or anonymous "authors"); a work cannot be copyrighted unless it is "fixed" (which excludes a wide range of improvised works and works of oral tradition); copyright does not extend to works that are not "original" (which rules out protection for folkloric productions that are valued for their fidelity to tradition rather than their deviations from it); and copyright does not protect "basic" components of cultural productions (which bars protection of, say, the rhythms that are most characteristic of both traditional musical forms and certain contemporary forms such as rap and hip-hop).

But while the law participated in the construction of the modern "author," it has yet to be affected by the structuralist and poststructuralist "critique of authorship" that we have been witnessing in literary and cultural studies for several decades. The exclusive tendencies inherent in the law's essentially Romantic conception of authorship operate both *within* the developed countries of the Americas and Western Europe and *between* developed and developing countries, and the conventional law of international copyright is one of the principal agencies through which those tendencies are realized. At least since 1886, the date of the first Act of the Berne Convention for the Protection of Literary and Artistic Works, international copyright has been premised on a vision of "authors' rights" that carries with it the full range of Romantic associations. Neither Berne nor any other major international agreement requires signatory states to afford legal protection to works falling outside the purview of authorship in the modern, Romantic sense we have described.

This essay grows out of an ongoing collaborative project, the aim of which is to extend and deepen the critique of authorship just sketched through a series of foundational investigations that place the phenomenon of cultural authority in social, economic, and historical perspective.[1] The project was launched at an interdisciplinary conference on Intellectual Property and the Construction of Authorship organized by the Society for Critical Exchange in 1991.[2] It has since been carried forward in numerous forums, including a seminar sponsored by the Rockefeller Foundation in 1993 which brought together twenty-five lawyers, cultural historians, policy makers, anthropologists, development specialists, and representatives of culture industries from the developed and developing worlds to ponder Cultural Agency/Cultural Authority: Politics and Poetics of Intellectual Property in the Post-Colonial Era. The "Bellagio Declaration" (see Appendix), which emerged out of this seminar, demonstrates another objective of our collaborative project: to operationalize the critique of authorship. By renewing the conversation between the law and literary theory that seems to have broken off in the nineteenth century, we are agitating for the development of more equitable models of intellectual property protection.[3]

We noted above that cultural production necessarily draws upon previous creative accomplishments. For the better part of human history this derivative aspect of new work was thought to contribute to, if not virtually to constitute, its value. Writers, like other artisans, considered their task to lie in the reworking of traditional materials according to principles and techniques preserved and handed down to them in rhetoric and poetics. It was only in the course of the eighteenth century, and then primarily in Western Europe, that an alternative vision of creative production focusing on the endowments and accomplishments of the individual "genius" emerged. In a sharp departure from the self-understanding of writers of previous generations, authors in the new Romantic mode viewed their task as one of transforming the materials of personal sense experience through the operation of their unique, individual genius. This change of emphasis mystified the writing process, obscuring the reliance of these writers on the work of others.

The new Romantic construction of creative production is illustrated in Wordsworth's famous lyric of 1807 which begins "I wandered lonely as a cloud." In this poem, commonly known as "Daffodils," creative production is presented as a solitary, originary process; however, the genesis of the poem suggests otherwise.[4] With the publication of the journals of Wordsworth's sister, Dorothy, it became clear that far from emerging from the operation of the solitary imagination on the raw materials of experience, "Daffodils" evolved collaboratively. Recording the sights and sounds of an after-dinner walk with William, Dorothy notes in her journal:

> When we were in the woods beyond Gowbarrow Park we saw a few daffodils close to the water-side. We fancied that the lake had floated the seeds ashore, and that the little colony had so sprung up. But as we went along there were more and yet more; and at last, under the boughs of the trees, we saw that there was a long belt of them along the shore, about the breadth of a country turnpike road. I never saw daffodils so beautiful. They grew among the mossy stones about and about them; some rested their heads upon these stones as on a pillow for weariness; and the rest tossed and reeled and danced, and seemed as if they verily laughed with the wind, that blew upon them over the lake; they looked so gay, ever glancing, ever changing. This wind blew directly over the lake to them. There was here and there a little knot, and a few stragglers a few yards higher up; but they were so few as not to disturb the simplicity, unity, and life of that one busy highway.[5]

A good deal both of the letter and of the spirit of this entry is assimilated into William's later poem, but without any reference to its author. Dorothy's substantial contribution—indeed, her very participation—has been completely effaced —her five "we's" assiduously replaced by "I's," transforming the couple's collective experience into a solitary one. The resulting poem relates the poet's moving experience of a phenomenon of nature which produces renewed pleasure whenever it is relived in memory:

> I wandered lonely as a cloud
> That floats on high o'er vales and hills,
> When all at once I saw a crowd,
> A host, of golden daffodils;
> Beside the lake, beneath the trees,
> Fluttering and dancing in the breeze.

Continuous as the stars that shine
And twinkle on the milky way,
They stretched in never-ending line
Along the margin of a bay:
Ten thousand saw I at a glance,
Tossing their heads in sprightly dance.

The waves beside them danced; but they
Out-did the sparkling waves in glee:
A poet could not but be gay,
In such a jocund company;
I gazed—and gazed—but little thought
What wealth the show to me had brought:

For oft, when on my couch I lie
In vacant or in pensive mood,
They flash upon that inward eye
Which is the bliss of solitude;
And then my heart with pleasure fills,
And dances with the daffodils.[6]

In the final stanza the poet's pleasurable recollection of his experience of the daffodils becomes a metaphor for the poetic process per se, constructing it as an operation not of several minds in collaboration but of a single, individual mind in interaction with the natural world. Ironically, the very lines in which this vision is set forth were supplied—as William elsewhere confirms—by his wife, Mary Hutchinson: "They flash upon that inward eye / Which is the bliss of solitude."[7]

The case of "Daffodils" is instructive because it exposes the element of collaboration at the heart of creative production generally even as it dramatizes the process by which such collaboration gets denied. We inevitably draw on the work of others in our creative activities—if not contemporaries working in close proximity, then those working at some temporal remove whom we may or may not acknowledge as "influences." The laws of copyright encourage us to deny others' contributions to our creative production by awarding the exclusive right to exploit it economically to "authors"—understood, thanks in no small measure to Wordsworth himself, as essentially *solitary* originators. Although a profoundly collaborative work, "Daffodils" was confirmed as William's property upon publication, and nobody, not even Dorothy or Mary, could have reproduced it in whole or in part without his permission. Today this process of authorial appropriation can produce even more extreme results: a modern-day Dorothy would run the risk of being charged (albeit erroneously) with infringement of William's copyright for publishing her prior prose description of the daffodils.

The acquisitiveness that Wordsworth displays in the "Daffodils" episode may surprise readers who know him chiefly as joint author with Samuel Taylor Coleridge of *Lyrical Ballads* (1798), the slim volume that revolutionized English poetry. For *Lyrical Ballads* was an intensely collaborative project—the most famous collaboration in English literature—and it was first published *anonymously*—as if in acknowledgment of its debt to the English people of the "middle and lower classes" whom the poets credit in the Advertisement at the beginning of the volume for much of the material and especially the style of the poems therein.[8]

However, by the time it was completed Wordsworth had asserted "a strong proprietary interest in the book," and so completely did he take control of the second edition, Stephen Gill writes, "that *Lyrical Ballads* 1800 bears only residual marks of the collaborative effort of 1798."[9] The most striking mark of his assertion of authorial control is the appearance in the new edition of Wordsworth's name on the title page. It appears there alone. In this new edition the short Advertisement has also been expanded into a lengthy Preface containing a defense of the poetics underlying the volume's experimental contents. Coleridge was intimately involved in the conceptualization of this Preface, if not directly in its composition, yet the only trace of his input is the attribution to "a Friend" of certain of the poems contained in the collection, followed by the remark, "I should not . . . have requested this assistance, had I not believed that the poems of my Friend would in a great measure have the same tendency as my own, and that, though there would be found a difference, there would be found no discordance in the colours of our style; as our opinions on the subject of poetry do almost entirely coincide."[10]

The Preface was to be the most substantial and influential statement of his theory of poetry that Wordsworth would produce. It is here that, even as he was effacing the traces of its collaborative provenance, Wordsworth first set forth his vision of *genuine* authorship as a secular priesthood which sets the poet apart from and above other creative producers. In a new section devoted to the question "What is a poet?" that he added to the Preface for the third edition of 1802, Wordsworth would elaborate, pronouncing poetry the "breath and finer spirit of all knowledge," and the poet

> the rock of defence of human nature; an upholder and preserver, carrying every where with him relationship and love. In spite of difference of soil and climate, of language and manners, of laws and customs, in spite of things silently gone out of mind and things violently destroyed, the Poet binds together by passion and knowledge the vast empire of human society, as it is spread over the whole earth, and over all time. The objects of the Poet's thoughts are every where; though the eyes and senses of man are, it is true, his favourite guides, yet he will follow whersoever he can find an atmosphere of sensation in which to move his wings. Poetry is the first and last of all knowledge—it is as immortal as the heart of man.[11]

These are extravagant claims. At a moment of radical ferment in every domain from physical science to political theory, Wordsworth declares poetry "the first and last of all knowledge." This, as Gill observes, "is more than a declaration of the importance of humane learning, more than an assertion of the imagination against the pressure of a sceptical, scientific, or utilitarian ethos. Wordsworth confers upon the poet the roles of chronicler and preserver, of comforter and moral guide, of prophet and mediator." To Pope "such exalted affirmations would have seemed ravings," Gill concludes, and Samuel Johnson, "who defined the poet as 'an inventor; an author of fiction; a writer of poems; one who writes in measure,' would have thought them nonsense, probably blasphemous nonsense."[12]

Even as he was articulating this heroic vision of his vocation Wordsworth was systematically erasing the traces of Coleridge's contribution. This peculiar blend of self-aggrandizement and strategic suppression of others characterizes our modern enactments of "authorship."

≡≡≡

The concept of authorship enacted in these episodes operates today in the laws of countries around the world to mediate the process by which acts of cultural appropriation yield legal rights in the appropriator, and Wordsworth and his associates played a crucial practical role in bringing this about. When the first copyright statute, the 1710 Statute of Anne, recognized the "author" as the person in whom textual rights initially vest, it created a convenience to publisher-booksellers, whose business practice (before and after the legislation) usually involved purchasing writers' manuscripts and incidental rights for a single lump sum. For the first century and a quarter of British copyright the author-figure of English law was, in short, an indistinct one.[13] But it was filled in, with Romantic coloration, during a campaign for copyright law reform—and, in particular, copyright term extension—which culminated in the Copyright Act of 1842.[14]

This campaign, initiated in Parliament by the lawyer–litterateur Thomas Noon Talfourd, was more or less directly inspired by Wordsworth, who had been complaining privately since at least 1808 that the short term of copyright served only the interests of "the useful drudges in Literature, . . . flimsy and shallow writers, whose works are upon a level with the taste and knowledge of the age," while "men of real power, who go before their age, are deprived of all hope of their families being benefited by their exertions."[15] Wordsworth's preference was for perpetual copyright, but he was practical enough to realize that this goal presented political problems. So, from 1837, when Talfourd's first bill calling for an expanded copyright term of an author's life plus sixty years postmortem was introduced, Wordsworth was privately and publicly involved in promoting the legislation: he not only coached Talfourd, providing material for his speeches, but personally wrote to dozens of Members of Parliament and other influential acquaintances to drum up support for the legislation, wrote several anonymous letters to newspapers, organized a campaign of petitions from well-known authors, and ultimately even petitioned Parliament in his own name. The terms of the eventual 1842 legislation, which compromised on a term of protection that Wordsworth undoubtedly still found inadequate, established postmortem copyright as an author's legacy to the next generation. Its specific provisions are less important in the present context, however, than the rhetoric of the debate leading up to the legislation, which brought to center stage the High Romantic author-figure who, in Talfourd's words, "persevere[s] in his high and holy course, gradually impressing thoughtful minds with the sense of truth made visible in the severest forms of beauty, until he . . . create[s] the taste by which he shall be appreciated."[16] This vision of authorship as a kind of secular prophecy, the product of "true original genius" operating on the raw materials of experience to create something new and unanticipated, has informed British copyright (and, by extension, that of other English-speaking countries) for the last century and a half.

Similar accounts of originary genius had provided the rationale for authorial entitlement in various Continental legal systems from the late eighteenth century on, and by the middle of the nineteenth century this vision of authorship was also exercising a shaping influence on the European campaign for a comprehensive international law of copyright. Until at least the first Act of the Berne Convention (1886), individual authors and authors' organizations took prominent roles in this campaign, and notions of inherent entitlement linked to the Romantic vision of authorship figured prominently in its rhetoric.

In 1838, the first British international copyright legislation was justified on the grounds that British authors had a right to the same protection abroad that British inventors already enjoyed. It was, said the Member of Parliament who introduced the bill, a

> matter of notoriety that works were [being] pirated abroad as soon as they made their appearance at home: that no sooner were productions sent to the press in this country, than the utmost efforts were exerted to purloin proof-sheets for the purpose of sending them to America, France, Belgium, or Germany. Pirated editions were published at once in those countries and circulated over those countries forthwith, by which means the authors were deprived of the fair fruits of their labour—of those legitimate pecuniary rewards for which they were reasonably entitled to look.[17]

The legislation authorized the Crown to enter into agreements with other states for the mutual protection of copyright, and with it Great Britain joined the growing number of European countries that were concluding bilateral copyright treaties with one another—often on terms that varied considerably from one agreement to the next.

The protection which such a network of bilateral treaties could offer authors in countries other than their own was far from comprehensive or systematic.[18] It fell short of being a truly "universal" scheme—and it was for such a scheme that authors began to campaign in earnest in the 1850s, commencing with the nongovernmental Brussels Congress on Literary and Artistic Property of 1858, which issued a series of resolutions introduced by the statement: "The Congress is of the opinion that the principle of international recognition of the property of authors in their literary and artistic works should be enshrined in the laws of all civilized countries." [19] The clear suggestion is that any country which fails to recognize the rights of authors cannot fairly lay claim to civilization.

This exalted view of authors' rights is further revealed in the final communiqué of another important international congress held in Paris in 1878, with Victor Hugo in the chair and authors (and publishers) from around the world in attendance. Its first two resolutions read:

> 1.The right of the author in his work constitutes, not a concession of the law, but one of the forms of property which the legislature must protect;
> 2.The right of the author, his beneficiaries and legal representatives is perpetual. [20]

In this view copyright is a natural and indefeasible right which arises in the first instance—without the intermediation of the state—from the very act of "authorship" itself.

The International Literary Association (later the International Literary and Artistic Association, or ALAI), which would prove to be such a powerful voice for "universal copyright," grew out of the 1878 congress. Membership was open to literary societies and writers of all nationalities; Hugo initially served as chair, and the association's first "committee of honor," nominated in 1879, consisted of Longfellow, Emerson, Tennyson, Trollope, Disraeli, Gladstone, de Lesseps, Dostoyevsky, Tolstoy, Auerbach, the Emperor of Brazil, the Prince of Wales, the King of Portugal, and the President of France. [21] Thus began an eight-year political and public relations campaign that ultimately produced the first Act of the Berne Convention.

From its inception the Berne Convention has been more than a treaty in the conventional sense—more, that is, than an agreement through which a group of states acknowledges certain finite obligations among themselves. In the domain of international law the most unusual feature of Berne (and one that it retains today in its sixth iteration, the Paris Act of 1971) is the first Article, which provides that signatory countries "constitute a Union for the protection of the rights of authors in their literary and artistic works." This legal device makes the Berne Convention an agreement with a cause, so to speak—the cause of promoting and extending authors' rights, however these may be secured in the national laws of countries around the world. [22] By the same token, interests which cannot readily be conceptualized in terms of "authorship," as that concept has been understood in Western laws since the mid-nineteenth century, find no place in the scheme of the Berne Convention.

The provisions of subsequent agreements notwithstanding, the organizing discourse of international copyright has retained its attachment to the Romantic conception of the author. This is true despite the fact that even before 1886 the drive for "universal" copyright had been substantially co-opted by publishers, for whom such an international legal regime represented an important precondition for a world market in books.[23] Today, in the wake of new agreements coming more than a century after the first Act of the Berne Convention, the international copyright system is being revised to address commercial concerns about the openness and fairness of the world trading system. But new agreements which treat intellectual property as an international trade issue simply perpetuate and extend the traditional emphases of copyright.

Late in 1993 representatives of 124 developed and developing countries signed the Final Act of the Uruguay Round of the General Agreement on Tariffs and Trade (GATT). One of the annexes to that instrument, the so-called Agreement on Trade-Related Aspects of Intellectual Property (TRIPs), brought to fruition more than five years of campaigning by the United States, Europe, and Japan to combat growing intellectual property "piracy," especially in the poorer nations of Asia, Africa, and South America, by revising international trade law so as to expand its historically exclusive focus on manufactured goods to include trade in certain intangibles as well. A prime motive for this campaign was the desire of the United States and other "net exporters" of commercial cultural productions for a set of international intellectual property norms with "teeth"—in contrast, for example, to the century-old Berne Convention. Like most other intellectual property treaties, Berne has relied entirely on moral suasion to bring about the desired effects on national laws. As the TRIPs provisions take effect, however, failure by a signatory state to enact or enforce intellectual property laws which measure up to the minimum standards decreed in the GATT becomes an "unfair trade practice," opening the non-complying state to a variety of sanctions—in particular, retaliatory action by other signatories.

The new domains incorporated by TRIPs include "Copyright and Related

Rights," "Trademarks," "Geographical Designations," and "Patents."[24] All but the first of these categories begin with a comprehensive definition of the included subject matter; however, the article dealing with "Copyright and Related Rights" (Article 9) begins by stating merely that "members shall comply with Articles 1 to 21 and the Appendix of the Berne Convention (1971)." So it is to Berne—a treaty which grew out of agitation on the part of mid-nineteenth-century European authors' organizations for greater international recognition of "authors' rights"—that one must look in the first instance for the meaning and scope of the new TRIPs norms.

Article 1 of the 1971 Act of the Berne Convention (like its prototype in the original Act of 1886) provides that "the countries to which this convention applies constitute a Union for the protection of the rights of authors in their literary and artistic works," and Article 2 itemizes these works:

> The expression "literary and artistic works" shall include every production in the literary, scientific and artistic domain, whatever may be the mode or form of its expression, such as books, pamphlets and other writings; lectures, addresses, sermons and other works of the same nature; dramatic or dramatico-musical works; choreographic works and entertainments in dumb show; musical compositions with or without words; cinematographic works to which are assimilated works expressed by a process analogous to cinematography; works of drawing, painting, architecture, sculpture, engraving and lithography; photographic works to which are assimilated works expressed by a process analogous to photography; works of applied art; illustrations, maps, plans, sketches and three-dimensional works relative to geography, topography, architecture or science.[25]

Despite its apparent comprehensiveness, this itemization of protected types of works has some important shortcomings from the standpoint of the United States, Europe, and Japan, which instigated the TRIPs agreement. Specifically, it fails to include several of their most characteristic, most valuable, and most vulnerable cultural productions. Standing alone, it leaves up to each signatory country whether or how to protect computer software, musical recordings, and databases from unauthorized duplication.

However, the reference to Berne in Article 9 of TRIPs does not exhaust the definition of "Copyright and Related Rights." Article 10 provides that "computer programs, whether in source or object code, shall be protected as literary works under the Berne Convention." Acceptance of this formulation by the GATT signatories marked the successful conclusion of a decade-long international campaign by software manufacturers and the countries where they are headquartered to achieve global acquiescence to the proposition that despite their utility, and the collaborative nature of the process by which they are produced notwithstanding, computer programs should be construed as works of individual creative genius—considered, that is, works of authorship within the core protection of national laws of copyright and authors' rights rather than the subject of peripheral or secondary legal schemes. The TRIPs agreement also indicates that "compilations of data or other material, whether in machine readable or other form, which by reason of the selection or arrangement of their contents constitute intellectual creations, shall be protected as such."[26] Thus have databases, too, been brought into the fold of Romantic authorship.

Moreover, TRIPs is the first major multiparty international agreement to cover the field of "related" or "neighboring" rights—that is, rights in sound recordings, performances, broadcast signals, and other productions akin to but conceptually distinct from the subject matter of traditional copyright and authors' rights. In the theory of intellectual property law this acknowledged "relationship" provides the rationale for assimilating the former to the latter for most purposes. Although the elitist view of "authorship" that prevails in much of Western Europe has so far prevented these productions from being considered fully eligible for protection as copyrightable works, they do achieve under Article 14 of TRIPs a sort of cadet status in international law.

For even longer than the U.S. software industry has been lobbying for recognition of computer programs as works of authorship, less developed countries have been making the case for stronger international protection of their characteristic cultural productions. But just as surely as the TRIPs agreement incorporates strong protections for the most significant exports of the information and entertainment industries of the most developed countries, by identifying them as (or assimilating them to) works of authorship, it leaves other forms of cultural expression without any significant recognition in international intellectual property law. Thus the content of national cultural traditions and what may broadly be termed "folkloric works" (including stories, images, and sounds) do not find pro-

tection under an authorship-centered regime on account of their collective
character—their content is not attributable to identifiable individuals—and
because by their very nature they lack "originality," the necessary characteristic of "authorship" in the legal as well as the general cultural sense of
the term. Not coincidentally, these are works which the culture industries
of the United States and Europe have been accustomed, since at least the
mid-nineteenth century, to regard as naturally occurring "raw materials"
available for appropriation. In their effect, then, the positive commands of
the TRIPs agreement, along with its strategic silences, codify and reinforce
essentially imperialistic patterns in North–South cultural relations—not
only helping to structure markets in the less developed countries for the
exports of the developed ones, but also assuring the conditions for a continued steady flow of free content, which can be improved and shaped into
recognizable works by the industries of authorship.

Some years ago the gift shop of the Museum of African Art in Washington, DC, offered a coffee mug decorated with a characteristic East African
motif: black, highly stylized figures of animals on a red field. The bottom of
the mug bore two legends: "Made in South Korea" and "© Smithsonian Institution." The community in which this imagery originated had taken no
part in, and derived no benefit from, its commodification. But the Smithsonian, which had employed both Korean production workers and American product designers to produce the mugs, claimed rights in the outcome
of their efforts. Nor was this claim necessarily an empty one. While the
Western models of copyright to which Berne and TRIPs give international
reach may provide little or no protection to elements of the traditional culture from which the motif was extracted, the marginal "value added" of
the designer of the mug itself would constitute original authorship, justifying a copyright in the result as a so-called derivative work.

The commercial environment of the West is rich in such instances of cultural appropriation abetted by national and global laws of intellectual property that assign high relative value to the characteristic productions of the
cultural–industrial complex while treating the heritage of other peoples—
including indigenous groups within Western societies—as naturally occurring raw materials. Close to home, while shopping for a child's birthday
gift, one of us recently came across a striking example—a $7.99 "Morning

Mist Dream Catcher" craft kit containing "everything you need to make your own Dream Catcher wall hanging." The front of the package (one of a number of similar items on display in this particular store) is prominently decorated with a representation of a beadwork strip incorporating the word "INDIAN," followed by the trademark symbol (™), and just below it the slogan: "A Native American Craft." The back features a descriptive paragraph which begins: "Do you know what a 'DREAM CATCHER' is? Indian folklore believes that dreams are messages sent to us from sacred beings during our sleep." Further legends include a statement that the product "voluntarily complies with all known safety regulations," the words "Packaged and Printed in the U.S.A. Parts from Taiwan, China and U.S.A.," and a copyright notice in the name of "Pastime Industries, Inc. Hauppauge, N.Y." Nowhere is there any indication that any individual Indian, let alone any tribal group, participated in or will profit from the venture.

Mail-order catalogues abound in examples of such rip-offs of Native American cultural traditions. A recent issue of *Coldwater Creek* features on a single page:

— jewelry incorporating a traditional Hopi trickster figure: "Here, the rascal Kokopelli comes alive on a sprightly pair of hand-polished sterling dangle earrings made in the USA." (Elsewhere, the same catalogue informs us that "'Buy American' is more than a slogan around here.")

— a watch cagily described as the "peerless work of New Mexico artisans who loop 10 slender strands of fine silver beads through each side of this silver-plated quartz timepiece. . . . Native-strung in the USA, with imported movement."

— a machine-washable "rolled half-sleeve sweater" decorated with Indian-derived designs by an artist "moved to create, in patterns inspired by Native America, turning each of these V-neck pullovers into a hand-printed work of art."[27]

Again, nowhere does the catalogue claim that any Native American individual or group has endorsed or will profit from these acts of cultural commodification.

Trivial in isolation, instances of this phenomenon cascade to form a significant pattern. A particularly pernicious recent example is the unauthorized commercial invocation of the revered Lakota Sioux figure Tasunke

Witko—or Crazy Horse—in the promotion of a "niche" alcoholic beverage brand. Introduced in 1992, the "Original Crazy Horse Malt Liquor," which is sold nationwide by the New Jersey–based firm of Ferolito, Vultaggio & Sons (who also market AriZona brand iced teas), has a high alcohol content (5.9%) and is packaged in a large, whiskey-style bottle. Besides its most obvious cultural reference, the label makes additional use of Native American symbolism and imagery, featuring a generic Indian in a headdress, along with beadwork designs and sacred Lakota symbols such as the "medicine wheel." Nor does this exhaust the merchandisers' effort to associate the product with Native American tradition; the label on the bottle reads (in part):

> The Black Hills of Dakota, steeped in the history of the American West, home of Proud Indian Nations. A land where imagination conjures up images of blue clad Pony Soldiers and magnificent Native American Warriors. . . . A land where wailful winds whisper of Sitting Bull, Crazy Horse, and Custer.

During his lifetime, as Nell Jessup Newton notes, Tasunke Witko denounced the introduction of alcohol into Indian communities, and he also forbade the representation or reproduction of his image.[28] In this case, his heirs and the representatives of tribal communities with which he was associated have a simple objective: to put an end to this unauthorized use of the Crazy Horse name and supposed likeness. So far, however, they have met with little success.[29] Were another distributor of alcoholic beverages to copy the design of the "Original Crazy Horse Malt Liquor" bottle or label, Ferolito, Vultaggio could—and presumably would—bring suit for both trademark and copyright infringement, claiming that their creative reprocessing of traditional materials had given rise to precisely the kind of economic value which U.S. intellectual property law protects.[30] Meanwhile, the descendants of Tasunke Witko have filed an action in Lakota tribal court asserting, in addition to various claims under tribal law, two claims based on "Anglo" theories of recovery from outside the mainstream of intellectual property: defamation and infringement of the "right of publicity" (the latter more often mobilized against unauthorized impersonators of celebrities like Elvis and Madonna). The outcome of the litigation remains uncertain. What is clear is that conventional intellectual property law, with its emphasis on original authorship, provides no grounds for relief.

Indigenous peoples' efforts to deploy mainstream intellectual property law to control the exploitation of their heritage are generally unavailing. Anthony Seeger has described his efforts in the early 1980s to preserve and protect the musical heritage of the Suyá Indians of the Brazilian Matta Grosso. When his recordings were released, they carried the legend (translated here from the Portuguese): "This recording was made with the knowledge and approval of the Suyá. The selections are artistic productions of this society. Royalties will be forwarded to the community, and must be paid. The unauthorized use of these recordings is prohibited not only by law, but by the moral force against the exploitation of these artists." But it did not work, as Seeger recounts:

Although I arranged for generous royalties to be forwarded to the Suyá [by the company which originally issued the records], we didn't control the further use of the recordings. The Suyá chief was staying in our house in Rio de Janeiro when we heard, to our immense surprise, a Suyá song played behind an advertisement for Rio educational television. I looked at him with considerable concern, and he grinned and said: "It's beautiful, everyone is hearing our music. . . ." The next time I heard Suyá music on television was not so benign, however. But they didn't see the program; I didn't make a copy of it. . . . Had we explored the matter, we would have found little help in existing copyright law.[31]

Probably the best-known example of the failure of mainstream intellectual property law to recognize the value of the cultural heritage of indigenous peoples is one which moves the discussion some distance (though not too far) from copyright. As Western pharmaceutical companies begin searching in earnest for traditional cures which can be "transformed" through the "inventiveness" of chemical and genetic engineers into mass-market medications, we can see that patent laws too are skewed toward rewarding the creative genius (here figured as the "inventor" rather than the "author") who reworks and transforms naturally occurring raw materials. The difficulty with applying this model to the case of prescription drugs derived from wild plants, of course, is that the sheer number of plant species (which probably approaches 750,000 worldwide) makes random "prospecting" for those with pharmacological potential completely infeasible. David Newman of the National Cancer Institute's natural products branch estimates that no more than one in 10,000 plant substances will become a usable product.[32] Only by relying on the knowledge of traditional medicine can drug researchers expect to succeed—and drug companies to profit. For an estimated three-quarters of the plants that provide the active ingredients in prescription drugs originally came to the attention of researchers because of their use in traditional medicine.[33]

As Jack Kloppenburg, Jr., observes, "Genetic and cultural information has been produced and reproduced over millennia by peasants and indigenous people," but "like the unwaged labor of women, the fruits of this labor are given no value despite their recognized utility. On the other hand, when such information is processed and transformed in the developed nations, the realization of its value is enforced by legal and political mandate." Kloppenburg continues:

Thus it is that I can read an article about the uses of an Asian tree [for pest control] in the academic journal *Economic Botany* . . . and a year later find an article in the Madison, Wisconsin *Capital Times* titled "State Man's Pesticide on Road to Fame." The latter article describes how "Businessman Tony Larson has impressed industrialists and government officials with his one-man campaign to provide the world's farmers with a pesticide made from seeds of an Asian tree." Somehow Asian farmers' pesticide has become "state man's pesticide." And not just rhetorically, but quite literally, since Larson has a patent on his formulation of neem extract which he calls "Margosan-O."[34]

To date, ethnobotanical prospecting has led primarily to the development of "new drugs" which employ chemicals harvested from plants as their active ingredients. In the future we can expect more and more drugs to employ synthetic versions of compounds originally isolated from wild plants rather than actual derivatives. In either case, what is appropriated in the process is not so much the botanical materials as something more abstract: indigenous peoples' knowledge of their beneficial properties. In the most general sense this is the sort of commodity of the mind that intellectual property law values and protects. But where indigenous "bioknowledge" is concerned, specific Western models of intellectual property, which reward the transformation of naturally occurring raw materials by inspired genius, simply don't apply.

This is not to say that the creation of new intellectual property rights in bioknowledge would be a panacea for the unfairnesses of current ethnobotanical drug development—as the familiar example of the rosy periwinkle illustrates. This plant species was first harvested in Madagascar for pharmaceutical use, and the two complex alkaloids isolated from it (vinblastine and vincristine) now form the bases of compounds used in anticancer chemotherapy. Formulations of these active ingredients have proved particularly effective against childhood leukemia and Hodgkin's disease and now earn the Ely Lilly pharmaceutical company an estimated $100 million a year.[35] But while Lilly still harvests the periwinkle to produce these medicines, it has left Madagascar behind. Lilly no longer relies on the island as the primary source of this "raw material." The plant, which grows readily in warm climates throughout the world, is now widely cultivated in the Philippines and Texas. Carrying this process of alienation one step farther, in a trend that almost certainly represents the future of drug development,

France's Pierre Fabre Laboratories has created an entirely synthetic version of one of the periwinkle-derived alkaloids for the treatment of bronchial and breast cancers.[36]

As a result, the people of Madagascar have received nothing of significance in connection with the development of these powerful drugs—not even an assured income from the sale of the plants themselves. These desperately poor islanders are thus rapidly deforesting their country to gain arable land on which to grow subsistence and market crops. Today, less than 20 percent of the original forest cover remains. And although ethnobotanical teams of African scientists and students are hurrying to record popular knowledge about the curative properties of other plants, it seems inevitable that much of this lore will be lost along with the island's biodiversity.

Ironically, the information about the properties of the rosy periwinkle that first drew Eli Lilly's researchers to Madagascar did not even come from the indigenous knowledge base of that society. As it turns out, investigation of the periwinkle began because Filipino and Jamaican folklore suggested that a tea brewed from its leaves could be a remedy for diabetes.[37] If anyone deserves compensation for appropriated bioknowledge in the case of the periwinkle, then, it is perhaps the Filipino and Jamaican communities in which this folklore was preserved rather than the people of Madagascar.

The 1992 Convention on Biological Diversity, concluded at the Rio "Earth Summit," represented a partial response to the dilemma of countries in Madagascar's position, but it did little to address the more fundamental issues raised by the appropriation of indigenous peoples' knowledge of the curative properties of plants. Signatory countries agreed to "share in a fair and equitable way the results of research and development and the benefits arising from the commercial and other utilization of genetic resources." Thus the treaty emphasizes *national* rights rather than the interests of *peoples*. Moreover, it conceptualizes "genetic resources" as raw materials like coal or mineral deposits rather than as properties of the mind. This is a backhanded tribute to the tenacity of the exclusive vision of individual originary genius which has shaped Western—and international—laws of intellectual property since their inception. But it leaves out entirely cultures that supply only bioknowledge and no actual botanical materials to the new drug-development process.

The treatment of genetic resources as raw materials implies that even those countries that qualify for a "share" of the benefits may receive relatively little. Their returns will be capped, according to one recent article, by the availability of multiple sources for a protected genetic material, by the low initial value of such material, and by "the extensive research and development process required to commercialize it."[38] In other words, the persistence of traditional intellectual property concepts which stress the importance of the "value added" by the transformation of naturally occurring raw materials operates to limit potential recoveries.

A different—and perhaps more promising—way to recognize the value of indigenous peoples' bioknowledge may be found in the initiative of one private company, San Francisco–based Shaman Pharmaceuticals, which describes its drug-development practices as follows:

> Given the limitations of random mass screening, Shaman has developed a process designed to provide significant time and cost savings in the discovery, development and commercialization of new classes of pharmaceutical products. The process is driven by the science of ethnobotany, or how native peoples use plants. Shaman uses data provided by a network of ethnobotanists and physicians engaged in ongoing field research—in Africa, the South Pacific, Southeast Asia and in Central and South America—to provide initial direction for its efforts. Working with traditional healers of various rainforest cultures allows Shaman access to the largest *in vivo* laboratory in the world.[39]

Shaman is publicly committed to sharing revenues with its local collaborators, but designing a program to accomplish this goal poses difficulties of its own. Even given the head start on new drug development which its approach ensures, only a few of the many promising ethnobotanical leads a company like Shaman will follow are likely to produce a marketable new drug. Indeed, of all the possible products the company has explored over its five years of existence, only one (the antiherpes drug Virend, based on a traditional South American remedy) has reached Phase 3 clinical trials— the last significant hurdle to commercialization. Obviously, a decision to compensate only those indigenous peoples whose bioknowledge actually led to a marketable product would mean that most of Shaman's collaborators would go uncompensated. Thus, the company has pledged to "return a portion of profits to *all* the communities and countries in which we have worked, no matter where in the world the plant or information we developed into a product originated. . . . In a financially unpredictable industry such as ours, spreading the benefits and risks among all Shaman contributors increases the opportunities for compensation and hastens compensation returns."[40]

The plans for delivering such compensation that are being developed between the Healing Forest Conservancy, a nonprofit foundation established by Shaman, and representatives of the countries and communities in which the company has worked, do not emphasize cash payments. They entail, rather, funding initiatives aimed at

> supporting land rights by demarcating historic territories to [sic] indigenous communities; strengthening indigenous peoples' organizations and fostering communication between indigenous groups and the outside world; integrating local people into programs for the collection, identification and inventory of local genetic resources by merging indigenous and modern scientific methods; promoting sustainable, ecologically sound development through local harvesting of products from forests as alternatives to clearcutting for timber; and linking public health and welfare of indigenous cultures and tropical forests.[41]

The model of intellectual property which underlies this program for compensation is radically different from the received Western paradigm. It treats traditional knowledge as a source of value rather than as a kind of raw material to which value must be added. But in doing so it does not seek to recast the bioknowledge of indigenous peoples in the mold of "authorship" or "invention": it emphasizes collective rather than individual entitlement.

Where the goal is achieving recognition of indigenous peoples' interests in folkloric and other traditional cultural materials, as distinguished from their bioknowledge, a review of the comparatively sparse literature published to date likewise suggests that new models of intellectual property will be required—models which acknowledge an "intermediate sphere" between "individual rights, on the one hand, and the national or international public domain, on the other."[42] For example, the Australian government's exhaustive 1981 *Report of the Working Party on the Protection of Aboriginal Folklore* explained why copyright neither is nor could easily become an adequate vehicle for the vindication of Aboriginal interests: "Although it is accurate, in moral terms, to speak of Aboriginal folklore as belonging to

Aboriginal groups, or members of them, there is in Aboriginal customary law no right of ownership which is distinct from other rights and is equivalent to the concept of property rights under Commonwealth law."[43] Thus, to impose a conventional intellectual property regime would be a colonialist act. Instead, the *Report* proposed passage of a special "Aboriginal Folklore Act" that would incorporate Aboriginal notions of collective control and customary use, but would also provide for compensation in cases of commercial exploitation of folkloric materials. However, this recommendation for the creation of a new legal hybrid has never been implemented.

In the same vein, the 1993 "Mataatua Declaration on Cultural and Intellectual Property Rights of Indigenous Peoples," issued by an assembly of over 150 delegates from fourteen countries, calls on indigenous peoples to "define for themselves their own intellectual and cultural property," and on states to

> develop in full co-operation with indigenous peoples an additional cultural and intellectual property rights regime incorporating the following:
> —collective (as well as individual) ownership and origin
> —retroactive coverage of historical as well as contemporary works
> —protection against debasement of culturally significant items
> —co-operative rather than competitive framework
> —first beneficiaries to be the direct descendants of the traditional guardians of that knowledge
> —multi-generational coverage span.[44]

Although some themes of this declaration are familiar features of the conventional discourse of intellectual property, others (particularly the emphasis on a "co-operative framework") are new and significant additions to it.

Also in 1993, the Bellagio Declaration (see Appendix) called for experimentation with "special regimes"—based on, but not identical to, those of Western intellectual property law—for the protection of "folkloric works," "works of cultural heritage," and "the biological and ecological 'know-how' of traditional peoples." But this was not the only—or even the primary—message of the Bellagio Declaration. More fundamentally, it emphasized the distributional inequities that are "built into the basic structure and assumptions of intellectual property" insofar as these have been shaped by the "notion of the author as an individual, solitary and original creator." It remains to be seen whether experiments in adapting intellectual property law to new purposes will succeed in overcoming these structural limitations.

Over the course of the "U.N. Decade of the World's Indigenous Peoples" (1994–2003), we may expect to see a variety of such experiments. It would obviously be premature to attempt to predict their outcomes. But it is sobering to note that in the domain of bioknowledge, where most efforts to adapt intellectual property law to new purposes have been focused in recent years, disillusionment with that project appears to be spreading among advocates for biodiversity and the interests of indigenous peoples. In his recent essay "Can the Intellectual Property Rights System Serve the Interests of Indigenous Knowledge?" Surenda J. Patel comes to the following radical—even utopian—conclusion:

> We should make an 180-degree about-face on empty debates on using and modifying the intellectual property rights system. The course followed so far is a dead end. . . . The reversal would require demanding a progressive decommercialization of [intellectual property rights in] technology, and eventually making technology the common heritage of humanity, as is the position now of all science and indigenous knowledge. It will then create the great trinity of indigenous knowledge, science, and technology, which could be harnessed to the attainment of the major aspirations of humanity—the conquest of poverty, illiteracy, ill health, ill housing, and inequalities among peoples, nations, races, genders, and religions.[45]

Patel's point may have broader validity. Ultimately, it may prove impossible—or unfruitful—to reshape intellectual property law so as to incorporate new kinds of rights and new categories of owners. Rather than refiguring traditional knowledge as the product of solitary, originary genius, we may have to reimagine the familiar subject matter of Western intellectual property as the outcome of collective, collaborative social activity.

Appendix

The Bellagio Declaration
STATEMENT OF THE BELLAGIO CONFERENCE
CULTURAL AGENCY/CULTURAL AUTHORITY: POLITICS AND POETICS OF
INTELLECTUAL PROPERTY IN THE POST-COLONIAL ERA
March 11, 1993

We, the participants at the Bellagio Conference on intellectual property, come from many nations, professions, and disciplines. We are lawyers and literary critics, computer scientists and publishers, environmentalists and scholars of cultural heritage.

Sharing a common concern about the effects of the international regime of intellectual property law on our communities, on scientific progress and international development, on our environment, on the culture of indigenous peoples. In particular,

Applauding the increasing attention by the world community to such previously ignored issues as preservation of the environment, of cultural heritage and biodiversity. But

Convinced that the role of intellectual property in these areas has been neglected for too long, we therefore convened a conference of academics, activists, and practitioners diverse in geographical and cultural background as well as professional area of interest.

Discovering that many of the different concerns faced in each of these diverse areas could be traced back to the same oversights and injustices in the current international intellectual property system, we hereby

Declare the following:

First, Intellectual property laws have profound effects on issues as disparate as scientific and artistic progress, biodiversity, access to information, and the cultures of indigenous and tribal peoples. Yet all too often those laws are constructed without taking such effects into account, constructed around a paradigm that is selectively blind to the scientific and artistic contributions of many of the world's cultures and constructed in *fora* where those who will be most directly affected have no representation.

Second, Many of these problems are built into the basic structure and assumptions of intellectual property. Contemporary intellectual property law is constructed around a notion of the author as an individual, solitary and original creator, and it is for this figure that its protections are reserved. Those who do not fit this model—custodians of tribal culture and medical knowledge, collectives practicing traditional artistic and musical forms, or peasant cultivators of valuable seed varieties, for example—are denied intellectual property protection.

Third, A system based on such premises has real, negative consequences. Increasingly, traditional knowledge, folklore, genetic material and native medical knowledge flow *out* of their countries of origin unprotected by intellectual property, while works from developed countries flow *in*, well protected by international intellectual property agreements, backed by the threat of trade sanctions.

Fourth, In general, systems built around the author paradigm tend to obscure or undervalue the importance of "the public domain," the intellectual and cultural commons from which future works will be constructed. Each intellectual property right, in effect, fences off some portion of the public domain, making it unavailable to future creators. In striking respects, the current situation raises the same concerns raised twenty years ago by the impending privatization of the deep-sea bed. The aggressive expansion of intellectual property rights has the potential to inhibit development and future creation by fencing off "the commons," and yet—in striking contrast to the reaction over the deep-sea bed—the international community seems unaware of the fact.

Fifth, We deplore these tendencies, deplore them as not merely unjust but unwise, and entreat the international community to reconsider the assumptions on which and the procedures by which the international intellectual property regime is shaped.

In general, we favor increased recognition and protection of the public domain. We call on the international community to expand the public domain through expansive application of concepts of "fair use," compulsory licensing, and narrower initial coverage of property rights in the first place. But since existing author-focused regimes are blind to the interests of non-authorial producers as well as to the importance of the commons, the main exception to this expansion of the public domain should be in favor of those who have been excluded by the authorial biases of current law.

Specifically, we advocate consideration of special regimes, possibly in the form of "neighboring" or "related" rights regimes, for the following areas:

— Protection of folkloric works.
— Protection of works of cultural heritage.
— Protection of the biological and ecological "know-how" of traditional peoples.

In addition, we support systematic reconsideration of the basis on which new kinds of works related to digital technology, such as computer programs and electronic data bases, are protected under national and international intellectual property regimes. We recognize the economic importance of works falling into these categories, and the significant investments made in their production. Nevertheless, given the importance of the various concerns raised by any such a regime—concerns about public access, international development, and technological innovation—we believe that choices about how and how much to protect data bases should be made with a view to the specific policy objectives such protection is designed to achieve, rather than as a reflexive response to their categorization as "works of authorship."

On a systemic level, we call upon states and non-governmental organizations to move towards democratization of the *fora* in which the international intellectual property regime is debated and decided.

In conclusion, we declare that in an era in which information is among the most precious of all resources, intellectual property rights cannot be framed by the few to be applied to the many. They cannot be framed on assumptions that disproportionately exclude the contributions of important parts of the world community. They can no longer be constructed without reference to their ecological, cultural, and scientific effects. We must re-imagine the international regime of intellectual property. It is to that task this Declaration calls its readers.

Signatories

This document was framed by lawyers, anthropologists, environmental-ists, computer experts, literary critics, publishers, and activists. Inevitably, each of us would change some word or phrase, or shift some emphasis. Its signatories agree, however, to the central themes and spirit of this Decla-ration and to the urgent sense of concern that motivated it. Institutional affiliations are provided for identification purposes only.

Upendra Baxi (University of Delhi)
Jay David Bolter (Georgia Institute of Technology)
James D. A. Boyle (Washington College of Law, American University)
Rosemary Coombe (University of Toronto School of Law)
Margreta de Grazia (University of Pennsylvania)
Peter Jaszi (Washington College of Law, American University)
Smadar Lavie (University of California, Davis)
Mary Layoun (University of Wisconsin, Madison)
Andrea Lunsford (Ohio State University)
Nébila Mezghani (University of Tunis)
J. Hillis Miller (University of California, Irvine)
Patrick J. O'Keefe (University of Sydney)
Albrecht Götz von Olenhusen (Freiburg i. Br., Germany)
Heiki Pisuke (University of Tartu, Estonia)
Mark Rose (University of California, Santa Barbara)
Pamela Samuelson (University of Pittsburgh School of Law)
Akin Thomas (Ibadan, Nigeria)
Martha Woodmansee (Case Western Reserve University)
Charles Zerner (Rainforest Alliance, New York)
Zheng Chengsi (Chinese Academy of Social Sciences, Beijing)

Notes

1   For some representative contributions to the project, see Martha Woodmansee, "The Genius and the Copyright: Economic and Legal Conditions of the Emergence of the 'Author,'" *Eighteenth-Century Studies* 17 (1984): 425–48; and *The Author, Art, and the Market: Rereading the History of Aesthetics* (New York, 1994); Mark Rose, "The Author as Proprietor: *Donaldson v. Becket* and the Genealogy of Modern Authorship," *Representations* 23 (1988): 51–85; and *Authors and Owners: The Invention of Copyright* (Cambridge, MA, 1993); Andrea Lunsford and Lisa Ede, *Singular Texts/Plural Authors: Perspectives on Collaborative Writing* (Carbondale, 1990); Pamela Samuelson, "Digital Media and the Changing Face of Intellectual Property Law," *Rutgers Computer and Technology Law Journal* 16 (1990): 323–40; and, with Randall Davis, Mitchell D. Kapor, and J. H. Reichman, "A Manifesto Concerning the Legal Protection of Computer Programs," *Columbia Law Review* 94 (1994): 2308–2431; Peter Jaszi, "Toward a Theory of Copyright: The Metamorphoses of 'Authorship,'" *Duke Law Journal* (1991): 455–502; Margreta de Grazia, *Shakespeare Verbatim: The Reproduction of Authenticity and the 1790 Apparatus* (Oxford, 1991); James Boyle, "A Theory of Law and Information: Copyright, Spleens, Blackmail and Insider Trading," *California Law Review* 80 (1992): 1415–1540; and *Shamans, Software, and Spleens* (Cambridge, MA, 1996); Niva Elkin-Koren, "Copyright Law and Social Dialogue on the Information Superhighway," *Cardozo Arts and Entertainment Law Journal* 13 (1993): 345–411; and Rosemary Coombe, "Challenging Paternity: Histories of Copyright," *Yale Journal of Law and the Humanities* 6 (1994): 397–422. The project as a whole and many of these contributions to it have been shaped by Michel Foucault's seminal essay "Qu'est-ce qu'un auteur?" (1969); see "What Is an Author?" in *Textual Strategies*, ed. Josué Harari (Ithaca, 1979), 141–60. One common theme of these studies is the demystification of the concept of originality. So it seems appropriate to note that some of the ideas discussed in early sections of this essay were either introduced or treated at greater length in other writings by us cited here and below. See, especially, our introduction to *The Construction of Authorship: Textual Appropriation in Law and Literature*, ed. Martha Woodmansee and Peter Jaszi (Durham, 1994), 1–13.

2   For a selection of papers from the conference, see Woodmansee and Jaszi, eds., *Construction of Authorship*.

3   Another argument for the urgency of renewing this interdisciplinary conversation may be found in Martha Woodmansee and Peter Jaszi, "The Law of Texts: Copyright in the Academy," *College English* 57 (1995): 769–87.

4   While we draw different conclusions, we learned about this collaboration from David Gewanter, "'Daffodils' and Authority: Wordsworth's Collaborative Lyric" (paper presented at the conference on Intellectual Property and the Construction of Authorship, Cleveland, 1991).

5   Dorothy Wordsworth, *The Grasmere Journals*, ed. Pamela Woof (Oxford, 1991), 84–85.

6   William Wordsworth, *Poems, in Two Volumes and Other Poems, 1800–1807*, ed. Jared Curtis (Ithaca, 1983), 207–8.

7   Wordsworth ascribed these lines to Hutchinson in a note dictated to Isabella Fenwick (ibid., 418).

8   William Wordsworth, *Lyrical Ballads, and Other Poems, 1797–1800*, ed. James Butler and Karen Green (Ithaca, 1992), 738.

9   Stephen Gill, *William Wordsworth: A Life* (Oxford, 1989), 184–85.

10   Wordsworth, *Lyrical Ballads*, 741–42. On the genesis of the Preface, including Coleridge's involvement, see Mary Moorman, *William Wordsworth: The Early Years* (Oxford, 1957), 492–96. Cf. Richard Holmes, *Coleridge: Early Visions* (New York, 1989): "Wordsworth, from a position of apparent weakness, had ruthlessly come to dominate the terms of the collaboration. Having used Coleridge—even, one might think, having exploited him—as advisor and editor, drawing him up to the Lakes for that very purpose, he had entirely imposed his own vision of the collection on the final text" (285).

11   Wordsworth, *Lyrical Ballads*, 752–53. At this time, and also in regular consultation with Coleridge, Wordsworth was attempting to articulate these ideas in the long poem that was eventually published as *The Prelude*. Here Wordsworth repeatedly acknowledges his friend's contribution; however, he did not publish this poem in his lifetime, but instructed that it be released posthumously. By the time it appeared in 1850, the year of Wordsworth's death, Coleridge had been dead for sixteen years.

12   Gill, *William Wordsworth*, 197.

13   See Jaszi, "Toward a Theory of Copyright," 468–71.

14   For a fuller treatment of this campaign, see Martha Woodmansee, "The Cultural Work of Copyright: Legislating Authorship in Britain 1837–1842," in *Law in the Domains of Culture*, ed. Austin Sarat and Thomas R. Kearns (Michigan, forthcoming).

15   William Wordsworth to Richard Sharp, 27 September 1808, in *The Letters of William and Dorothy Wordsworth: The Middle Years, 1806–1811*, ed. Ernest de Selincourt and Mary Moorman (Oxford, 1969), 266.

16   Thomas Noon Talfourd, Speech to the House of Commons, 18 May 1837, *Parliamentary Debates*, 3d series, vol. 38 (1837), col. 877.

17   Poulett Thomson, Speech to the House of Commons, 20 March 1838, *Parliamentary Debates*, 3d series, vol. 41 (1838), col. 1098. See James J. Barnes, *Authors, Publishers and Politicians: The Quest for an Anglo-American Copyright Agreement, 1815–1854* (London, 1974).

18   See Sam Ricketson, *The Berne Convention for the Protection of Literary and Artistic Works: 1886–1986* (London, 1987), 39.

19   Ibid., 42.

20   Ibid., 46.

21   Ibid., 48 n. 28.

22   Ibid., 144–46.

23   See N. N. Feltes, *Literary Capital and the Late Victorian Novel* (Madison, 1994).

24   "Uruguay Round Agreement on Trade-Related Aspects of Intellectual Property Rights, Including Trade in Counterfeit Goods (TRIPs)," in William Patry, *Copyright and the GATT: An Interpretation and Legislative History of the Uruguay Round Agreements Act* (Washington, DC, 1995), A-3–A-31.

25   "Berne Convention for the Protection of Literary and Artistic Works," 24 July 1971; rpt. in Ricketson, *Berne Convention*, 929–55; quotation from 930.

26   "Uruguay Round Agreement," A-7.

27   *Coldwater Creek: A Northcountry Catalog* ("First Thaw" 1996): 4.

28 See Nell Jessup Newton, "Memory and Misrepresentation: Representing Crazy Horse," *Connecticut Law Review* 27 (1995): 1003–54; quotation from 1017.

29 Ibid., 1028. In response to tribal protests, the beer's distributors have argued *both* that in their marketing of this product they simply seek to "celebrate the greatest leader of his people in modern times" *and* that Crazy Horse's reputation is being overstated by opponents of the beer: "The acceptance of Crazy Horse's role, whatever his role may have been, among Native Americans, was not, and is not, universal" (ibid.).

30 Indeed, the distributors have argued that a proposed regulatory ban on the use of the Crazy Horse name would be a "confiscatory 'taking' by the federal Government of private property trademark rights, for which taxpayers ultimately must pay" (ibid., 1028 n. 101).

31 Anthony Seeger, "Singing Other Peoples' Songs," *Cultural Survival Quarterly* 15 (1991): 36–39; quotations from 36.

32 See Kathleen Day, "Rain Forest Remedies: More Drug Companies Turning to Tribal Healers for Medicines," *Washington Post*, 19 September 1995, E-4.

33 See Steven R. King, "The Source of Our Cures," *Cultural Survival Quarterly* 15 (1991): 19–22, esp. 19.

34 Jack Kloppenburg, Jr., "No Hunting!" *Cultural Survival Quarterly* 15 (1991): 14–18; quotation from 16.

35 See Edward O. Wilson, "Threats to Biodiversity," *Scientific American* (September 1989): 108–16.

36 Anne Jeanblanc, "Fighting Cancer on Many Fronts," *World Press Review* (May 1993): 42–43.

37 Karen Ann Goldman, "Compensation for Use of Biological Resources under the Convention on Biological Diversity," *Law and Policy in International Business* (January 1994): 695–726, esp. 717 n. 131.

38 Ibid., 716 n. 127.

39 Shaman Pharmaceuticals, "Ethnobotany Accelerating Drug Discovery," press release, April 1995, 2.

40 Steven R. King and Thomas J. Carlson, "Biocultural Diversity, Biomedicine and Ethnobotany: The Experience of Shaman Pharmaceuticals," *Interciencia* 20 (1995): 134–39; quotation from 135.

41 Ibid., 136.

42 Janice G. Weiner, "Protection of Folklore: A Political and Legal Challenge," *International Review of Industrial Property and Copyright Law (IIC)* 18 (1987): 56–92; quotation from 92.

43 Department of Home Affairs and Environment, *Report of the Working Party on the Protection of Aboriginal Folklore* (Canberra, 1981), 34.

44 "The Mataatua Declaration on Cultural and Intellectual Property Rights of Indigenous Peoples," First International Conference on the Cultural and Intellectual Property Rights of Indigenous Peoples, June 1993, 2–4.

45 Surenda J. Patel, "Can the Intellectual Property Rights System Serve the Interests of Indigenous Knowledge?" in *Valuing Local Knowledge: Indigenous People and Intellectual Property Rights*, ed. Stephen B. Brush and Doreen Strabinsky (Washington, DC, 1995), 305–22; quotation from 319.

Adam Zachary Newton

From Exegesis to Ethics:
Recognition and Its Vicissitudes
in Saul Bellow and Chester Himes

> We were the end of the line. We were the children
> of the immigrants who had camped at the city's back
> door . . . we were Brownsville—*Brunsvil*, as the old
> folks said—the dust of the earth to all Jews with money,
> and notoriously a place that measured success by our
> skill in getting away from it. So that when poor Jews
> left, even Negroes, as we said, found it easy to settle
> on the margins of Brownsville.
> —Alfred Kazin, *A Walker in the City*

> These were the poorest people of the South, who
> poured into New York City during the decade follow-
> ing the Great Depression. . . . They felt as the Pilgrims
> must have felt when they were coming to America.
> But these descendants of Ham must have been twice
> as happy as the Pilgrims, because they had been catch-
> ing twice the hell. . . . The children of these disillu-
> sioned colored pioneers inherited the total lot of their
> parents—the disappointments, the anger. To add to
> their misery, they had little hope of deliverance. For
> where does one run to when he's already in the prom-
> ised land?
> —Claude Brown, *Manchild in the Promised Land*

Certain pairings of texts from different literary
or cultural traditions—say, Conrad's *Nostromo*

The *South Atlantic Quarterly* 95:4, Fall 1996.
Copyright © 1996 by Duke University Press.

and García Márquez's *Hundred Years of Solitude*, or Gogol's story "The Overcoat" and Melville's "Bartleby the Scrivener"—make a natural kind of sense, marriages, if you will, born of more than just creative matchmaking. But Saul Bellow and Chester Himes? A high-cultural Nobelist and an equally driven, willful ex-convict, the one a testament to the ideology of literary man as *thinker* and of Jew as "humanist," the other to that of writer as raw *force* and Black man as art—"my form, *myself*"?[1]

Imagine a line extending from the totemic fiction of Malamud's *Tenants* at one end to the polemic friction between Blacks and Jews, as replayed by Harold Cruse and Cynthia Ozick, at the other.[2] Call it a single narrative of *blackjewishrelations* (which I spell as one word to emphasize the inflated quality of this particular piece of symbolic capital)—a literary history of sorts, short but bitter. Haven't the organizing structures of fiction and journalism, then, already beaten literary criticism to the punch? Where, in other words, is there space on that "line" for another "point," another story?

With its hypertrophied Jew and its elemental Black, Malamud's novel alone would seem to consign the unlikely conjunction of real-life writers like Bellow and Himes to the twilight zone of the uncanny. Ozick's and Cruse's (albeit dated) analyses of the cultural politics pitting Black intellectuals against Jewish undercut the very idea. No doubt Bellow (and Himes, were he still alive) would chafe at being so associated even on the accessory, ad hoc plane of "representational thematics," the interpretative school to which my "thematics of recognition" belongs.

Nevertheless, of all possible paired texts by American Black and Jewish authors, *If He Hollers Let Him Go* and *The Victim* seem to me one of the most apropos, for *in conjunction* they uncannily convert exegesis into political, and ethical, exigency, into an ethical-politics of *recognition*. If we regard literary history and criticism alike as venues of "social space," a space formed by the ligatures, the binding ties, which interventive readings forge or create, then "intertextuality" signifies a critical task as much as a property of texts themselves.[3]

Whether the lived realities of anti-Semitism and racism can be double-tracked (and I do not gainsay the need to do so, if I do not feel sanguine about the outcome), an identity politics which cordons off these texts from one another or backlights them against the separate horizons of "African American" and "Jewish American" literature makes for a pinched and hamstrung criticism. A dynamic of engagement, however, places these novels in a relationship of genuine tension, facing off in a textual encounter. Such "dialogizing" of literary invention by Blacks and Jews does not necessarily carry over into public discourse or *Lebenswelt*. (Gloss, not glass, best describes representation's relation to the Real anyway, as Brecht knew when he endorsed cigarette smoke interposed before his aesthetic "mirrors."[4]) But neither is literary criticism *merely* academic with recognition as the shared optic for reading these texts, bending their combined light toward a critically engineered public space. To the degree that "the public" is the vector generated by points, or acts, of ethical encounter, literary analysis of this sort should have genuine ethical force.

Accordingly, the term "face," a recurrent motif in these texts, functions as part of a "thematics of recognition," a representational grammar internal to the texts themselves. But as a metaphor for staging ethical encounter, it also serves as an external hinge between their African American and Jewish American imaginaries, hence *facing* Black and Jew. "Face" functions in a frankly Levinassian mode here as well, with the role assigned to ethics in my formulation "an ethical-politics of recognition." With the qualifying adjective supervening in the phrase, "politics" becomes the more dependent and anchored term. "Ethical-politics" thus signifies a politicizing of specifically Levinassian themes and categories here, and the "politics of recognition" consequently undergoes a certain skewing, at least so far as its terms have been defined by Charles Taylor and others.[5]

If we take the title of Emmanuel Levinas's essay "Politics After!" at *face* value, "politics" becomes the supervening term in an already ethical formulation; the political moment, while crucial, arrives *late* (or *prematurely*, as the case may be). Even if we grant, with Roger Simon, that the politics of recognition is "based on the assumption that the public assertion of the collective history to which one belongs is supposed to serve as a corrective to some deficit in self-esteem,"[6] selfhood's esteem already labors under a deficit incurred vis-à-vis the Other. To put it another way, before victimization becomes badge, flag, or redoubt, it is grasping hand and seeing eye, the phenomenal constitutiveness of human encounter. "The articulation of identities," as Simon notes, "cannot be reduced to a personal desire for cultural acknowledgment. What's at stake must be written in different terms."[7]

═══

Asa Leventhal, one of several candidates for the titular condition of Bellow's *Victim*, comes not from Brownsville but from Hartford, Connecticut, that is, from one of those "middle class districts that showed the way to New York" rather than from somewhere truly impoverished. Still, having for a time drifted on New York's Lower East Side, "starved and thin," he has learned that Kazin's "getting away from it" can also mean getting away *with* it: "He had almost fallen in with that part of humanity of which he was frequently mindful (he never forgot the hotel on lower Broadway), the part that did not get away with it—the lost, the outcast, the overcome, the effaced, the ruined."[8] In Kazin's terms, Bellow's protagonist has come to mark a division between a "they" and a "we," and we must conclude with him that "to settle on the margins" promises a less than happy ending, tantamount as it is to being set apart, singled out, enclosed.

"Even," *pace* Kazin, for "Negroes." Take, for instance, Bob Jones, the titular—though elided—"nigger" in Himes's *If He Hollers Let Him Go*. Conversant, like Leventhal, with the dilemmas of marginality, of the "end of the line," of *they* and *we*, Jones too learns hard lessons of mis-placement. And, in a sense, he also knows what getting away from/with it means. But his fate remains far more penumbral than Asa's, and he catches "twice the hell," since for Bob *place* rhymes much more than accidentally with *race*. Framed for rape at the end of the novel (a trumped-up charge in which the court colludes), he is given "a break" by the judge and allowed to enlist in the army rather than be incarcerated:

> "If I let you join the armed forces—any branch you want—will you give me your word you'll stay away from white women and keep out of trouble?" I wanted to just break out and laugh like the Marine in my dream, laugh and keep on laughing. 'Cause all I ever wanted was just a little thing—just to be a man. But I kept a straight face, got the words through my oversized lips. "Yes sir, I promise." . . . Two hours later I was in the Army.[9]

That is how Himes's novel ends, and a similar mood of éminence grise and scene of escort occurs in the last paragraph of *The Victim*:

> "Wait a minute, what's your idea of who runs things?" said Leventhal. But he heard Mary's voice at his back. Allbee ran in and sprang up the stairs. The bell continued its dinning, and Leventhal and Mary were still in the aisle when the houselights went off. An usher showed them to their seats.[10]

How it feels to be "Colored" (or *Jewish*) *me/Jewish* (or *Black*) *like me: we,* in contradistinction to *you,* in relation to *they*—that most durable of tropes in the literature of ethnic auto/biography. Kazin and Brown sketch it in my epigraphs as the difference between identity's home and its beyond. Bellow's and Himes's texts, however, begin in situ, taking the otherness of place for granted as merely laying the ground for the otherness of person—or of self. Even a matter as ostensibly benign as pronominal deixis— the marking out of *you* or *your, those* or *my,* "people"—in these novels demonstrates an equally underlying politics and poetics; indeed, pronouns and proper nouns could, in a way, be considered their twin "theme"—the discursive machinery, the "attack-words," in Elias Canetti's phrase, of anti-Semitism and racism.[11]

A related but even more embodied thematic pattern in these two novels, however, propels *The Victim* and *If He Hollers Let Him Go* from their very first pages: a persistent, even obsessive, concern with the human *face* as subject and object, as tenor and vehicle, ultimately as field for *recognition.* Bellow's novel begins with two epigraphs, a parable of accountability from *The 1001 Nights* and the following quotation from Thomas de Quincey's *Confessions of an English Opium Eater:* "Be that as it may, now it was upon the rocking waters of the ocean the human face began to reveal itself; the sea appeared paved with innumerable faces, upturned to the heavens, faces imploring, wrathful, despairing; faces that surged upward by thousands, by myriads, by generations." In the case of Himes's text, the novel proper opens with a series of hallucinatory visages. In the first of five dream–set pieces corresponding to the five days of the story's action and telescoping the novel's propulsive anatomy of racial animosity, Jones dreams of a Black man given the task of "look[ing] at the dead body of Frankie Childs in the face." Jones then turns over in his sleep and conjures up a second tableau of humiliation, a dream which centers on his own excruciated fascination with two white faces persistently laughing at his own. Upon waking, Jones laments that he has been recently greeting the day with fear and trembling, which he correlates with the "handicap" of race, now brought home to him all the more powerfully by recalling "the look of people's faces when you asked them about a job." [12]

In fact, the differentia specifica of figure, physiognomy, and hue runs absolutely riot in Himes's novel, an obsessive feature of the text's descriptive field:

> The first to be called was a medium-sized, well built, fast walking dark brown man of about thirty-five.
>
> . . . .
>
> She was a full-bodied, slow-motioned home girl with a big broad flat face, flat nosed and thick-lipped; yellow but not bright.
>
> . . . .
>
> He was a thin, wiry nervous Irishman with a blood-red, beaked face and close set bright blue eyes.
>
> . . . .
>
> [I] straightened up, face to face, with a tall white girl in a leather welder's suit . . . a peroxide blonde with a large-featured, overly made-up face, and she had a large, bright-painted fleshy mouth, kidney shaped.
>
> . . . .
>
> A short, dumpy, brown-skinned girl with slow-rolling eyes and a tiny pouting mouth let us in.
>
> . . . .
>
> A light-complexioned, simple-looking girl with a pretty face and dangling hair sat on the arm of an empty chair. . . . A slim, good-looking fellow about her colour with conked yellow hair and a hairline mustache sat on the middle of the davenport.[13]

At the same time, the novel compulsively stages scenes of face-to-face "recognition":

> Something drew her gaze and she looked up into my eyes. We held gazes until I stopped just in front of her.
>
> . . . .
>
> Looking up, I caught a young captain's eye. He didn't turn away when our gazes met; he didn't change expression; he just watched us with the intent stare of the analyst.
>
> . . . .
>
> The white woman next to me stopped talking and looked around. I could feel her gaze on me. . . . Our eyes met. . . . She looked away after a moment and I looked into the mirror and met the eyes of the man on the other side of her.
>
> . . . .
>
> We both jumped back from pure reflex. Then recognition came into his eyes and his face turned greenish white. It froze him, nailed him

to the spot. For a moment I was stunned. I'd never seen a white man scared before, not craven, not until you couldn't see the white for the scare.[14]

In the case of Bellow's novel, albeit less blatantly than Himes's, the entire narrative and its imagistic tension follow, one could say, from the looks traded by and the prolonged mutual "studying" of two faces—Leventhal's and his nemesis, Allbee's—a *Jewish* and a *non-Jewish* face, the one delineated as such, the other through implicit contrast (we are told mainly that Allbee is tall and blonde):

> Some such vague thing was in Leventhal's mind while he waited his turn at the drinking spout, when suddenly he had a feeling that he was not merely looked at but watched. Unless he was greatly mistaken a man was scrutinizing him, pacing slowly with him as the line moved.
>
> . . . .
>
> Well, now you've found out that I still exist and you're going home, is that it? . . . I mean that you just wanted *to have a look at me . . . wanted to see me.*
>
> . . . .
>
> But now and then, moving from cage to cage, gazing at the animals, Leventhal, in speaking to Philip, or smoking, or smiling, was so conscious of Allbee, so certain he was of being scrutinized, that he was able to see himself as if through a strange pair of eyes: the side of his face, the palpitation of his throat. . . . Changed in this way into his own observer, he was able to see Allbee, too . . . his raggedly overgrown neck, the bulge of his cheeks, the color of blood in his ear.
>
> . . . .
>
> He had a particularly vivid recollection of the explicit recognition in Allbee's eyes which he could not doubt was the double of his own.[15]

While these passages may suggest merely descriptive contours for a thematics of "face," Levinas's phenomenological ethics can provide more elaborate exegetical possibilities. Extending "face and recognition" in Levinassian ethics to the thematics of ethnic literature also politicizes Levinas's work in turn, thereby allowing us to trace one path from exegesis to ethics and back again, "from ethics to exegesis," in Levinas's terms.[16]

In Levinas's philosophy, "ethics" means more than an account of norms for human sociality; it is *first philosophy* (and therefore prior to ontology) because it marks the very ground of being, its power lying precisely in its ab-original character. Levinassian ethics sees "in justice and injustice a *primordial* access to the other beyond all ontology."[17] This is not justice as fairness, as Rawls has defined it.[18] The "original position" for Levinas is not predicated upon a veil of ignorance which guarantees each person a similarity of position to, but not vis-à-vis with, all the others; neither is it the rationally willed categorical imperative of a Kantian moral agent vis-à-vis objective norms of social relation. Nor, finally, is it the communitarian ideal of a society rooted in attachments, hydra-headed in its collective vis-à-vis. Instead, this "original position" is simply, and radically, *vis-à-vis*: the intersubjective drama of face-to-face encounter, the independent self "unseated" from selfhood by the moral claim posed by the other person in his/her *alterity*. As lived obligation, as relatedness "undergone," ethics, then, is featured and bodied forth by *visage*. Ethics is presystematic because it stands above all as *manifested*, that is, as directly experienced through the concrete, immanent, and sensuous encounter with the Other. And it is the human face, a primordial "upsurge," which marks the site of such encounter. "Even when he does not regard me," Levinas fondly quotes the Song of Songs, "he regards me."

Along with its power to show forth—its phenomenal character—the face is defined for Levinas by its capacity for language. The face as primordial manifestation speaks, and in so doing enjoins responsibility; it says, "You will not kill." As Levinas explains,

> "Thou shalt not kill" or "Thou shalt love thy neighbor" not only forbids the violence of murder: it also concerns all the slow and invisible killing committed in our desires and our vices, in all the innocent cruelties of natural life, in our indifference of "good conscience" to what is far and what is near, even in the haughty obstinacy of our objectifying and our thematizing, in all the consecrated injustices due to our atomic weight of individuals and the equilibrium of our social orders.[19]

The biblical topos here is not incidental to the argument, for Levinas has particularized the metaphysical thrust of all his work—independent of his philosophical writings—in a series of essays on Jewish identity and in Talmudic commentary.[20] But particularity serves as both problem and problematic here. On the one hand, Levinas typically identifies it with privileged (i.e., "seated") positions of autonomy, a positionality that he castigates:

> The original perseverance of being in its being, of the individualism of being, the persistence or insistence of beings in the guise of individuals jealous for their *part*, this *particularism* of the inert, substantivized into things, particularism of the enrooted vegetable being, of the wild animal fighting for its existence, and of the soul, the "owner and interested party" Bossuet speaks of, this particularism exacerbated into egoism or into political "totalities," ready or readying themselves for war, is reversed into "Thou shalt not kill," into the care of one being for another being, into non-in-difference of one toward the other.[21]

Or, to put it another way, the "narcissism of little differences" (Freud) simply picks up where primary narcissism leaves off. Yet, on the other hand, Levinas just as consistently privileges the specific textual and prophetic traditions of Jewish peoplehood as uniquely embedded particulars grounding a universal drive toward justice: Israel as "a *figure* in which a primordial mode of the human is revealed."[22] Elsewhere, he explicates "Judaism" as follows:

> As a prophetic moment of human reason where every man—and all of man—end[s] up redefining one another, Judaism would not mean simply a nationality, a species in a type and contingency of History. Judaism, rather, is a rupture of the natural and the historical . . . as if Jewish destiny were a crack in the shell of imperturbable being and the awakening to an insomnia in which the inhuman is no longer covered up and hidden by the political necessities which it shapes, and no longer excused by their universality.[23]

A similar argument can be—and has been—made about race, such as Frantz Fanon's analysis of hypostatized Blackness: "[The Jew] and I may be separated by the sexual question, but we have one point in question. Both of us stand for evil."[24] As even the sexual distinction drawn here is debatable, the unifying point, I think, is symbolic capital, the capacity to "stand for," to represent *both* particularly *and* universally. And indeed, Levinas expressly concerns himself with the presymbolic, or what we might call the precultural—ethics as a dimension of height which arrests and contests the laterality, or mutual translatability, of independent realms and nation-hoods.[25] Height is ascribed to ethics but also, more vexedly, to "Judaism"—a singular witness to the irruption of ethics into being and, more concretely, of what Levinas calls "Holy History" into the ongoing formation and dissolution of cultures.[26]

Now, reckoning seriously with such an emphatic defense of exceptionality as the "formation and expression of the universal"—and Jewish exceptionality, at that—would seem to upend the very question of a pluralism of texts and of peoples; even to *juxtapose* culturally specific documents, as I do here, would be to incur Levinas's punning and double-edged charge of "disorientation": a distracting "saraband" of contrived diversity.[27] Moreover, his solution—the specificity of Judaism—offers, it seems, no wider interpretative applicability, not least in the domain of secular, culturally particular literatures. Longitude, not latitude, plots the always prior place of Jewish particularity for Levinas.

Indeed, both of our texts here may be read as fortuitously dramatizing Levinas's metaphor of "awakening to an insomnia": each of the five days which comprise the action of *If He Hollers Let Him Go*, for example, begins with Bob Jones's awakening from disturbed sleep to the greater nightmare of everyday racism; and throughout *The Victim* Asa Leventhal either has his sleep interrupted by visits from his nemesis or has felt "threatened by something while he slept." Even so, neither novel develops its particular, ethnically specific "case" after the fashion of Levinas's paradoxically transcendental/exceptionalist model.

Or does it? Is there any approach that would both unify the texts and extend, perhaps challenge, Levinas's work? Two obstacles in Levinas's thought seem to hamper its usefulness for a criticism-as-ethical-politics: (1) "face" is identified not with culturally marked features but with "abstract man disengaged from all culture";[28] and (2) "particularity" signifies not difference but uniqueness (the particularity of *goi echad*, of a "unique nation," as in the petitionary [*Tachanun*] prayer of the Jewish daily service). The second is admittedly the thornier difficulty, as Levinas plainly demonstrates in a section of "Judaism and Revolution" entitled "Politics and Violence": "We [the people of Israel] are a vineyard more complicated than a plot of land that is cultivated; only its owner, sublime particularism, is equal to the task of removing the thorns."[29] That is, G-d acts singularly, and redemptively, in Jewish history. This is not the place to assess such a claim, but certainly other grand narratives of cultural and ethnic misfortune can claim the identical privilege of defining collective identity through the particularist removal of historically contingent thorns. More succinctly and pointedly, a *universal* moral indemnity vibrates through, and rescues, *human* history.

The other obstacle (and the more relevant one here) has already been extensively redressed in *Narrative Ethics*, where I argue for the constitutive "dress" of what appear to metaphysicians' eyes, perhaps, to be subsidiary accoutrements of identity. Thus in Stephen Crane's story "The Monster," Melville's *Benito Cereno*, and Richard Wright's *Native Son*, ethical homicide, in Levinas's sense—"the indifference of 'good conscience' to what is near and what is far"—means the murder done to *Black* faces by *White* eyes. The failure, or abrogation, of recognition in these texts devolves upon an impaired moral faculty which perceives (and dehumanizes) faces that are racially and culturally *particular*. If "violence can aim only at a face" (in Levinas's memorable phrase), at the emblem and core of humanity, the exterior feature of interiority par excellence, then (in homage to Ralph Ellison) violence aimed at Black or Jewish faces would limn Black or Jewish masks.[30]

We often process physiognomic information in fiction as simply the establishing material of *vraisemblance*; this, the text is telling us, is a fully featured "character." And yet, in *The Victim*, Bellow renders faces and face-to-faces with an exactitude unremarkable in itself perhaps, but which gathers piquancy in light of the ambient air of mystification hovering about the plotted circumstances of recognition.[31] *Something* here is flagging our attention:

> Leventhal's figure was burly, his head large, his nose, too, was large. He had black hair, coarse waves of it, and his eyes under their intergrown brows were intensely black and of a size unusual in adult faces. . . . They seemed to disclose an intelligence not greatly interested in its own powers, as if preferring not to be bothered by them, indifferent; and this indifference appeared to be extended to others. He did not look sullen but rather unaccommodating, impassive.[32]

Bellow's eye for the discrete particular notwithstanding, this text (whose burden is being "summoned" to account) works *in particular* by soliciting us directly to look at its dynamics of looking:

> The park was even more crowded than before, and noisy. There was another revivalist band on the corner, and the blare of the two joined

confusingly above the other sounds. The lamps were yellowed, covered with flies and moths. On one of the paths an old man, sunburned, sinewy, in a linencap, was shining shoes. The fountain ran with a green, leaden glint. Children in their underclothing waded and rolled in the spray, the parents looking on. Eyes seemed softer than by day, and larger, and gazed at one longer, as though in the dark heat some interspace of reserve had been crossed and strangers might approach one another with a kind of recognition. You looked and thought, at least, that you knew whom you had seen.[33]

Immediately after this description, Kirby Allbee (Leventhal's antagonist in the full classical sense) accosts him. Leventhal muses, "My god, my god, what kind of fish is this? One of those guys who wants you to think they can see to the bottom of your soul." A dance of eyes, faces, and recognitive looks fills out the episode, reaching a pitch in the following passage:

Leventhal grimly looked at him in the light that came through the leaves. He [Allbee] had been spying on him, and the mystery was why! How long had he been keeping watch on him and for what reason— what grotesque reason? Allbee returned his look, examining him as he was examined, in concentration and seriousness. . . . And in the loom of these eyes and with the warmth of the man's breath on his face, for they were crowded together on the beach, Leventhal suddenly felt that he had been singled out to be the object of some freakish, insane process, and for an instant he was filled with dread.[34]

Now, certainly, alternative phenomenologies of "the look" can be brought to bear here, as plausibly from, say, Hegel or Sartre, or even Erving Goffman, as from Levinas. But, in the context of the idea that "strangers might approach one another with a kind of recognition" (what Levinas will call *l'approche du prochain*) and a sensation of being "singled out" (what Levinas will call "the subject . . . unseated by a wordless accusation"), the recognition scene at this juncture in the text seems nothing short of uncanny— as, in truth, it does to Leventhal himself:

Any derelict panhandler or bum might buttonhole you on the street and say, "The world wasn't made for you any more than it was for me, was it?" The error was to forget that neither man had made the arrangements, and so it was perfectly right to say, "Why pick on me?

I didn't set this up any more than you did." Admittedly there was a wrong, a general wrong. Allbee, on the other hand, came along and said, "*You!*" and that was so meaningless. For you might feel that something was owing to the panhandler, but to be directly blamed was entirely different.[35]

In fact, the plot progressively indicates to Leventhal and readers alike that he does bear a certain irrecusable responsibility—that the unfamiliar betrays more than a little familiarity through one of life's inveterate *unheimlich* maneuvers—direct "blame" or not.

Face-to-face interactions in *If He Hollers Let Him Go* are more flagrantly polarized, and in that sense perhaps more "political," than those in *The Victim*, but they really illustrate only another—and analogous—kind of existential harrowing:

> The red light caught me at Manchester; and that made me warm. It never failed; every time I got in a hurry I got caught by every light. . . . When the light turned green it caught a white couple in the middle of the street. . . . But when they looked up and saw we were coloured they just took their time, giving us a look of cold hatred. . . . I sat there looking at the white couple until they had crossed the sidewalk giving them stare for stare, hate for hate. . . . My arms were rubbery and my fingers numb; I was weak as if I'd been heaving sacks of cement all day in the sun.[36]

I am struck here especially by the ambient pressure of arrest—the "light *caught me*"; "it *caught* a white couple"—the absorption *into the body* of the pained weight of scrutiny (something Bellow's text also features—or better, figures), and, of course, the charged and contestatory gazing itself. As in Fanon's repeated motif of specular aversion in "The Fact of Blackness"— "Look, a Negro!; Mama, see the Negro!"[37]—being Black in this novel means fundamentally *to be seen*. And while Levinas's favored trope may marshal its power from the ethical urgency of speech and vision conjoined in the human face, each signifying both entreaty and command, its peculiar relevance for this novel, it seems to me, centers on the way in which faces act as either weapons or targets of racism's negative proof (or political corrective) for the ethics of encounter. That is, in the concrete, physiognomic facts of Blackness (or Jewishness, or any particularized humanity, for that matter), Levinas's transcendental ethics may find its political objective correlative.[38]

Now, it should be evident that I have been invoking Levinas *thematically* here, borrowing against the rich and capacious pledge of image and figure that valorizes his argumentation throughout, taking his ever-more intense drive toward the material content of ethical encounter as legitimation for my own restricted focus on trope and image. Or (to remotivate a distinction drawn earlier), in thus bending it, I get demonstrably away from—though not "with"—strict Levinassian ethics. (Clearly, my critical approach *responds* to Levinas, as witness the noninterchangeable and asymmetric facing of texts which guides my readings here.)

Levinas often adverts to the biblical formula *hineni* ("here I am") in its French translation—*me voici*—in order to emphasize what he cleverly terms the "accusative" aspect of subjectivity; selves assume a place already marked out by obligatedness and thus occupy, as it were, an ethical terminus ad quem. Instead of the "merely" ethical deixis expressed by *here I am*, however, the racialized subjects of Himes's and Bellow's novels might be said to exclaim *let me go*, a quite different trope of accusation, but one which has its biblical precedent too—in an archetypal narrative of bondage and culturally legitimated persecution. To be the protagonist of such a text means to be literally *agonized*—the victim of unreasonable and yet unaccountably personalized prejudices.[39] Not classical, but rather the most modern subjects of cultural tragedies, American Jews and Blacks in these respective novels are the objectified subjects in the unreconstructed grammar of racism: trapped ("let him go"), outraged ("if he hollers"), ontologically slotted ("victims").

That both novels traffic in victimization does not *necessarily* make them congruent anatomies of race-hatred (nor does it align them with the more recent, simpleminded agitprop of "victimese," the rhetoric of injury). They tell different stories, regardless of any points of contact I might instigate here. Bellow's title names no referent, so it could just as plausibly designate Allbee, the novel's putative malignity, the subplot of Leventhal's sister and dying nephew, or the assorted urban anonyms who fail to "get away with it"—a bum, a peddler, a dishwasher, a Filipino busboy, a dying man on the subway tracks.[40] By contrast, the anonymous third-person pronoun "captured" by the doggerel title of *If He Hollers Let Him Go* draws ironic attention to Bob Jones's singular nonperson double bind as both first-person narrator and second-person "phobogenic object"[41]—in either case, the only and unequivocal victim of *his* story. To paraphrase Mikhail Bakhtin, since

Bob Jones cannot simply be himself, he must cite himself—with a vengeance, which is as much a self-catching as a letting-go:

> I wanted to tell him I didn't want to go to bed with her, I wanted to black her eyes; but just the idea of her being a white woman stopped me. I felt flustered, caught guilty. I couldn't realize what was happening to me myself. It was funny in a way. I couldn't tell him that I *didn't* want her because she was a white woman and he was a white man, and something somewhere way back in my mind said that that would be an insult. And I couldn't tell him that I *did* want her, because the same thing said that that would be an insult.
>
> . . . .
>
> Every white person I come into contact with, every one I have to speak to, even those I pass on the street—every goddamn one of them has the power of some kind of control over my own behavior. Not only that but they use it—in every way.[42]

While the second passage above arguably describes another textual dilemma—the seizurelike quality of Jones's narration—the first conveys a communicative paradox from which his narrative is not exempt. Does the narrator's "penning" (in Stanley Cavell's *aperçu*) spell release or just another kind of incarceration?[43] I think the novel's answer to that question is finally equivocal, but of the two texts *If He Hollers* certainly draws a far bleaker picture of the racialized subject-as-prison-house.

Bellow seems to work off of the more broadly Levinassian premise that a kind of indefeasible guilt attaches to selfhood *ab initio*, even though Allbee assuredly aims his violence at Leventhal's specifically *Jewish* face; despite being singled out through—or better perhaps, along with—anti-Semitism, Leventhal meets it, face to face, with an excessive obligatedness and answerability. Indeed, this very polarity of surpluses—the "remainder" of selfhood which is ethnic particularity and the extra weight which is the Other—defines the thematic tension between both novels and Levinas's philosophy which is the "politics of recognition"—the self alienated from within by *its own* exorbitant otherness, while still pledged outward.[44]

It is closer to the pole of "ethical responsibility," then, that *The Victim*'s sequence of events seems to cluster. (*The Victim* taps long-patent metaphysical and allegorical veins of American fiction, especially in its play with figures of substitution and doubling; my interpretative recourse to the "transcendental" is, accordingly, not outside the purview of either this novel or Bellow's work generally.) The very first time Allbee descends upon Leventhal, for example, the two initially fail to make contact—conspicuously so: "He had already taken off his shirt and was sitting on the bed unlacing his shoes when there was a short ring of the bell. Eagerly he pulled open the door and shouted, 'Who is it?' The flat was unbearably empty. . . . There was no response below. He called out again, impatiently."[45] If there is a kerygmatic text that stands behind this scene (using "kerygmatic" in Levinas's sense of the summoning quality of encounter), it is less likely existentialist than biblical—Song of Songs (5:2–6): "I was asleep, but my heart was awake; hark my beloved is knocking. . . . I opened to my beloved, but my beloved had turned away, had gone. . . . I sought him, but I could not find him. I called him, but he did not answer me." Whether Bellow intended the allusion or not, the point is the ritualized *staging* of encounter. Indeed, Levinas uses this very same trope of (mis)recognition to evoke the way in which the other person intrudes unbidden on the complacencies of selfhood, arresting it in its *pouvoir de pouvoir*,[46] or, perhaps more appositely in this case, its *boudoir de pouvoir*.

When Leventhal and Allbee finally meet in the park shortly afterwards, the vector from summoning to facing is drawn and scored with Asa's "feeling that he was not merely being looked at but watched." Allbee's second visit even more obviously lays bare the metaphysic of "intrusion" on which the novel can be said to turn:

> "Now who in the name of hell would ring like that?" he said. But he already knew who it was. It was Allbee. . . . He knew that he had come in; nevertheless he controlled his desire to turn. . . . To enter without a knock or invitation was an intrusion. Of course the door was open, but it was taking too much for granted all the same not to knock. "I *owe* him hospitality, that's how he behaves," passed through his mind.[47]

Now, if "intrusion" is understood as a cognate of "recognition," interpreted in the double sense of "facings" within and between texts, what *The Victim* rehearses *is* precisely Leventhal's indemnity, irrespective of any actual impact he may have had on Allbee's life; and the latter's anti-Semitism is ultimately formulated as "something very mysterious, namely a conviction or illusion that at the start of life, and perhaps even before a promise had been made."[48]

But what has happened to the *politics* of recognition? What of the pole of ethnic/racial/religious surplus, of "particularity"? Surely, Allbee's anti-Semitism—its content and motivation—is not incidental to *The Victim*'s "metaphysic of intrusion," its recognitive plot of target, pursuit, and capture:

> "Why do you sing such songs?" he said. "*You* can't sing them. . . . You have to be bred to them. . . . Sing one of the psalms. I'd love to hear it . . . [or] any Jewish song. Something you've really got feeling for. Sing us the one about the mother."
>
> . . . .
>
> She has that proud look that's proud without being hard. You know what I mean. It's a serious look. You see it in *Asiatic* sculpture. . . . It's apparent enough; it doesn't need any investigating. Russia, Poland, I can see at a glance. . . . I've lived in New York for a long time. It's a very Jewish city, and a person would have to be a pretty sloppy observer not to learn about Jews here.
>
> . . . .
>
> "And try to imagine how New York affects me. Isn't it preposterous? It's really as if the children of Caliban were running everything. . . . I go into the library once in a while to look around, and last week I saw a book about Thoreau and Emerson by a man named Lipschitz. . . . A name like that?" Allbee said this with great earnestness. "After all, it seems to me that people of such background simply couldn't understand."
>
> . . . .
>
> You people, by and large—and this is only an observation, nothing else, take it for what it's worth—you can only tolerate feelings like your own.[49]

Allbee (is the name portentously "ontological" or simply an exclamation of surprise?) bears down on Leventhal throughout *The Victim*, both as the imagined cause of all his misfortune and as a Jew—two contingent facts—the accidentally particular and the peculiarly particular—that intertwine. Allbee never approaches or reproaches Leventhal on any basis apart from the "stain" of "you people-hood." But does the text? What weight does it assign to ethnic difference in its own discomfiting of Leventhal's subjectivity?

Looking for an answer, I turn again to Himes. The crux of *If He Hollers*

Let Him Go is what can only be called an extended face-off between Bob Jones and Madge, his White co-worker at the wartime shipyard, the "tall white girl in a leather welder's suit" with whom Jones comes "face to face":

> We stood there for an instant, our eyes locked, before either of us moved; then she deliberately put on a frightened, wide-eyed look and backed away from me as if she was scared stiff, as if she was a naked virgin and I was King Kong. It wasn't the first time she had done that. I'd run into her on board a half-dozen times during the past couple of weeks and each time she'd put on that scared-to-death act. . . . But now it sent a blinding fury through my brain. Blood rushed to my head like gales of rain and I felt my face burn white-hot. It came up in my eyes and burned at her; she caught it and kept staring at me with that wide-eyed phoney look. Something about her mouth touched it off, a quirk made the curves change as if she got a sexual thrill, and her mascaraed eyelashes fluttered. Lust shook me like an electric shock; it came up in my mouth, filling it with tongue, and drained my whole stomach down into my groin. And it poured out of my eyes in a sticky rush and spurted over her from head to foot. The frightened look went out of her eyes and she blushed right down her face and out of sight beneath the collar of her leather jacket, and I could imagine it going down over her over-ripe breasts and spreading out over her milky-white stomach. When she turned out of my stare I went sick to the stomach and felt like vomiting. I had started toward the ladder going to the upper deck, but instead I turned past her, slowing down and brushing her. She didn't move. I kept on going, circling.[50]

Behind the lurid and hard- (or pot-) boiled style (though the sexualization of racial difference is hardly unimportant here), Himes has skewed Levinas's "rectitude" of the face-to-face relation in a very interesting way: *the face* becomes *the look* as the rules of engagement yield to the rules of performance. The scene of recognition, in other words, has been overtly dramatized, its inherent potential for theatricality realized.

Several pages later, the narrator and his new nemesis square off once again: "She had her back to me and her hood up so it covered her hair, so I didn't recognize her right off . . . . I saw that she was the big, peroxide blonde I'd run into on the third deck earlier; and I knew the instant I recognized her that she was going to perform then—we would both perform." And, needless to say, the ensuing story-length, full-cast performance follows the familiar script to the letter. Madge says the magic words which expressly countermand the Torah injunction against murder (even when such homicide is "ethical" or "merely" discursive): " 'I ain't gonna work with no nigger!' she said in a harsh, flat voice."[51]

The novel's deliberately, extravagantly potboiling plot boils over, with Jones eventually arrested for a non-rape that he and Madge "perform" through several acts. (As Fanon, an obvious admirer of the novel, puts it, "So it is with the character in *If He Hollers Let Him Go*—who does precisely what he did not want to do."[52]) And institutionality, finally, plays its part in the denouement as Bob Jones gets "escorted" from dockside labor to armed service—the more sinister sense of being "let go." In fact, this last development is anticipated at the very beginning of the novel, when Jones, reflecting on the recent internment of Japanese Americans, says, "It was taking a man up by the roots and locking him up without a chance. Without a trial. Without a charge. Without even giving him a chance to say one word. It was thinking about if they ever did that to me, Robert Jones, Mrs. Jones's dark son, that started to get me scared."[53] Thus even the novel's narrative thrust knowingly performs itself, telegraphing, predicting, always driving toward its inevitable ending. Written on the heels of *Native Son* (Bob Jones even refers to Wright's novel), *If He Hollers Let Him Go* flaunts a whole repertoire of signifyin(g), sending itself up as it brings its "hero" down. No wonder, then, that each of the plot's five units of action begins with *dreamwork*, the hard realities of racial prejudice literaturized, fictioned from within and from the start.

"Good acting is what is exactly human," says a character in *The Victim*. (Later, Leventhal reapplies this maxim to the exigencies of his own situation: "He liked to think 'human' meant accountable in spite of many weaknesses—at the last moment, tough enough to hold."[54]) Indeed, Bellow's novel trades as often as Himes's does on metaphors of acting and performance. (A subplot involves Leventhal's attempt to get Allbee hired by a talent scout; an ensemble discussion of acting takes place at the dead center of *The Victim*; and it ends with a recognition scene in a theater, where Leventhal reencounters Allbee on the arm of a "famous actress.") And much like the coupled characters of *If He Hollers*, Leventhal and Allbee subtend degrees of facing with angles of masking—all of it intensely physicalized:

Leventhal remarked to himself that there was an element of performance in all that he [Allbee] was doing. But suddenly he had a strange,

close consciousness of Allbee, of his face and body, a feeling of intimate nearness. . . . He could nearly feel the weight of his body and
the contact of his clothes. Even more, the actuality of his face, loose
in the cheeks, firm in the forehead and jaws, struck him, the distinct-
ness of it; and the look of recognition Allbee bent on him duplicated
the look in his own.[55]

I alluded earlier to Erving Goffman, whose treatment of face-to-face
interaction is, of course, relevant to the thematics of recognition in both
Levinas's work and the two novels at hand.[56] Faces—and especially those
distinguished by, say, racial or ethnoreligious characteristics—to the degree that they are "presented," could be said to *perform* rather than simply
manifest themselves. In Goffman's more pragmatic model of social phenomenology, "frame analysis" is applied to precisely those particularized
features of human encounter which Levinas's philosophy would bracket:
the "antiethical" devices (Levinas might say) of self-masking that cush-
ion and keep at bay the *proximity* and *approach* of "the neighbor." Thus,
in an important essay entitled "Reality and Its Shadow," Levinas speaks
of the doubled, shadowed, even "caricatured," relationship that continually haunts personal identity: "A being is that which reveals itself in its
truth, and, at the same time, resembles itself, is its own image."[57] In other
words, an external veneer of semblance (i.e., of both resemblance and dis-
sembling) glosses the baseline level of signification—selfhood which is
answerable, prima facie, to others—what Levinas calls the "nudité" of the
face, in a companion essay to "Reality and Its Shadow":

> The absolute nakedness of a face, the absolutely defenseless face,
> without covering, clothing, or mask, is what opposes my power over
> it, my violence, and opposes it in an absolute way, with an opposition
> which is opposition in itself. The being that expresses itself, that faces
> me, says *no* to me by his very expression. . . . The face is the fact that
> a being affects us not in the indicative, but in the imperative, and is
> thus outside all categories.[58]

All of Levinas's philosophy is devoted to the ethical epiphany of unmasking, of showing forth, of facing. If *exposure* defines contact with the Other,
then, conversely, a sort of *double exposure* describes the ambiguous nature
of identity left to its own devices. And yet here again we encounter the
"faces that we meet" in Himes's and Bellow's novels as political object les-

sons of ethical transcendence in human relations. For in *The Victim* and *If He Hollers Let Him Go*, to be seen or addressed or pursued as a "Jew" or a "nigger" is to be ineluctably double-exposed. Levinas's ethics of imperative intersubjectivity does not always (or perhaps can never fully) transcend the specificity of this or that person who is "culturally" singled-out—the person, in other words, whose face will lend itself involuntarily to the indicative mode of "an Asiatic" cast or a "flat-nosed, thick-lipped" mien. In being a "Black" or "Jewish" face, in other words, Bob Jones's or Asa Leventhal's face is thematized, allegorized, from within.

Double exposure, double-talk, double consciousness: these represent the shadow-graphs that limn a politics of recognition. When James Weldon Johnson referred, in *The Autobiography of an Ex-Coloured Man*, to the "freemasonry of race,"[59] he was adumbrating the masque or performance which (in Levinas's sense) turns the ethnic or racial subject into an allegory of itself, into its own image, into the "remainder of selfhood" described above. To put it another way (paraphrasing *The Victim*), in the literature of ethnic entrapment, *acting*—good or bad, willed or forced—is what is exactly *Black* or *Jewish*.

In his analysis of contemporary French Jewish identity, Alain Finkielkraut says that for a certain segment of "Jewish romantics these days . . . the word 'Jew' is worn like a brooch on a dark gray suit."[60] I appreciate this conceit not only because of its wonderful turn on identity as adornment, but also for the way it resonates with the same sort of recognitive bric-a-brac that crams the texts (and glosses the faces) of *The Victim* and *If He Hollers Let Him Go* like so much theatrical makeup:

> [Leventhal] was on a boardwalk. . . . On his left, there was an amusement park with ticket booths. . . . He entered a place that resembled a hotel . . . but proved to be a department store. He was here to buy some rouge for Mary. The salesgirl demonstrated various shades on her own face, wiping each off in turn with a soiled hand towel and bending to the round mirror on the counter to draw a new spot. There was a great, empty glitter of glass and metal around them. What could this possibly be about? Leventhal wondered.[61]

Or, as Himes renders it in the climactic rape-charade:

> "*Help! Help! My God, help me! Some white man, help me! I'm being raped.*" I saw the stretch and pop of her lips, the tautening of her throat

muscles, the distortion and constriction of her face . . . as if her face were ten feet high. . . . My eyes felt as if they were five times their natural size; as if they were bursting in their sockets, popping out of my head. *"Stop, nigger! Don't, nigger. Nigger, don't. Oh, please don't kill me, nigger."* [62]

Like a brooch on a dark gray suit.

At the end of *The Victim*, Leventhal is redescribed: "His obstinately unrevealing expression had softened. His face was paler and there were some gray hairs in his hair, in spite of which he looked years younger." In this same chapter, the assignment of one's place in life is called a "promise" which is either a "conviction or [an] illusion":

In thinking of this promise, Leventhal compared it to a ticket, a theater ticket. And with his ticket, a man entitled to an average seat might feel too shabby for the dress circle or sit in it defiantly or arrogantly; another, entitled to the best in the house, might cry in rage to the usher who led him to the third balcony. And how many more stood disconsolately in the rain and snow, in the long line of those who could only expect to be turned away? But no, this was incorrect. The reality was different. For why should tickets, mere tickets, be promised if promises were being made—tickets to desirable and undesirable places? There were more important things to be promised. Possibly there was a promise, since so many felt it. He himself was almost ready to affirm that there was. But it was misunderstood. [63]

Inflecting this metaphor—already grounded in the theatrical—toward the Levinassian renders tickets the "illusion" that is the necessary obverse of "conviction." Tickets operate as the evidence-checkpoint of objectified surface which interrupts otherwise unimpeded passage, thereby forcing a kind of occlusion of depth—"a glass darkly" anterior to any promise of "face-to-face" encounter. Pop-eyes, thick lips, and big noses are "mere" features that "thematize" the "absolute nakedness of a face without covering, clothing, or mask." For Levinas, the face speaks, and says, "NO." But it more typically says, "Kick me, Kike me," [64] or "catch a nigger by the toe," or "you people." As with Kazin's "even Negroes" and Claude Brown's "scrubbing 'Goldberg's' floor," language, too, fails the test of transparency, always clutching the tickets to, and thereby carrying with it, the places it has been.

"Recognition" in Bellow's and Himes's novels shows how and where the ostensibly transcendent encounter between two human faces trips over particularity. In Levinas's terms, while the ethnic or racial face may indeed affect us in the imperative, it does so *within*, not outside of, categories—categories which are as often linguistic as they are visual. Hence, finally, the paradox of transcendent visage "sealed in blackness" (Fanon's phrase)—or Jewishness—reaching its logical conclusion at the end of *If He Hollers Let Him Go*, where *hollering*—the cry of the victim—means, precisely, being *caught*.

> "Wait, I'll let you in," I shouted above the din. "Wait, this woman is crazy!" A guy leaned over the hole and swung at my head with a ball-peen hammer. . . . I saw the guy's face, not particularly malevolent, just disfigured, a white man hitting at a nigger running by. I hadn't even tried to rape her. I'd been trying to get away from her. . . . She'd kept me there, cornered me, hadn't let me go.[65]

Notes

1 My quotation is from Bernard Malamud's novel *The Tenants* (New York, 1971), 68, and, perhaps needless to say, my characterization is meant ironically: once fiction becomes a gloss for life, reflexivity cannot be far behind. In his autobiography *The Quality of Hurt* (New York, 1972), Himes himself reflexively calls his first novel "my bitter novel of protest" (75), a description echoed two pages later in a broadside against his publisher's less than enthusiastic marketing: "The whole episode left me very bitter" (77). A contemporary "review" of *If He Hollers Let Him Go* from an editorial in *Ebony* (November 1947), however, makes "bitter" an understatement: "an invidious, shocking, incendiary . . . virulent, malicious book full of venom and rancor [that] substitutes emotions for intelligence, dictates thinking with the skin rather than the brains" (44). The reception for Bellow's 1947 novel, on the other hand, was highly favorable, although Bellow presumably regards *The Victim* as an "early" effort that still holds up.

2 See Harold Cruse, *The Crisis of the Negro Intellectual* (New York, 1967), especially "Negroes and Jews—The Two Nationalisms and the Bloc(ked) Plurality" (476–97); and Cynthia Ozick, "Literary Blacks and Jews" (her updated reflections on Malamud's "fiction of blows"), in Paul Berman, *Blacks and Jews: Alliances and Arguments* (New York, 1994), 43–75.

3 See Adam Zachary Newton, *Narrative Ethics* (Cambridge, 1995), especially the introductory discussion of Levinas in "'Creating the Uncreated Features of His Face': Face and Monstration in Crane, Melville, and Wright," 179–235; and *Facing Black and Jew:*

Re-Imagining American Literary History (forthcoming). See also Simon Critchley, *The Ethics of Deconstruction: Derrida and Levinas* (Oxford, 1992); cf. the introduction to Tobin Siebers, *The Ethics of Criticism* (Ithaca, 1988), for a concise genealogy of this critical imperative.

4 Bertolt Brecht, *Shriften zum Theater* (Frankfurt, 1957), 1: 165.

5 See Charles Taylor, *Multiculturalism and the "Politics of Recognition": An Essay* (Princeton, 1992). Taylor explicitly concerns himself here with the competing claims of disparate constituencies and the institutional structures that govern or mediate responses to them—hence the force of *politics*. Accordingly, he deploys the linguistically allied phrases "politics of universalism" and "politics of difference" in a characteristic (and characteristically cogent) historicizing of communal claims on representation and visibility. His *Essay* is not without its points of arguability, as the accompanying response pieces in the volume attest. But in terms of my own difference from Taylor, what I mean by the "politics of recognition" is an unavoidable *surplus* of identity borne by actors in intersubjective dramas of recognition which italicize, as it were, their "particularity," namely, as *Blacks* or *Jews*. Ethics would be the phenomenon, then, and politics its epiphenomenal shadow; or, in Taylor's terms: "We must be open to comparative cultural study of the kind that must displace our horizons in the resulting fusions" (73), where "displacement" signifies for me an ethical troubling of intact political "fusions." For alternative approaches, see *Multiculturalism: A Critical Reader*, ed. David Theo Goldberg (Cambridge, 1995); and David Hollinger, *Postethnic America: Beyond Multiculturalism* (New York, 1995).

6 Roger Simon, "Face to Face with Alterity: Postmodern Jewish Identity and the Eros of Pedagogy," in *Pedagogy: The Question of Impersonation*, ed. Jane Gallop (Bloomington, 1995), 90–105; quotation from 90. See also S. P. Mohanty, "Us and Them: On the Philosophical Bases of Political Criticism," *Yale Journal of Criticism* 2 (1989): 1–31.

7 Simon, "Face to Face with Alterity," 90.

8 Saul Bellow, *The Victim* (New York, 1975 [1947]), 21, 27.

9 Chester Himes, *If He Hollers Let Him Go* (New York, 1986 [1945]), 203.

10 Bellow, *Victim*, 256.

11 From the essay of the same title in Elias Canetti, *The Conscience of Words*, trans. Joachim Neugroschel (New York, 1976), 140–44. Since these are experiential as much as discursive issues, socio-phenomenological analyses like those of Jean-Paul Sartre, Frantz Fanon, and Alain Finkielkraut gloss these texts as readily as any literary criticism might. See Jean-Paul Sartre, *Anti-Semite and Jew (Reflections on the Jewish Question)*, trans. George J. Becker (New York, 1948); Frantz Fanon, *Black Skin, White Masks*, trans. Charles Lam Markmann (New York, 1967); and Alain Finkielkraut, *The Imaginary Jew*, trans. Kevin O'Neill and David Suchof (Lincoln, 1995); see also the essays in *The Anatomy of Racism*, ed. David Theo Goldberg (Minneapolis, 1990).

12 Himes, *If He Hollers*, 2, 3.

13 Ibid., 5, 7, 17, 19, 65.

14 Ibid., 129, 59, 39, 127.

15 Bellow, *Victim*, 31, 33 (my emphasis), 99, 151.

16 See Newton, *Narrative Ethics*.

17   Emmanuel Levinas, *Totality and Infinity: An Essay on Exteriority*, trans. Alphonso Lingis (Pittsburgh, 1968), 89; my emphasis.

18   Cf. John Rawls, *A Theory of Justice* (Cambridge, MA, 1971); and *Justice as Fairness* (New York, 1991).

19   Emmanuel Levinas, "From Ethics to Exegesis," in *In the Time of Nations*, trans. Michael B. Smith (Bloomington, 1994), 109–13; quotation from 110–11.

20   See, for example, Emmanuel Levinas, *Beyond the Verse: Talmudic Readings and Lectures*, trans. Gary D. Mole (Bloomington, 1994).

21   Levinas, "Ethics to Exegesis," 110. Compare the following critique of politicized plural-ism from "Phenomenon and Enigma," in *Collected Philosophical Papers*, trans. Alphonso Lingis (Dordrecht, 1987), 65–73: "The saraband of innumerable and equivalent cultures, each justifying itself in its own context, creates a world which is, to be sure, deocci-dentalized, but also *disoriented*. To catch sight, in meaning, of a situation that precedes culture, to envision language out of the revelation of the other . . . in the gaze of man aiming at a man precisely as abstract man disengaged from all culture, in the naked-ness of the face . . . is to find oneself able to judge civilizations on the basis of ethics" (101). See also Emmanuel Levinas, "The Rights of Man and the Rights of the Other," in *Outside the Subject*, trans. Michael B. Smith (Stanford, 1994), 116–25; and the essays in *Difficult Freedom*, trans. Seán Hand (Baltimore, 1990).

22   Levinas, "Ethics to Exegesis," 110.

23   Emmanuel Levinas, "Demanding Judaism," in *Beyond the Verse*, 3–10; quotation from 4.

24   Fanon, *Black Skin, White Masks*, 180. Cf. these remarks: "I am the slave not of the idea that others have of me but of my own appearance" (116); "with the Negro the cycle of the *biological* begins. . . . The Negro is the genital" (161–62); "the Negro is comparison" (211). Even more pointedly: "The Jew is attacked in his religious identity, in his his-tory, in his race, in his relations with his ancestors and with his posterity; . . . But it is in his corporeality that the Negro is attacked" (163). "Is this the whole story? Unfor-tunately not. The Negro is something else. Here again we find the Jew" (180). See also Sander Gilman, *Jewish Self-Hatred: The Hidden Language of the Jews* (Baltimore, 1986); and *The Jew's Body* (New York, 1991). What makes the role of representation so tricky here, however, is its duality: on one hand, it can take the form of an unreflective pro-cess of symbolization (anti-Semitism/philo-Semitism, Negrophobia/Negrophilia), and, on the other, it is sustained by a wholly otherwise, second-order level of ethical judg-ment and political critique. Still, *any* gesture toward some kind of ethnic Imaginary will almost inevitably betray the long arm of fiction, another reason why Himes's and Bel-low's novels gloss Levinas's ethics as aptly as *it* applies to *them*.

25   As Levinas says elsewhere, "The approach to the face is the most basic form of respon-sibility. As such, the face of the other is verticality and uprightness: it spells a relation of rectitude. The face is not in front of me (*en face de moi*) but above me"; quoted in Richard Kearney, "Dialogue with Emmanuel Levinas," in *Face to Face with Levinas*, ed. Richard A. Cohen (Albany, 1989), 13–33; quotation from 24.

26   For Levinas Jewish particularism is always a historicized particularism. Yet he oscillates (as does Jewish self-understanding generally) between two legitimating explanations:

a nationhood founded on sacred responsibility ("You shall be holy for I am holy"), *and* responsibility ensuing from the continued travail suffered as, or in, peoplehood. Answerability for the other is first enjoined on Mounts Moriah and Sinai, then earned as the dialectic response to repeated political scourgings and ethnic cleansings. "The congenital universality of the Jewish spirit," Levinas writes in "Assimilation and New Culture" (*Beyond the Verse*, 196–201), "involves an ineffaceable moment of isolation and distancing. This peculiarity is not simply the fruit of exile and the ghetto, but probably a fundamental withdrawal into the self in the awareness of a surplus of responsibility towards humanity. . . . This is undoubtedly what the awareness of being chosen is," as opposed to "an irremediable particularism, a petitioning nationalism" (198). See also "Judaism and Revolution," in *Nine Talmudic Readings*, trans. A. Aronowicz (Bloomington, 1990), 94–119, where Levinas syllogizes "Judaism or responsibility for the entire universe, and consequently a universally persecuted Judaism" (115). The *particular* particularism, in this case of Jewish peoplehood, derives from its being absolutized from both within and without.

27 See note 21; and David Theo Goldberg's helpful essay "Multicultural Conditions," in Goldberg, ed., *Multiculturalism*, 1–41.

28 These matters certainly warrant more than cursory attention since, even within the strict confines of Levinas's oeuvre, they pose real structural difficulties. For him, the overriding cultural distinction is between Jewishness and the West or "Hebrew" and "Greek." The "Orient," in other words, denotes Israel. His political loyalties as a French national, his directorship of the Westernizing Ecole Normale Israelite Oriental, and his resolute "Europocentrism" all lend a significant bias to the terms he dignifies for argumentation, as well as underwriting the ideological assumptions on which he proceeds. The "other" in Levinas is thus not entirely pre- (or even post-) cultural; alterity is implicitly Western and masculine. A wider ambit for considering this conceptual shibboleth is offered in Ernst Simon, "The Neighbors Whom We Shall Love," in *Modern Jewish Ethics: Theory and Practice*, ed. Marvin Fox (Columbus, OH, 1975), 29–56; and Jacob Katz, *Exclusivism and Tolerance* (Oxford, 1961).

29 Levinas, "Judaism and Revolution," 113. The point of reference here is a debate on revolutionary politics in the tractate *Baba Metzia*, 83a–83b, of the Talmud. See also the essays in the "Politics" section of *The Levinas Reader*, ed. Seán Hand (Oxford, 1989).

30 See Ralph Ellison, "Twentieth Century Fiction and the Black Mask of Humanity," in *Shadow and Act* (New York, 1964), 24–44.

31 Cf. Roland Barthes's analysis of verbal precision in *The Pleasure of the Text*, trans. Richard Howard (New York, 1975): "The exactitude in question is not the result of taking greater pains, it is not a rhetorical instrument in value, as though things were *increasingly well* described—but of a change of code: the (remote) model of the description is no longer oratorical discourse (nothing at all is being 'painted'), but a kind of lexicographical artifact" (26–27). But in Bellow's case, the language of the text *does* in fact take greater pains.

32 Bellow, *Victim*, 20.

33 Ibid., 31.

34 Ibid., 36.

35   Ibid., 77.

36   Himes, *If He Hollers*, 12–13.

37   Frantz Fanon, "The Fact of Blackness," in *Black Skin, White Masks*, 109–40. See also the following passage from Himes, *If He Hollers*: "I just had time to see him: a tall young blond guy about my age and size. His mouth was twisted down in one corner so that the tips of his dogteeth showed like a gopher's mouth and his blue eyes were blistered with hate. I'll never forget that bastard's eyes. Then that sick, gone feeling came in the pit of my stomach—just a flash. And a blinding explosion went off just back of my eyes as if the nerve centres had been dynamited. I had the crazy sensation of my eyes popping out of my head. . . . Bile rolled up in my stomach and spread out in my mouth. I started retching and caught myself. The sun beat down on my head like showers of rain. My skin was tight and burning hot, but it wouldn't sweat. Only in the palm of my hand holding the knife did I sweat" (33, 35).

38   Levinas, of course, would insist on the necessary contradiction between ethics and politics (or the subordination of one by the other) in this sense. See "Ideology and Idealism," in Hand, ed., *Levinas Reader*, 235–47: "The otherness of the absolutely other is not just some quiddity. Insofar as it is a quiddity, it exists on a plane it has in common with the quiddities that it cuts across. . . . Absolute *difference* cannot itself delineate the plane common to those that are different. The other, absolutely other, is the Other [*L'autre, absolument autre, c'est Autrui*]. The other is not a particular case, a species of otherness, but the original exception to order. It is not because the Other is novelty that it 'gives room' for a relation of transcendence. It is because the responsibility for the Other is transcendence that there is something new under the sun" (245). When asked in an interview about Israelis and Palestinians as each others' paradigmatic "Other," Levinas replied, "My definition of the other is completely different. The other is a neighbor, who is not necessarily kin, but who can be. And in that sense, if you're for the other, you're for the neighbor. But if your neighbor attacks another neighbor or treats him unjustly, what can you do? Then alterity takes on another character, in alterity we can find an enemy, or at least we are faced with the problem of knowing who is right and who is wrong, who is just and who is unjust"; see the interview with Levinas, Finkielkraut, and Shlomo Malkr on Radio Communauté, 28 September 1987, in *Les Nouveaux Cahiers* 18 (1982–83): 1–8. What can one say but that Levinas finesses the issue of particularity in a not altogether unambivalent fashion, at times disallowing it and at times appealing to it.

39   To be sure, victimization—real persecution predicated on ethnic hatred—explicitly enters Levinas's philosophy only in his treatment of historical Jewish identity. Yet it almost surely serves as an implicit model for the recasting of terms he introduces in *Otherwise Than Being; Or, Beyond Essence*, trans. Alphonso Lingis (The Hague, 1978), where subjectivity becomes a "persecution" and a "wounding" by the Other, with the self "held hostage" by the claim of alterity in a steady state of unwilled "substitution."

40   See Bellow, *Victim*, 33, 95, 96, 119, 198.

41   Fanon, *Black Skin, White Masks*, 151.

42   Himes, *If He Hollers*, 119, 16.

43   Cf. the similar—and self-conscious—predicament described by Alfred Kazin, *A Walker*

in the City (New York, 1951): "It troubled me that I could speak in the fullness of my own voice only when I was alone on the streets, walking about. There was something unnatural about it; unbearably isolated. I was not like the others! I was not like the others!" (24).

44 Apropos of the cleft without and the fissure within, see Julia Kristeva, *Strangers to Ourselves*, trans. Leon S. Roudiez (New York, 1991): "Strangely, the foreigner lives within us: he is the hidden face of our identity, the peace that wrecks our abode, the time in which understanding and affinity founder. By recognizing him within ourselves, we are spared detesting him in himself. A symptom that precisely turns 'we' into a problem, perhaps makes it impossible. The foreigner comes in when the consciousness of my difference arises, and he disappears when we acknowledge ourselves as foreigners, unamenable to bonds and communities" (1). Charles Taylor comes at this dialectic of interiority and exteriority from a similar (though differently historicized) angle of approach in *Multiculturalism and . . . "Recognition"*: "What has come about with the modern age is not the need for recognition but the condition in which the attempt to be recognized can fail" (35).

45 Bellow, *Victim*, 29.

46 Levinas, *Totality and Infinity*, 198. For the allusion to Song of Songs, see *Otherwise Than Being*, 141–42. See also Jacques Derrida, "At This Very Moment in This Work Here I Am," in *Re-Reading Levinas*, ed. R. Bernascon and S. Critchley (Bloomington, 1991), 11–48, which begins, "*He will have obligated* . . . as after the passing of some singular visitor, you are no longer familiar with the places, those very places where nonetheless the little phrase—Where does it come from? Who pronounced it?—still leaves its resonance lingering" (11 [Levinas's emphasis]).

47 Bellow, *Victim*, 66.

48 Ibid., 249.

49 Ibid., 34, 70, 131, 179.

50 Himes, *If He Hollers*, 19.

51 Ibid., 27. For a comprehensive analysis of racism as language, see David Theo Goldberg, "The Social Formation of Racist Discourse," in Goldberg, ed., *Anatomy of Racism*, 295–318.

52 Fanon, *Black Skin, White Masks*, 140.

53 Himes, *If He Hollers*, 3.

54 Bellow, *Victim*, 75.

55 Ibid., 144. In the dream sequence that follows, Leventhal has "an unclear dream in which he held himself off like an unwilling spectator; yet it was he who did everything" (150).

56 See especially Erving Goffman, *Interaction Ritual: Essays in Face-to-Face Behavior* (Garden City, 1967); and *The Presentation of Self in Everyday Life* (Garden City, 1959).

57 Emmanuel Levinas, "Reality and Its Shadow," in *Collected Philosophical Papers*, 1–12; quotation from 6. See also Newton, "Face and Monstration," in *Narrative Ethics*.

58 Emmanuel Levinas, "Freedom and Command," in *Collected Philosophical Papers*, 13–22; quotation from 21.

59 James Weldon Johnson, *The Autobiography of an Ex-Coloured Man* (New York, 1927), 21–22.

60 Finkielkraut, *Imaginary Jew*, 71.

61 Bellow, *Victim*, 245.

62 Himes, *If He Hollers*, 183.

63 Bellow, *Victim*, 249. Tickets of admission form a motif in their own right here; cf. pages 27, 30, 112, 150, 155, and 186.

64 Lyrics of "They Don't Care About Us" by Michael Jackson, from his recent CD *HIStory*, Epic Records, MJJ Productions, New York, 1995: "Sue me, Jew me, everybody do me / Kick me, Kike me, don't you black or white me." These lines have since been revised for a second pressing.

65 Himes, *If He Hollers*, 184.

Claude Lefort

Sade: The Boudoir and the City

*J*ouissance, cruelty, knowledge of nature through *jouissance* and cruelty, all these themes are interlaced with that of corruption in *La Philosophie dans le boudoir*.

This novel—but is it a novel?—stands out in Sade's work in a paradoxical way, that is, both for its lightness and for its theoretical and political ambition. Here Sade tells us what the Republic should be. What could seem more serious? We are in the Thermidorian period, right after the fall of Robespierre and Saint-Just. Debate is lively between those who think the Revolution is over and those who favor a return to Jacobinism. True, Sade does not speak in his own name. The ideal republic is described in a pamphlet that one of the characters in the boudoir presents to his friends. It is entitled *Français, encore un effort si vous voulez être républicains* (Yet Another Effort, Frenchmen, If You Would Be Republicans). This text has so whetted the interest of Sade critics that they treat it as an independent tract, and it was even published under separate cover some

The *South Atlantic Quarterly* 95:4, Fall 1996.
"Sade: Le Boudoir et la cité," *Ecrire: A l'épreuve du politique* by Claude Lefort © Fondation Saint-Simon, 1992; © Calmann-Lévy, 1992. Translation published by permission of Calmann-Lévy.

years ago by Jean-Jacques Pauvert.[1] The fact is that the few political writings by Sade from when he was secretary of the Parisian Section of Piques (1793) do not stand out among the revolutionary writings of the era, although his activity was not negligible. In contrast, *Français, encore un effort* proceeds from an extraordinary will to subvert all established order. I know of no scandalous satire [*libelle*] that testifies to such an upheaval of thought, to such a smashing down of the barriers of the thinkable, to such a ground-swell that carries off everything in its path: all positions of authority, the foundations of religious despotism, political despotism, the despotism of opinion, and the despotism that society itself exercises over its members.

Without any doubt, the work bears the mark of the spirit of revolution, but one would have no hope of understanding Sade's designs if one forgot that *Français, encore un effort* has its place in *La Philosophie dans le boudoir*. True, the relationship between the pamphlet and the dialogues, both cruel and lighthearted, that precede its reading appears somewhat baffling, which is why the famous Sade biographer, Gilbert Lély, imprudently—that is, without proof—surmised that the author had inserted this text, after the fact and arbitrarily, into "an exquisitely constructed whole."[2] Yet one need only read *Français, encore un effort* somewhat attentively to notice that the pamphlet pursues on the political level the theme of corruption, a theme that is present from the beginning of the work and right up to the very end. Let us not forget that corruption is a great theme of political philosophy. The distinction between a well-ordered society living in conformity with nature and a corrupt society is one of the foundations of classical political philosophy, the philosophy of Plato and of Aristotle. Moreover, as unsettled [*ébranlé*] as the classical teachings have become in modern times, the political critique of corruption has not ceased to be formulated and reformulated each time one placed tyranny in the dock or charged a monarchy with creeping absolutism, each time one denounced the arbitrary power that the supposed representatives of the people had arrogated to themselves or described the degradation of peoples who had become accustomed to their servitude.

To take some initial bearings here, we might recall how important the concept of "corruption" was in the Florentine age of civic humanism at the beginning of the fifteenth century and later in the work of Machiavelli. Recall, too, the mobilizing power of the puritan critique of corruption in seventeenth-century England and, in the eighteenth century, the polemics launched by the radical Whigs, the far Left of the period. An obsession with corruption also haunted the American and French Revolutions. Finally—and especially important to the appreciation of Sade's thought—is the characteristically modern idea of a corruption that could taint not only a city or a particular nation but humanity per se: a sense of corruption concealed beneath the trappings of civilization, beneath the trappings of material progress, of luxury, of refinement and culture. The thing is so well known that it hardly needs emphasizing.

To return to Sade, the author begins to confront us with the question of the corruption of mores by inviting us into his boudoir, an enclosed space, one that is apparently foreign to the city. Four principal characters will develop there: Mme de Saint-Ange, who has initiated the meeting; her brother, "the Chevalier"; the latter's friend, Dolmancé, a great speechmaker and an expert in the art of *jouissance*; and, finally, an ingenue, Eugénie. It is the desire to corrupt that, at the beginning of this work, guides Mme de Saint-Ange's singular project to initiate the delicious Eugénie in the liberties of *jouissance*. After being assured by her brother that his friend, whom she does not yet know, "is really the most totally and thoroughly corrupt person, the most evil individual, the greatest scoundrel in the world,"[3] she becomes enchanted with the idea of making Dolmancé her accomplice.

What is *La Philosophie dans le boudoir*? A sort of novel, in the form of dialogues, presented as a theatrical show; it is a dramatic composition whose theatrical character is underscored by the stage directions given for the actors' movements and by their asides, which are indicated in parentheses. The theme is the education of a young girl or, as I have just said, her initiation in the liberties of *jouissance*. This undertaking, as the lady who has drawn her into the boudoir jokingly says, requires both theory and practice. The practice will induce the most varied exercises, of which Eugénie will be object, agent, and witness. The theory will allow the treatment of similarly varied problems, at the initiative of these wicked instructors, but nonetheless in response to the ingenue's insatiable curiosity.

I'll pass over the elementary teachings. Eugénie wants to know the name and function of everything she is allowed to see, touch, and smell. What is a "prick"? she asks. What are "testicles," a "clitoris," a "vagina"? She acts like a child eager to learn new words. What is "come"? What does "whore" mean? Her philosophical curiosity is no less anchored in the childish desire to know everything; it is she who wants to be enlightened on the utilitarian value of the virtues and who insists that her teachers return to the theme of religion, which they went over too quickly for her liking.

Discussion, however, is interrupted several times for practice in some equally instructive exercises that lead her from discovery to discovery—but without the dialogue ever ceasing. Everything that is done is said. Well before Dolmancé proclaims the "right to say everything"—a formula that Maurice Blanchot emphasizes,[4] but only in relation to Sade's rage for writing—there is an incessant flow of speech. Nothing contracts or discharges in the bodies of the characters, or in their minds (Dolmancé says at one point: "What an imagination . . . she discharges from the head"[5]), nor is there any contact or coupling, without the accompaniment of a voice. The quest for explanations, which the young girl pursues, conquers all. Thus does Eugénie, deflowered by the Chevalier and then penetrated simultaneously from the front and from behind by the young gardener called to the rescue and by Dolmancé—Eugénie on the brink of annihilation, Eugénie in ecstasy—suddenly recover her voice and find the strength to pose another question. With disarming gravity, the schoolgirl declares: "I would like to know whether mores are truly necessary in a government, whether their influence carries any weight with regard to the genius of a nation?"[6] Now, it is at this point, we should recall, that Dolmancé, the most corrupt man, produces the pamphlet he has found (or so he says) at the Palais-Egalité, one of the spots where everyone who is anyone in revolutionary Paris meets.

Sade neglects no detail in what Lély called this "exquisitely constructed whole." The reading of *Français, encore un effort* follows the double rape of Eugénie—who believed herself to be, after her deflowering, at the end of her pains and her joys—and is entrusted to the "fine organ" of the Chevalier, he who had the privilege of executing that most noble task. Eugénie's last cry had been, "Oh, yes, I swear in my present state of drunkenness that I would go, if I had to, and get myself fucked in the middle of the street."[7] The space of the boudoir has thus already opened onto the space of the city. Finally, I myself shall not miss picking up one further indication: before the Chevalier takes hold of the pamphlet, Mme de Saint-Ange dismisses the young gardener, the only character who owed his admission to the boudoir merely to the unusual size of his member, the only one who was not an accomplice but simply an instrument of pleasure: "Out with you, Augustin, this is not for you; but don't go too far—we'll ring when we want you to come back."[8]

Why, then, shouldn't Augustin listen? To put it another way, what is Sade trying to tell us, the readers, with this stroke? What complicity is he seeking to establish with us, such that he feels no need to justify the exclusion of the man of the people—an exclusion that occurs, moreover, at the very moment when the philosophy of the boudoir opens onto the philosophy of the city? The sign should be kept in mind, whatever its meaning. Something is going to be said that is undoubtedly more serious, something that goes beyond the remarks already made, as scandalous as these have been to a gardener's ears. Could it be that political philosophy exposes one to greater dangers, or is it simply that this "oaf," as Eugénie called him, had already shown that he did not have an ear for listening, so impatient was he to come? At this point, theory diverges from practice; the presence of a body without ideas, as the excellent Sade critic Annie Le Brun says, becomes inopportune.[9] Such little questions are enough to show us that the work is very cleverly conceived—for the pleasure and astonishment of the reader.

I would suggest that the reader who has followed the early dialogues of *La Philosophie dans le boudoir* and indulged in the spectacle is disposed in an entirely different way from the reader who approaches *Français, encore un effort* without having been prepared for it and who stumbles upon the first few sentences read by the Chevalier: "I come to offer great ideas. They shall be heard. They shall be given due reflection. If not all of them please, surely a few will. I thus shall have contributed something to the progress of Enlightenment and I therefore shall be content."[10] To be sure, this reader's expectations will be sorely tried when he learns, soon thereafter, upon what foundations the Republic is to be established. But for now, and even for awhile longer, he will adopt the tone that the philosophe's speech has insinuated into him, the tone of the Enlightenment thinker. (And how often will we hear about "the torch of philosophy"!)

What I mean to say, in short, is that every reading of a text implies, for the one who reads it, some manner of saying it to oneself—and, always already, some manner of interpreting it, simply by the inflection one gives to the words, the rhythm to the phrase, by a modulation of speech that in oneself remains unpronounced. One does not read Molière as one reads Racine or Descartes. But the difference is not dictated entirely by the text; it also arises from the operations performed by the reader. Indeed, what would be the point of learning to read if not to decipher and to communicate what are called "messages"? The thing is well known, but usually everything happens as if this knowledge served no purpose. Ordinarily, we are reluctant to admit that the interpretation based on one's understanding, the learned interpretation, is inseparable from this first sensible interpretation of which every reading is made. And there is an indefinable shuttling back and forth between them. It is one's manner of reading that leads to understanding, and it is also one's understanding that leads to rereading, to rearticulating, to scanning the text in another way. Of course, the distance between the actor–performer [*l'interprète–acteur*] on stage and the scholar–interpreter may be unbridgeable, but there is still a sort of mediation: the art of reading, which is impossible to define. And since I have just advanced the idea that the manner of reading is not dictated entirely by the text, I must qualify this statement by adding that it is nevertheless from the power of a piece of writing that a reading draws its power. For the reader knows that there has to be a proper reading [*une bonne lecture*].

Why this digression? There are certainly no writers, by which I mean genuine writers, who exempt us from the task of interrogating ourselves about our manner of reading, no writers whom we do not have to reread and reread again in an effort to harmonize our voices with theirs—unless we just collide against them, which sometimes happens. And it is not some knowledge about what genre their literature, their writing, belongs to that will deliver us from the insecurity of reading. But, this being granted, we still must recognize that among these writers are a few who throw us into a state of the greatest insecurity. Sade is one of them. Not primarily because he escapes all academic classification, but because even *the abysses he opens up are not always reliable*; and because, by the same token, we cannot always rely, either, on the operation whereby we think we have discovered in the damned part of his work the sacred part, or in the omnipotence of the desire he affirms the pure denial of the law, or, yet again, in the exorbitance of what he calls "insurrection" the "intransigence" of Saint-Just. (I am alluding here to an interpretation advanced by Blanchot, an otherwise admirable critic.[11]) But as it is neither among my intentions nor within my power to pronounce on the work as a whole, I will return to the manner of reading *Français, encore un effort*—to the manner of reading that I believe I have learned in letting myself be guided by the early dialogues of *La Philosophie dans le boudoir*.

These dialogues are highly troubling due to the variety of impressions they procure. I have already mentioned the variety of exercises practiced and the variety of themes subjected to discussion, but now it is time to note the relationship that Sade establishes with us, his readers. He allows us no rest. He exacts from us an extreme agility, suggesting this or that position only to yank us immediately out of it. "Dissolved positions [*Attitudes rompues*]," he says once, speaking of his characters. This is a theatrical term, but it also applies to us, the readers, for he is constantly disrupting our own progress. For brevity's sake, I shall simply say that this agility is stimulated by the devices of comedy. Le Brun rightly observes that *La Philosophie dans le boudoir* is a "very merry [*gai*] book."[12] To me, it seems somewhat more than that. It is at times irresistibly funny, despite its cruelty—which does not mean that it is not serious and, again, even somewhat more than that: in short, it is a book that torments our thought. What is this torment?

The first words exchanged between Mme de Saint-Ange and the Chevalier are those of libertines. They presage an intrigue that is consonant with an established tradition. Our expectations are undone as soon as Mme de Saint-Ange discloses her project—a kind of education—and her intentions: "I'll have two pleasures at once: that of enjoying [*jouir*] these criminal lecheries myself and that of giving the lessons, of inspiring a taste for them in the sweet innocent I am luring into our nets." She adds: "Of course, I'll spare nothing to pervert her, degrade her, upend in her all the false ethical principles people might already have used to dazzle her."[13] Seducing an ingenue in order to enjoy her and to see her deflowered and sodomized, thereby satisfying one's own criminal desires—the game is not surprising when one knows about libertinism, the literature of libertinism. On the other hand, the reader is caught in the net when wickedness and education, initiation into *jouissance* and emancipation, come to be conjoined. The net's mesh may seem too large, too visible, for Sade is obviously inverting the old Socratic formula: *No one does evil voluntarily*; but it becomes clear in what follows that, beginning with the premises he has laid down, Sade is empowering himself to seize upon those ideas that are considered the most noble, those that are the attainments of civilization—and this he does precisely in order to discredit the principles of morality. These fine and noble ideas partly contradict the ones that guide Eugénie's emancipation, yet he does not wish to do without them, and perhaps he cannot do without them. He must invoke natural law, liberty, and equality—essential attributes of human nature.

But what is human nature, if "nature" implies no norm? What is liberty, if the sexual drive alone dictates the worth of any act? And what is equality, if it excludes the recognition of like by like? And the whirlwind does not stop there, for we cannot forget Mme de Saint-Ange's desire: "I want," she says of Eugénie, "to make her as wicked as I am . . . as impious . . . as debauched."[14] The object of her desire, in other words, is Eugénie's desire, but in a quite particular way. To want to corrupt her is to want to form her in one's own image, to seek to see oneself in her. This whirlwind has already dizzied the reader. But there are several sorts of dizziness: the image of the educator–corrupter is also troubling. There is, in fact, in every educational undertaking a sort of violence that cannot be measured, that lies hidden, that is only indicated by the *obligatory* distance between teacher and pupil; it is only indicated by the resistance that the teacher opposes to the drive for knowledge so as to neutralize it, to temper a drive that could get the better of the student. And, correspondingly, this undertaking entails a violence in the pupil's expectations: an impatience for what, beyond the things the pupil is told, his senses are avid to know. This is, indeed, the twofold relationship that Sade makes manifest, that he is showing us.

The bodies embrace, interpenetrate, and the movement of thought couples upon the movement of the organs. From the erogenous zones emerge ideas. But the characters' words are just as troubling, these words that accompany and that name the movements of the bodies and the successive combinations of positions, governed always by the orgasmic imperative [*l'impératif de la jouissance*]. For, starting with injunctions, responses, commentaries, and exclamations, a sense of bewitchment such as few physical spectacles produce overtakes us, the readers. Then the boudoir, the enclosed space of pleasure, captivates the reader, who becomes the target of the desire to corrupt. Yet this is only one moment of the reading process. What could be more comic than this schoolgirl who is so quick to satisfy her sense of perversity, so enchanted with her own progress: "Oh, how well I now understand what evil is . . . how much my heart desires it!" Or: "How easily do I see that what you exact is for my own good?" And one cannot help but laugh again when, after having justified murder, rape, incest, and parricide, Mme de Saint-Ange, hoping to free Eugénie from all scruples toward her mother, solemnly declares: "During this age when the Rights of Man have been broadened at so great a cost, girls ought not to continue to think that they are the slaves of their families."[15] Or, yet again:

Let us hope that people's eyes will be opened and that, in guaranteeing freedom for all, the fate of these unhappy girls will not be forgotten; . . . they will soon triumph over custom and opinion. Man, becoming wiser because he will be freer, will sense the injustice that would exist in heaping scorn on girls who act thus. May the act of yielding to nature's impulses, which a captive people viewed as a crime, no longer be so regarded among a free people.[16]

All this noble talk—which is attributed to an ignoble character—how can we read it, and hence say it to ourselves, without adopting a declamatory tone, as I have just done? Even more, how can we avoid seeing in the statements, the refined speeches delivered by Dolmancé, which are placed in the service of the critique of morality, the pretensions and the dogmatism allegedly connected with the ideology of the age?

La Philosophie dans le boudoir is a title that by itself is already blasphemous. Where it finds a site to work, philosophy plies its trade within a learned society. No doubt, during that century philosophy was also widely practiced in the salons. But it went there without—at least in the eyes of its faithful supporters—losing sight of its primary destination. To philosophize in the boudoir, on the other hand, presupposes a singular manner of conceiving wisdom: what the ancients called "a life lived in conformity with nature"—which presupposes an even more singular manner of testing principles in the light of facts. This entails not only, as someone will later say, bringing philosophy down to Earth from the heavens, but setting it in a place of lust.

But knowledge does not lose its rights for all that. In the boudoir, one discusses virtues and vices; one discusses, too, the foundations of religions, the paths to happiness, the classical distinction between nature and convention. Nevertheless, the great traditional themes are subjected to the viewpoint of the boudoir. Philosophy in the boudoir is philosophy sifted through the screen of the boudoir. True, just as in a learned society, the society of the boudoir includes members who hold some title that authorizes them to participate in the dialogue. It requires walls that separate it from the vulgar. Perhaps this is why the gardener is chased out. Nevertheless, this society is also distinguished by the fact that it is a secret society and one that intends to remain so, since its debauchery contradicts the rules of every political society.

Although Eugénie's curiosity provokes her to ask whether mores are truly necessary to a government, and although Dolmancé—as an enlightened man with views on all subjects—would not want to leave any question unanswered, it is unclear what motive would drive the tiny world of the boudoir to develop the model of a Republic that would respond to its wishes. Surely, the society that would come closest to its wishes is precisely the one that would ignore it. Moreover, Sade very cleverly introduces political philosophy here through the reading of a pamphlet that comes from outside the boudoir. Not only does this device meet a need, but it also serves a ruse that momentarily disconcerts us, the readers.

To summarize, as briefly as possible, the pamphlet's argument: From his very first words, the author of the pamphlet appears to be a patriot and a staunch republican, as well as an ardent defender of the Revolution—with, however, one reservation, namely, that he deems the Revolution unfinished (hence his appeal to the French: "Yet another effort!"). He speaks, at length, the language of virtue; then, while examining the best means to found the Republic, or rather to set it upon indestructible foundations, his words again link up, little by little, with the words uttered in the boudoir, those of Dolmancé, those of Mme de Saint-Ange. The anonymous author, a stranger to the boudoir, in some sense reinvents it, proposing to multiply this boudoir under the form of establishments created by the government. Men and women who noticed some attractive individual in the street could summon that person to appear and assert their right to take their pleasure [*jouir*] with him or her, ultimately to use him or her as they liked in guaranteed secrecy. Finally, there is a description of licentiousness, which is defined as the condition for the safety of the Republic. What makes this even more comic is that the point of departure for this new philosophical, or philosophico-political, agenda is the opposite of the previous one, that is, the one at the beginning of the dialogue. We are led back, under the sign of pure reasoning, to a panegyric on corruption. Ignominy was evident from the start of the dialogues, although not without being combined, at times, with the new themes of emancipation: liberty, equality, and natural law. Here, the ignoble is first concealed under a pompous display of grand principles, then it reappears innocently draped in the folds of virtue. Simply speaking, virtue is transformed into vice. Now, if we do not recognize that this is a deliberate move on Sade's part, we will inevitably fail to grasp a weakness in his arguments. That is, we will fall into the trap of attributing to him ideas which he seizes upon only to pervert, of taking literally arguments and maxims from the first part of the text—the section on religion and the one on mores—without noticing his playfulness there. I have already quoted the beginning of the very first sentence: "I come to offer great ideas"—which many other phrases later echo. For example: "Let us therefore annihilate forever everything that might one day destroy your work. Imagine that the fruits of your labors were reserved only for your grandchildren; duty and probity command that you bequeath to them none of those seeds of disaster that could plunge your descendants back into the chaos from which we have with such pain just escaped." Or: "Rather than fatigue your children's young organs with deific stupidities, replace them with social principles of surpassing value; . . . teach them to cherish the virtues you scarcely ever mentioned in former times . . . ; make them feel that this happiness consists in making others as fortunate as we ourselves desire to be." Finally, and I shall stop here: "Return next to the utility of morality: give them [your pupils], on this vast subject, many more examples than lessons, many more demonstrations than books, and you will make good citizens of them; you will make them into fine warriors, fine fathers, fine husbands. . . . Patriotism will then shine in all spirits."[17]

Each and every one of these sentiments will be contradicted in the rest of the pamphlet, not a word of which proves credible. The generations to come merit only indifference, we learn; morality is not only useless, but dangerous; the family is destined for destruction; children will not know their fathers. It thus seems to me that Blanchot is mistaken when he chalks up to reason in Sade—a reason that is always in excess, he says—what must really be seen as "the most shameless contradictions, arguments that turn into their opposites, statements that do not hold up," yet adds: "Sade speaks in order to convince. He is searching, he is always manifesting, here and there, his sincere conviction."[18] To say this is to run the risk of passing Sade off as either a madman or an imbecile. I maintain, again, that it suffices to set the tone in order to give these phrases the effect the author is expecting from them.

In short, I maintain that Sade exploits philosophico-revolutionary discourse in order to bring out the consequences that undermine its principles. Moreover, once we uncover this process (which again draws on the art of the theater), we must grant that the author never stops exploiting it, even when he seeks to demonstrate that vices exist in conformity with the laws of nature (in the classical sense) or with natural law (in the modern sense) or with the ultimate ends of the Republic. It is not only revolutionary discourse that Sade deliberately distorts, but philosophical discourse in general and republican humanism in particular. While Sade does not mention Plato, he invokes the theory of the community of women—but only to distort it by basing the legitimacy of incest on it. He does not mention Machiavelli, but he follows the latter in observing that Rome was founded upon crime; and while affirming that an old and corrupt republic cannot save itself by virtue, he neglects to recall what Machiavelli viewed as the greatness of the Romans, that is, the fact that law thrives only when it is combined with the desires of a free people. He also forgets that corruption cannot be abolished by granting individuals a license to indulge their private pleasures. He does not mention Hobbes, but he makes his own the thesis that the state of nature is a war of all against all—except that he takes care not to point out that civil society originates and evolves from man's inability to sustain this war, this terrible ordeal. He does not mention Rousseau (whom he invokes only apropos of the death penalty and adultery), but he makes his own the case against civilization—except that he uses this case to serve an end that runs contrary to Rousseau's since he denies man's natural goodness.

Sade's concern is not to subject the ideas of the philosophes to examination, but to extract formulas from them that will allow him to dress up his own discourse in philosophical garb or rather to drape himself in the tatters of philosophy. He renders this travesty of philosophy almost convincing by throwing about himself some of the references in which it is clothed. He makes the legislators of Greece, along with Seneca, Charron, Plutarch, and many others, shine, one after another. He does so, however, in order to exculpate calumny, rape, and sodomy. Why speak of contradictions? Contradiction, because it reestablishes the exigencies of logic, is a serious thing. Now, it seems to me that in Sade this is an authorial ruse. Philosophical discourse, moreover, has never been exempt from such tricks. The Platonic dialogues or the works of Machiavelli offer some great examples. It is not certain (nor has it been disproved) that Sade was inspired by them, but he is pleased above all to *divert* [*détourner*]—I insist upon this term because it had so much success in 1968—ideas from their original destination, and he endeavors in other respects to weaken the authority of the argument, of all argument. He does so by advancing, with equal seriousness, a thesis and its contrary, or by thoroughly exploiting the resources of an infantile intelligence.

Take incest. It is not an evil, he tells us, since procreation, a fact of nature, does not result in any tie between the child and those who begot it. And furthermore, experience proves how this purely conventional relationship can arouse feelings of hatred. Nor is incest an evil, he tells us later, because it is quite natural that a being should feel attracted by its closest object, the one that resembles it most. Take another example: the defense of calumny. The slanderer has every merit on his side. If he attacks a perverse man, he usefully attracts attention to the latter, and, in imputing to that man crimes he did not commit, the slanderer helps to unmask him before public opinion; if he attacks a virtuous man, he goads that man to redouble his zeal in order to defend his honor. After this, can we say that Sade wants to convince anyone? And yet I note that Jacques Lacan, who did not ordinarily lack a sense of humor, complained that in this case the demonstration was a bit abrupt.[19]

What there is no doubt about is that before or behind the arguments, Sade is pursuing his own designs. The determined, deliberate movement of his discourse does not lead one to believe that it is just some incoherent blathering. The cumulative effect produced by the pamphlet seems to me quite remarkable. Indeed, the philosophical demonstrations come to resemble the exercises practiced in the boudoir. The ideas copulate, part, and are rearticulated in accordance with the multiple positions of the person speaking. The learned profligacy seems aimed precisely at arousing the reader to orgasm [*une jouissance*]. I am not talking about metaphysical orgasm. Sade employs *jouissance métaphysique* once when denouncing the vanity and horror of the kind of love that fosters a disagreeable burning sensation, he tells us, in the absence of all real pleasure, which is to say, a love that corrupts. No, it is rather an orgasm that proceeds from excitation of the head—this head that "discharges," to use Dolmancé's expression— an orgasm that is apt to spread into the body and one which, perhaps, was already brewing within the body.

In a sense, the reader is put into a state somewhat reminiscent of Eugénie's condition. Mme de Saint-Ange confided to her brother that she wanted to upend [*culbuter*] all the false principles of morality in Eugénie. Does not Sade want to upend philosophy in the reader? Of course, Eugénie and the reader do not occupy the same place; the reader is not necessarily an ingenue. Indeed, Sade is probably counting on the reader's complicity, perhaps even more on his complicity than on his conversion. Provoking laughter from the reader is already a way of corrupting him, for laughter is not always the best medicine, contrary to what is often said. In luring him into this debauchery of ideas, Sade is seeking to stir up an agitation of the body that is already simmering within the reader, to insinuate into thought the drives that thought restrains. And in fact he suggests at one point, in the voice of Dolmancé, that his philosophical saraband contains seething desires. Dolmancé has just expounded a long dissertation on *jouissance*, the will to domination that accompanies it, and the absurdity of wanting to thwart it. Suddenly, he exclaims: "Fuck! I'm hard again! . . . I beg you to call Augustin [the gardener] back in here. 'Tis amazing how this fine lad's superb ass does preoccupy my mind while I talk! All my ideas seem involuntarily to relate back to that masterpiece, Augustin."[20]

Be that as it may, we should not lose sight of Sade's relationship to the Revolution and the Republic, to which I now return. I do not want to give the impression that Sade was counterrevolutionary, antirepublican, or indifferent to politics. I doubt that his radical critique of religion has ever been equaled; his rejection of all forms of deism, his attraction to all forms of insurrection, necessarily puts him on the side of the Revolution. The general uprising, the tremendous upheaval in institutions, all that has stirred up a new phantasmagoria—raging floods, volcanic eruptions, earthquakes—none of this was alien to him. Yet he detested the revolutionary ideology and everything that smacked of new, constraining norms, of pretensions to virtue. On the other hand, without being republican, he was nonetheless biased, I would say, toward this regime due to his hatred of royalism and of the eighteenth-century aristocracy. In order to try to catch up with his thought, we need to focus on the passage in the pamphlet where its author calls for, indeed demands, immoral citizens. At this point, the argument is aimed at defending the thesis that prostitution, adultery, incest, rape, and sodomy should not be considered offenses.

> We certainly should not for one moment doubt that all those so-called
> morals crimes . . . would be of absolutely no importance under a gov-
> ernment whose sole duty consists in preserving, by whatever means

necessary, the form essential to its continuance: there you have a republican government's sole morality. But, since the republic is permanently menaced by the despots surrounding it, one cannot reasonably imagine that the means for its preservation might be *moral means*, for the republic will be preserved only by war, and nothing is less moral than war. I ask now how one will succeed in demonstrating that, in a State rendered *immoral* by its very obligations, it is essential that the individuals who make up this State be *moral*. I will go further: it is a very good thing that they are not. The Greek lawgivers perfectly appreciated the capital necessity of corrupting the member-citizens so that, their *moral dissolution* influencing the dissolution useful to the machinery of State, there resulted the kind of insurrection that is always indispensable to a government that, perfectly happy like a republican government, must necessarily arouse hatred and envy in all that surrounds it. Insurrection, these sage legislators thought, is not at all a *moral* condition; it nevertheless has got to be a republic's permanent condition. Hence it would be no less absurd than dangerous to require that those who are to insure perpetual *immoral* upheaval in the machinery of State themselves be very *moral* beings, for the *moral* state of a man is one of peace and tranquillity, whereas the *immoral* state of a man is one of perpetual unrest that brings him nearer to that necessary state of insurrection in which the republican must always keep the government of which he is a member.[21]

This passage is also quoted by Blanchot, who draws conclusions from it that I do not share.[22] First of all, Sade attributes to republican government a characteristic that he ought to acknowledge as true of any government. Indeed, that its sole duty consists in preserving itself is a formula that has a Machiavellian resonance to it—although the Florentine did not express himself in those terms—but the author of *The Prince* did deem, as Aristotle did before him, such an imperative indispensable to any power. It is equally obvious that, whatever the regime, a State is surrounded by potential enemies and forced to have recourse to immoral means and that, therefore, it encourages a tendency toward violence among its members that is alien to the virtues celebrated by philosophy. If Sade wants to distinguish the Republic from other regimes, he has undoubtedly made it his target because it claims a morality that it can only fall short of achieving; it pretends to obey the animating principles of virtue, and not those of fear or of honor, as Montesquieu noted. Sade counters this pretense with the idea that liberty implies a permanent state of insurrection—that is, not harmony, as republicans presume, but, one would think, a constant state of agitation among its citizens, each one of whom is ready to rise up against the threat of oppression. After all, this language could still be considered Machiavellian while also recalling that of numerous revolutionary writers equally convinced since the seventeenth century that the people should never prostrate themselves before a master, nor even before their own representatives, mere delegates at risk of turning into tyrants. Nevertheless, those writers never associated insurrection with immorality; insurrection is the sign of the desire for liberty, whereas vice is the weapon of despotism. To understand what Sade means by insurrection, one must read on a little further and pause at his examination of lust: "We must endeavor to introduce some order into this sphere," he then writes, and "establish all the security necessary so that, when need draws the citizen near the objects of lust, he can give himself over to doing with them all that his passions demand, without ever being chained down by anything, since there is no other passion in man that has so great a need for full and free extension as this one."[23] Then, after having recommended the creation of those famous establishments I mentioned earlier, Sade suddenly lets his own views break through:

> Although, as I told you just a moment ago, no passion has a greater need of the widest horizon of liberty than has this one, none, doubtless, is more despotic: here it is that man likes to command, to be obeyed, to surround himself with slaves compelled to satisfy him. Now, whenever you withhold from man the secret means whereby he exhales the dose of despotism nature instilled in the depths of his heart, he will return to exercising this despotism over objects near to him and he consequently will trouble the government.[24]

In contrast, if "his tyrannical desires"[25] are satisfied, he will conduct himself as a citizen. Sade turns this argument over again and again, but I do not want to quote it at too great a length; his attitude toward the Republic, it seems to me, is sufficiently enlightening here. He violently weds the Republic, joining with it on the ruins of a regime that he hates. But somehow he penetrates it to touch bottom, what he thinks is the bottom: the despotism of the human being, which only the Republic can authorize. I say *touch bottom*, but it would be better to say *open an abyss*. There is for Sade, in effect, an abject despotism, which is that of the prince. Man makes an idol of the prince, just as he makes an idol of a despotic god. But then man is unaware of his abjection. In contrast, the despotism of passion, if made his own, leads man to discover his abjection. Why, one might ask, is Sade interested in the political? But is it not precisely because the possibility of conceiving despotism depends on the form of government—depends on the Republic? The Republic does not institute a virtuous community for itself. When it claims to do so, the Republic in turn becomes a machine for producing idols: the very machine that Robespierre tried to restore. No, the true merit of the Republic is its fitting out, or furnishing, the space of people's solitudes. Therefore, it is hardly possible to affirm freedom. The liberty to take one's pleasure is achieved, is won, only through the blooming, through the blossoming forth, of tyrannical desires. But it is also impossible to affirm equality, for if it is true that each person naturally possesses the same right, the exercise of that right is accomplished by the enslavement of others.

The speech Dolmancé addresses to Eugénie echoes these sentiments from the pamphlet:

> What is it that one desires when taking one's pleasure? That everything around us be concerned with nothing but ourselves, think of naught but us, care for us only. If the objects that serve us know pleasure too, you can be very sure that they are less concerned for us than they are for themselves, and lo! our own pleasure is consequently disturbed. There is not a man alive who does not wish to play the despot when he is hard; . . . the idea of seeing another enjoy as he enjoys reduces him to a kind of equality with that other, which impairs the unspeakable charm that *despotism* caused him to feel.[26]

These sentences no longer seem to me to pertain to what I called a "philosophical saraband." Sade's own thinking breaks through, as it does when he has Dolmancé say: "So long as the act of coition lasts, I may, to be sure, continue to need that object [the other] in order to participate in the act. But as soon as the need is satisfied, what, I beg you to tell me, remains between me and that object? And what real obligation will bind the result of this commerce to it or to me?"[27]

This is, let us note, a good summary description of the Cartesian notion of a space that is *partes extra partes*; it is the notion of a "time pulverized into instants" that comes back to us via the unexpected detour of a theory of eroticism. Pure exteriority of one person in relation to another, pure discontinuity, pure contact of self with self: such would be the "original truths." But at this point mustn't we grant that Sade's thesis, if thesis there be, is virtually overtaken or turned inside out by his work? Indeed, his own characters do not couple with each other like mere automatons. The movement of bodies is associated with the imagination of figures and also with the imagination of orgasmic pleasure. They speak, they are caught up in the duration of the dialogue. Ultimately, the work itself addresses readers and requires at some unspecified future time the renewing presence of an interpreter. It triggers in each reader a process whereby one incorporates thoughts that have escaped the author's mastery.

But perhaps this conclusion at which I am tempted to halt, shouldn't it too be doubted? Is Sade entirely captivated by the image of the individual despot? And by the image of a humanity populated with beings who are strangers to each other? Does he not know that he is writing? Why does the idea of corruption matter so much if freedom merges with the expression of tyrannical desires? And, in terms of this hypothesis, what does the desire to write, Sade's desire to write, signify?

Does not Sade suggest that the desire to corrupt exceeds the desire to take one's pleasure and to dominate in taking one's pleasure? Assuming that this last desire would be natural, the first must be deviant since the desire to corrupt recreates a tie with the other, tends to make of the other an accomplice, and in a certain manner remakes sociability. And furthermore, if civilization is the process of corruption and if moral teaching is the perversion of the human being, what are we to make of a corruption that is a counter-corruption? Is not Sade exploiting the phantasmagoria of the revolutionary era, the phantasmagoria of plot and counterplot?

I thus return, in conclusion, to my initial remarks about the role that the concept of "corruption" plays in political life. Classical philosophy as well as modern philosophy, though in a different way, established the distinction between nature and corruption via an idealization of nature, by which I mean via a purification or purging of the idea of nature. Sade does not abolish the distinction, let us note, but he reestablishes it via an idealization of corruption. Whereas Plato arrived at the analysis of real society by starting from an idea of the nobility of human nature, Sade returns to real society by disclosing what is basest in human nature.

In doing so, he renders the distinction obscure; its terms can no longer be grasped. We, the readers, are deprived of the image of a "good society." We are incited to reject ideology of any kind whatsoever as we glimpse the abyss that ideology covers over. But I do not want to say any more for fear of attributing to Sade a new moralism; and I would much rather preserve his enigmas.

—Translated by David Ames Curtis

Notes

Trans. note: Claude Lefort (1924–) is a former contributor to Jean-Paul Sartre and Maurice Merleau-Ponty's political journal *Les Temps Modernes*, as well as cofounder, with Cornelius Castoriadis, of *Socialisme ou Barbarie* and, with Pierre Clastres, of *Libre*. He is the author of numerous philosophical and political works, including *Un homme en trop: Réflexions sur l'Archipel du Goulag* (1976), *Les Formes de l'Histoire: Essais d'anthropologie politique* (1978), *Sur une colonne absente: Ecrits autour de Merleau-Ponty* (1978), *Eléments d'une critique de la bureaucratie* (1979), *L'Invention démocratique: Les limites de la domination totalitaire* (1981), *Essais sur le politique: XIXᵉ–XXᵉ siècle* (1986), *Le Travail de l'oeuvre: Machiavel* (1986), and, with Cornelius Castoriadis and Edgar Morin, *Mai 68, La Brèche/Vingt ans après* (1988).

"Sade: Le Boudoir et la cité" was originally published in *Petits et grands théâtres du Marquis de Sade*, ed. Annie Le Brun (Paris, 1989). It was reprinted in *Ecrire: A l'épreuve du politique* (Paris, 1992), a collection of Lefort's essays exploring the political dimensions of literary texts and the literary dimensions of political texts, which has not yet found an American publisher.

1   *Français, encore un effort*; preceded by Maurice Blanchot, "L'Inconvenance majeure" (Paris, 1965).

2   Gilbert Lély, *Vie du marquis de Sade*, 3d ed. (Paris, 1982).

3   *La Philosophie dans le boudoir (Les Instituteurs immoraux)*; Preface by Gilbert Lély (Paris, 1972), 19.

   Trans. note: I have consulted and made use of Richard Seaver and Austryn Wainhouse's translation, "Philosophy in the Bedroom," in *The Marquis de Sade: The Complete Justine, Philosophy in the Bedroom and Other Writings* (New York, 1965), but I take responsibility for the final form of the translations from Sade quoted in the text; all page references are to the French edition cited above.

4   See Blanchot, "L'Inconvenance majeure," 20.

5   *Philosophie*, 180.

6   Ibid., 189–90.

7   Ibid., 189.

8   Ibid., 190.

9 Annie Le Brun, *Soudain un bloc d'abîme: Sade* (Paris, 1986); see also *Sade: A Sudden Abyss*, trans. Camille Naish (San Francisco, 1991).

10 *Philosophie*, 190.

11 See Blanchot, "L'Inconvenance majeure," 32–38.

12 Le Brun, *Soudain un bloc d'abîme*, 257.

13 *Philosophie*, 24, 25.

14 Ibid., 25.

15 Ibid., 91, 60, 66.

16 Ibid., 68.

17 Ibid., 194, 204, 207.

18 Blanchot, "L'Inconvenance majeure," 11, 10.

19 Jacques Lacan, "Kant avec Sade," in *Ecrits* (Paris, 1966), 765–90; quotation from 788; see also "Kant with Sade," trans. James B. Swenson, Jr., *October* 51 (1989): 55–75.

20 *Philosophie*, 279.

21 Ibid., 224–25; Sade's emphases.

22 See Blanchot, "L'Inconvenance majeure," 29.

23 *Philosophie*, 227.

24 Ibid., 228.

25 Ibid.

26 Ibid., 276–77.

27 Ibid., 173.

Richard H. Weisberg

The Text as Legislator:
Devoir and the Millennial Stendhal

We know that Stendhal enjoyed reading a couple of pages of the *Code Napoléon* every night to calm his soul and inspire his talents. To us who are near the millennium, this seems aberrational. We all need quiet and we all crave inspiration. But who among us would voluntarily crack the spine of any legal code written under Western skies, much less delve into it for creative guidance? The modern rift between letters and law seems most striking in the difference, say, between the Internal Revenue Code and our favorite novel. Although Karl Llewellyn, the European-born drafter of the American Uniform Commercial Code, looks like a latter-day Stendhal when he writes about codification, he stands as one of the few twentieth-century disciples of a sparse but eminent nineteenth-century Continental school.

Stendhal's nocturnal predilection constitutes a reversal of his contemporary Shelley's famous dictum—"poets are the unacknowledged legislators of the world"—for the Frenchman believed that the legislator influenced the artist, not necessarily that the poet's individual brilliance created unlegislated rules superseding those en-

The *South Atlantic Quarterly* 95:4, Fall 1996.
Copyright © 1996 by Duke University Press.

acted by elected lawmakers. Yet once he got beyond his beloved codes, Stendhal seems to have had a more modern view of law, one aligned to the normative indictment of legal language by such novelists as Dickens (especially *Bleak House*, but also *Great Expectations*), Faulkner (i.e., *Intruder in the Dust* and *Sanctuary*), and Camus (*L'Etranger* to some extent, but *La Chute* even more so). Through Julien Sorel in *Le Rouge et le noir*, Stendhal exhibits no greater disdain—and this is to say a good deal—than for the lawyers and judges whose careers have made them central to French justice, as when Julien speaks in *style indirect libre* about his own capital trial:

> Ces juges si formalistes, si acharnés après le pauvre accusé. . . . Je me soustrairais à leurs injures en mauvais français, que le journal du département va appeler de l'éloquence. . . . L'avocat général faisait du pathos en mauvais français sur la barbarie du crime commis. . . . L'éloquence plate de l'avocat général augmenta ce sentiment de dégoût.

> (These judges, who are so formalistic, so dogged in their pursuit of the poor accused. . . . I should escape from their power, from their insults in bad French, which the local newspaper will call eloquence. . . . The assistant public prosecutor was indulging in pathos in bad French on the barbarity of the crime that had been committed. . . . The assistant public prosecutor's insipid rhetoric heightened this feeling of disgust.)

Individual lawyers often speak—and even more often write—poorly. We know this. But what we have forgotten is Stendhal's nightly dose of Napoleonic legislation: for him, the great *codes of law* evoked a magnificent response. In the Stendhalian space between exalted law code and debased law talk may lie much wisdom. For while the practicing lawyer or judge epitomizes the petty and pragmatic trend of an individual "career," the codes present a public challenge to lend one's talents to the improvement of a structured *community*. Public discourse may serve no other end than the completion of a professional function for the lawyer, but for the codifier public discourse creates a series of *devoirs*—"duties" that both constrain and liberate individual talent.

═══

Julien Sorel is the sole transgressing protagonist in modern fiction who knows even before consulting a lawyer under which section of the Criminal Code he is likely to be prosecuted. His interests are more general and extended, however, better suited to an age when law and letters habitually merged. As a Latin scholar in the seminary his interests reflect those of his creator, who was drawn to Cicero, Virgil, and Horace. (This seminarian rarely speaks of the New Testament!) These models indicate Julien's attraction to the last European epoch in which law and letters—action and eloquence—could be merged in a single orator or statesman. It is to these classical figures that the heroic spirit turns, as to Napoleon the codifier. For as Nietzsche observed in *Zur Genealogie der Moral*:

> Wie ein letzter Fingerzeug zum *anderen* Wege erschien Napoleon, jener einzelnste und spätestgeborene Mensch, den es jemals gab, und in ihm das fleisch-gewordene Problem des vornehmen Ideals an sich—man überlege wohl, was es für ihn ein Problem ist—Napoleon, diese Synthesis von Unmensch und Übermensch.

> (Like a last signpost to the *other* path, Napoleon appeared, the most isolated and late-born man there has even been, and in him the problem of the *noble ideal as such* made flesh—one might well ponder *what* kind of problem it is: Napoleon, this synthesis of the *inhuman* and *superhuman*.)

Julien's skeptical and scornful nature finds only this Napoleon, the hero and the codifier, a "signpost" to that better—one might say, that classically coherent—world. The creative and forceful nature needs the constraint provided by both heroes and law codes, for no meaningful action is possible except "in obedience to *one* constraint [in *einer* Richtung]," as Nietzsche puts it in *Jenseits von Gut und Böse*. Achievement beyond the norm first requires a reverence for the norm. It is one's devoir, one's *duty*, to master the text which most promises that constraint. For Julien, as for his creator, that inspirational text is a noble code of laws, and he has apparently committed Napoleon's laws to memory as faithfully as he once memorized his Cicero.

Now if Nietzsche accorded Stendhal a respect he extended to few other nineteenth-century storytellers, it may well have been due to their shared belief that a code might emerge from a creative act (or series of acts) and that such a code would thereafter guide society in accordance with the just values of the codifier. While this may sound very un-Nietzschean to a falsely attuned postmodern ear—one which prefers not to find reverence in him for either law or text—consider the language of this key passage from the *Genealogie*, in which Nietzsche strives to dissociate justice from vengeance and petty pragmatism, or *ressentiment*:

> In welcher Sphäre ist denn bisher überhaupt die ganze Handhabung des Rechts, auch das eigentliche Bedürfnis nach Recht auf Erden heimisch gewesen? Etwa in der Sphäre reaktiven Menschen? Ganz und gar nicht: vielmehr in der der Aktiven, Starken, Spontanen, Aggressiven. Historisch betrachtet, stellt das Recht auf Erden . . . den Kampf gerade *wider* die reaktiven Gefühle vor, den Krieg mit denselben seitens aktiver und aggressiver Mächte, welche, ihre Stärke zum Teil dazu verwendeten, der Ausschweifung des reaktiven Pathos Halt und Mass zu gebieten und einen Vergleich zu erzwingen.

> (To what sphere is the basic management of law, indeed the entire drive toward law, most connected? In the sphere of reactive people? Absolutely not: much more so in the realm of the active, strong, spontaneous, aggressive. Historically understood, the place of justice on Earth is situated as a battle *against* the reactive emotions, a war waged by means of that active and aggressive power that here uses a part of its strength to quiet the ceaseless rumblings of *ressentiment* and to enforce a settlement [my translation].)

Here, Nietzsche claims for the hero a lawmaker function. Only through positive action does law assert itself positively, stanching the forces of ressentiment that otherwise constantly bubble over in Christian societies. The *actor*—think of Moses, the French revolutionaries, or some recent feminists—devotes some of her time to *codewriting*!

> Das Entscheidenste aber, was die oberste Gewalt gegen die Übermacht der Gegen und Nachgefühle tut und durchsetzt—sie tut es immer, sobald sie irgendwie stark genug dazu ist—, ist die Aufrichtung des *Gesetzes*, die imperativische Erklärung darüber, was überhaupt unter ihren Augen als erlaubt, als recht, was als verboten, als unrecht zu gelten habe; . . . von nun an wird das Auge für eine immer *unpersönlichere* Abschätzung der Tat eingeübt, sogar das Auge des Geschädigten selbst (obschon dies am allerletzten).

> (The most decisive move, however, made by the higher power against the predomination of grudge and spite is the establishment of *the law*, the imperial elucidation of what counts in [the codifier's] eyes as per-

mitted, as just, and what counts as forbidden and unjust; . . . from then on, the eye will seek an increasingly *impersonal* evaluation of the deed, even the eye of the victim himself, although his will be the last to do so [my translation].)

This is a remarkable text—and one which considerably undermines the postmodernist program for Nietzsche (e.g., Derrida's, in *Eperons/Spurs*), which has insisted on his relativism and his hermeneutic radicalism. (Even the pragmatist's Nietzsche, however closer to the mark he seems here, cannot hold up against this passage; but more about Nietzsche's quite unpragmatic place in the current discourse on the private/public distinction shortly.) What we find here, rather, is a Stendhalian admirer of Napoleon positing the possibility in each generation of a superb lawgiver whose creative impulses in the domain of action extend to the promulgation of a text by which others may be led to just behavior "on Earth." (This twice-used rhetorical flourish in the Aphorism suggests, of course, Nietzsche's abhorrence of the Christian idea that justice must be put off until the next world, a notion he ascribes to the resentful nature of Christian theology and hermeneutics.) Even the injured party, Nietzsche tells us, will come to view his situation impersonally—which brings us back to Julien Sorel.

Consistent allegiance to a codified text requires the happy coincidence in one's life of *both* a "noble" code to provide boundaries and guidelines for even the creative, imaginative spirit *and* a community of peers alive to the justness of that code. So Julien waits and waits, without violating the written law. For the Stendhalian hero, there is time to try out a life that might remain true to the codifier, without replicating the latter's own spilling of blood. It is therefore of some importance that, unlike Dostoyevsky's Raskolnikov, Julien associates devoir with *lawful* behavior until very late in the story. (For the heroic law student of *Crime and Punishment*, there is no model for action that would not instantly move one beyond the bounds of the law: *prestupleni'e*, the Russian word for "crime," means a "stepping across." Raskolnikov's crime occurs before we have completed even a fifth of the novel.)

Since there is no community receptive to Julien's mediated notion of Napoleonic heroism, he finds an outlet, ultimately, in transgression. But even as he pulls the trigger on Mme de Rênal, he wants to be punished under the code: "'I caused death with premeditation,' Julien told [the judge]. '. . . Article 1342 of the Penal Code is explicit; I deserve death and I am ready for it.'" Julien, like his creator, has memorized Napoleon's Code and, prior to the "murder" of Mme de Rênal, has felt constrained to follow the rules. But allegiance to the code also depends on others in one's field of relations exulting in the code's generous spirit, and here Julien (again, like his creator) is disappointed.

Seeking a *constrained* outlet for his ambitions, Julien associates heroism on a smaller scale with each act of duty—each *devoir*—that he imposes on himself in the domains of romance, politics, and thought: embracing Mme de Rênal; furthering the marquis de la Môle's Restorationist scheme while attempting to cool Mathilde de la Môle's passion for him; and persistently, even excessively, criticizing himself. Conscientiously memorizing and following the code, he attempts (wearing both the red and the black) to fulfill his *devoir*. He might have survived his less than heroic times had not Mme de Rênal—she to whom he first devoted his full creativity in the domains of *physical* and *spiritual* duty—contrived to undo him by revealing their love affair in her letter to the marquis. In response, however, Julien abruptly transgresses all codes—by shooting her in a church. This breach of the code he so reveres comes on the heels of one disappointment after another with his contemporaries. A theme of the novel, this disparagement of the nineteenth century places prudence, ambition, and avarice in sullen opposition to devoir—a despicable triad that is also associated with the practice of law—for placing himself in the hands of lawyers after his rash act is far less acceptable to Julien than submitting to the great code itself.

Julien's complete absence of ressentiment, as well as his ultimate allegiance to the codifier, thus becomes instantly palpable after the shooting. Indeed, his "injured eye," to paraphrase Nietzsche, now perceives Mme de Rênal's epistolary vengeance "coolly," and he surrenders to the law under the appropriate section of the Napoleonic Code. The would-be hero, brought down as much by his "prudent" times as by any personal failing, leaves the world insisting on the justice of his penalty, and without regret. He has performed his devoir. He has, finally, remained true to the actor-lawgiver model instantiated first by the Israelites and the Romans, then by Napoleon, the "last signpost" to that ideal.

=====

In *Contingency, Irony and Solidarity* (1989), Richard Rorty lucidly identifies what he sees as an unbridgeable gap between the private person striving for individuality and the public person engaged in social improvement. For Rorty, Nietzsche exemplifies—along with Baudelaire and Proust—the quest for the self-created life, the striving for "private perfection." Thinkers like Marx, Dewey, Habermas, and Rawls, on the other hand, contribute to a "shared, social effort—the effort to make our institutions and practices more just and less cruel." Between these poles, Rorty situates the pragmatic "liberal ironist," who is resigned to the unalterable difference between the two types, a difference that Rorty couches in the strongest terms: "We shall only think of these two kinds of writers as *opposed* if we think that a more comprehensive philosophical outlook would let us hold self-creation and justice, private perfection and human solidarity, in a single vision. There is no way in which philosophy, or any other theoretical discipline, will ever let us do that."

The Stendhalian Nietzsche, however, is precisely that figure who bridges the gap otherwise filled only by postmodernist irony. This nineteenth-century model redeems classical notions of the polity that must be revived as we look back on our own dismal century and strive toward a more just world. Through this figure, we can advance a set of positive personal values in the domain of public expression, even of social legislation. However "untimely" such a model may be, from a purely theoretical point of view, in these otherwise diminishing times it opens up the possibility of our meeting ethical challenges which the elite in particular no longer has any right to ignore or—worse still—to obscure with self-denying verbiage.

Rorty's privately creative actor was once a classical legislator and could still become one today. In the classical model, public virtue reflected but was essentially distinct from any private sphere of behavior; as a result of being considerably less important to the *polis* then, the private person enjoyed freedoms unthinkable now in his or her public display of communal duty and wisdom. Yet the varieties of speech and act that were possible in the private realm were thought harmonious with civic virtue in that no private miscreant could finally enjoy (for he could never earn) public respect. Thersites, in the *Iliad*, is "the ugliest man who ever came under Ilion," but not because of any physical deformity; his private malefaction is of a piece with his public persona, and his cowardly words suffice—without any inquiry into the details of his private life—to disqualify him for public stature.

In the twentieth century, however, classical virtue has yielded to pluralistic "values," and there is far less assurance that anyone's public behavior can be gauged without close scrutiny of the private deeds that alone can reveal the actor's "values." Precisely reversing the classical model, public performance is distrusted as a signpost of the private individual, and private habits and associations must be exposed to unpack the "true" identity of the presumptively false public person. Perhaps the only remnant of the ancient model becomes evident when a public person errs grotesquely by making a negative, extreme statement. But *positive* public pronouncements are no longer taken seriously.

The result for ethical politics is calamitous. And equally disheartening is the effect upon culture, which once displayed through stories the community's aspirations and fears, but now appeals to "truth" in its rawest and most extreme forms: in endless confessions of increasingly bizarre behavior and in the substitution of "real" events for the rich stories that formerly inspired and undergirded the ethical lives of public actors. In just one exemplifying area—but a vital one—law becomes a form of entertainment rather than a search for justice. The public arena of dispute resolution yields to the private excesses of passion, as jurors and litigants, lawyers and defendants, journalists and observers join forces in displays of mutual resentment, fear, anger, and even fury. With our theaters uninspiring and empty, our courtrooms—and our political conventions—now function along with confessional talk shows as laboratories of "values"; meanwhile, public, civic virtue dissolves or—worse still—devolves into the competing voices of religious, media, and political "leaders" whose appeals to fear and prejudice capitalize on the timidity of the more enlightened even to broach the question of ethics.

Can it be that what those enlightened ones have learned from the shattering events of our waning century is to retreat from the obligation to define and to actualize *public* virtue? Did the hideous totalitarianism of fifty years ago preempt the public sphere, leaving men and women too petrified to strive together, to make of their multiple voices a harmonious sound of forwardness and of inspiration? It may be that sensitive people have privatized themselves first to avoid the gluttonous gaze of the media, but finally because the strongest public men in recent memory have only infected our private consciousness with images of previously unimaginable horror. I am haunted by the thought that Hitler may have posthumously vanquished us by petrifying our collective and structural instincts.

Returning to literature, it is also noteworthy that Stendhal's conception of noble legislation died as soon as Flaubert made lawmaking everywhere a symbol of ressentiment, particularly through his priestly Schahabarim (in *Salammbô*) and his mediocre law student Frédéric Moreau (in *L'Education sentimentale*). Since then, a line of strong storytellers from Dostoyevsky to Melville to Kafka to Camus has seen lawmaking, lawyering, and adjudication in the darkest terms, part of the demonry that distances our private ambition from the ground of public participation.

Nietzsche once allowed that it would be "some time" before his *Genealogie* would be read correctly. Perhaps that time has come, perhaps with a little help from Stendhal. Everywhere concerned in his stories with the notion of devoir, Stendhal fires our imagination as a *public* weapon for good. His characters' drive to act well is not, on this model of devoir, purely *self*-generated. Instead, devoir imposes on each protagonist an externally inspired set of affirmative and negative constraints. Heroic action, in both the private and the public sphere, is defined in Stendhal's world as both self-willed and socially constructed by external models, particularly by the model of a noble legislator, or codifier. But what is the autonomous individual bound to do when both a noble code and a harmonious community of fellow citizens is lacking? This is apparently the dilemma of a postmodernist world, and I do not believe that it occurred to Stendhal. For him, the mediocrity embodied in pragmatism, which is everywhere contrasted with devoir, is best expressed by the banal prose of practicing lawyers. For us, all that appears to have survived is that baleful jargon.

There is no escape. Each of us must conceive of a story in which our own best-developed private persons may find some unironic expression in the public sphere.

Note

Unless otherwise indicated, quotations in English of Stendhal's *Le Rouge et le noir* (Paris, 1958 [1830]) are from *The Red and the Black*, trans. Catherine Slater (New York, 1991); quotations of Nietzsche's *Zur Genealogie der Moral*, Vol. 76 of *Sämtliche Werke* (Stuttgart, 1964), are from Walter Kaufmann's translation, and those of *Jenseits von Gut und Böse* (Aphorism 188), Vol. 76 of *Sämtliche Werke* (Stuttgart, 1964), are from Marianne Cowan's translation.

For related discussions, see my *When Lawyers Write* (Boston, 1987); *The Failure of the Word: The Protagonist as Lawyer in Modern Fiction* (New Haven, 1989 [1984]); "On the Use and Abuse of Nietzsche for Modern Constitutional Theory," in *Interpreting Law and Literature*, ed. S. Levinson and S. Mailloux (Chicago, 1988), 181–92; and "De Man Missing Nietzsche: *Hinzugedichtet* Revisited," in *Nietzsche as Postmodernist: Essays Pro and Contra*, ed. Clayton Koelb (Albany, 1990), 111–26.

Rey Chow

We Endure, Therefore We Are: Survival,
Governance, and Zhang Yimou's *To Live*

If there is a metanarrative that continues to
thrive in these times of metanarrative-bashing,
it is that of "resistance." Seldom do we attend a
conference or turn to an article in an academic
journal of the humanities or the social sciences
without encountering some call for "resistance"
to some such metanarrativized power as "global
capitalism," "Western imperialism," "patriarchy,"
"compulsory heterosexuality," and so forth. In
many respects, "resistance" has become the rhetorical support of identitarian politics, the conceptualization that underwrites the discourses of
class, racial, and sexual identity.[1] As an imaginary appealing especially to intellectuals, "resistance" would have to come from somewhere. It
follows that resistance is often lodged in something called "the people" or one of its variants,
such as "the masses," "the folk," or, at times, "the
subalterns." What is implicitly set up, then, is a
dichotomy between the pernicious power on top
and the innocent, suffering masses at the bottom, whose voices await being heard in what is
imagined as a corrective to the abuses of political power.

What is often missing in such an imaginary of

The *South Atlantic Quarterly* 95:4, Fall 1996.
Copyright © 1996 by Duke University Press.

popular resistance is the crucial notion of a mediating apparatus, a specifically defined public space, that would serve to regulate the relationship between those who have political power and those who do not. The *absence* of such a mediating apparatus has vast implications for the conceptualization of political governance. Here, I would like to explore some of these implications in terms of the ideological conditions in contemporary China, particularly as such conditions appear in Zhang Yimou's 1994 film *Huozhe (To Live).*[2]

In twentieth-century China, the figure of "the people" has likewise been invested with the value of political resistance.[3] The overthrow of the ancient, monarchical form of political power in 1911 was accompanied by theorizations of *min*—"the people"—and it was on the basis of three principles— the people's race/ethnicity, livelihood, and sovereignty—that they were henceforth to be governed. "The people" as such was figured in the naming of the new political order founded in 1912 by Sun Yat-sen—*Zhonghua minguo* (literally, "the Chinese people's state"). Even though the English translation of this name, "the Republic of China," does contain the idea of governance by the populace through the etymology of the word "republic," it does not highlight "the people" as prominently as the literal meaning of the Chinese phrase. (*Zhonghua minguo* is the name that continues to be used by the Taiwan government today.) In the decades subsequent to 1912, as the Chinese Communists gained control over the nation, the idea of "the people" was further defined in terms of the oppressed classes, in particular the rural peasants and the urban proletariat. Overturning the Confucian class hierarchy that had placed peasants and workers below scholars, the Chinese Communist conceptualization of society would put such subaltern classes at the very top, as the core of the new nation. In the era after 1949, when China proudly reestablished its status among the nations of the world, the collective rhetoric employed both inside and outside China was that the new China was a modern, *because* class-conscious, political state, a state founded on *popular resistance* to the feudalist corruption of the former elite classes of ancient China as well as to the imperialism and capitalism represented by the United States and Western Europe. The construction of national identity under communism, then, was firmly girded by "the people" and their "resistance," as the nation's new name,

Zhonghua renmin gongheguo—"The People's Republic of China"—still emphatically declares. As a means not of reflecting but of producing reality, the practice of naming extended far beyond the title of the new nation. As slogans such as *geming wuzui, zaofan youli* ("it is not criminal to make revolutions, it is right to rebel") became part of the everyday vocabulary during the frenzy of revolution, and as streets, hotels, hospitals, restaurants, department stores, and other public places acquired new appellations such as "Revolution," "People," "Friendship," "Struggle," "Proletariat," and their like, human relations, too, were being reformed through renaming. Titles based on the traditional kinship system (with its complex hierarchical differentiations) gave way to the nondifferentiating "comrade," a form of address that announced the egalitarian basis of Chinese social relations.

Since the Cultural Revolution (mid-1960s to mid-1970s), the ideals of the Communist revolution have been challenged and, in many cases, abandoned.[4] However, even as Chinese intellectuals have come to realize, in disillusionment, that revolution and dictatorship are part of the same power structure, they have nonetheless continued to be fascinated by that entity called "the people." In the writings and films of the post–Cultural Revolution period, "the people" have once again become a site of utopian interest, a site to which writers and filmmakers repeatedly turn for inspiration. We think of the stories of Bai Hua, Mo Yan, Su Tong, Ah Cheng, Han Shaogong, Gao Xiaosheng, and Chen Zhongshi, among other authors, while contemporary films with rural, folkish, and popular themes by such directors as Wu Tianming, Chen Kaige, Tian Zhuangzhuang, Zhang Nuanxin, Xie Jin, and Xie Fei are known even to audiences who are not otherwise acquainted with contemporary China.[5]

In many of the fictional representations by these writers and filmmakers, the turn to "the people" is accompanied by the portrayal of suffering. Following their literary and filmic predecessors in their frequent recourse to melodrama and sentimentalism, contemporary Chinese writers and filmmakers explore suffering as an alternative political language, thus giving their works the appearance of affirming "individual rights and freedoms against totalitarianism."[6] But if this apparent interest in individual rights and freedoms is future-oriented and forward-looking, it is also nostalgic. In their discontent with current circumstances, Chinese intellectuals seem to be seeking in the "ordinary folk" a source of knowledge that has remained uncorrupted by the lies and errors perpetrated in the decades of bureaucratized revolution. Inscribed in representations of China's remote areas and often illiterate populations, the search for such uncorrupted knowledge stems from a wish, in the post–Cultural Revolution period, for enlightenment through what is considered "primitive" and "originary." In terms of a shared political culture, therefore, this unmistakable nostalgia is not simply nostalgia for "the people" as such; it is also nostalgia for the *ideals* of popular resistance that once inspired political revolution. The continued fascination with "the people" suggests an attempt to cling to the beliefs that lay at the foundation of modern Chinese national identity. Yet precisely because the turn to "the people" is nostalgic as much as utopic— a desire for home as much as for change—it inevitably reencounters all the problems that are fundamental to that turn.

For instance, the invocation of "the people" in modern China has often gone hand in hand with another invocation—"the West." During the Great Leap Forward, the rhetoric of *chao ying gan mei* (literally, "overtaking England and catching up with the United States") was used to mobilize the entire country to labor hard for national self-strengthening.[7] Specifically, England and the United States stood for technological advancement, an area in which China needed to improve. Acknowledging the necessity of "Western technology," however, undermined belief in "the Chinese people" as the ultimate source of national empowerment in a fundamental way. For if China did in fact need *external* input in order to attain the status of a world-class nation, then what did that make "the people," the supposed mainstay of national identity? To solve the problem raised by this inconsistency, the Chinese Communists have resorted—in spite of their claims of overthrowing tradition—to a formulation that has been used by Chinese politicians since the nineteenth century: "Let us adopt science and technology from the West, but let us preserve Chinese culture"; "let us modernize, but let us modernize with Chinese characteristics"; "let us adopt capitalism, but we will call it Chinese socialist capitalism." Such variations on the nineteenth-century dictum *zhong xue wei ti, xi xue wei yong* ("Chinese learning for fundamental principle, Western learning for practical use") point to an ambivalence that structures the conceptualizing of a political culture based on an unmediated notion of popular resistance.

In such conceptualizing, "the people" become a fantastical stand-in for national specificity—in this case, for what is "Chinese." On the one hand, this thing that is "the Chinese"—their people, their culture, their value—

is thought to be unique and self-sufficient; on the other hand, it is in need of preservation and protection from outside forces. "The Chinese"—people/culture/value—is what makes China China—that is, what no one can change or take away; at the same time, "the Chinese" is what "the West" can endanger—that is, what someone *can* change and take away. Caught between cultural pride and cultural necessity, the investment in national and cultural specificity as the basis of political identity is marked by an impossible rift from the beginning. To patch over this rift, a particular kind of *essentialism* has to be introduced, one which often takes stunningly provocative forms, demonstrating the logic of a well-lived, though tattered, ideology.

Consider the People's Republic's notorious manner of handling human rights. Here, China's foremost problem of governance, overpopulation, is approached not as a problem that can and should be solved gradually, but rather as an immutable fact—an immutable fact that is, moreover, cast in the form of an *essential lack*, the (potential) lack of food. Such, then, is the attitude of the Chinese authorities: it is inconceivable that the West tell China what to do on the issue of human rights because *human rights in China* simply means having enough to eat. Since the People's Republic has done more than any previous Chinese government to feed the Chinese people, it is already honoring human rights *in the Chinese way*. Human rights as insisted upon by Westerners—in the form of, say, freedom of speech and trial by law—amounts to foreign interference in Chinese *internal* affairs. China—in the position of a victim—must resist such imposition, invasion, and so forth.

Instead of being used as an occasion to rethink the fraught relationship between the governing and the governed, the problem of overpopulation becomes a justification for the abuse of political power, an excuse to stop, rather than to begin, any consideration of alternative forms of governance. What is interesting is that such a justification for the abuse of political power must be aimed at an external target. In the world of postcolonial awareness, the intransigent attitude of the Chinese gerontocracy toward political governance conveniently finds its guise in the form of national self-determination against "the West."

A number of important implications are revealed in this process, all following from the fantastical construct of a "self-sufficient" China/Chineseness that can and must govern itself. First, this need for self-governance

is defined, paradoxically, by way of an essential lack—the lack of food—
and thus as a matter of biological survival: the need for self-sustenance.
Although China's long periods of starvation in the past might have had
much to do with government policy and with the unequal distribution of
food among different classes, history is bypassed in favor of an essentialist
survivalism. Second, as the reduction of human rights to a matter of having
enough to eat indicates, issues of political representation can be likewise
reduced to—and abstracted as—something potentially lacking/missing.
Accordingly, while it is this potentially lacking/missing thing that defines
China's uniqueness, that makes China China, "the people" are in effect
just a bunch of gaping mouths and, as such, are precluded from having
political representation. In the vicious circle of "political rights"–cum-
biological needs, "the people" are literally held hostage by themselves—
by their "essential need" to survive. Instead of being recognized as something done to or against "the people," the denial of political rights will thus
always be *condoned* in their best interests. Third, the continual abuse of
power, secured as it is by the structure of this vicious circle, can legitimate
and perpetuate itself on the grounds of "Chinese" internal affairs. Cultural
and national identity, which is the crux of the relationship between the
governing and the governed, is then simply a matter of cumulation, com-
pounded by acts of essentializing, acts of absorbing and assimilating every
problem inward—into the entrails of the physical body, into the interior of
the nation, into the systemic propriety of the culture—and redefining it as
"Chinese."

The people, popular resistance, and the relationship between such resistance and political governance are among the issues Zhang Yimou examines in his film *To Live*. Based loosely on the novella of the same title by
the contemporary mainland author Yu Hua, *To Live* is, on first reading and
viewing, very much a story of its time.[8] Like many examples of fiction and
film produced since the mid-1970s, *To Live* looks *back* to events of the past
through a look *at* some ordinary people—the Xu family—whose saga runs
from the late 1940s to the 1970s (the period after the peak of the Cultural
Revolution).

The film begins in a gambling house. Xu Fugui, the only son of a well-off
family, is already heavily in debt, as recorded in a log kept by the dealers.

Refusing to pay heed to the advice of his parents and his pregnant wife, Fugui squanders the family fortune, including the ancestral home which is sheltering them. Having thus lost his house, his father (who dies after signing the house away), and his wife (Jiazhen, who, in despair, has left with their daughter and gone to her own family), Fugui is reduced to making ends meet by selling the few possessions he still owns. Many months pass before Jiazhen returns with their daughter, Fengxia, and a newborn son, Youqing. With the help of Long'er, the man who took over his ancestral home, Fugui begins a new career as a singer and player in a shadow-puppet theater, making his living by performing with a troupe. He and Jiazhen go through a series of epochal events—the Civil War between the Nationalists and the Communists, the Communist Liberation of China, the Great Leap Forward, the Cultural Revolution—and lose both their children in the process. At the end, four members of the family survive—Fugui, Jiazhen, their son-in-law (Wan Erxi), and their grandson (Mantou/Little Bun).[9] By this point, conditions in China are seemingly improving.

At one level, the ability "to live" can undoubtedly be understood as the basic resistance of the common people to the random disasters befalling them under a political system that has failed in its mission. However modest, the plea for the condition of "living" serves in this instance as a metacriticism, a critique of the critical imperatives of the political regime, which was itself founded on the ideas and ideals of resistance and struggle. Because this political regime has resorted time and again to violence and murder in order to realize its dreams, and has replicated the authoritarianism it once sought to resist, the film's sympathetic portrayal of "living" is made in the spirit of a resistance to bureaucratized resistance, a struggle against the state-sponsored struggle of official rhetoric. To be able to live through—and *in spite of*—disasters should in this light be seen as a "back to basics" approach in what I have elsewhere called the post-catastrophic discourse of contemporary China.[10] After the grandiose messages of revolution, for which millions of lives have been lost in the name of salvation, it is as if the sheer possibility of simply living has become cause enough for celebration and respect. The commonplace "to live," then, has the same nostalgic function as the figure of "the people" in that it, too, asserts the value of a return to something fundamental. Having lived through years of war, poverty, separation, illness, fatal accidents, and the loss of loved ones, ordinary people now prefer to occupy themselves with the mundane and the banal—such as eating, for instance. The film concludes with the survivors of the family's three generations gathering for yet another meal.

———————

As in Zhang's other films, the shift in the medium of representation— from literary writing to film—offers a significant clue to his reading of the "original" subject matter. The major change introduced by Zhang is the elimination of Yu Hua's first-person narration.[11] Hence, while our understanding of the events in the novella relies on Fugui's memory and narration, in the film Fugui becomes simply one among many characters. From the perspective of reception, the effect is that of a shift from a single voice which predominates and guides (the reading) to multiple characters, events, and discourses. This shift, though perhaps a technicality, is crucial nonetheless because it introduces a departure from the ideological implications of the novella. Yu Hua's literary style, which uses simple, matter-of-fact prose, presents the past in the form of what is already past. With Fugui as the only survivor in (and of) his own tale, the feeling of closure, of a story and a history having been completed and come to an end, is put across with the certainty of a retrospective—"it all happened this way." Zhang's film, by contrast, forgoes the relative stability of a kind of writing based on the remembrance of things past. By abandoning the nostalgic perspective of a sole surviving narrator, Zhang opens up the narrative in terms of temporality—"it is still going on; it is to be continued." What is perhaps foreclosed in the retrospective narration of Yu Hua's novella is conversely supplemented by the story's unfolding on the screen, the presentness of which transforms the significations of "living," of what it means "to live."

Moreover, by eliminating the story's monological narration, the film enables the interactions among the characters to surface much more readily, and it is through such interactions, which can no longer be attributed or confined to the understanding of a single character, that a very different kind of narrating unravels alongside the realistic one. To be sure, Zhang, like all good popular artists who understand the importance of popular appeal, does make ample use of the current interest in the lives of "common people" to tell a moving and entertaining story on the screen with the full coherence of illusionism.[12] But he has also done something more: by taking seriously the Chinese Communist dictum of paying attention to "the people," Zhang has produced a film which literally takes a long, hard look at "the people," one that reveals them as sentimental, loving, and filial, but also as petty, small-minded, and, above all, *ready to sacrifice others in order to protect themselves.* Unlike the Party officials and the many Chinese intellectuals who continue to idealize "the people" by invoking them poetically as the bearers of revolution, resistance, and hope, Zhang gives us an unglorified portrait of the people—not exactly as the embodiment of evil but, more disturbingly, as a host for the problems that have beset China's construction of its "national" identity through political governance. If Zhang's film is a critique of the ideology of the Chinese regime, as I believe it is, it is a critique that materializes by reinforcing the critical terms legitimized by that regime—"the people" and their "resistance"—to the hilt.

In a cultural context in which food occupies such a central physical and imaginary place, what better way to look hard at "the people" than through the event of eating, an event which is fully resonant with the theme "to live"? Zhang's handling of eating is, as I will argue, nothing less than extraordinary. In Yu Hua's novella, food is central to the narrative action in that it serves to propel the plot, deepen characterization, and intensify conflict. Among the novella's most memorable scenes are those depicting starvation and the search for edible things in the countryside.[13] In Zhang's film, however, food takes on a drastically different set of connotations. While he never neglects the physical appeal of food—as what fills the stomach—Zhang also *desentimentalizes* the representation of food as a fundamental lack. Instead of using food—or its absence—as a means of mobilizing the narrative action, Zhang represents it as an indigestible detail—as what does not quite go "in," what does not get eaten with satisfaction. Remaining thus in a relation of *exteriority* to the human bodies that are supposedly its "end," food is decoupled from the essentialist survivalism to which it has always been attached and becomes an occasion for the staging of another kind of consumption—the consumption of political oppression. In the following three examples, food assumes not so much the form of a substance to be ingested as the form of the leftover, the absurd, or the weapon.

Jiaozi (Meat-Filled Dumplings). One morning, Youqing is abruptly awakened from a deep sleep and forced to go to school—his classmates have come by on their way to remind his parents that all students are expected to show up early to learn about steelmaking. Having just brought home their family's share of jiaozi from the town as a reward for their hard work,

Jiazhen proceeds to prepare a lunchbox for her son, making sure that he has plenty of the mouth-watering dumplings. That same day, Youqing is killed in an accident. Still tired, he has fallen asleep against a wall; when a vehicle crashes into the other side of the wall, it collapses on the little boy. Youqing never has a chance to open his lunchbox. When we see the jiaozi again, they have been left cold and untouched, their culinary appeal completely superseded by the grief at Youqing's graveside, a place where food is traditionally displayed as a way of paying one's respects to the dead.

Mantou (Steamed Wheat Buns). Fengxia gives birth to her son in a hospital the management of which has been assumed by the youthful Red Guards, who are as contemptuous of the older and more experienced medical doctors, whom they consider "reactionaries," as they are complacent about their own ability to handle medical emergencies. Such attitudes quickly change with the onset of Fengxia's postpartum hemorrhaging. Earlier, hoping to ensure a safe delivery, the Xu family had gone against hospital rules and brought in a top gynecologist, Professor Wang, pulling him from a procession in which he and other intellectuals were being paraded as symbols of "feudalist corruption." But Professor Wang has not eaten for three days. When he is offered some mantou, he gorges himself so hastily that he becomes almost comatose—a condition aggravated by the water he is then given by those who are trying to help. In the absence of any medical intervention, Fengxia bleeds to death.

Already, in these two brief examples, the handling of food suggests that eating is something other than "filling the stomach." What is normally welcome is in both cases associated with the sacrifice of innocent children. Would Youqing have died if his parents had not forced him to go to school early in conformity with others? The meat-filled dumplings, a rare treat during the days of the Great Leap Forward, become in the end *leftovers*—the waste of ideological abuse, undoubtedly prepared with parental love and patriotic loyalty, which find their ultimate victim in the young child. The most familiar and familial items of consumption—jiaozi being best when homemade and always served during festivities—here take on a defamiliarized and defamiliarizing relation to what they normally signify. Rather than being eaten and absorbed, the lumps of dough and meat now stand as reminders of a life that has been irrecuperably wasted.

Similarly, would Fengxia have died if intellectuals and skilled professionals such as Professor Wang had not been mindlessly abused during the madness of the Cultural Revolution? The mantou, meant to ease Professor Wang's hunger so that he can assist in the childbirth, rehydrate and expand within his starvation-shrunken stomach. Failing thus to be properly incorporated, the mantou indirectly kill Fengxia. However well-intentioned, "filling the stomach" in this case leads to death, with food emphatically marked by the errors and terrors of history. Toward the end of the film, as the Xu family visits the graves of both children, Fugui reflects on the past, lamenting the fact that he had given Professor Wang too many mantou—otherwise, he says, the professor could have saved Fengxia's life. Or else, he adds, it was the water that they should not have given him. Fugui even supplies a mathematical elaboration: "People say that once you drink water, one mantou in the stomach turns into seven. Professor Wang ate seven mantou. Seven times seven is forty-nine. That'd knock anyone out of action!" When they learn that Professor Wang has since then avoided anything made from wheat, eating only rice, which is more expensive, Jiazhen exclaims—in what comes across as an utterly bizarre conclusion to this tale of epochal crisis and sorrow—"What a food bill he must have every month!"

Statements such as Fugui's and Jiazhen's seem absurd not because they reduce great suffering to mathematics and economics, but because such reductions confront us with a stark discontinuity in emotional experience. From anticipating the birth of a grandchild with both anxiety and hope to witnessing the death of one's child, then mourning, followed by a return to "normal" life, and finally the ritualized family visit to and conversation at the grave—the changes and reversals of emotional intensity that occur around food play off one another in such a way as to reveal what—for the lack of a better term—must be called a dialectic, whereby moments of poignancy swing between a tone of sentimental vulnerability, on the one hand, and of absurdist irony, on the other. There is no tragic moment, as a result, that does not simultaneously border on the comic and the ridiculous, or vice versa.

Noodles. Of all the moments related to eating, the most compelling one is a scene which features Youqing during the Great Leap Forward period. Fengxia, as we learn earlier in the film, became deaf and mute after a childhood fever. She is the object of ridicule among the town schoolboys, who mock her with malicious tricks such as shooting at her behind with a sling-shot and then waiting in hiding for her response. Incensed by such abusive behavior, little Youqing has attempted to protect his older sister. One day when the families in the town gather for a meal in the communal dining hall, Youqing gets himself a big bowl of noodles laced with hot chili sauce and walks up to the boy who leads his gang in abusing Fengxia. Climbing up on a chair behind the boy, who is busily eating, Youqing raises the bowl and, in a gesture that resembles the offering of a sacrament, pours the noodles and sauce over his enemy's head. Outraged, the boy bursts into tears, while his father quickly calls the crowd's attention to the Xu family. Fugui, greatly embarrassed by Youqing's incomprehensible behavior, scolds his son, demanding that he apologize. When Youqing refuses, Fugui grabs him, spanking him until Jiazhen and others separate them. Only later, when they are alone at home and Jiazhen has explained the background to Youqing's act, does Fugui realize that he has wronged his son.

This scene of collective food-sharing comments provocatively on two distinct forms of *political* behavior. What is the difference between Youqing's act and Fugui's act? One is an attempt, albeit childish, to demand social justice for a person who cannot speak for herself. The other is a public punishment of a child by an adult who succumbs to crowd pressure. Because solidarity between father and son would threaten the father's status, he must distance himself from his son by punishing him. At the same time, though, this face-saving act of distancing also reestablishes and reaffirms the father's linkage with—his possession of and authority over—his child. In terms of food, we could say that whereas Youqing goes without food in order to use it as a weapon of "disorderly conduct," Fugui attempts to restore order so that the group, including himself and his family, can resume eating.

Implicitly patriarchal, Fugui's act is typical of a certain attitude toward the community. The fear of ostracization means that the process of socialization—of learning to live with others—is one of punishment and discipline, and such punishment and discipline invariably entail sacrificing the minor, the innocent, the oppressed. The more unreasonable the community, the more relentless it will be in sacrificing such underclasses. Hence, the measures taken by Fugui *against* Youqing are intended less to discipline the child than to identify with the community—to demonstrate Fugui's own worth within the community. Sacrificing the minor, the innocent, or the oppressed in exchange for the acceptance of the community ultimately constitutes an act of *self*-empowerment and *self*-governance.

═══════

The close links between sacrifice and socialization raise questions about the way "the public" is conceived and, accordingly, the way governance is practiced and mobilized. Like "the people," "the public" is, theoretically, an empty space, a space to be manipulated. In the political culture of a nation such as China, which is governed by "strong men" rather than through the mediation of law, and where, as one critic puts it, the political machine "serves at the same time as a judicial apparatus," "the public" becomes simply a space for the use of those who hold political power.[14] For the ordinary person afraid for his own life, then, "the public" functions much more as a space in which to submit to authority and to hide oneself than as an arena in which to speak out against injustice and to propose political alternatives. As modern Chinese history has demonstrated time and again, those who dare to tell the truth are more often than not sacrificed.[15] The vigilance of "the public" is wholly aimed at *conformity and invisibility*, not dissent and intervention.

This requisite conformity and invisibility has prevailed to such a degree that even an event as revolutionary as the appearance of the Red Guards in the "public space" during the 1960s amounted to just another version of the oppression and persecution of the innocent. Conceived of as a groundbreaking intervention in China's tradition, the Red Guards were supposedly the opposite of the patriarchal social order. Behind their mobilization was an uncompromised idealism: let our children, our oppressed classes speak up; let them overthrow corrupt forms of power; let them tell us what to do; let them create a new social space! And yet at the same time, the fundamental conceptualization of "the public" went unchallenged, so the fervor of the Red Guards simply degenerated into the very same self-righteous abuse of political power that had characterized their elders.

This conception of "the public" as a space in which to conform with the powerful is recognizably different from that to which those living in the West are accustomed. In the West, the public is arguably also a space of governance—but with a significant difference. With the mediation of law, "the public" functions in the latter context as a constraint on those who exercise power, subjecting them to scrutiny and holding them accountable.

What this means is that the space of the public is no longer at the disposal of only those with political power; it is also where multiple discourses, reflecting vastly divergent, at times opposing, perspectives, achieve legitimacy solely through a continual competition for power. Any attempt to manipulate the public space in an authoritarian fashion will simply have too many hurdles to overcome and will thus be much less likely to achieve any extended dominance.[16]

Time and again, the West's habituation to this legally bound "public" has blinded it to China's alternative conception. During the Tiananmen Massacre of June 1989, for instance, even as the West was imagining that its intense gaze would check the Chinese authorities' display of authoritarianism, these authorities were reacting in exactly the opposite manner. They reacted as if they had been provoked into action in a public space where their authority had been challenged and needed to be reestablished. Thus it was precisely the West's attention, aimed at discouraging militaristic violence, that helped to generate this violence. The Chinese authorities had to prove that they, proprietors of their own political power, were in control of the public space, and they did so by slaughtering their own "children."[17]

In this regard, the scene in which the father publicly punishes the son in *To Live* can be read as a miniaturized rerendering of that dramatic punishing scene watched by the entire world in June 1989. In both situations, demands for social justice lead to protests and demonstrations, which in turn catch the attention of a crowd. Like Fugui under the pressure of public attention, the Chinese authorities reacted by striking out at the children who had embarrassed them, crushing them with tanks and gunfire. To this day, these acts of violence continue to be justified in terms of sustaining peace and prosperity—that is, of restoring "social" order.

These conflicting views of the public and of governance are replayed every time an outspoken person emerges to criticize the political regime in Beijing. Fang Lizhi, Wei Jingsheng, Martin Lee, Szeto Wah, Christine Loh, Emily Lau, and Harry Wu are just a few who come to mind.[18] In order to do what they seek to do, which is to bring about democracy in territories under (or soon to be under) Chinese rule, these radicals must act as though they were ignorant of the concept of the public that is implicit in that rule. In doing so, they have time and again provoked the Chinese authorities' profound anger. What is maddening to these authorities is not merely what the radicals say in their speeches and writings about China's various acts of social injustice, but also the defiant, "uncouth" manner in which they voice their criticisms in public. When that public is international, their "misbehavior" becomes unpardonable. In keeping with the circular reasoning of their essentialist governing ideology, the Chinese authorities typically handle such defiance by turning the radicals into outcasts, through criminalization and imprisonment or through deportation and ostracization. Often, such "outcasting" is put in explicitly nationalistic and ethnic terms, with troublemakers accordingly labeled "traitors" who have betrayed China to the "foreigners," the "Western imperialists."[19]

With its overtones of absurdity and sentimentalism, the scene in which Fugui spanks his son in submission to the pressuring public gaze is hence emblematic of the predicament of governance in Chinese political culture. Such governance is driven by a public sphere that, unable to serve as the site for a potentially autonomous opposition, readily collapses into a mechanism for coercion by brute force. Without the effective intervention of a restraining legal apparatus, this public space requires the individual to assume a subordinate position vis-à-vis "public opinion," a position enforced by discipline and punishment. The patriarchal implications of such subordination include the fact that its enforcement will always be aimed at the powerless, who must always be disciplined and punished regardless of the grounds on which their discontent is voiced. The governing–governed relationship in this context becomes tripartite: governance is enforced not only by soliciting the governed to serve the arbitrary and brutal interests of the *public*, but also by manipulating them into willingly sacrificing those who are disadvantaged—in the name of the *public good*. In turn, these disadvantaged members of the public may internalize such governance as *self*-governance—by either becoming as violent as their governors (if they succeed in procuring power for themselves) or submissively enduring violence to themselves (if they remain "ordinary citizens"). Since the majority of society must remain "ordinary citizens," governance means, ultimately, the dissemination of a political culture in which people are always prepared to tolerate violence and to accommodate further violence. It is under such patterns of governance and self-governance that "endurance" excels as the foremost moral virtue in the struggle "to live." Perhaps nowhere is the violence that goes into the making of this virtue more evident than

in the Chinese character for "endurance"—*ren*—which is composed of a
"knife" above the "heart."

———

Technically, how can a critique of an abstract quality such as "endurance"
be made on the movie screen? With his usual penchant for understanding
what works in the medium of film, Zhang added a series of events which
are not found in Yu Hua's novella. This "supplement" not only contributes
to the spectacular cinematic visuality that is a hallmark of all of Zhang's
films, but also exemplarily allegorizes the contradictions inherent to the
people's "survival."

Near the beginning of the film, after Fugui has reduced his family to
poverty, he goes to Long'er for help. Having won the Xu family's ancestral
home that Fugui gambled away, Long'er refuses to lend him any money,
but instead offers him the loan of a box containing some bric-a-brac from
the past—a set of shadow puppets.[20] From then on, Fugui, who, in an
earlier scene, showed off his singing talent in the gambling house, will
make his living by singing with a traveling troupe of puppeteers.

During one performance near the end of the Civil War, Fugui and his fellow performers are conscripted into the Nationalist army by force. Because
the puppets are on loan from Long'er, Fugui insists on lugging them along
in their heavy box. When the Nationalists are defeated by the Communists,
Fugui, like many others, becomes a prisoner of war only to discover that his
burdensome puppets have suddenly become a treasure: accidentally picked
up by the bayonet of a Communist soldier, the figures, dazzling against the
sun, provide a means of entertainment for the troops. In performing for
the soldiers and giving them some relief from the dull wartime conditions,
Fugui becomes a minor hero and is awarded a certificate for having served
the People's Liberation Army. When he is finally able to return home, this
certificate provides proof that he and his family are "exemplary" citizens at
a time when others, especially landowners, are being hounded. (Long'er,
for instance, is dragged off to be executed before Fugui's eyes.)

Then, during the Great Leap Forward, when every household's iron is
confiscated for smelting as part of the national self-strengthening effort,
Fugui's puppets are, once again, threatened. But just as they are about to
be confiscated, Jiazhen makes a suggestion to the town chief: Why not
use the puppets to entertain the workers? Fugui's livelihood is thus sal-

vaged a second time. Finally, during the Cultural Revolution, when relics of the past become dangerous to own because of their association with a "corrupt" ideology, Fugui is advised to burn his puppets before they are discovered. Even then, the wooden box in which the puppets had been stored is transformed into something useful: a nest for the chicks to be raised by Fugui's grandson. What he had once told Youqing, Fugui now tells Mantou: When the chicks grow big, they will turn into geese; when the geese get big enough, they will turn into lambs; when the lambs have grown, they will turn into oxen. . . . As life gets better and better, the little boy will no longer ride on the back of an ox but on trains and airplanes.

As a means of making a living, the shadow puppets are richly suggestive of the complex significance of "the people" and "popular resistance." The puppet theater is, first and foremost, a practice of the past—an art form associated with premodern China. Yet in spite of its anachronism, the puppet theater is a resilient cultural mode that continues to be performed in various regions where it is associated with local folk traditions. In terms of the pedagogical mission of the political regime, it is precisely such relics as the shadow-puppet theater that interest Chinese Communist historians, for they are part of the "popular material culture" that constitutes the new conceptualization of revolutionary China. Furthermore, as a symbol of the people's tradition, the puppets in To Live endure, surviving one disaster after another. Even after they are finally destroyed, the box which once held them survives and nurtures new life. Are these puppets not the best testament to the common people's will to live? Instead of merely affirming this, Zhang's film makes us reflect on the nature of endurance itself: What exactly is "endurance," and what does it tell us about the way China is governed?

Like the puppets, the characters in the film show a remarkable ability to persist through trying circumstances. Not only do they adapt to the physical hardships of life, but they seem equally capable of accommodating themselves to the ideological manipulations of the state. Once wealthy landowners, the Xu family adjusts to the low status of "poor townsfolk," settling in and deliberately conforming with every move they make. In an early episode, for instance, Fugui and Jiazhen learn from the town chief that Long'er, the new owner of their ancestral home, refused to surrender the house to the authorities and instead burned it down in an act of "counterrevolutionary sabotage." Fugui's first reaction is one of shock at the destruction—after all, all that sturdy timber used to belong to the Xus. But, remembering that he is in public, he quickly adds that it is not their timber but "counterrevolutionary timber." Jiazhen gets the message immediately: "Yes," she echoes, "it's counterrevolutionary timber." In another episode, as the family sits down for a meal, Erxi, the son-in-law, mentions that their old friend Chunsheng, who had been an important cadre member, has been arrested and is in the process of being purged, so they should keep their distance (*hua qing jie xian*—literally, "draw a clear line") from him. Once again, Fugui readily acquiesces, glancing anxiously at the picture of Chairman Mao that was Chunsheng's wedding present to his daughter.

Such small incidents, comments, and details, which pass almost unnoticed because they are such a "natural" part of the story, cumulatively amount to an alternative reading of "the common people." This reading does not celebrate the common people's ability to live—to adapt to and endure harsh circumstances—as an unequivocal virtue; rather, it problematizes it as China's most enduring *ideology*.[21] In Zhang's film, the conventional notion of endurance as a strength is not simply reproduced but consciously staged, and it is through such staging, such dramatization or melo-dramatization, that a crucial fantasy which props up "China"— whether as a culture, a nation, a family, or a common person—is revealed. "We, the Chinese, are the oldest culture, the oldest people in the world," this fantasy says. "The trick of our success is the ability to stick it out— to absorb every external difficulty into ourselves, to incorporate even our enemies into our culture. We endure, therefore we are."

Like the structure of all powerful ideologies, endurance–cum–identity works tautologically: the ability to endure is what enables one to live, but in order to endure one must stay alive. "To endure" and "to live" thus become two points of a circular pattern of thinking which reinforce each other by serving as each other's condition of possibility. In accordance with this circular, tautological reasoning, the imperative "to live" through endurance becomes what *essentially* defines and perpetuates "China." As such, it operates as a shield in two senses: "Living" protects China from destruction at the same time that it prevents China from coming to terms with reality. That is, "China"—preoccupied exclusively with its own survival—is *in reality* its own worst enemy because that preoccupation is precisely what has led China's political history, with all its catastrophes, to be repeated ad infinitum.

The best demonstration of this self-perpetuating ideology of endurance and survival in *To Live* is none other than the shadow puppets, whose capacity for survival becomes most evident, ironically, in their destruction. For if, as the town chief points out, the stories performed by the puppet theater are all "classic feudal types"—all about *dihuang jiangxiang, caizi jiaren* ("emperors, kings, generals, ministers, scholars, and beauties")— and that is why the puppets must be burned, then isn't the fascination with such stories reproduced in the very act of burning, which is, after all, an act performed in filial worship of Mao Zedong (as an "emperor") and in mindless obedience to the Party and the Revolution? Although the puppets are destroyed on account of their feudalist ideological import, *feudalist ideology itself is kept alive in the very event that seeks to extinguish it.* Moreover, tradition, now an empty box, nonetheless continues "to live" by supporting new life—both the grandson and his chicks. And, this new life is imagined in the form of a fantastic, progressive *telos*—from chickens to geese, to lambs, to oxen, even to trains and airplanes—of a life that keeps getting "better and better" without ever getting any better at all.[22]

By abandoning the singular perspective of one character and by foregrounding interactions among different characters over such additional, apparently "technical" elements as the shadow-puppet theater, Zhang enables a radically nonconforming view of endurance and survival to emerge. His approach is, strictly speaking, an *ethical* one insofar as it is an approach to the *ethos*—the way of life of a group of people—in this case "the Chinese." Ethics in this sense is not the abstract moral/philosophical sphere of Western modernity but the structure, dynamics, and values of social life in a specific community. More than any of Zhang's other films, *To Live* focuses on social practices in the context of the Chinese ethos, elaborating—as it exposes—China's "national" ideology. Through this most accessible, chronological narrative of the lives of "common people," Zhang raises the most profound political question: How is China governed, managed, and fantasized as a collective? The answer proposed by his film is equally profound, and remarkable: China is governed, managed, and fantasized as a collective by the self-fulfilling, self-perpetuating ideology of endurance and survival—of an ethical insistence on staying alive at all costs. And yet, such an insistence, despite its nobility, is not *ethical* enough, for it can be and frequently has been co-opted by precisely the forces it seeks to resist. The ideology of endurance and survival has been so thoroughly and "naturally" incorporated into "the imaginary relation" between the Chinese and their real living conditions that the government can blatantly disregard human rights in the name of human rights,[23] since, after all, "human rights" means "having enough to eat," and China's food supply is an essentially "internal affair." When any intervention in China's handling of this crucial issue can be successfully dismissed as "Western imperialism"—yet another external threat to be endured and survived by the Chinese—a time-honored form of governance remains in full force.

If my reading of this fundamental critique of Chinese society in Zhang's film is at all tenable, then it should not be surprising that a saga with so many heart-rending episodes would also have many funny and farcical, indeed absurd, moments. If a film can be said to have an affect, that of *To Live* can only be described as the affect of excess. This excess stems from the criss-crossing of various modes of emotional intensity: melodrama and sentimentalism (with many tear-jerking interludes), comedy (with belly laughs at unexpected moments), and scenes that provoke other strong feelings (such as those generated by the wonderfully performed intimate relations among the various family members). But the affect of excess also points to the presence of an otherness, a chord of emotional dissonance struck from within the realistic narrative that neither tragedy, farce, nor familial bonding manages to muffle.

This emotional dissonance is the result of a narrative structure that alludes to the possibility of an alternative reading as it unfolds, so that the experience of "seeing" the film becomes one of virtually looking at a hologram. While there is undoubtedly a cohesive frame of reference, which allows us to follow the story, there is at the same time another configuration that is equally present on the surface, waiting to be seen. What is crucial is that the recognition of this other configuration inevitably disrupts, destabilizes, and distorts the more obvious one, although we can choose to "see" only that one and to ignore the other. Coming from a director who has lived for decades in a totalitarian state where the authorities continue to obstruct his work,[24] this holographic mode of storytelling is, we may surmise, a tactic for smuggling subversive messages past censors. As I have already mentioned, such subversive smuggling is often achieved by means of passing incidents, comments, and details.

It is achieved by means of minor characters as well. For instance, little Youqing, who disappears halfway through the film, subverts the predominant message of survivalist endurance more than once. After being wrongly punished in the communal dining hall, Youqing decides to play a practical joke on his father, at the suggestion of his mother. During one of Fugui's performances, Youqing serves his father a bowl of tea—laced with large amounts of vinegar and chili sauce. Drinking the tea unawares, Fugui chokes and spits it out, splashing the puppet theater screen and making everyone laugh. In a scene filled with the most infectious feelings of warmth and fun, thus, the son's mischievous act—another spin-off of the idea of unincorporable food—provokes the father into a momentary "revolt." A person who usually "swallows" everything, Fugui finally acts in a way that is, in terms of the ideological structure of the story, the opposite of endurance.

The other character in Zhang's film besides Youqing who represents the possibility of an alternative behavioral code is Chunsheng. As Fugui's sidekick in the gambling house and the traveling puppeteer troupe, then during the Civil War, Chunsheng is kept in the role of a character on the side, a character who, unlike Fugui, is not central to the story. He sometimes strikes us as a bit crazy, such as when he claims—on a battlefield covered with corpses—that he wants to drive a car so much he would gladly die for that experience. Years later, Chunsheng unexpectedly reappears as the district chief who has accidentally killed Youqing, and whom the Xu family (Jiazhen, in particular) refuses to forgive. As a result, Chunsheng is relegated to the position of a suspect outsider. On important occasions, such as Fengxia's wedding, he is neither formally invited to join the celebration nor served tea as a guest in the house.

During the Cultural Revolution, like many officials of standing, Chunsheng is tried and persecuted as a "capitalist running dog." One night, after his wife has apparently committed suicide, he comes to see Fugui and confesses in despair, "I don't want to live any more!" As Chunsheng bids him farewell, Fugui urges him to be strong and to go on living. For the first time since Youqing's death, Jiazhen softens and asks Chunsheng to come into the house. She reminds him that he owes their family a life, a debt that endows his own life with value. Chunsheng, however, neither agrees nor disagrees. Although we hear the admonition "to live" loud and clear, Zhang's film leaves it unclear as to whether Chunsheng will accede to this imperative. His disappearance into the dim light at the end of the street, an image of melancholic uncertainty, marks a departure from co-erced survival at all costs.

As someone who even considers refusing to endure, "to live," Chun-sheng can be linked to some of Zhang's most defiant characters, such as the peasant woman, Judou, in *Judou* and the maid, Yan'er, in *Raise the Red Lantern*. In terms of the ideological structure of *To Live*, Chunsheng's walking away introduces a distance, a chasm, within the picture of a con-tinuous collective "living" and offers a glimpse of the possibility of an alternative to China's governance and political culture. It is, however, no more than a glimpse. The working out of the implications of this barely glimpsed alternative would have to be a long-term intellectual, political, and ethical project.

Notes

1 John Guillory has offered a thorough critique of the assumptions and consequences of the use, currently in vogue in the U.S. academy, of identity politics in debates about literary canon formation. Guillory argues that, in assuming a certain transparency be-tween "identities" and "works," those who reduce problems of the canon to excluded social identities tend to neglect the issues of access to literacy, the means of production of what he calls "cultural capital"; see his *Cultural Capital: The Problem of Literary Canon Formation* (Chicago and London, 1993). On the problematic of resistance and litera-ture, see the interesting alternatives to "resistance-thinking" discussed in Ross Cham-bers, *Room for Maneuver: Reading (the) Oppositional (in) Narrative* (Chicago and London, 1991). Instead of "resistance," Chambers proposes the notion of "oppositionality," which he defines as a tactic that works within power, but that seeks to make changes in the desires involved in power. The medium that Chambers adopts for an oppositional prac-tice is narrative-reading.

2 Zhang Yimou, dir., *Huozhe* (*To Live*), produced by Century Communications, U.S. dis-tribution by Samuel Goldwyn, 1994.

3 On the affinities between events in modern China and events in the contemporary Western academy, see Rey Chow, *Writing Diaspora: Tactics of Intervention in Contempo-rary Cultural Studies* (Bloomington and Indianapolis, 1993), 1–26.

4 For a thoughtful and informative historical discussion of events in Communist China, see Maurice Meisner, *Mao's China and After: A History of the People's Republic*, rev. and exp. ed. of *Mao's China* (New York, 1986 [1977]). Readers unacquainted with contem-porary Chinese history are referred to James M. Ethridge's summary account of the

Cultural Revolution in *China's Unfinished Revolution: Problems and Prospects since Mao* (San Francisco, 1990), 247–52:

> Most people believed that the need for class struggle . . . had essentially passed with the completion of land reform and socialist transformation of private enterprise in the fifties. However, Mao continued to see (as he had for years) a constant need for permanent, unrelenting, widespread—and sometimes violent—class struggle to combat the rise of a new bourgeoisie. . . . He encouraged such class struggle in the Socialist Education Movement . . . which began in 1962 and was merged with the Cultural Revolution in 1966. During the same period, Mao's status as a demigod was enhanced by the compilation of the "Little Red Book" containing hundreds of quotations from his speeches and writings. The book was an immediate sensation and strengthened the personality cult that was to make Mao even more formidable in days to come. "The Great Proletarian Cultural Revolution," as the movement was called officially, was launched in a speech by Zhou Enlai at a huge May Day celebration in Beijing in 1966. (248)

5 Works by some of these authors in English translation include Bai Hua, *The Remote Country of Women*, trans. Qingyun Wu and Thomas O. Beebee (Honolulu, 1994); Mo Yan, *Red Sorghum*, trans. Howard Goldblatt (New York, 1993); and *Explosions and Other Stories*, ed. Janice Wickeri (Hong Kong, 1991); Ah Cheng, *Three Kings: Three Stories from Today's China*, trans. Bonnie S. McDougall (London, 1990); and Han Shaogong, *Homecoming? and Other Stories*, trans. Martha Cheung (Hong Kong, 1992); see also the short stories by some of these authors in the following anthologies: *Spring Bamboo: A Collection of Contemporary Chinese Short Stories*, comp. and trans. Jeanne Tai, foreword by Bette Bao Lord, introduction by Leo Ou-fan Lee (New York, 1989); *Worlds of Modern Chinese Fiction: Short Stories and Novellas from the People's Republic, Taiwan and Hong Kong*, ed. Michael S. Duke (Armonk, 1991); *Running Wild: New Chinese Writers*, ed. David Derwei Wang, with Jeanne Tai (New York, 1994); *The Columbia Anthology of Modern Chinese Literature*, ed. Joseph S. M. Lau and Howard Goldblatt (New York, 1995). Chinese films known to Western audiences include Wu Tianming's *Old Well*; Chen Kaige's *Yellow Earth* and *Farewell My Concubine*; Tian Zhuangzhuang's *Horse Thief* and *The Blue Kite*; Zhang Nuanxin's *Sacrifice Youth*; Xie Jin's *Hibiscus Town*; and Xie Fei's *Girl from Hunan*.

6 See, for instance, Nick Browne's discussion of Xie Jin's *Hibiscus Town* in "Society and Subjectivity: On the Political Economy of Chinese Melodrama," in *New Chinese Cinemas: Forms, Identities, Politics*, ed. Nick Browne, Paul G. Pickowicz, Vivian Sobchack, and Esther Yau (Cambridge, 1994), 40–56: "Suffering is linked ultimately to the injustices of the political administration of social power. In this sense, subjectivity is part of a new political language of the post–Cultural Revolution period. It indicates an aspect of the person beyond that of the citizen" (53).

7 On the Great Leap Forward, see Ethridge, *China's Unfinished Revolution*:

> By mid-1957, shortly before the Great Leap Forward began, land reform and socialist transformation of most private enterprises had been accomplished. The First

Five-Year Plan had been completed with satisfactory success. Continued steady, if not spectacular, progress seemed entirely possible.

For some reason not entirely clear, however, the government (and apparently Mao in particular) felt some compulsion to achieve a dramatic advance in economic development at that time. Specialists in Chinese affairs themselves differ in their perspectives on the forces behind the Great Leap Forward. . . .

For whatever reason, the Party, beginning early in 1958, launched the heady, radical, inspiring, and catastrophic Great Leap Forward, a movement calculated, to cite one slogan of the time, to "Overtake and surpass Britain within fifteen years in the output of steel and other important products!" Other slogans were more memorable and emotional, such as "Dare to storm the heavens!" . . .

But, just as there was great progress there was also great waste, great expense, and near exhaustion. Crops failed . . . problems in the countryside multiplied. . . . The steel that was made in hundreds of thousands of makeshift furnaces was useless, and much new construction was of poor quality. . . . By the end of 1959, what Frank K. M. Su has called "a romantic period in China's socialist construction" was over. Its wisdom and consequences are still debated. (259–60)

8   Yu Hua, *Huozhe* (Hong Kong, 1994). (I am grateful to Shan Qiang He for my copy of the novella.) *Huozhe* originally appeared in the P.R.C. literary journal *Shouhuo* (Harvest), No. 6 (1992). Yu Hua also coauthored the screenplay with Lu Wei. For a discussion in English of other works by Yu Hua, see Lu Tonglin, *Misogyny, Cultural Nihilism, and Oppositional Politics: Contemporary Chinese Experimental Fiction* (Stanford, 1995), 155–79. Lu argues that Yu Hua's writings replicate the structures of patriarchal violence they seek to transgress.

9   In Yu Hua's novella, Fugui is the only survivor.

10   See my "Pedagogy, Trust, Chinese Intellectuals in the 1990s—Fragments of a Post-Catastrophic Discourse," in *Writing Diaspora*, 73–98, especially my discussion of Ah Cheng's novella *King of the Children*.

11   There are actually two first-person narrators in Yu Hua's story—the character Fugui and the narrator who records Fugui's tale, which constitutes the bulk of the narrative.

12   For a more detailed discussion of Zhang's tactics as a popular artist, see Rey Chow, *Primitive Passions: Visuality, Sexuality, Ethnicity, and Contemporary Chinese Cinema* (New York, 1995), 142–72. Zhang is reported to have said, in relation to the making of his 1995 film *Yao ah yao! yao dao waipo qiao* (*Shanghai Triad*), "In the past, our Fifth Generation directors were fascinated with such [intellectual] things, introducing history, culture, and philosophy into films. . . . These are precisely the things I want to avoid now"; see Wang Bin, "Feature," *Dianying shuangzhoukan* (*City Entertainment*), 1 June 1995, 37; my translation.

13   See Yu Hua, *Huozhe*, esp. 164–82.

14   Browne, "Subjectivity and Society," 46. See Ethridge, *China's Unfinished Revolution*, 268–72, for a summary account of China's legal system. Among other things, Ethridge notes that the Chinese legal system differs from those of many Western countries in that "there is no presumption of innocence at a trial (just the opposite, in fact, because

preliminary investigation is supposed to have already established the need for having a trial); there are no rules of evidence; there is no independent judiciary; and there is no expectation that a judicial decision will necessarily be made according to precedents offered by similar cases" (269). He also quotes from "a surprisingly frank article" that appeared in the *Beijing Review* "after the conservatives took over" (i.e., after 4 June 1989): "'Not many people say outright that power is bigger than the law. But actually nowhere in the country has a mechanism yet been established capable of restricting power abuse in the true sense of the word. There are no hard and fast rules which can subject power-holders to legal restrictions or bring power-abusers to justice. Some power-wielders, who think themselves superior, always take it for granted that laws are something designed for other people, the rank-and-filers, while they themselves stand high above the law, far out of its reach, and do not need to be limited by it'" (271).

15 See my discussions in *Writing Diaspora*, 73–98. Zhang's 1992 film, *The Story of Qiuju*, depicts a peasant woman's stubborn fight for justice through the many levels of bureaucracy. Although it has a more or less happy ending, the film is a direct comment on the difficulty of telling the truth in public in China.

16 Lest I give the impression that I am simply applauding the Western conception of the space of the public, let me add that, living in the United States, I am fully aware of the problems at the other end of the spectrum from China—the problems that result from the systemic legislation of every aspect of life, including the most private and personal. This "public space of litigation," however, is not my focus here.

17 For a related discussion, see my opening arguments in "Media, Matter, Migrants," in *Writing Diaspora*, 165–80.

18 Wei Jingsheng and Fang Lizhi are two of the People's Republic's most outspoken dissidents. Both have been punished for demanding democracy. Wei, a worker, had been imprisoned since 1979 before being briefly released in September 1993; he was detained again in April 1994, formally charged in November 1995 with attempting to overthrow the Chinese government, and sentenced in December 1995 to another fourteen years in prison. Fang, an astrophysicist, was held under house arrest at the U.S. Consulate in Beijing until he was allowed to leave the country in June 1990 after signing an affidavit saying that he would not criticize the Chinese government; he now teaches in Arizona. Martin Lee, Szeto Wah, Christine Loh, and Emily Lau are among the most outspoken politicians fighting for the continuation of democratic rule in Hong Kong after China's resumption of sovereignty in 1997; among the most contentious issues on which they have opposed and criticized the Chinese authorities are those to do with *rule by law*, such as China's murky handling of the Basic Law Agreement (concerning the future administration of Hong Kong) and the question of whether a Court of Final Appeal will be established in Hong Kong before 1997. Harry Wu is a human rights activist who spent nineteen years in a labor camp before he left China. Now a U.S. citizen, Wu has been disseminating information in the West about China's abuse of political prisoners. Arrested in the summer of 1995 on one of his clandestine trips into the country to collect more information, he was sentenced to fifteen years in prison, but then was expelled by the Chinese authorities.

19 "Outcasting" is, of course, simply the other side of a coercive "unifying" of all people,

territories, and things "Chinese," so that any public demonstration of departing from this Chinese "oneness" must be penalized. This is why the U.S. visit of Li Denghui, Taiwan's president, in the early summer of 1995, for instance, provoked such heated debates in Chinese newspapers. As part of an attempt to counter and contain this public challenge to the idea of "one China," the People's Republic has been threatening, since Li's visit, to invade Taiwan—such as by ostentatiously practicing missile launches across the Taiwan Straits during the summer of 1995.

20 In Yu Hua's story, Long'er offers Fugui a few acres of land.

21 My reading of the relationship between ideology and representation (literary or otherwise) follows Pierre Macherey's in *A Theory of Literary Production*, trans. Geoffrey Wall (London, 1978).

22 I should clarify at this point that my reading of Zhang's critique of the will "to live" as an ideology is not intended as a demand for living at a "higher" level, for attaining something more "noble" and "dignified" than mere survival. In other words, my reading is not based on a kind of humanist imperative to distinguish human beings from "lower" life forms, but rather on the assumption that it is, indeed, a human condition to be preoccupied with survival and that *that* is the ideological problem. Unlike nonhuman animals, which, in their complete absorption in life, are not concerned with "survival" as such, humans, in their struggles "to live," are always fantasizing a "better" future for which absolute sacrifice and absolute accommodation are always required. My criticism of the imperative "to live," then, proceeds from the premise that preoccupation with survival is not honorably animalistic but pejoratively humanistic because such a preoccupation can be and has been exploited by totalitarian regimes for purposes of massive organized violence, violence that is, moreover, legitimized as sacrifice for a "better" human life to come.

23 See Louis Althusser, "Ideology and Ideological State Apparatuses (Notes towards an Investigation)," in *Lenin and Philosophy and Other Essays*, trans. Ben Brewster (New York and London, 1971), 127–86: "What is represented in ideology is . . . not the system of the real relations which govern the existence of individuals, but the imaginary relation of those individuals to the real relations in which they live" (165).

24 For instance, Zhang's films have been censored more than once in China. When *To Live* was entered in the 1994 Cannes Film Festival without the permission of the Chinese government, Zhang was penalized by being forbidden to collaborate with foreign investors for the next two years.

Victoria Kahn

Political Theology and Reason of State in *Samson Agonistes*

In his treatise on *Political Theology* of 1922, Carl
Schmitt defined the sovereign as "he who decides on the exception."[1] Schmitt, a conservative
scholar of constitutional law during the Weimar
Republic and later a supporter of the Third Reich,
was interested in the paradox that the sovereign
both "stands outside the normally valid legal system, [and] nevertheless belongs to it, for it is he
who must decide whether the constitution needs
to be suspended in its entirety. . . . The essence of
the state's sovereignty [is] not . . . the monopoly
to coerce or to rule, but . . . the monopoly to
decide." While modern constitutionalist thought
tends, according to Schmitt, to eliminate "the
sovereign in this sense," the seventeenth-century
tradition of natural law recognized the exception:
"The classical representative of the decisionist
type [of juristic thought] . . . is Thomas Hobbes,"
with his maxim *auctoritas, non veritas facit legem.*[2]
The sovereign is he who has the power to decide
what counts as the norm and the exception, as
true and false, in the political sphere. The sovereign also has the right to suspend positive law
for the good of the people or the preservation
of the state. In the idiom of seventeenth-century

The *South Atlantic Quarterly* 95:4, Fall 1996.
Copyright © 1996 by Duke University Press.

political theory the problem of the exception is the problem of reason of state.

Although Schmitt distinguished between the monopoly to coerce and the monopoly to decide, it is clear that for him the latter presupposed the former. It is perhaps for this reason that Schmitt was interested in Walter Benjamin's early essay "The Critique of Violence"; both viewed the foundation of law as a "coup de force," a performative or interpretive violence for which there is no prior justification.[3] Similarly, according to this logic, it is impossible to say that a decision is just if it merely conforms to a prior rule of law (which would be mere legality, not justice); rather, to the extent that the law has to be enacted, it is reinvented each time.[4] Here we see that reason of state does not necessarily reinforce the status quo: because it does not identify justice with positive law, it may also criticize existing relations of power.[5] Not surprisingly, given his account of the fiat behind all legal order, Schmitt believed that all modern concepts of the state are secularized theological concepts: "The exception in jurisprudence is analogous to the miracle in theology."[6] Perhaps for similar reasons, Benjamin associated the violence of founding a new political order with divine violence.

Samson Agonistes is Milton's—and Samson's—attempt to think the exception in the realm of politics and theology. In doing so, it necessarily takes up the relations of the law and violence, of reason and reason of state—issues that Milton had addressed with considerably more equanimity, even optimism, in *The Tenure of Kings and Magistrates* and the first *Defence*. Although in these prose tracts of the late 1640s and early 1650s Milton assimilated reason of state to Aristotelian or Thomistic natural law, in *Samson Agonistes* reason of state comes to represent a crisis of rationality and of the will. As Arthur Barker noted long ago, while in principle the law of right reason and nature is different from divine grace, in practice "that theoretical distinction was difficult to preserve, especially when reason and faith, natural and spiritual law, were together involved in the dispute over the rights of conscience." In radical puritan thought, reasoning about the exception on the basis of natural law and the inner promptings of grace came to involve far more than "the mere natural law of self-preservation": at stake was the relationship of unwritten natural law to the law of the spirit and thus, I would add, the power and authority of reason itself.[7] In Milton's late drama, the norms of conscientious action and the sanction for violence are themselves the subject of debate: Gewalt—the authority for violence, the power to decide—is now a problem rather than simply a solution. This is a problem of political theology, on the one hand, and of genre, on the other. In the first case, it points to the voluntarism of Milton's theology, according to which God gave us the power freely to choose—not least of all in the realm of politics.[8] In the second, it points to the genre of tragedy, a genre which dramatizes the tensions and ambiguities of human decision-making, of "man in his condition as an agent"—not least of all, in relation to the divine.[9]

In the preface to *Samson Agonistes* Milton tells us his model is "tragedy, as it was anciently composed," which, according to Aristotle, has the "power by raising pity and fear, or terror, to purge the mind of those and such like passions, that is to temper and reduce them to just measure with a kind of delight."[10] With this last subordinate clause, Milton enters the Renaissance debate concerning the political effects of catharsis. While Aristotle had made no particular, explicit claims for the political uses of tragedy, Italian Renaissance commentators regularly discussed its social and political consequences. Central to the debate was whether catharsis purged or merely tempered the passions, and whether purgation created quiescence or something more like stoic resolve. Giacopo Mazzoni, whom Milton mentions in *Of Education*, took a conservative position on the political effects of tragedy, which he saw as moderating the hubris of the great, extinguishing sedition and preserving peace. In his *L'arte poetica* of 1564, Antonio Minturno argued for the more complicated effect of patience and resourcefulness: "The recollection of the grave misfortunes of others not merely makes us quicker and better prepared to support our own, but wiser and more skillful in escaping similar evils." Tragedy, in this view, may both purge and moderate the passions; it may encourage both "patience" and heroic acts of "invincible might," to quote the chorus of *Samson Agonistes*. As Merritt Hughes noted, although Milton does not explicitly cite Minturno in the preface to *Samson*, he seems to have subscribed to a similar view of the complicated, politically bracing homeopathic effect of tragedy.[11]

A more pointed recognition of the ambivalent effects of tragedy is signaled by Milton's reference in the preface to Paraeus's commentary on the tragedy of Revelation. As Barbara Lewalski has argued, Paraeus was not alone among Protestant commentators in "locat[ing] the tragedy of Revelation in the sufferings and agons of the Church under Antichrist: 'the forme of this Prophesie . . . representeth Tragicall motions and tumults of the adversaries against the Church of Christ.'"[12] Samson, in this light, is not so much a type of Christ as a warfaring saint who "under the conditions of this life . . . cannot escape suffering and death, or the knowledge that [his] own guiltiness deserves it."[13]

In both Italian and English conceptions, tragedy is dialectical. In the Italian Renaissance commentaries that Milton knew well, tragedy works by contraries: it solicits the passions only to purge or modify them; it stages the representation of death and destruction so that the spectator will be elevated by experiencing the powerful and lively emotions of pity and fear. Like the rhetorical category of the sublime to which it is often allied (in both Renaissance and modern discussions), tragedy makes the theatrical representation of violence the condition of the spectator's pleasurable experience of the marvelous and of self-preservation.[14] But the conjunction of Italian commentators on Aristotle with Protestant commentators on the tragedy of Revelation also points to a conception of tragedy which is dialectical, in the sense of dramatizing contradiction, equivocation, ambivalence—not just in the contrast between the fortunes of the spectator and actor but within the drama itself. In this view of tragedy, the protagonist's exercise of the will is the occasion of unintended suffering. Volition may appear to be indistinguishable from violence; the agent is acted upon; "bloody instructions," to quote *Macbeth*, "return to plague the inventor." The political effects of tragedy are complicated by a dramatization of the problems of agency and imitation.

If Renaissance reflections on reason of state engage some of the same contradictions as contemporary reflections on tragedy, as I believe they do, then in *Samson Agonistes* reason of state—reasoning about the exception—becomes the tragedy of political thought, and the ambivalent experience of tragedy the literary equivalent of the cognitive dilemma signaled by reason of state. As we will see, reason of state appears to be in excess of the law and takes the form of an exercise of extraordinary power that is justified by reference to a "higher" natural law of reason. But this reference to a higher law is problematic since reason of state can be feigned to justify lowly considerations of expedience and self-interest. Thus reason of state fascinates because it involves the potentially illegitimate transgression of the norm—of justice and ethical behavior, of divine law: it is a figure of the effect of power in all its ambivalence. Here we can begin to discern the difference between Milton's reason of state and Schmitt's political theology. For Schmitt, "theology" is a metaphor: deciding the exception can never involve an illegitimate transgression of divine law since in all important respects the human sovereign is the law. For Milton, legitimacy is of the essence precisely because theology is not simply a metaphor for secularized political sovereignty; instead, it refers to our all-too-human knowledge of divine sovereignty. In contrast to Schmitt, for the late Milton political theology involved the ambivalent human experience of the divine, an experience which—by the time of *Samson Agonistes*—had come to seem irreducibly tragic. That tragedy cannot be understood without an exploration of the tension between natural law and conscience in seventeenth-century debates about reason of state.

≡≡≡

For Milton and his contemporaries, reason of state is the form of reasoning that deliberates about exceptional political cases in which *salus populi*—the good of the people, the preservation of the state—demands the violation of positive and/or moral law.[15] Reason of state thus poses distinctive ethical and epistemological problems. It emerges as an ethical problem when the preservation of the state is perceived to be at odds with the norms of justice—as Carl Friedrich noted, "Only when there is a clash between the commands of an individual ethic of high normativity and the needs and requirements of organizations whose security and survival is at stake can the issue of reason of state become real."[16] Yet, as the ambiguity of salus populi suggests, reason of state also emerges as an ethical problem when true justice seems to require the violation of positive or moral law.

The dilemma of reason of state is epistemological as well as ethical since, from the outset, reason of state involves a series of potentially equivocal relationships between reason and decision, discretion and necessity, justice and force, law and conscience. Although in one sense reason of state simply applies the natural law or rational principle of self-preservation to the political sphere, in another sense it explodes the distinction between rational norm and application since it concerns exceptions that cannot be subsumed under ordinary reason. If they could, there would be no need to invoke a rationality intrinsic to politics (as opposed to ethics)—a supplement to reason that may take the form of divine inspiration. If, in the first case, reason of state is part of an older natural-law tradition grounded on the belief in self-evident principles of reason, in the second case it comes close to being a skeptical or instrumental approach to politics, one that could be aligned with a radical puritan belief in divine grace.[17]

We can begin to get a sense of the equivocal epistemological and ethical status of reason of state by examining debates between royalists and parliamentarians about discretionary political power in the years leading up to and including the Civil War. These were debates not simply about de facto power but also about legitimate authority. While "reason of state" was sometimes a term of abuse, it also served to justify the exercise of emergency powers. And, for royalists and parliamentarians alike, the Nazarite Samson functioned as an important example of these powers.[18]

On the royalist side, what Friedrich has described as the ethical "issue" of reason of state was resolved by assimilating it to the tradition of the *arcana imperii*: the king was privy to the secrets of empire that verged on and were at times explicitly identified with a God-given insight into political matters.[19] Only the king had the knowledge to decide what was in the public interest; his decisions could therefore not be constrained—nor his conscience troubled—by considerations of merely human law. Reason of state was, in the view of James I, not so much a problem as a solution, another name for divine-right absolutism. So James argued in a 1621 letter to the House of Commons defending his discretionary power in matters of policy, which "were of necessity secret, unpredictable, and peremptory."[20] In 1628, in response to the Petition of Right, Serjeant Ashley similarly declared that "kings rule not only by the common law but also by 'a law of state,' and added that 'in the law of state their acts are bounded by the law of nature'" rather than by positive law. In the Commons Francis Nethersole argued that "for reason of state the king could imprison [and tax] without showing cause."[21] Not surprisingly, given this use of reason of state to justify impositions and imprisonment at the king's will, Sir Edward Coke remarked that "a Reason of State is a trick to put a man out of the right way; for, when a man can give no reason for a thing, then he flieth to a higher Strain, and saith it is Reason of State." In the parliamentary debates of 1628, one George (or John) Browne similarly declared that "reason of state is a meere chimera."[22]

By the 1640s, however, parliamentary critics of the king were invoking reason of state in defense of their own policies, identifying it not with divine right absolutism but with nascent constitutionalism. Charles Herle, a Presbyterian clergyman, argued that "mixt Monarchy" was the best form of government and that *"Reason* or *wisdom of State . . .* first *contriv'd* [the mixture]."[23] Reason of state also had the more particular connotation of discretionary power in matters of necessity and self-preservation, now identified as resistance to the king. For critics of absolute monarchy such as Henry Parker and Milton, God-given reason dictated not only that government be based on an original covenant or contract with the ruler, but that this contract be revocable when the ends of government—self-preservation as well as preservation of the state—were not being served. Thus in *The Contra-Replicant, His Complaint to His Majestie,* Parker justified reason of state as a supplement to contract, one that achieves a kind of sublime—even an imperial—transcendence of the law:

> Lawes ayme at *Justice,* Reason of state aimes at *safety . . . .* Reason of State goes beyond all particular formes and pacts, and looks rather to the being, then the well-being of a State. . . . Reason of state is something more sublime and imperiall then Law: it may rightly be said, that the Statesman begins where the Lawyer ceaseth; for when warre has silenced Law, a kind of dictatorian power is to be allowed to her; whatsoever has any right to defend it selfe in time of danger is to resort to policy in stead of Law.[24]

Parker's remarks suggest that he recognized reason of state could be a dangerous supplement to any fixed conception of mixed monarchy or government based on law, contract, and consent. Yet, for Parker, precisely because reason of state is concerned with the "right" of self-defense, it proves to be the underside of any legitimate model of contractual obligation.

Milton made a similar argument in *The Tenure of Kings and Magistrates* and the first *Defence,* stressing even more forcefully than Parker the compatibility of natural law and reason of state not simply with "safety" but with true justice. In both texts, government is established and preserved by the exercise of God-given reason in accordance with "that law of Nature and of God which holds that whatever is for the safety of the state is right and just."[25] Thus, in *The Tenure,* Milton argued that the regicide—which violated positive law—was justified by natural law, which dictated above all the safety of the people.[26] And in defending the actions of Parliament and the army, he referred to "the glorious way wherin *Justice and Victory* hath set them; the only warrants through all the ages, next under immediat Revelation, to exercise supream power." [27] In the first *Defence*, Milton asserted that absolute obedience to positive law amounted to an idolatrous submission to tyrannical or de facto political power without concern for justice. In contrast, reason, justice, morality, and the natural law of salus populi all demand that tyrants be punished by violence. [28] In both texts exceptions to or suspensions of positive law are normalized by reference to right reason and the law of nature. At the same time, in both texts reason of state involves critical judgment rather than an appeal to absolute authority; as such, it transforms the exercise of what Parker called "arbitrary power," making it an instrument of justice rather than legality, of revolution rather than the status quo. [29]

And yet contemporaries were acutely aware that reason of state and the necessities to which it claimed to respond could be abused or feigned. In such cases, reason of state was not grounded in God-given reason and natural law; rather, it represented a kind of Machiavellian supplement to reason, a usurpation of the divine prerogative to suspend the moral law. In these cases, the invocation of reason of state involved equivocation or false casuistry. In his *Lectures on Conscience and Human Law*, Bishop Sanderson warned in particular against the equivocal interpretation of salus populi, promoted by "a class of men [who] have used their leisure in a luckless way, to invent and import a new scheme of *politics* into the *State* . . . under the pretence of *Christian liberty*, or of *liberty of Conscience*." After explaining that the word *people* is properly understood to include both the king and his subjects, he added,

> I have explained these particulars with precision . . . [for two reasons]; the first, that we may not suffer ourselves to be deceived and imposed upon by a fallacious construction of an ambiguous word; the other, in order that there may be no force in the mere sound of the word *people*, to prejudice the sovereign of the community, and the ruler of the nation. [30]

Sanderson might well have had in mind someone like John Goodwin, who in *Right and Might Well Met* identified the interest of the people with the army and the Independents, and who defended the army's illegal actions on the ground that

> the law of nature, necessity, and of love to their country, . . . being the law of God himself written in the fleshly tables of men's hearts,

hath an authoritative jurisdiction over all human laws and constitutions whatsoever, a prerogative right of power to overrule them and to suspend their obliging influences in all cases appropriate to itself. Yea many of the Lawes of God themselves, thinke it no disparagement unto them, to give place to their elder Sister, the Law of necessity, and to surrender their authority into her hand, when shee speaketh.[31]

For Goodwin, as for many of his contemporaries, reason of state could involve the suspension of divine as well as positive law for reasons of necessity. To the objection that it is difficult to judge what is necessary, Goodwin replied that we are obliged by our consciences to do so even though our judgment may be fallible: "The neglect, or non-exercise of that judging faculty or power, which is planted in the soules and consciences of men by God, upon such terms, and with references to such ends as these, draweth along with it that sin, w[hi]ch the Wise man called, the *despising of a mans wayes* . . . . Every man is bound to consider, judge, and determine, what is meet, and necessary for him to doe, either to, with, for, or against, all other men."[32] Whereas Goodwin asserted that the effort to judge could not be condemned even though a particular judgment might be faulty, contemporary treatises on casuistry stressed that a right intention could not justify an immoral act. Yet for Sanderson the problem was not chiefly one of misconstruction but of deception: as Goodwin himself admitted, necessity may be feigned as well as misinterpreted; and when it is feigned, the new politics begins to look strangely like an attempt to use the fiction of necessity as a rationale for merely human transgressions of divine law.

This dynamic of freedom and necessity, of divine and human law, may explain the fact that Samson regularly served as a counter in royalist and parliamentary discussions of this extralegal power to determine the exception. Discussing Bate's Case (1606), which had upheld the king's right to levy impositions by arguing that the king's power was "supra-legal, so that he might for reason of state act contrary to the common law," Sir John Davies compared the strength of the king's absolute prerogative to Samson's:

The King's Prerogative in this point is as strong as *Samson*, it cannot be bound; for though an Act of Parliament be made to restrain it, and the King doth give his consent unto it, as *Samson* was bound with his own consent, yet if the Philistines come, that is, if any just or important occasion do arise, it cannot hold or restrain the Prerogative, it will be as thred, and broken as easie as the bonds of Samson.[33]

For Davies Samson is exemplary of sovereign power because his strength is so great that he cannot be restrained by any other force: he can only bind himself ("bound with his own consent"). Yet Davies also notes almost parenthetically that the occasion of breaking the bonds of Parliament must be "just or important," thereby suggesting that the king's arbitrary power is guided by considerations of justice above and beyond the law. In doing so, he implicitly suggests the rhetorical question which Milton's Samson asks in his first soliloquy: "What is strength without a double share of wisdom?" Or, less rhetorically, on the basis of what knowledge should the king or any individual subject break his bonds?

In *The Reason of Church Government*, Milton inverted the kind of argument made by Davies, comparing Samson's locks to the Mosaic law (allegorically: English law) rather than exclusively to royal prerogative:

> I cannot better liken the state and person of a King then to that mighty Nazarite *Samson*; who being disciplin'd from his birth in the precepts and the practice of Temperance and Sobriety, without the strong drink of injurious and excessive desires, grows up to a noble strength and perfection with those his illustrious and sunny locks the laws waving and curling about his god like shoulders. . . . But laying down his head among the strumpet flatteries of Prelats, while he sleeps and thinks no harme, they wickedly shaving off all those bright and waighty tresses of his laws, and just prerogatives which were his ornament and strength, deliver him over to indirect and violent councels . . . and make him grinde in the prison house of their sinister ends and practices upon him.[34]

Whereas Davies compared Samson's strength to Charles's unconstrained prerogative, Milton implies that both strength and prerogative are a function of the law. And he warns that when "Law and Right" recover their "wonted might," they will "thunder with ruin upon the heads of [Charles's] evil counsellors, but not without great affliction to himself."[35] Here too the law is an instrument of critical judgment as well as strength, of justice as well as arbitrary power. Milton suggests a similar linking of criticism and strength in the first *Defence*, where he describes Samson as a heroic tyrannicide who "thought it not impious but pious to kill those masters that were tyrants over his country."[36] Yet, in describing Samson as one who "made war single-handed on his masters . . . whether prompted by God or by his own valor," Milton also raises the question of the divine authority for Samson's decision—the question, that is, of his calling.

═══

Reason of state is often assumed to be a secular rationale of expedient political action, one that is incompatible with the rule of the saints. Yet, as Milton's description of the pious Samson in the first *Defence* suggests and as a number of scholars have observed, the Protestant doctrines of the covenant and the calling proved to be particularly hospitable to reason of state in all its ambiguity.[37] On the one hand, the voluntarism of such doctrines seems to have contributed to a rational view of this worldly experience, including politics and the exigencies of reason of state. On the other hand, this same voluntarism, along with the notion of the specific calling, served to isolate politics from other kinds of activities and, at least in some cases, to make politics less a matter of shared rational deliberation than of individual decision and of the will. This is particularly the case with Samson the Nazarite, whose struggle to understand his calling—his individual covenant with God—is intimately bound up with his meditation on reason of state.

At least since Weber, the idea that Protestantism (particularly Calvinism) fostered a rational view of this worldly activity has been a familiar one. Weber famously argued for the connection between Protestantism and capitalism, but others have modified his views by extending them— and claiming that they apply chiefly—to the sphere of politics.[38] According to this view, the Protestant doctrine of God's covenant with man informs and serves as a model for this worldly government conceived of as a contract established by human volition and choice—precisely what Milton argued in both *The Tenure* and the first *Defence*. Such a doctrine also served to articulate, and undoubtedly for some believers to resolve, the tension between coercion and consent in human experience. Just as the theological covenant reconciles divine predestination and human agency by making God's gift of grace an offer to which the believer must consent, so the Christian commonwealth reconciles coercion and free will by making the subordination of our interests to the public interest a matter of consent and individual conscience.[39]

While all saints were called in general to be conscientious and obedient citizens of the Christian commonwealth, some were called in particular to perform the duties of magistracy or political office. It is here that the Protestant notion of the vocation isolated the realm of government as a separate calling, one which has its own rules of conduct, its own *ratio* or rationale, separate from the sphere of religious devotion. Luther illustrated this separation when he observed, "I fulfill the commands of the Lord when I teach and pray, the plowman when he listens and does his farm work diligently; and the prince and his officials do not fulfill them, when they cannot be found when needed, but say that they must pray—for that means to withdraw from God's true service in the name of God."[40] What is true of the prince is true of his soldiers as well, whose vocation Luther defends in "Whether Soldiers, Too, Can Be Saved." The occupation of the soldier, including the exercise of violent force, is as legitimate as any other occupation, as long as the soldier realizes that "no one is saved as a soldier but only as a Christian."[41]

Of particular relevance to Samson is the fact that the Protestant notion of the calling could be used to justify not only the social and political status quo, but also exceptions to that rule precisely because it hovered between vocation and work; or rather, it made one's work into a vocation by infusing it with faith and conscience. Like the notion of the covenant, it adjudicated between predestination and works, coercion and consent, by making one's vocation appear to be a response to being called.[42] It was precisely this infusion of conscience—this conversion of work into "works of faith"—that made the notion of the calling equivocal and unstable: ostensibly a justification of social and political hierarchy, a calling could also be used to justify extraordinary actions "above the form of law or custome."[43] Thus, in William Perkins's *Treatise of the Vocations or Callings of Men*, we learn that there are two kinds—the calling of the Christian believer, which is determined by God's general providence, and the individual calling or profession (king, subject, merchant, plowman), which is determined by God's specific providence. Although the two callings should be performed together, "a particular calling must give place to the general calling of a Christian when they cannot both stand together."[44] Precisely because the doctrine of the calling raises the specter of an individual called to be a "public person," an individual who acts according to conscience rather than in accordance with his place in a social and political hierarchy, it stands at the intersection of norm and exception, contract and reason of state. Like

the notion of contract, that of a calling attempts to negotiate a conflict between coercion and consent, divine and human will; like reason of state,
being "called" could justify exceptions to the rule.

The doctrine of a special calling and of a rationality intrinsic to politics gave rise to what Michael Walzer (following George Mosse) has called
a "political casuistry." If casuistry is the art of reasoning about difficult
moral cases, of adjudicating between conflicting moral principles, political
casuistry is the art of reasoning about political cases that are not easily—
or usefully—subordinated to either positive or moral law. And one of the
goals of this political casuistry was to effect precisely the sort of divorce
between public and private persons mentioned above. Yet, as manuals of
casuistry acknowledged, it was often impossible to separate matters of
policy from matters of conscience, for in cases where there was an absolute conflict between obedience to the sovereign and obedience to God the
latter took precedence. Hence Luther's and Calvin's insisting that resistance, for example, could only be undertaken by public persons who were
lesser magistrates, not by private individuals acting according to their own
consciences. Hence also the fear that casuistry would actually foster resistance by helping to create conscientious subjects.[45]

This dilemma of conscientious action "above the form of law or custome" is the subject of Luther's tract *On Secular Authority*, which takes up
the casuistical question of "whether a Christian can even wield the secular Sword and punish the wicked [himself], seeing that Christ's words 'Do
not resist evil' seem so peremptory and clear." Luther solves this case of
conflicting moral principles, as a good casuist would, by distinguishing
between contexts: while the sword cannot be used "over or among Chris-
tians," "a Christian use" can be made of the sword to punish or restrain the
wicked.[46] Similarly, while the sword cannot be used to revenge or benefit
oneself, it may be used in "the service of others":

> And so the two [principles] are nicely reconciled: you satisfy the de-
> mands of God's kingdom and the world's at one and the same time,
> outwardly and inwardly; you both suffer evil and injustice and yet
> punish [the wicked]; you do not resist evil and yet you do resist it. As
> to you and yours, you keep to the Gospel and suffer injustice as a true
> Christian. But where the next man and what is his are concerned, you
> act in accordance with the [command to] love and you tolerate no in-

justice against him. And that is not prohibited by the Gospel; on the contrary the Gospel commands it elsewhere.[47]

The criterion of Christian usage then raises the further question of whether "I can use the Sword for myself and my own concerns, provided I am not out for my own good, but merely intend that evil should be punished?"[48] According to Luther, this is the case of conscience exemplified by Samson. On the one hand, Samson represents the vocation of "the sword," which, like other callings, can be used in the service of God. On the other hand, Samson sets a dangerous precedent for ordinary reason because he "used his private concerns as a pretext for declaring war against [the Philistines]," even though he "did not do it to avenge himself or to seek his own advantage, but to help [the Israelites] and punish the Philistines." Thus Luther warns, "Where [ordinary human] reason wants to do likewise, it no doubt pretends that it is not seeking its own advantage, but the claim will be false from top to bottom. The thing is impossible without grace. So if you want to act like Samson, then first become like Samson."[49] As readers of *Samson Agonistes* know, this "becoming like Samson" is something which even Milton's Samson has to achieve.

―――

From the very beginning of *Samson Agonistes*, Samson's task is to understand himself as an exception, both in the sense of an exceptional individual called by God to do exceptional acts and as an individual who has singularly failed to live up to his calling. In meditating on his equivocal status as deliverer, Samson thus necessarily addresses what we have come to understand as the problem of reason of state: the problem of the relationship of the exception to the rule, of power to legitimate authority, of justice to positive law. Precisely because reason of state involves not only *reasoning* about the exception but also *deciding* what counts as an exception, it exemplifies as well the problematic relationship of the law to the individual conscience, and of reason to the will.[50]

Samson's reasoning about his own exceptional status is dramatized in his soliloquy on the prophecy of his role as deliverer, a prophecy that he is unable to interpret correctly:

> Promise was that I
> Should *Israel* from *Philistian* yoke deliver;

> Ask for this great Deliverer now, and find him
> Eyeless in *Gaza* at the Mill with slaves,
> Himself in bonds under *Philistian* yoke;
> Yet stay, let me not rashly call in doubt
> Divine Prediction; what if all foretold
> Had been fulfill'd but through mine own default,
> Whom have I to complain of but myself? [51]

Samson struggles to make sense of his condition by revising his understanding of prophecy: he first interprets the prophecy that he would deliver
Israel as a "prediction," a "promise" that God has failed to fulfill, then reverses his understanding, blaming himself for his fate: "Whom have I to
complain of but myself?" No sooner has he done so than he begins to im-
pugn the justice of God's creation: "O impotence of mind, in body strong! /
But what is strength without a double share of wisdom?" He then recoils
from this question, asserting that God's will is just, though inaccessible to
human reason: "But peace, I must not quarrel with the will / Of highest
dispensation, which herein / Haply had ends above my reach to know." [52]
Struggling to decide between these alternatives, yet incapable of doing so,
Samson despairs of making sense of his experience in terms other than
those of simple irony: dark amid the blaze of noon, he suffers a living
death. He is not so much an exception as an example of the incomprehen-
sibility of God's ways. Irony is here for Samson simply the other side of his
either/or mode of reasoning, neither of which allows him to understand
his calling or the conditional nature of God's prophecies and covenants.
On the one hand, covenants are not predictions because they are not unilateral. On the other hand, because covenants are not unilateral, Samson
cannot by himself bring about the fulfillment of the prophecy. [53]

This initial soliloquy sets the pattern for the rest of the play, in which
Samson and his visitors struggle to interpret the equivocal signs of his condition. Particularly striking are the repeated failure to recognize Samson as
being like his former self (here Samson is the exception to the prophecy)
and the repeated attempts to erase the exception by reading Samson as an
"example" of some general law or truth of the human condition. In this
second case, exemplary reading has the effect of curtailing efforts to understand both Samson's responsibility for his decisions and God's justice.

The chorus unwittingly sums up the problem of turning Samson the exception into the rule when it describes Samson as a *"mirror* of our fickle

state, / Since man on earth *unparallel'd*," but goes on to resolve this paradox by casting him simply as an "example" of the reverses of fortune.[54] Samson describes himself as an "example" of a neglected deliverer, of fallen pride, and of the betrayed husband.[55] Like the chorus, Manoa reads him as an example of our fickle state and, like Samson in his first soliloquy, glosses this state in terms of the simple irony of the "good / Pray'd for, [which] often proves our woe." Harapha sees Samson as an example of a fallen hero.[56] Thus the chorus ascribes Samson's condition to fortune; Samson alternately complains that he was not given enough knowledge to use his strength correctly or that he was "overpow'r'd" by Dalila; Manoa describes Samson as "ensnared" by Dalila and unjustly punished by God; and the chorus exempts Samson of responsibility by pronouncing both that God may dispense with his own laws and that we should not reason vainly about divine justice.[57] In every case, doing away with Samson's responsibility for his decisions involves giving up on God's justice or, at the very least, identifying his justice with his absolute authority or arbitrary power.[58]

Samson, however, continues to reason about the exception—both his calling and his weakness of the will. In contrast to his interlocutors, he struggles to make sense both of God's justice and his own actions, exploring in the process the equivocal status of reason of state as both reason and decision. The dilemma of Samson's calling is not resolved by greater knowledge, however, or by choosing one more rationally compelling interpretation over another. Instead, what the conclusion dramatizes is the necessity of decision. Crucial to our understanding of this necessity are those exchanges in the poem in which Samson discusses his own decisions, past and present, and in which he explicitly takes up the argument from reason of state.

It makes sense that, in reasoning about his past decisions, Samson should explicitly address the argument from reason of state since he had used it to justify his own violation of positive law in marrying an infidel. Through his reflections on reason of state in his encounters with Dalila, Harapha, and the Philistine officer, Samson gradually comes to understand that such reasoning about the exception involves a critical act of judgment, a negative dialectics which (against James I) refuses to equate authority with legitimacy, power with justice.[59] These encounters thus amount to a kind of metadiscourse on the exception, an ironic commentary on any discourse that turns the exception into a rule in an attempt to obviate the necessity for a decision. Conversely, they show us that decisions are necessary precisely because arguments from authority (even the authority of natural law) are deeply equivocal, subject to parody, ironic manipulation, and reinterpretation. Finally, as Samson comes to understand, the equivocal signs of experience are less to be reasoned away than embraced as the condition for any true decision: equivocation and decision are two sides of the same coin.

Samson first appeals to reason of state in response to a question from the chorus about his marriages to "*Philistian* women," which violated Jewish law. According to Samson, his marriage to the woman of Timnah was dictated by God's concern for the salus populi of the Jews: Samson was "motion'd . . . of God" so that he might "begin *Israel's* Deliverance." This first exception to Jewish law then serves as an authorizing precedent and makes the marriage to Dalila less of an exception than an example: "I thought it lawful from my former act, / And the same end; still watching to oppress / *Israel's* oppressors."[60] Yet, by definition, true exceptions cannot be authorized by precedent; nor can they serve as legal precedents, if by this we mean authorities that obviate the necessity of a decision in the present. It is fitting, then, that Dalila should later throw Samson's argument back in his face, effectively claiming that she thought her betrayal of him was lawful from his former act, his own example. Here, as elsewhere, arguing from precedent and example serves to diminish responsibility: "To what I did thou show'd'st me first the way"; "ere I to thee, thou to thyself was cruel."[61] Even Samson's abandoning the woman of Timnah is pressed into the service of Dalila's self-justification:

> I saw thee mutable
> Of fancy, fear'd lest one day thou wouldst leave me
> As her of *Timna*, sought by all means therefore
> How to endear, and hold thee to me firmest.[62]

Finally, Dalila glosses her love for Samson as a kind of erotic reason of state: "These reasons in Love's law have pass'd for good, / Though fond and reasonless to some perhaps."[63] The "law" of love excuses reasons which from another perspective violate reason itself.

The next exchange further explores the opposition of authority and decision. In justifying her own betrayal of Samson, Dalila once again tries to turn the exception into the rule, this time by explicitly invoking reason of state or "public good" as the authorizing precedent for her actions. Describing the pressure exerted upon her by the Philistine "Magistrates / And Princes," she concludes:

> . . . at length that grounded maxim
> So rife and celebrated in the mouths
> Of wisest men, that to the public good
> Private respects must yield, with grave authority
> Took full possession of me and prevail'd;
> Virtue, as I thought, truth, duty so enjoining.[64]

Although Dalila uses the elevated language of public good, she reasons in a fashion that suggests instead the constraints of self-preservation: she "yields" when "grave authority" takes "possession" of her. For Dalila, reason of state does not involve deciding the exception; rather, it functions as the Hobbesian authority of magistrates and princes that usurps judgment and coerces submission.

Samson's reply suggests that he has learned from Dalila's parody of his earlier argument. In response to her own argument from authority, Samson makes reason of state a matter of critical judgment: he recasts her implicit argument about protection and obedience, contending that in her married state Dalila was no longer a Philistine and therefore owed obedience to Samson rather than to her former countrymen:

> Being once a wife, for me thou wast to leave
> Parents and country; nor was I their subject,
> Nor under their protection but my own,
> Thou mine, not theirs: if aught against my life
> Thy country sought of thee, it sought unjustly,
> Against the law of nature, law of nations,
> No more thy country, but an impious crew
> Of men conspiring to uphold thir state
> By worse than hostile deeds, violating the ends
> For which our country is a name so dear;
> Not therefore to be obey'd.[65]

Although Samson invokes the authority of the "law of nature, law of nations," he also makes it clear that Dalila has failed to reason correctly about reason of state, for he subjects the terms of her argument—not only self-preservation but also love, justice, nation, and obedience—to an immanent critique. Dalila's country is not her nation, "but an impious crew"—not to be obeyed since she has married Samson, but also because in seeking injustice they have violated the proper ends of nationhood. Thus his distinction between positive law and natural law discriminates between true and false interpretations of the law of nature as well.[66]

Samson's response to Harapha illustrates even more powerfully that natural law cannot serve as a standard of justice and rule of action that obviates decision.[67] Although Samson first defends the Hebrews' right of resistance in terms of reason of state and the maxim of natural law—"vim vi licet repellere" (force may be repelled with force)—he justifies his own particular role as liberator by reference to his calling:

> My nation was subjected to your Lords.
> It was the force of Conquest; force with force
> Is well ejected when the Conquer'd can.
> But I a private person, whom my Country
> As a league-breaker gave up bound, presum'd
> Single Rebellion and did Hostile Acts.
> I was no private but a person rais'd
> With strength sufficient and command from Heav'n
> To free my country.[68]

To the argument from natural law the objection could be raised that Samson was merely a private person who had wrongly (according to the standard Protestant argument) arrogated to himself the right to resist that belonged to public persons or "lesser magistrates." The justice of the argument from reason of state—the application of natural law—thus requires a decision about Samson's own exceptional status. Here too, in response, Samson does not so much reject his critics' argument as redescribe it: he does not justify his acts by reference to his public position as a judge of Israel but by a claim of individual conscience.[69] As in Luther's description of Samson in *Secular Authority*, private persons may be public persons and may perform actions for reason of state if they are divinely called to do so.

Samson's deliberations about whether to go with the Philistine messenger dramatize more powerfully than any of his previous encounters the intersection of reason of state and the doctrine of a calling. As in his previous exchanges, here too Samson reasons about reason of state, exploring its equivocal status as reason and decision, the natural law of self-preservation and the determination of justice. But Samson also begins here to link this equivocal status itself to the necessity of a decision: whereas for Dalila an exception could be subsumed under a rule, Samson has come to understand that an exception resists easy categorization; it prompts casuistry and equivocation precisely because it is itself equivocal—open to more than one description. In accepting this openness, Samson understands his calling as an exception for which there can be no precedent, if by that we mean an authority that resolves ambiguity and obviates the need for a decision. Reason of state—reasoning about the exception—becomes an emblem of the equivocal nature of human attempts to act justly in the absence of authoritative knowledge.

The equivocal nature of reason of state emerges as Samson rehearses its potential meanings. At first he argues that it is lawful to serve the Philistines with his labor, because they have him "in thir civil power," but unlawful to be present at "idolatrous rites":

> Where outward force constrains, the sentence holds;
> But who constrains me to the Temple of *Dagon*,
> Not dragging? the *Philistian* Lords command.
> Commands are no constraints.[70]

The first line sums up one view of passive obedience—obedience "where outward force constrains"—with particular attention to the argument from self-preservation. The next lines draw out an implication of this view: that one may refuse actively to serve an illegitimate power.[71] Yet, shortly after this, Samson asserts that God permits an exception to these rules, one that paradoxically makes active obedience a form of active resistance:

> Yet that he may dispense with me or thee
> Present in Temples at Idolatrous Rites
> For some important cause, thou needst not doubt.[72]

God, that is, can equivocate about reason of state, calling his servants to perform exceptions to the law which are nevertheless "not forbidden in our Law." Immediately after asserting this, Samson begins to feel "the rousing motions . . . which dispose / To something extraordinary" and decides to go to the temple, convinced that he will do "nothing . . . that may dishonor /

Our Law, or stain my vow as *Nazarite*."[73] Whether the reason of state that calls Samson to "go along" with the messenger is divine or not, it clearly allows Samson to reason dialectically about the law, to see the law as containing its own negation and higher preservation, and thus to equivocate.

This equivocation at the heart of reason of state (as obedience or resistance) is nicely dramatized by Samson's own casuistical reply to the messenger:

> Because they shall not trail me through thir streets
> Like a wild beast, I am content to go.
> Master's commands come with a power resistless
> To such as owe them absolute subjection;
> And for a life who will not change his purpose?[74]

Practically every word in these lines is ambiguous; even the enjambment in the first line looks both ways, suggesting the ferocity behind Samson's "content." The statement that "Master's commands come with a power resistless / To such as owe them absolute subjection" only raises the question of to whom we owe absolute subjection. Finally, in mocking the argument for self-preservation, Samson also forces us to consider what is meant by "life" in "And for a life who will not change his purpose?"[75]

In linking equivocation to the possibility of rebellion, Milton was articulating the worst fears of many of his contemporaries at the same time that he was radically revising traditional notions of reason of state.[76] In the 1650s, supporters of the Commonwealth feared that royalists would engage in equivocation or mental reservation when swearing allegiance to the new government; after 1660, supporters of the Restoration suspected a similar equivocation on the part of those who resisted it. In *Leviathan* Hobbes registered his fears of just such a figurative, otherworldly understanding of "life" as Samson suggests, observing that the belief in "eternal life" was more powerful than the fear that one might lose one's physical life: thus belief in a metaphorical kingdom of God could incite rebellion against the literal kingdom of the sovereign.[77] And Milton justified Hobbes's fears in the first *Defence* when he asserted that "Christ . . . took upon himself . . . the form of a slave, so that we might be free. I do not speak of inward freedom only [but also] political freedom."[78] In this light, Samson's response to the messenger is not so much a simple rejection of Dalila's reason of state as a dialectical revision of it: a purposeful equivocation that subjects the notion of literal or corporeal self-preservation to an ironic critique while suggesting a more sublime conception of what it might mean to preserve the self—a more sublime conception of reason of state.

This more sublime conception of reason of state is one that cannot be fully grasped by reason. Samson reasons up to a point, but his decision to go to the Philistine temple does not follow upon the conclusion that God has in this case dispensed with him. Rather, it follows upon "rousing motions." In the end, Samson's about-face in going to the temple suggests that, while rules can be instantiated, and examples imitated, an exception must be decided. A decision is necessary precisely because exceptions are by definition equivocal: there is no single, a priori rule of interpretation— whether the belief in antinomianism or in absolute obedience to de facto political power—that will allow us to reason them away. Decisions are also deeply equivocal since they require that we act in the absence of certainty, and in ignorance of the full meaning of our acts.[79]

Whereas Samson's equivocation to the messenger is deliberate and strategic, his decision to go with the messenger and his final act in the temple dramatize what I would call the deeper casuistry of tragedy: the irreducible amphiboly or equivocation at the heart of reason. If in *The Tenure of Kings and Magistrates* reason of state is simply one instance of the application of natural reason to the sphere of politics, in the course of *Samson Agonistes* reason of state comes to stand for that which is necessarily in excess of reason: as a supplement to reason, reason of state suggests reason's deficiencies, its self-division, its inability to ground or coincide with itself. For reasoning about justice does not simply involve an application of moral law but a decision to act, one that—insofar as it is free—occurs in the absence of any authorizing precedent. From one theological perspective, we might call this deficiency irony; from another, it is tragedy.[80]

Samson's final decision to pull down the temple is notoriously available to conflicting interpretations. In his final words to the Philistines, Samson distinguishes between his "reason," which has led him to obey their commands, and his "own accord," which now moves him to a different trial of his strength.[81] The description of Samson bowing his head "as one who prayed" makes this final act of conscience an act of Gewalt in all its ambiguity—for we are unsure, as Milton certainly intended us to be, whether

Samson's political act is an expression of divine authority or of merely human violence. Precisely because it involves an act of faith, deciding this point is ultimately a theological act; yet the surplus of possible meanings also dramatizes the lack of sure coincidence between politics and theology, human action and divine authority.

From one perspective this conclusion might appear to conform to Milton's argument about tyrannicide in *The Tenure*. Taking up the example of Ehud, the slayer of King Eglon (Judges 3:12–26), Milton argued that evidence of Ehud's divine inspiration is irrelevant to our understanding of his deed since he acted "on just principles, such as were then and ever held allowable."[82] As Martin Dzelzainis has commented, "A divine command establishes that a given action is lawful but is not itself what constitutes the grounds of its lawfulness; for that we must look to natural reason."[83] In this light Manoa's final judgment that God did not part from Samson but favored and assisted him to the end and the chorus's belief that God "unexpectedly return[ed] / . . . to his faithful Champion" are also irrelevant.[84] For, following *The Tenure* and the first *Defence*, we might surmise that here too Samson's natural reason has justified his exceptional act, "above the form of law or custome."

And yet, the feeling we are left with in the end is not that Samson's act has been rationally justified, but that it has been made more mysterious, less accessible to reason, more difficult to imitate; for the lack of coincidence between divine authority and human will is represented both as the condition for action and as self-violence. On the one hand, Manoa describes Samson's act of fulfilling the prophecy in terms of his imperfect identity: in a world where all interpretation must be in excess of the law, where there is no secure foundation for acts of conscience, Samson can only quit himself *like* Samson; he must always be an exception even to himself.[85] On the other hand, the equivocal final scene in which Samson is, in Manoa's words, "over-strong against [him]self," or, in the words of the chorus, "self-kill'd / not willingly," shows that this lack of identity may be experienced as violence.[86] We might even conjecture that Milton intends a dark parody of the union of coercion and consent in contemporary rational theories of political contract. Whereas, according to Milton and, in a different way, Hobbes, we consent to be coerced when we transfer our power to the sovereign, Samson's final act shows us that the will is itself a mysterious locus of coercion and consent, the intersection of human decision and divine *arcana imperii.* In the end, *Samson Agonistes* is a tragedy precisely because the exception and the will as the locus of decision are deeply implicated: the exception is the condition for any meaningful decision at the same time that its incoherence (its availability to contradictory interpretations) dramatizes the violence, including the self-violence, involved in any decisive imposition of sense. Hell, Augustine said, is not being able to decide;[87] tragedy, for the late Milton, is having to—is what our decisions look like.

This was the case partly for historical reasons, for the Restoration was a tragedy to Milton, a stage on which the armed saint was compelled to act alone, without fellow citizens. But the act of deciding the exception also looks like tragedy because Milton was not content, as Hobbes was, to equate justice with de facto authority. Precisely because justice is not simply a matter of authority, there is room for the conscientious individual to reason about the exception—specifically, about the justice of our individual acts; but because, in the words of *Areopagitica*, truth has been "hewed . . . into a thousand pieces," there is also room for the tragedy of the will. *Samson Agonistes* thus gives us a tragic version of *Areopagitica*'s "reason is but choosing."

If, in contrast to Schmitt and Hobbes, Milton presents the voluntarism of political theology as tragedy, he also—as his readers would expect—uses tragedy to teach us a lesson of political theology. God is ultimately the sovereign who decides the exception, but in this world Samson's act is open to our proximate interpretation. In this respect, it is very much like those actions of *Paradise Lost* that "do not express their own meaning for either the characters involved or the reader," and in response to which the reader is "radically individualized by being compelled freely to judge."[88] In obscuring the grounds of Samson's decision, Milton puts the reader in Samson's position of deciding the meaning of his act. It is this interpretive reticence on Milton's part which helps to make reading *Samson Agonistes* such an ambivalent experience, for the mixture of attraction and repulsion, coercion and consent, identification and differentiation that characterizes the spectator's experience of tragic catharsis is rendered here as an interpretive ambivalence as well. Confronted with a Samson who is both judge and victim, and whose grounds for deciding the exception are unknowable, the reader experiences not only pity and fear but what Angus Fletcher has described as "the mixture of pain and pleasure" in the uncertainty of exegesis.[89]

Some readers will resolve this uncertainty by deciding that Samson is an exception and, for that reason, not to be imitated. Other readers, "like Samson," will read Samson as "a mirror . . . unparallel'd," an example of exceptional commitment that they too can decide to embrace. Like the regicide in the first *Defence* and like Samson in Luther's treatise *On Secular Authority*, Milton's Samson reveals the conditional structure of any exception, which is exemplary if we have the grace to make it so. In a revolutionary gloss on Schmitt's maxim that the "sovereign is he who decides the exception," Milton implies that it is not the sovereign but the conscientious subject whose task it is to differentiate between positive law and true justice and to act accordingly. The conscientious subject is ideally the true sovereign. The conclusion of *Samson Agonistes* thus illustrates Bishop Sanderson's fears about the revolutionaries' equivocal gloss on the word "people" to the prejudice of the king as "ruler of the nation," but only at the price of turning Samson himself into an example of tragic casuistry: to paraphrase Luther's remarks (quoted above from *Secular Authority*), Samson experiences the conflicting demands of God's kingdom and the world's at one and the same time, outwardly and inwardly; he both suffers evil and injustice and yet punishes the wicked; he both resists evil and yet does not resist it. Whether he thereby "satisfies" the demands of both God's kingdom and the world is something neither Samson nor we can know. But it is a question, Milton insists, that we ought not fail to ask.

≡≡≡

Coda. Carl Schmitt's treatise on political theology interested radical as well as conservative thinkers of the 1920s and 1930s. Both Otto Kirchheimer and Franz Neumann, members of the left-wing Frankfurt Institute for Social Research, were drawn to Schmitt's critique of the Weimar constitution and Weimar liberalism. Recently, interest in Schmitt (and in Schmitt's affinity for the early work of Walter Benjamin) has revived among leftist political philosophers and literary critics, who are drawn to his work not only for its political analysis but also, I suggest, for the sublime frisson of his fascination with violence.[90] In a recent book, William Scheuermann insists that it is all the more important to recapture the legacy of thinkers such as Kirchheimer and Neumann who, after an initial appreciation of Schmitt, argued strenuously for the importance of the liberal rule of law. Milton (*pace* some recent efforts) is not a liberal thinker, and Samson is not an example of the liberal individual resisting the encroachment of

Philistine tyranny; faith and natural law rather than formal legal procedure are the keys to Milton's concern with the sanctity of individual conscience. But if *Samson Agonistes* cannot provide a liberal rebuttal of Schmitt (and it's not clear why we should want it to), it can at least remind us that Schmitt's equation of seventeenth-century reflections on reason of state with Hobbesian authoritarianism is tendentious—both in narrowing the historical field to Hobbes and in its interpretation of Hobbes himself. In contrast to Schmitt's "monological, unfettered fascist will, acting according to 'a pure decision not based on reason and discussion and not justifying itself,'"[91] Milton and Hobbes both occupy a universe in which rational justification is a crucial aspect of political action. Milton's tragedy (and perhaps tragedy in general) is much more a product of this effort to make rational sense of our experience than it is a celebration of the irrational will.

Notes

I am grateful to Vassilis Lambropoulos and Victoria Silver for comments on earlier drafts of this essay.

1 Carl Schmitt, *Political Theology*, trans. George Schwab (Cambridge, MA, and London, 1985), 5. "The decision on the exception is a decision in the true sense of the word. Because a general norm, as represented by an ordinary legal prescription, can never encompass a total exception, the decision that a real exception exists cannot therefore be entirely derived from this norm. . . . What is argued about [sovereignty] is the concrete application, and that means who decides in a situation of conflict what constitutes the public interest or interest of the state, public safety and order, *le salut public*, and so on. The exception, which is not codified in the existing legal order, can at best be characterized as a case of extreme peril, a danger to the existence of the state, or the like. But it cannot be circumscribed factually and made to conform to a preformed law" (ibid.).
2 Ibid., 6, 13, 33; quoting Thomas Hobbes, *Leviathan* (London, 1651), chap. 26.
3 On Schmitt and Benjamin, see Jacques Derrida, "Force of Law: The 'Mystical Foundation of Authority,'" in Deconstruction and the Possibility of Justice, a special issue of *Cardozo Law Review* 11 (1990): 919–1046, esp. 941, 943; cf. Schmitt, *Political Theology*, 10, where decision rather than norm is held to be the basis of legal order. Derrida notes that the German title of Benjamin's essay is "Zur Kritik der Gewalt," and that *Gewalt* may be translated as either violence or legitimate power, justified authority, thus raising the question of their relationship ("Force of Law," 927).
4 See Derrida, "Force of Law," 961, 963.
5 This may explain in part the interest of left-wing writers such as Otto Kirchheimer and Franz Neumann, as well as Benjamin, in Schmitt's early work. See William E. Scheuermann, *Between the Norm and the Exception: The Frankfurt School and the Rule of Law* (Cambridge, MA, and London, 1994), esp. chap. 1.
6 Schmitt, *Political Theology*, 36.

7   Arthur E. Barker, *Milton and the Puritan Dilemma* (Toronto, 1942), 148–49.

8   By Milton's voluntarism I do not mean "the Protestant tradition of voluntarism which held that whatever God commands is just simply because it is the will of God," as Martin Dzelzainis defines it in his introduction to John Milton, *Political Writings*, ed. Martin Dzelzainis, Cambridge Texts in the History of Political Thought (Cambridge, 1991), xv; I mean instead the belief in the efficacy of the human will.

9   Jean-Pierre Vernant, "Intimations of the Will in Greek Tragedy," in Vernant and Pierre Vidal-Naquet, *Myth and Tragedy in Ancient Greece*, trans. Janet Lloyd (New York, 1990), 49–84; quotation from 79. See also Jean-Pierre Vernant, "Tensions and Ambiguities in Greek Tragedy," 29–48, in the same volume.

10 John Milton, *Samson Agonistes*, in *Complete Prose and Major Poems*, ed. Merritt Y. Hughes (Indianapolis, 1984 [1957]), 549–93; quotation from 549.

11 Giacopo Mazzoni, *On the Defense of the Comedy of Dante* (1587), trans. Robert L. Montgomery (Tallahassee, 1983), 105–6; Antonio Minturno, *L'arte poetica* (1564), in *Literary Criticism*, ed. Allan H. Gilbert (Detroit, 1962), 290; see also 289. In his note on the preface to *Samson Agonistes*, Merritt Hughes observes that Minturno "came close to Milton's 'agonistic' conception by adding that tragedy is properly a kind of spiritual athletic discipline like the hard physical training of the Spartans, and that it trains men to endure reversals of fortune" (Milton, *Samson Agonistes*, 549 n. 3). Other Italian Renaissance commentators also noted that tragedy could police the passions, while implying (in some cases despite themselves) that it could also channel them into a potentially subversive stoicism. On the debate about catharsis, see Baxter Hathaway, *The Age of Criticism: The Late Renaissance in Italy* (Ithaca, 1962), 205–302.

12 Barbara K. Lewalski, "*Samson Agonistes* and the Tragedy of the Apocalypse," *PMLA* 85 (1970): 1050–62; quotation from 1051.

13 Milton, *Samson Agonistes*, 1062.

14 Renaissance commentators on imitation and on Aristotle's *Poetics* regularly discuss the pleasure that results from the catharsis of pity and fear in terms of a recognition of one's distance from the threat of violence (which is thus a recognition of self-preservation). In this context Lucretius's passage on the pleasure we take in observing a shipwreck from afar is often cited or alluded to; see, for example, Giangiorgio Trissino, *Poetica* (1563): "That evil which does not come on ourselves, as Lucretius says, is always pleasant to observe in others" (Gilbert, ed., *Literary Criticism*, 227).

15 Camille Wells Slights notes, in *The Casuistical Tradition* (Princeton, 1981), that "the maxim *salus populi suprema lex* was invoked variously in Henry Parker, *Observations upon some of his Majesties Late Answers and Expresses* (1642); in Samuel Rutherford, *Lex, Rex* (1644); in John Goodwin, *Right and Might Well Met* (1648); in Milton, *The Tenure of Kings and Magistrates* (1649); and in Thomas Hobbes, *Leviathan* (1651). Robert Sanderson devotes two of his ten lectures on casuistry to explaining it. See *Several Cases of Conscience Discussed in Ten Lectures* (1660)" (276 n. 26).

16 Carl Friedrich, *Constitutional Reason of State* (Providence, 1957), 4.

17 On the ambiguous position of reason of state between older and newer conceptions of politics, see Michel Foucault, "Governmentality," in *The Foucault Effect: Studies in Governmentality*, ed. Graham Burchell, Colin Gordon, and Peter Miller (Chicago, 1991),

87–104; and "Omnes et singulatim: Towards a Criticism of 'Political Reason,'" in *The Tanner Lectures on Human Values, 1981*, ed. Sterling M. McMurrin (Salt Lake City and Cambridge, 1981), 225–54. Foucault overemphasizes the degree to which the concept of reason of state is divorced from natural law ("Omnes et singulatim," 244); he also does not discuss the intersection of this newer conception of politics with puritanism.

18 Christopher Hill cites a number of the references to Samson in contemporary political debates, in *Milton and the English Revolution* (London, 1977), 428–30. See also Joseph Wittreich, *Interpreting "Samson Agonistes"* (Princeton, 1986), chap. 4.

19 On the link between reason of state and *arcana imperii*, see Ernst H. Kantorowicz, "Mysteries of State," *Harvard Theological Review* 48 (1955): 65–90; Francis D. Wormuth, *The Royal Prerogative, 1603–1649* (Port Washington, NY, and London, 1972 [1939]); and Jonathan Goldberg, *James I and the Politics of Literature* (Baltimore, 1983).

20 Wormuth, *Royal Prerogative*, 74. James I argued: "These are unfit Things to be handled in Parliament, except your King should require it of you: for who can have Wisdom to judge of Things of that Nature, but such as are daily acquainted with the Particulars of Treaties, and of the variable or fixed Connexion of Affairs of State, together with the Knowledge of Secret Ways, Ends and Intentions of Princes, in their several Negotiations?" (75).

21 Quoted by J. P. Sommerville, *Politics and Ideology in England, 1603–1640* (London and New York, 1986), 167–68. J. G. A. Pocock notes that Ashley was rebuked by Parliament for his invocation of "a law of state"; see *The Ancient Constitution and the Feudal Law*, 2d ed. (Cambridge, 1987 [1957]), 290.

22 Coke is quoted by Wormuth, *Royal Prerogative*, 78; Browne is quoted by Sommerville, *Politics and Ideology*, 166. On the role of reason of state in parliamentary debate, see also David Berkowitz, "Reason of State and the Petition of Right," in *Staatsräson*, ed. Roman Schnur (Berlin, 1975), 165–212; Richard Tuck, *Philosophy and Government, 1572–1651* (Cambridge, 1993), 202–79; and Alan Craig Houston, "Republicanism and Reason of State: From Royal Prerogative to the Rule of Law," in *The Politics of Necessity: Reason of State in Modern European Political Discourse* (Cambridge University Press, forthcoming).

23 Quoted in Tuck, *Philosophy and Government*, 234.

24 Henry Parker, *The Contra-Replicant, His Complaint to His Majestie* (London, 1642), 18–19.

25 John Milton, *A Defence of the English People* (1651), in *Collected Prose Works*, 8 vols., ed. Don M. Wolfe et al. (New Haven and London, 1953–82), 4, 1: 317–18.

26 Precisely because the people delegate or entrust their power to the sovereign in order that the state be preserved from the conflict of particular interests, the people may for reasons of state violently depose him and reassume their power when the sovereign violates this trust; see Dzelzainis, introduction to Milton, *Political Writings*, xvii–xviii, on Milton's use of the language of trusteeship rather than contract in *The Tenure* in order to avoid the implication that the king is an equal party with equal rights.

27 John Milton, *The Tenure of Kings and Magistrates* (1649), in Wolfe et al., eds., *Collected Prose Works*, 3: 194.

28 Milton, *Defence*, 4, 1: 397, 459. As Arthur Barker noted long ago, Milton's final justification for the king's execution "was provided by 'that general and primary law' which, according 'to the will of God, to nature, and to reason,' made the people's good the supreme law of the state" (*Puritan Dilemma*, 147).

29 Parker, *The Contra-Replicant*: "For if it be lawfull for both Houses of Parliament to defend themselves, it must of necessity follow, that they may and must imprison, levye
moneyes, suppresse seditious preachers, and make use of an arbitrary power according
to reason of state, and not confine themselves to meere expedient of Law" (29).

30 *Bishop Sanderson's Lectures on Conscience and Human Law*, ed. Christopher Wordsworth
(London, 1877), 273–74, 278; see 278–79, on the interpretation of "people" in the phrase
"salus populi" as excluding the king: "I observe . . . that the word *people* . . . may be
taken either *collectively*, as it includes the whole community of the State, the sovereign
and the *subjects* together; or *disjunctively*, as it implies the *subjects only*. . . . It is therefore
a most dangerous mistake (not to call it a malicious design) to wrest and to apply what
is said of the people *collectively* in the *first sense*, as it includes the *whole community* [in-
cluding the king], to the *people* in the *latter* acceptation, as it signifies the *subjects only*, to
the exclusion of the sovereign." Sanderson's lectures were delivered in 1647.

31 John Goodwin, *Right and Might Well Met* (London, 1648), 15.

32 Ibid., 16.

33 Sir John Davies, *The Question Concerning Impositions*; quoted in Wormuth, *Royal Prerogative*, 72. Wormuth notes that "the book was written toward the end of the reign of
James I, but was not published until 1656." According to Wormuth, the "three great
constitutional issues in the period 1600–1660" all involved the crown's appeal to reason
of state: "the king's right to levy impositions, decided in Bate's Case (1606); the king's
right to arrest for reason of state without alleging a cause, decided in the Five Knights'
Case (1627); the king's right to levy taxes without the consent of Parliament, on the plea
of necessity, decided in Hampden's case (1638)."

34 John Milton, *The Reason of Church Government* (1641), in Wolfe et al., eds., *Collected
Prose Works*, 1: 858–59.

35 Ibid.

36 Milton, *Defence*, 4, 1: 401–2. See also the reference to Samson in *Areopagitica*, in Wolfe
et al., eds., *Collected Prose Works*, 2: 557–58. On Milton's arguments from reason of state
in *The Tenure*, see Victoria Kahn, "The Metaphorical Contract in Milton's *Tenure of Kings
and Magistrates*," in *Milton and Republicanism*, ed. David Armitage, Armand Himy, and
Quentin Skinner (Cambridge, 1995), 87–112. For an analysis of Milton's views on reason of state which arrives at different conclusions, see Steven Jablonski, "'Evil Days':
Providence and Politics in the Thought of John Milton" (Ph.D. diss., Princeton University, 1993), chap. 4.

37 See George Mosse, *The Holy Pretence: A Study in Christianity and Reason of State from
William Perkins to John Winthrop* (Oxford, 1957); Friedrich, *Constitutional Reason of State*;
and Michael Walzer, *The Revolution of the Saints* (Cambridge, MA, 1965).

38 See Walzer, *Revolution of the Saints*; Albert O. Hirschman, *The Passions and the Interests:
Political Arguments for Capitalism before Its Triumph* (Princeton, 1977), who argues that
Weber's account of the rise of capitalism needs to be supplemented by attention to spe-
cifically political arguments; and Friedrich, *Constitutional Reason of State*, esp. chap. 4.

39 See Walzer, *Revolution of the Saints*, 47, 167.

40 Quoted in Friedrich, *Constitutional Reason of State*, 57.

41 Martin Luther, "Whether Soldiers, Too, Can Be Saved" (1526), in *Luther's Works*, 55 vols.,

ed. Jaroslav Pelikan and Helmut T. Lehmann; Vol. 46, ed. Robert C. Shultz (Philadelphia, 1967), 135.

42 The relevance of the doctrine of the calling to *Samson Agonistes* is explored in John Guillory, "The Father's House: *Samson Agonistes* in Its Historical Moment," in *Milton*, ed. Annabel Patterson (London, 1992), 202–25.

43 Milton, *The Tenure*, 3: 194.

44 William Perkins, *A Treatise of the Vocations or Callings of Men* (1603), in *The Works of William Perkins*, ed. Ian Breward (Appleford, UK, 1970), 456–76; quotation from 457. Perkins is also cited by Guillory ("The Father's House"), who is interested in the instability of the notion of calling as vocation or work in Luther and Perkins, and the tension between general and specific predestination—the called and the elect—in Calvin, but his chief concern is the way this instability adumbrates a bourgeois conception of the individual.

45 See Christopher Hill, "Covenant Theology and the Concept of 'A Public Person,'" in *Essays in Honour of C. B. Macpherson*, ed. Alkis Kontos (Toronto, 1979), 3–21. Hill shows that the criteria for defining a public person were themselves a subject of debate: for some a public person was anyone who held a representative public position, such as a Member of Parliament; for others "the godly were public persons because Christ was a public person, and they were part of Christ" (18). On the fear that casuistry would create rebellious subjects during Elizabeth's reign, see Lowell Gallagher, *Medusa's Gaze* (Stanford, 1991), 77–80.

46 Martin Luther, *On Secular Authority* (1522–23), in *Luther and Calvin on Secular Authority*, ed. and trans. Harro Höpfl, Cambridge Texts in the History of Political Thought (Cambridge, 1991), 15; see also 16: "It is in this way that all the saints have borne the Sword from the beginning of the world: Adam and his descendants, Abraham when he saved Lot. . . . And Moses, Joshua, the Children of Israel, Samson, David, and all the kings and princes of the Old Testament acted in the same way." As Höpfl points out, the German title of Luther's treatise, *Von Weltlicher Oberkeit*, is ambiguous: "Oberkeit" is "an abstract term meaning . . . the status of having authority or power" (xxxii); in this respect it is like Benjamin's "Gewalt."

47 Luther, *Secular Authority*, 15; cf. Romans 13:4.

48 Ibid., 22.

49 Ibid., 16, 18, 22.

50 It is thus not surprising that Samson's meditations involve some of the standard cases of casuistry (marriage with an infidel, attending forbidden rites, suicide), as well as what Perkins described as "the greatest [case of conscience] that ever was: how a man may know whether he be the child of God, or no" (quoted in Slights, *Casuistical Tradition*, 293). Although Slights discusses the links between *Samson Agonistes* and traditional cases of conscience, she stresses that these are "less important than Samson's gradual enlightenment about how to resolve moral problems" (292). On *Samson Agonistes* as a drama of the will, see William Kerrigan, "The Irrational Coherence of *Samson Agonistes*," *Milton Studies* 22 (1986): 217–32.

51 Milton, *Samson Agonistes*, 37–45.

52 Ibid., 52–54, 60–62.

53 On either/or reasoning and its transformation into both/and by the end of *Samson Ago-
nistes*, see Joseph Summers, "The Movements of the Drama," in *The Lyric and Dramatic
Milton*, ed. Joseph Summers (New York, 1965), 153–75, esp. 157–60. See also Edward
Tayler, *Milton's Poetry: Its Development in Time* (Pittsburgh, 1979), who regards *Samson
Agonistes* as a Christian tragedy because "Samson guided solely by God is not 'tragic,' as
Samson guided solely by himself is not 'Christian'" (121).

54 Milton, *Samson Agonistes*, 164–66. Stanley Fish, in "Question and Answer in *Samson
Agonistes*," *Critical Quarterly* 11 (1969): 232–64, notes that the chorus tries to make Samson "a particular instance of a general and implacable truth" (242). Fish also notes how
the chorus turns Samson's unparalleled condition into a parallel, that is, an example;
see "Spectacle and Evidence in *Samson Agonistes*," *Critical Inquiry* 15 (1989): 556–86,
esp. 559–60.

55 Milton, *Samson Agonistes*, 241–76 and 290, 532, 765.

56 Ibid., 350–51, 1155ff.

57 Ibid., 169, 52–54, 206–8, 881, 365, 370, 293–324, 652–709.

58 On the chorus's fideism, see Joan S. Bennett, "Liberty under the Law: The Chorus and
the Meaning of *Samson Agonistes*," *Milton Studies* 12 (1978): 141–63.

59 I borrow the term "negative dialectics" from Theodor Adorno and Max Horkheimer, who
used it to refer to a method of dialectical thinking that is not teleological, but instead
engages in an "immanent critique" of the status quo; see Victoria Silver, *Milton and the
Predicament of Irony* (Princeton University Press, in press), on the relevance of this term
to Milton's ironic poetics. Here I want to suggest that Samson engages in a kind of immanent critique of others' arguments from authority, showing that any positive term
contains its own negation: dialectical thinking is reasoning about the exception (or the
difference at the heart of any identity) because it turns positive terms into their own
negation ("at variance" with themselves [line 1585]). In showing that every positive term
can become its opposite, dialectical thinking also suggests a kind of equivocation.

60 Milton, *Samson Agonistes*, 222, 225, 231–33.

61 Ibid., 781, 784.

62 Ibid., 793–96.

63 Ibid., 811–12.

64 Ibid., 850–51, 865–70.

65 Ibid., 885–95.

66 See Barbara Kiefer Lewalski, "Milton's *Samson* and the 'New Acquist of True [Political]
Experience,'" *Milton Studies* 24 (1989): 233–51. Lewalski remarks, "In some ways there
seems little to choose between Dalila's proclaimed motives and Samson's own, since his
marriage [was] intended to advance Israel's cause against the Philistines. Samson, however, challenges Dalila's relativism by appealing to widely shared human values. With all
the polemic of the English civil war echoing in the background, he flatly denies ultimate
authority to civil and religious leaders, or to *raison d'état*" (241). This is true in the obvious sense that "ultimate authority" in Milton's universe always resides with God. But
there is another sense in which Samson does not reject reason of state at all: he simply
redefines it as critical reasoning about the exception. As this redefinition suggests, in
arguing from reason of state Dalila is not so much Samson's opposite as his parodic

double. On this point, see Joan S. Bennett, "'A Person Rais'd': Public and Private Cause in *Samson Agonistes*," *Studies in English Literature* 18 (1978): 155–68, esp. 156. Slights also notes Dalila's false reasoning about the public good (*Casuistical Tradition*, 277).

67 Lewalski notes that "Samson's responses [to Harapha] echo the basic radical Puritan (and Miltonic) justifications . . . [including] appeals to the natural law, which always allows rebellion against conquerors" ("Milton's *Samson*," 243); but she doesn't see the relevance of these remarks to Samson's exchange with Dalila. Bennett, however, does, in "Person Rais'd."

68 Milton, *Samson Agonistes*, 1205–13.

69 See Slights, *Casuistical Tradition*, 280.

70 Milton, *Samson Agonistes*, 1369–72.

71 Slights quotes the Protestant casuist William Ames on how subjection doesn't necessarily imply obedience. Even the general rule of nonresistance was qualified by scriptural passages stating that (in cases of conflict) one should always obey God, not man (*Casuistical Tradition*, 285). See Luther's and Calvin's arguments for passive obedience or nonresistance, as well as their remarks justifying active resistance by lesser magistrates against unjust rulers, in Quentin Skinner, *The Foundations of Modern Political Thought*, 2 vols. (Cambridge, 1978), 1: 191–238 et passim.

72 Milton, *Samson Agonistes*, 1377–79.

73 Ibid., 1409, 1381–84, 1385–86.

74 Ibid., 1402–6.

75 Summers also makes this point about the ambiguity of "life" ("Movements," 172).

76 For a sixteenth-century illustration of this fear, see the *Arte of English Poesie* (1589), in which George Puttenham gives examples of *amphibologia*, or ambiguous speech, which associate it with rebellion. On this association, see also Steven Mullaney, "Lying Like Truth: Riddle, Representation, and Treason in Renaissance England," *English Literary History* 47 (1980): 32–47. (The role of equivocation in *Samson Agonistes* may explain the echoes of *Macbeth* in lines 34, 82, and 605.)

77 Hobbes, *Leviathan*, chap. 38.

78 Milton, *Defence*, 4, 1: 374.

79 Fish notes that when Samson says, "I with this messenger will go along" (line 1384), the *will* "stands not for the fixed position of a fully formed and independent self but for a self 'willing' to have its configurations transformed by a future it cannot read" ("Spectacle and Evidence," 579). For Fish, this amounts to a shift in emphasis from Samson's final act of pulling down the temple to his decision to go with the messenger. In my reading, both actions involve decisions which are equally mysterious.

80 On the theological context of Milton's irony, see Silver, *Predicament of Irony*; she also briefly discusses the relationship between tragedy and irony.

81 Milton, *Samson Agonistes*, 1641–43.

82 Milton, *The Tenure*, 3: 215–16.

83 Dzelzainis, ed., Milton, *Political Writings*, xv.

84 Milton, *Samson Agonistes*, 1719–20, 1750–51.

85 In this sense, Milton's Samson does live up to one seventeenth-century etymology of his

name: "there a second time"; see William Riley Parker, *Milton's Debt to Greek Tragedy in "Samson Agonistes"* (Hamden, CT, 1963 [1937]), 13 n. 35.

86 Milton, *Samson Agonistes*, 1590, 1664–65.

87 In book 8, section 9, of the *Confessions*, Augustine describes the effect of sin as the inability *ex toto velle* (literally, to will completely); quoted in Charles Taylor, *Sources of the Self* (Cambridge, MA, 1989), 185.

88 Carrol B. Cox, "Citizen Angels: Civil Society and the Abstract Individual in *Paradise Lost*," *Milton Studies* 23 (1987): 165–96; quotations from 176.

89 Angus Fletcher, *Allegory* (1964); quoted by Neil Hertz, "The Notion of Blockage in the Literature of the Sublime," in *The End of the Line: Essays on Psychoanalysis and the Sublime* (New York, 1985), 47. Fletcher observes that this "intellectual tension, [which accompanies] the hard work of exegetical labor . . . is nothing less than the cognitive aspect of ambivalence which inheres in the contemplation of any sacred object. Whatever is *sacer* must cause the shiver of mingled delight and awe that constitutes our sense of 'difficulty'" (ibid.).

    A number of critics have commented on what I would call the double focus of *Samson Agonistes*. A. S. P. Woodhouse argues that Milton presents Samson as armed both with "celestial vigor" and "plain heroic magnitude of mind" and that the poem represents the human tragedy of Samson's martyrdom before it subsumes the human into a larger, providential scheme; see "Tragic Effect in *Samson Agonistes*," *University of Toronto Quarterly* 28 (1959): 205–22; quotations from 213, 221. Virginia R. Mollenkott makes a similar argument about Milton's presentation of Samson as both an instrument of God and a flawed human individual; see "Relativism in *Samson Agonistes*," *Studies in Philology* 67 (1970): 89–103. William Kerrigan, in *Prophetic Milton* (Charlottesville, 1974), observes that Samson's "tragedy poses one pair of alternatives that can never collapse into harmony." On the lines "doubtful whether God be Lord, / Or Dagon," he comments: "This 'Or' cannot be compromised. What the catastrophe of *Samson* divides, [only] the Apocalypse will clarify once and for all" (250); *Samson* dramatizes "the 'brotherly dissimilitudes' of *Areopagitica*" (253).

90 For evidence of interest in (though not to be simply equated with approval of) Schmitt's work on the part of leftist intellectuals, see the "Special Section on Carl Schmitt and the Frankfurt School," *Telos* 71 (1987): 37–111; and *Telos* 72 (1987), a special issue on Carl Schmitt. Benjamin's "Critique of Violence" is a touchstone of many of the articles in Deconstruction and the Possibility of Justice, the special issue of *Cardozo Law Review* cited in note 3.

91 Scheuermann, *Between the Norm and the Exception*, 203; quoting Schmitt, *Political Theology*, 66.

Ian Hunter

Literary Theory in Civil Life

For those already interested in heading away from the discussions of "aesthetics and politics" or "literature and ideology" that have preoccupied thinking about the social uses of literature for the last three decades, an alternative field of discussion concerns the civic role played by academic literary culture as a particular ethos or style of life. The way to this field goes through a genealogy of modern criticism as a distinctive "spiritual exercise" or practice of the self. Before mapping this genealogy, though, we should consider some of the different ways in which it is possible to discuss the relations among literature, politics, and society. The following typology is intended as a framework for clarifying the particular way that the theme of literature and politics has been formulated in modern literary theory and criticism.

The first kind of relation is one where a literary *paideia* functions as a cultural qualification for the exercise of political and administrative power. Max Weber's discussion of the relation between Confucianism and the Chinese bureaucracy falls within this category.[1] More recently, Peter Brown has contributed a graceful essay

The *South Atlantic Quarterly* 95:4, Fall 1996.
Copyright © 1996 by Duke University Press.

on the role of the Greek rhetorical paideia in the governance of the late Roman Empire. By providing central administrators and provincial notables with a common set of discursive and moral reflexes, this paideia allowed the far-flung provinces to be governed through the medium of an elite cultural deportment. Composing themselves "as carefully as they composed their speeches," the rhetors and philosophers of the late Empire played a key role in the exercise of government. Their schools transmitted the ethical disciplines through which public conduct was groomed, dangerous rage contained, and frank political advice proffered to rulers possessing legally unlimited power.[2] Moreover, as Gerhard Oestreich's *Neostoicism and the Early Modern State* reminds us, such a relation between literature and politics is by no means confined to the ancient world. While differing significantly from the rhetorical paideia of late antiquity, the neo-Stoic pedagogy of an early modern humanist like Lipsius displays its own version of the relation between literary training and the exercise of power. What Lipsius took from Seneca and Cicero were the rhetorical and ascetic means of cultivating the virtue of "constancy," a specific political comportment comprised of inward self-restraint and outward calm and fortitude that was required for civil governance in a period of confessional division and religious civil war.[3]

A second kind of relation between literature and politics occurs when the exercise of power is associated with and dependent on the mass dissemination of certain kinds of literature. Largely confined to print cultures, in this category too the differences are as important as the similarities. In the early modern period the exercise of Protestant pastoral discipline was dependent on the religious and commercial distribution of works in a variety of genres—the Bible, moralizing broadsides, conduct books, devotional manuals, spiritual autobiographies, and, eventually, novels.[4] We can also note a filial relation that developed between the cultural and commercial channels thus opened and the nineteenth-century novels of social reform.[5] Through these channels and without having to exercise direct legislative muscle, British governments could find their health, welfare, and educational programs receiving publicity, support, and criticism among the reading publics organized by socially engaged journals and novels such as Dickens's *Hard Times*, with its sentimental depiction of elementary education and factory labor.

A third relation between literature and politics is exemplified by the historical circumstances in which "aesthetic education"—formerly an elite practice of literary self-cultivation—became embodied in the governmental school systems of northwestern European societies and their colonial offshoots.[6] This development, which began in the middle of the nineteenth century and was the enabling condition of modern literary pedagogy ("English"), might be treated as a further instance of the first type (the exercise of power through cultural qualification) except that it was more widespread and concerned the governed as much as the governors. Moreover, it is important to focus on the historical specificity and peculiarity of what occurs when a highly specialized practice of aesthetic self-fashioning is redeployed as a social discipline in modern "governmental" societies,[7] a point to which I will return.

The fourth literature/politics relation appears not to be based on any particular historical literary culture or dissemination. It authorizes itself instead through the theoretical positing of a general relation between the exercise of power and the operation of literary texts (language, discourse). The varieties of literary theory offer different construals of this operation, viewing it in terms of the formal relations among the elements of a linguistic or semiotic system (structuralism); in terms of the role of such relations in the "naturalization" of social structures (Marxism) or psychic processes (Lacanianism); or in terms of the text's role in masking the destabilizing oppositions ("aporia") on which it is based (deconstruction). These different construals, though, share a common mode of theorization, one that morally stigmatizes the exercise of power by vesting it in the inscrutability of the operation of literary texts (again, variously portrayed via such notions as ideology, the unconscious, or "logocentrism"). Thus, for example, Terry Eagleton claims that the role of literary theory is to analyze how various discourses "shape the forms of consciousness and unconsciousness, which are closely related to the maintenance or transformation of our existing systems of power."[8] Similarly, Jacques Derrida can insist that "if it is of any consequence," deconstruction is not just "a specialized set of discursive procedures, still less the rules of a new hermeneutic method that works on texts or utterances in the shelter of a given or stable institution," but "also, at the very least, a way of taking a position, in its work of analysis, concerning the political and institutional structures that make possible and govern our practices, our competencies, our performances."[9] While they may differ over the construal of the literary operation, then, both writers share the mode of theorization that identifies its "political" character with its (initial) inaccessibility to representation. This makes literature always and everywhere political in the same way. In short, the fourth relation between literature and politics is pan-hermeneutic and (because of this) pan-political.

It should already be clear that there are significant methodological, disciplinary, and ethical differences between the first three varieties of the literature/politics relation and the fourth. In contrast to the latter, the former can all be formulated in a manner that is historically particular, theoretically minimal, and morally undecided. That is, each can allow what is to count as literature, politics, and the forms of their relation to be determined through local historical investigations. These investigations need make no general theoretical stipulations regarding the nature of subjectivity or power and need have no general ethical predilections regarding the exercise of power or the practice of literary cultivation. The fourth relation, however, is ahistorical; embedded in general theoretical speculation regarding the nature of subjectivity, language, and power; and characterized by invariant ethical standpoints on the exercise of power and the role of the literary in human emancipation.

In fact, we have already identified the main reason for this difference. As an initial formulation, let us say that by vesting the political in the inscrutability of the literary operation, modern literary theory endows itself with a specific ("philosophical") conception of power as unconscious action and positions itself to recover the literary operation for consciousness: Eagleton's analysis of the discourses that "shape the forms of consciousness and unconsciousness"; Derrida's recovery of "the political and institutional structures that make possible and govern our practices, our competencies, our performances." If literary theory's conception of the literature/politics relation is ahistorical, that is because (in contrast to the other three relations) at its heart we, find not a particular historical comportment of the person but the universal figure of the subject. This figure is invoked as soon as the operation of literature is said to escape or subvert the consciousness of the reader or writer. For what is escaped or subverted—in fact, posited by the trope of inscrutability—is precisely the figure of the subject oriented to a pure contemplation of the (presently hidden) literary operation. Let us also be clear that it makes no difference whether one shares Eagleton's view that this operation will indeed be revealed to consciousness (through a theoretical representation of its material conditions) or Derrida's view that the moment of revelation will be permanently deferred (through the interminable oscillations of the aporia). What specifies the standpoint of literary theory is simply the teaching that the operation of literature is presently inscrutable; for this is what conjures up the subject as the universal longing for insight into that operation—a longing satisfied no less by the pathos of deferral than by the promise of revelation.

In characterizing literary theory (and its view of the literature/politics relation) in this manner, I am making use of a particular methodological turn taken by the disciplines of the history of philosophy and religion. Briefly, this turn entails shifting the axis of analysis from the truth of a philosophical discourse to the role of such a discourse in shaping a particular "spiritual comportment" or way of acceding to the truth. Equally, one might say that this is a shift in which the analysis of discourse as a theoretical representation is subordinated to the description of it as a "spiritual exercise" shaping the comportment of the "theorist" as a specialized persona or conduct of life.[10] Applying this descriptive strategy to literary theory leads to a similarly radical shift in the axis of analysis. Instead of asking how we can uncover the inscrutable operation of literature—and arguing over whether it is a linguistic, psychic, social, or phenomenological process—one asks a different question: What kind of relation to or comportment of the self is formed by teaching that the operation of literature is inscrutable? This question allows us to approach the latency of literary processes in a new way: not as a *theoretical problem* requiring clarification but as an *ethical problematization* requiring individuals to relate to themselves as in need of theoretical clarification. In short, we can suggest that the inscrutable character of literature arises not from theoretical reflection but from its pedagogical or "psychogogical" use as a discipline shaping the comportment of the one who reflects.

This changed perspective allows us to put a new set of questions to literary theory's pan-hermeneutic and pan-political relation between literature and politics. We can ask, for example, whether, like Brown's rhetorical paideia and Oestreich's neo-Stoic discipline, modern literary theory is itself a species of cultivation—one linked to the exercise of power not through a theoretical clarification of the unconscious but through the cultural qualification of the theorist as a being who seeks clarification. We can also ask whether the political salience of theory might arise less from its unmasking of power than from the historical circumstances—centered in the redeployment of aesthetic education as a governmental pedagogy—that have put the moral authority of the unmasking theorist to work in the field of social governance.

═══════

Edward Said situates his discussion of cultural imperialism by positing a fundamental "closure" of European discourses with regard to the experience of colonized peoples. Of interest here, however, is not the "postcolonial" content of the occluded experience, which other theorists have attributed to women, gays, ethnic minorities—and, not so long ago, to the working class—but the manner in which literature is implicated in this closure:

> Yet neither Conrad nor Marlow gives us a full view of what is *outside* the world-conquering attitudes [of imperial culture]. . . . By that I mean that *Heart of Darkness* works so effectively because its politics and aesthetics are, so to speak, imperialist, which in the closing years of the nineteenth century seemed to be at the same time an aesthetic, politics, and even epistemology inevitable and unavoidable. For if we cannot truly understand someone else's experience and if we must therefore depend upon the assertive authority of the sort of power that Kurtz wields as a white man in the jungle or that Marlow, another white man, wields as narrator, there is no use looking for other, non-imperialist alternatives; the system has simply eliminated them and made them unthinkable.[11]

Apparently, this closure is so complete that even today it defeats the efforts of all those who would appeal to something beyond its discursive horizon. It defeats the resentful subaltern voices of the colonized, who, in dismissing the European moral novel as so much "aesthetic frumpery," fail to work through it, thereby falling victim to their own assertiveness. And it defeats the empirical historians of colonialism. In presuming to offer a descriptive account of the reality outside the aesthetic discourse of the novel, these historians allegedly overlook their own entrapment within the symbolic violence of narrative form, with all the political distortion that this is supposed to entail.[12]

There is thus apparently no alternative but to read imperialism through the novel itself. For although it too is opaque to the real imperialism that lies outside its discourse, the novel is marked by a unique self-consciousness regarding its opacity. This self-consciousness, says Said, is expressed by a "dislocation" in the novel's discursive organization that, in the case of *Heart of Darkness*, takes the form of a gap between the narrator's point of view and the author's. Although this gap is not sufficient to allow the author access to the Real of colonialism or to the postcolonial future, it does open a space between the flux of the real and the assertive authority of representation, from which the future can emerge. In fact, this is how the novel overcomes the closure of representation: not through a more accurate depiction but by participating in the same reality as colonialism itself. For it appears that colonialism is nothing other than the metaphysical violence inflicted by representation upon an unrepresentable reality. The power of the "white man in the jungle" and the power wielded by the narrator have, it seems, the same source and potentiality—in metaphysics:

> By accentuating the discrepancy between the official "idea" of empire and the remarkably disorienting actuality of Africa, Marlow unsettles the reader's sense not only of the very idea of empire but of something more basic, reality itself. For if Conrad can show that all human activity depends on controlling a radically unstable reality to which words approximate only by will or convention, the same is true of empire, of venerating the idea, and so forth. . . . Conrad's genius allowed him to realise that the ever-present darkness could be colonised or illuminated . . . but that it also had to be acknowledged as independent. . . . [Kurtz and Marlow] (and of course Conrad) are ahead of their time in understanding that what they call "the darkness" has an autonomy of its own, and can reinvade and reclaim what imperialism has taken for *its* own.[13]

Still, while the novelist opens the gap between representation and being, thereby allowing the Other its autonomy, he nonetheless remains trapped within his own representation: "But Marlow and Kurtz are also creatures of their time and cannot take the next step, which would be to recognise that what they saw, disablingly and disparagingly, as a non-European 'darkness' was in fact a non-European world *resisting* imperialism so as one day to regain sovereignty and independence, and not, as Conrad reductively says, to reestablish the darkness."[14] It is left to the theorist, therefore, to fully admit the previously occluded Other to the sphere of representation by naming it (the "non-European world *resisting* imperialism"), but apparently not in a manner that subordinates it again to the assertive authority of (narrative–historical) meaning. The "task" of the theorist is thus to occupy neither the stable space of history nor the timeless space of aesthetics, but to move between them, in the space of dialectical transformation or becoming, revealing the future in the passage between an unrepresentable reality and an unavoidable representation.

From literary theory's treatment of the literature/politics relation, we can isolate three routine hermeneutic operations which, far from identifying literary theory as a modern idiosyncrasy, link it to an ancient spiritual exercise.

The first operation is that of *hermeneutic (self-)problematization*. The unannounced gesture that transports Said's reader across the hermeneutic threshold is the teaching that the text is not to be trusted—that its representations are too clouded by interest or desire to reveal the real, that it is closed and inscrutable. For it is this gesture that requires me to distrust my own representation or reading of the text by acknowledging that it too shares these distorting interests and desires. This in turn conditions my taking up a hermeneutic relation to myself, that is, of coming to think of my own truth as hidden by the distortion of representation and hence as in need of decipherment. At the same time, and as part of the same practice of self-problematization, the reader is subject to the doctrine that the real is not accessible outside the literary text either. Such is the effect of teaching that the ostensibly extratextual knowledges—of the text's literal–political truth and empirical–historical context—are themselves closed within the authority of *their* representations. The hermeneutic problematization thus renders the text both opaque to its outside (compelling the turn inward to self-decipherment) and inescapable (dictating that this decipherment take place only through interpretation of the literary text): "There is no way of doing such readings as mine, no way of understanding the 'structure of attitude and reference' except by working through the novel."[15] In short, by deploying the text as both inscrutable and inescapable, literary theory compels and motivates certain individuals—nowadays mainly humanities students—to search for their hidden selves in the hermeneutic decipherment of the text's hidden meaning.

The second operation is the *dialectical "practice of the self."* According to a long-standing metaphysics, it is not simply the failure of knowledge that occludes the real, but the nature of human ethical being as such, the interests and desires of which distort contemplation and make representation a self-regarding exercise of the will: "All human activity depends on controlling a radically unstable reality to which words approximate only by will or convention."[16] According to an equally long-standing moral anthropology, it is the divided character of human being that is responsible for this occlusion of the real: the person is split between an intellect that seeks an impossibly pure insight into the nature of the real and a sensibility whose interests and desires block this insight even while they motivate and give pleasure. The real thus may not be approached directly through a positive knowledge, but only via a transformation of human being that reconciles or overcomes this division. In other words, the practice of self-decipherment into which literary theory inducts its practitioners is also a practice of self-transformation, for tying the recessive character of the real to the divisions of the self means that true knowledge must wait on the overcoming of these divisions.

The theoretical reading thus takes the form of a dialectical practice through which the reader seeks to overcome the divisions of ethical being. This practice of the self is organized via the rhetorical formula of balanced antitheses. Far from being (as some of their plain-speaking critics allege) a specious complexification of thought, these antitheses or aporia, like their Stoic and Pyrrhonist prototypes, are in fact the discursive instruments for a particular work of the self on the self. The goal of this ethical labor is the achievement of an inner equipoise between two viewpoints, discursively positioned as contradictory yet inescapable.[17] Hence the theoretical reading constitutes a demanding but repetitive contrapuntal spiritual exercise. On the one hand, the reader is required to criticize the aesthetic text for its self-interested occlusion of the real: "We must not say that since *Mansfield Park* is a novel, its affiliations with a sordid history [of imperialism] are irrelevant or transcended." On the other hand, all direct representations of the real must also be criticized for failing to work through the interests and desires of the aesthetic text: "Does the aesthetic silence or discretion of a great novel in 1814 receive adequate explication in a major work of historical research a full century later? . . . *Mansfield Park* encodes experiences and does not simply repeat them." The object of the theoretical reading thus is not to achieve an "assertive" description of the text or its context. Rather, it is to stage a discursive equilibrium between the impossible disinterest of positive historical knowledge and the unacceptable self-enclosure of the aesthetic sensibility: "The task is to lose neither a true historical sense of the first, nor a full enjoyment or appreciation of the second, all the while seeing both together."[18] It is the pursuit of this equipoise as a spiritual goal that identifies the dialectical reading as a particular ethical task of behavior or ascetic work of the self on the self.

The third operation is the *moral stigmatization of the political.* As a result of the intellectualist imperative to subject all spheres of life to the regime of self-decipherment and self-transformation—"all human activity depends on controlling a radically unstable reality"—the political and governmental spheres lose their specific gravity and appear only as icons of hermeneutic failure. The exercise of political and governmental power is thus treated as a macroscopic projection of the same "assertive authority" and willful representation that is supposed to flow from the person's failure to be open to the Other. (Imperialism is an expression of representational closure.) Conversely, as the microcosm of bad politics, personal theoretical "errors"—empiricism, (nondialectical) "rationalism"—are stigmatized as the intellectual correlates of political oppression. (Positive knowledge is an armature of imperialism.) In accordance with the remorseless logic of the dialectical spiritual exercise, the "assertiveness" of politics is pinned to its alleged failure to reconcile being and thought: on the one hand, the political is identified with the premature attempt to sweep aside hermeneutics and gain direct access to empirical or transcendental realities; on the other, it is treated as symptomatic of enclosure within self-interested representational systems. Organized by the dialectical exercise, Said's political analysis works through a series of paired, mutually defined dialectical failures, or ethical mirror inversions: "Policy-oriented intellectuals [who] have internalised the norms of the state" thus find their mirror image in academic "cults"—"post-modernism, discourse analysis, New Historicism, deconstruction, neo-pragmatism"—whose self-interested and self-enclosed "jargon" cuts them off from the political world altogether, inducing "an astonishing sense of weightlessness with regard to the gravity of history and individual responsibility."[19] Similarly, the self-enclosed and self-serving images of Western media conglomerates (e.g., of Arab "terrorism" and "fundamentalism") generate their own inverse image: the anti-American resistance movements whose transcendent religious aspirations make them no less closed and intolerant than their imperial Other.

Not surprisingly, a true (secular, humane) politics is identified with movement, with the unfixing of the mirror oppositions—in short, with the playing-off of each side against the other. Said thus endorses a "negative dialectic" that would dissolve the frozen political identities and interests and would reunite humanity's warring camps: "What matters a great deal more than the stable identity kept current in official discourse is the contestatory force of an interpretative method whose material is the disparate, but intertwined and interdependent, and above all overlapping streams of historical experience."[20] In this way, in their restless movement through and beyond the oppositional fixities ("intellectual exile"), the hermeneutic exercises of the literary theorist can capture the migratory experience of the political refugee. Hence, "while it would be the rankest Panglossian dishonesty to say that the bravura performances of the intellectual exile and the miseries of the displaced person or refugee are the same," it is apparently not dishonest to suggest that such bravura performances embody this misery and its potential for liberation: "It is possible, I think, to regard the intellectual as first distilling then articulating the predicaments that disfigure modernity—mass deportation, imprisonment, population transfer, collective dispossession, and forced immigrations."[21]

─────

In early Christian monasticism, reading took its place alongside fasting, prayer, the keeping of vigils, and the making of pilgrimages as an ascetic practice performed by the spiritual athlete in training for holiness. Of interest here is not the doctrinal content of the holy books but the practice of reading to which they were subjected, one that constituted a specific spiritual exercise. Michel Foucault has provided a suggestive framework for approaching this exercise, contrasting it with the different (yet related) use of ethical literature in the pagan philosophical schools.[22] According to Foucault, the latter use was primarily *mnemonic*, comprising a series of techniques—meditation, repetition, memorization, autosuggestion—aimed at transforming the precepts of a particular master into ethical habits.[23] The Christian practice, however, was primarily *hermeneutic*, consisting of techniques of self-decipherment and self-purification intended to prepare the individual for contemplation of the divine.[24]

For John Cassian, the Scriptures, far from being transparent and ready for memorization, were themselves clouded by the frailties and illusions of human understanding. Hence Cassian recommended a fourfold technique for separating "the precious gold of Scripture" from the dross with which it is alloyed in the human understanding: first, by attending to the difference between the "painted" and the true gold of Scripture; second, by rejecting "counterfeit" religious thoughts; third, by detecting the alloy of "false and heretical meaning" in the Scriptures; and finally, by recognizing and rejecting those meanings corroded and debased by personal vanity. In this exercise the opacity of Scripture, arising from the corrupted capacities of human nature, could become the instrument of moral self-problematization. It was the means by which the monk would be required and motivated to turn inward, deciphering and transforming himself by discriminating the inner meaning of the holy books from the false impressions left in the corrupted medium of their human understanding:

> We should then constantly search all the inner chambers of our hearts, and trace out the footsteps of whatever enters into them with the closest investigation lest haply some beast, if I may say so, relating to the understanding, either lion or dragon, passing through has furtively left the dangerous marks of his track, which will show to others the way of access into the secret recesses of the heart, owing to a carelessness about our thoughts. And so daily and hourly turning up the ground of the heart with the gospel plough . . . we shall manage to stamp out or extirpate from our hearts the lairs of noxious beasts and the lurking places of poisonous serpents.[25]

In this manner, through a sedulous winnowing of the scriptural husk from its inner truth, the spiritual athlete could purify and clarify his inner self, preparing it for contemplation of divine things.

Is it the ghost of Cassian's inscrutable Scripture—darkened by the vanity of human reason and corrupted by the self-interest of human passion— that haunts Said's "closed" text? Without putting more weight on it than it can bear, and acknowledging its conjectural and provisional character, let us formulate a relation between the early Christian and the modern literary hermeneutics of the self as follows: In deploying ethical writings in the space of hermeneutic self-problematization—that is, by tying the hidden meaning of the text to the opacity of the reader's ethical being—modern literary theory emerges as a historical improvisation on the hermeneutic exercises associated with the Christian pursuit of holiness. Acknowledging that in any such improvisation the discontinuities will be as important as the continuities—and accepting that changes in the circumstances of their deployment will change the significance and force of the exercises themselves—it is possible nonetheless to suggest some lines of historical transformation linking the two practices of self-decipherment. For the sake of discussion at least, we can suggest four such lines running through Northern European intellectual and political life between the sixteenth and eighteenth centuries: (1) the "extra-monastic" (Reformation) dissemination of the hermeneutic exercises; (2) their philosophical "secularization"; (3) their aesthetic deployment; and (4) their use as a "counter-politics."

We can draw some lessons regarding the extra-monastic dissemination of Christian hermeneutics from Henning Reventlow's *Authority of the Bible and the Rise of the Modern World*. In tracking the genesis of the "modern" attitude to religion and biblical authority, Reventlow pays particular attention to what he calls the "spiritualist" wing of Christianity. Stretching back to patristic times and subject to periodic efflorescences since then, this tendency operates through a series of "neo-Platonic" dualisms—the visible and invisible church, inner and outer religion, the spirit and the letter of the holy books—oriented toward the critique of official religion from the standpoint of a personal ascetic pietism.[26] Not the least of its interests for our purposes is Reventlow's argument concerning the manner in which this spiritualist pietism could give rise to a kind of rationalism usually associated with the German *Aufklärung*. Once the distinction between the spirit and the letter allowed the literal–historical truth of the Scriptures to be read as the merely allegorical expression of an inner ethical truth, and once larger sectors of the population had been given access to this hermeneutic, divine law could be transformed into a moral imperative or a rational process occurring within the individual.[27] On this view the so-called Enlightenment—or at least its transcendental–rationalist variety—was really an extension of the "Christianization" of lay populations that began with the Reformation. Here we can do no more than gesture toward the complex interactions between proselytizing confessions and centralizing states that historians have identified with the Christianizing or "confessionalizing" of early modern Europe.[28] For the moment, let us regard these interactions—in which spiritual exercises were redeployed as social disciplines, and territorial states supported Christian pastoral school systems—as bridges across which devotional practices like the Christian hermeneutics of the self could march into the universities, journals, and salons of educated Europe, installing their regime in the name of rational self-reflection.

The secularization of Christian hermeneutics thus refers to its redeployment in a range of new civic–intellectual spaces. We might, therefore, equally think of this process as the Christianization of civic space, with monastic spiritual exercises mutating into the intellectual disciplines of a civic elite.[29] The "ethicizing" and individualizing of devotional practice accompanying this process can be glimpsed in Kant's distinction between statutory and moral doctrines:

> Now tenets of faith which are also to be conceived as divine commands are either merely *statutory* doctrines, which are contingent for us and [must be] revealed [if we are to know them], or *moral* doctrines, which involve consciousness of their necessity and can be recognized a priori—that is, *rational* doctrines [*Vernunftlehren des Glaubens*]. The sum of statutory teachings comprises *ecclesiastical faith* [or dogma]; that of moral teachings, pure *religious* faith.[30]

At one level, the transformation of devotional practice is clear enough. It is registered in the assertion that the force of divine commands is to be located no longer in the revealed will of a supernatural being but in the subject's consciousness of their rational necessity. What is less evident, though, is that the manner in which the subject becomes conscious of this rational necessity—or accedes to its truth—is itself dependent on the maintenance of a particular devotional practice: the (modified) Christian hermeneutics of the self. Two aspects of Kant's philosophical theology, as outlined in *Religion within the Limits of Reason Alone* and *The Conflict of the Faculties*, help to make this clear.

First, Kant redeploys the Christian hermeneutics of the self in its characteristic spiritualist form, distinguishing between the "sensuous" husk of the Scriptures and their "intellectual" kernel. Moreover, like Cassian, he ascribes the opacity of the husk to the fallen nature of man's ethical being, specifically, to man's "sensuous inclinations" that are satisfied by the self-regarding rewards promised in the "sensible vehicle" of Bible stories. Armed with this version of the hermeneutic, Kant produces a rationalist rereading of the central sacramental truths, treating the Incarnation, the Trinity, the Crucifixion, Holy Communion, and Baptism as so many allegorical expressions of moral ideas to be found only within human reason.

(Thus, for example, he argues that the figure of Jesus as the "God–man" expresses not the literal truth of God's embodiment in a real man but the ethical truth of the "idea of humanity in its moral perfection.") Following familiar Protestant, Deist precedents, Kant then proceeds to attack the visible or "ecclesiastical" religions of Judaism, Catholicism, and orthodox Protestantism for their sacramentalist belief in the literal, historical truth of biblical narratives. In pandering to the desire for sacramental salvation, he argues, such faiths reinforce people's self-regarding inclinations, which are precisely what must be overcome if they are to learn to act on the basis of rational insight into moral law.[31] At the same time, however, Kant extends the range of the hermeneutic to attack philological "scholarship," which, through the disciplines of comparative grammar and contextual analysis, was beginning to bring the Bible within the sphere of positive, historical knowledge. For Kant, the true or rational meaning of the Bible is not what may be discovered through a philological investigation of its historical authorship but what is "put there" by the hermeneutic reading, in which the reader's sloughing of the textual husk performs the work of self-purification/-clarification:

> In explaining the Bible to the people the preacher must be guided, not by what scholarship *draws out* of Scripture by philological studies, which are often no more than misleading guesses, but by what a moral cast of mind [*moralischer Denkungsart*] (according to the spirit of God) *puts into* it, and by teachings that can never mislead and can never fail to produce beneficial results. In other words, he must treat the text *only* (or at least *primarily*) as an occasion for anything morally improving that can be made from it, without venturing to search what the sacred authors themselves might have meant by it.[32]

The "Scriptural scholar" must therefore be subordinated to the "Scriptural interpreter," for philology is concerned only with scientific knowledge of the historical meaning and authenticity of the holy books, whereas interpretation gives access to a universal rational truth through the moral transformation of the interpreter:

> With regard to what is statutory in religion, we may require biblical hermeneutics (*hermeneutica sacra*)—which, since it has to do with a scientific system, cannot be left to the laity—to tell us whether the exegete's findings are to be taken as *authentic* or *doctrinal*. In the first

case, exegesis must conform literally (philologically) with the author's meaning. But in the second case the writer is free, in his exegesis, to ascribe to the text (philosophically) the meaning it admits of for morally practical purposes (the pupil's edification); for faith in a merely historical proposition is, in itself, dead.[33]

Or, more succinctly, "For the final purpose even of reading these holy Scriptures, or of investigating their content, is to make men better; the historical element, which contributes nothing to this end, is something which is in itself quite indifferent, and we can do with it what we like."[34]

Kant's "rational" interpretation of the Scriptures is thus actually inimical to philology's historical description of biblical texts and contexts. Seen in this light, the theoretical doctrine that the text has no fixed historical meaning—that true meaning is read in during the process of interpretation—is anything but a symptom of postmodern nihilism. On the contrary, the strategies by which modern literary theory renders the text inscrutable (by problematizing its literal historical truth) and inescapable (by privileging hermeneutic self-decipherment over philological description) apparently emerged with the early modern philosophical redeployment of the Christian hermeneutics of the self.

Second, Kant's version of the hermeneutic is supported by a special "dialectical" spiritual exercise. Kant might well claim to be moving the necessity of moral doctrine from supernatural to rational auspices, yet such doctrine still remains outside the sphere of positive knowledge and declarative statement. It must be approached asymptotically, through a series of painstakingly arranged antitheses or antinomies. In the *Conflict*, Kant organizes these antitheses around the opposition between (Lutheran) orthodoxy and Pietism, each of which is problematized from the standpoint of the other. Orthodoxy is thus made to represent the view that moral transformation can be achieved by adherence to the revealed, historical "letter" of the Scriptures, leading to sacramentalism and the formalist belief in salvation through mere "statutory" knowledge. Pietism is made to stand for the opposite view, that moral transformation comes about through the individual's direct experience of the spirit of the word in his own heart—a view identified with Illuminism and the voluntarist belief in salvation through the "feeling" of God's gratuitous grace.[35] The function of this opposition, however, is not to validate one position at the expense of the other; nor is it to invalidate both in favor of a new, positive doctrine. Its role instead is to require the reader to hold these two positions in intellectual equipoise—problematizing, simultaneously, orthodoxy's literalism and formalism from the standpoint of Pietism's direct experience of saving grace, and Pietism's Illuminist enthusiasm from the standpoint of orthodoxy's insistence on the revealed truth of the Scriptures. In fact, Kant's critical hermeneutic operates only *through* and *as* this spiritual balancing act. Thus, for example, it is only by counterposing the orthodox view of the Savior (as a historical reality) and the heterodox view of salvation (as a matter of inner illumination) that Kant arrives at the "critical" view of Jesus as a regulatory idea or "archetype lying in our reason":

> Even the Bible seems to have nothing else in view: it seems to refer, not to supernatural experiences and fantastic feelings which should take reason's place in bringing about this revolution [man's moral transformation], but to the spirit of Christ, which he manifested in teachings and examples so that we might make it our own—or rather, since it is already present in us by our moral predisposition, so that we might simply make room for it. And so, between *orthodoxy* which has no soul and *mysticism* which kills reason, there is the teaching of the Bible, a faith which our reason can develop out of itself. This teaching is the true religious doctrine, based on the *criticism* of practical reason, that works with divine power on all men's hearts toward their fundamental improvement and unites them all in one universal (though invisible) church.[36]

Here, we are not concerned with the content of the "true religious doctrine" that Kant purports to derive from the hermeneutic exercise (and which will soon be joined by various "true" aesthetic, historical, and political doctrines), but with the role of the exercise in forming a particular way of *acceding* to the truth of doctrine (of whatever kind). By aligning a dislocation in the text (vehicle versus meaning) with a dislocation in ethical being (sensibility versus intellect), the hermeneutic makes access to true doctrine dependent on a practice of self-reflection that is simultaneously a practice of ethical self-transformation because the dialectical refinement of the sensibility is intended both to reveal the pure moral idea and to give it power over self-interested desire. If the (hermeneutic) division of the text is between an opaque exterior vehicle and an unreachable interior meaning, while the (moral–anthropological) division of the person is between an impure sensibility and a pure intellect, then neither division is grounded in the *nature* of texts or of persons. Each is a purely historical mode of the hermeneutic practice of the self, operating as an instrument of self-problematization and self-shaping. The object of this hermeneutic is thus not knowledge of the text—which was becoming the province of philology—but the forming of a certain spiritual or intellectual comportment of the subject. For the moment, let us say that this comportment is one in which the reader, ceaselessly moving between a sensuous literalism and an intellectual intuitionism, approaches the point whereby refinement of the sensible vehicle and embodiment of the supersensible idea enable him to form a text and a self through which reason can transform the world. Kant's redeployment of the Christian hermeneutics of the self thus transfers the status of holiness to a new kind of (civic) intellectual. This figure, while eschewing supernatural guarantees in the name of rational self-reflection, inherits the prestigious disciplines of self-clarification/-purification that promise to illuminate the mundane world not through mere knowledge but through the attainment of a higher or more complete mode of ethical being.

It is in Schiller, however, that we find the move to identify this more complete mode of being with the "aesthetic." The unfamiliarity of this reconstructed term—in his First Critique Kant was still using it to name the forms of sense perception, while Baumgarten's *Aesthetica* construed it as "con-fused" or indistinct ideas—is reflected in a long footnote that Schiller appended to his *Aesthetic Education*:

> For readers not altogether familiar with the precise meaning of this word, which is so much abused through ignorance, the following may serve as an explanation. Everything which is capable of phenomenal manifestation may be thought of under four different aspects. A thing can relate directly to our sensual condition (to our being or well-being): that is its physical character. Or it can relate to our intellect, and afford us knowledge: that is its logical character. Or it can relate to our will, and be considered as an object of choice for a rational being: that is its moral character. Or, finally, it can relate to the totality of our various functions without being a definite object for any single one of them: that is its aesthetic character. A man can please us through his readiness to oblige; he can, through his discourse, give us food for thought; he can, through his character, fill us with respect; but finally

he can also, independently of all this, and without our taking into consideration in judging him any law or any purpose, please us simply as we contemplate him and by the sheer manner of his being [*Erscheinungsart*]. Under this last-named quality of being we are judging him aesthetically. Thus there is an education to health, and education to understanding, an education to morality, and education to taste and beauty. This last has as its aim the development of the whole complex of our sensual [*sinnlichen*] and spiritual [*geistigen*] powers in the greatest possible harmony.[37]

Schiller measured his distance from Kant's moral philosophy in his essay "On Grace and Dignity": In emphasizing the dignity of moral duty over the grace of aesthetic being, Kant had apparently taken a one-sided rationalist view, coercing the feelings in the name of the law. In doing so, argued Schiller, he had ignored the possibility of a true reconciliation of intellect and sensibility that would allow man to obey the law joyfully and without constraint.[38] Equally, we might mention Schleiermacher's *On Religion* as a second instance of the post-Kantian aesthetic turn, since he too saw Kant's moral law as repressing the feelings. For Schleiermacher it was the feelings, not reason, that connected man to the divine, and they did so through the immediacy with which they opened him to nature and to art.[39] And even today, the view that the post-Kantian turn to the aesthetic represented a fundamental critique of and alternative to "Kantianism" is not without its adherents.[40]

From our standpoint, though, the aesthetic turn is far from being a break with the spiritual exercises that Kant had helped to transport into the civil sphere. After all, Schiller's and Schleiermacher's demands for a less repressive or more harmonious relation between intellect and feeling call up the same divided ethical being—that is, the same moral anthropology—that Kant invokes. So too should their complaints about Kant's one-sidedness and their aspirations to a more complete mode of being be read as indelible signs of the same dialectical spiritual exercise that Kant had helped to refurbish for civil–intellectual use. In short, if Kant's moral philosophy can be seen (in part) as a philosophical redeployment of the Christian hermeneutics of the self, then Schiller's and Schleiermacher's aesthetics can be seen as historical variations or improvisations on the same ethical practice. It is in this sense that we can talk about an "aestheticization" of religious hermeneutics.

Schiller's *Aesthetic Education* can be regarded as the first fully developed program for deploying the Christian hermeneutics of the self in the aesthetic sphere. While Kant's philosophical modification of the hermeneutic exercises was driven by their pedagogical deployment in the university seminar, Schiller's improvisation sprang from a broader urban context— the milieu of literary journalism, friendship-cults, *Seelsorgegruppen*, and reading groups that linked the university and the seminary to the salons of an educated elite.[41] Here, with the ethicizing and individualizing of Christian spirituality generating a cult of "feeling," it became possible for intellectuals like Schiller to substitute literary fiction for the holy books and to adapt the hermeneutics of holiness to the cultivation of aesthetic inwardness.[42]

The marks of this transformation are clearly visible in Schiller's disposition of the literary text, which could not be approached as an object of rhetorical imitation, philological description, or doctrinal instruction because of the unique manner in which its meaning is "embodied" in its formal organization. But this teaching, which would pass into the New Criticism as the imperative of "form–content unity," is only a symptom of Schiller's aesthetic adaptation of the hermeneutic spiritual exercises. If the text suffers an internal dislocation, dividing into an empty form and a formless meaning, this is because man's ethical being is similarly divided into a "form drive" and a "sense drive," yielding a nature that is either "too tense" (didactic) or "too relaxed" (sensuous). In other words, the dislocation and unification of aesthetic form and content are features not of the literary text but of the practices of hermeneutic self-problematization/ -cultivation in which that text may be caught up. Lack of aesthetic unity in the text is thus a symptom of the reader's own failure to reconcile his form and sense drives:

> But it is by no means always proof of formlessness in the work of art itself if it makes its effect solely through its contents; this may just as often be evidence of a lack of form in him who judges it. If he is either too tensed or too relaxed, if he is used to apprehending either exclusively with the intellect or exclusively with the senses, he will, even in the case of the most successfully realised whole, attend only to the parts, and in the presence of the most beauteous form respond only to the matter. Receptive only to the raw material, he has first to destroy the aesthetic organisation of a work before he can take pleasure

in it, and laboriously scratch away until he has uncovered all those details which the master, with infinite skill, had caused to disappear in
the harmony of the whole. The interest he takes in it is quite simply
either a moral or a material [*physich*] interest; but what precisely it
ought to be, namely aesthetic, that it certainly is not.[43]

Like Kant's insight into the "true rational doctrine," Schiller's unity of form
and content refers not to a declarative truth of the text but to the grooming
of a particular spiritual comportment or mode of acceding to the truth. Of
course, Schiller differs from Kant in identifying this comportment with a
reconciliation of intellect and feeling that transforms morality into inclination rather than with an overcoming of inclination that allows conduct
to be governed by pure ideas. But from the standpoint of our investigation,
this difference, far from being fundamental, is symptomatic only of differences in the overlapping milieux—philosophy seminar and literary reading
group—for which the hermeneutic exercises were adapted and to which
they gave shape. The moral intensification of literary cultivation that would
flow through Romanticism and into modern literary pedagogy should thus
be seen as an outcome of the aesthetic adaptation of the Christian hermeneutics of the self. Hence, if Schleiermacher could advise the educated elite
to read the Bible as literature, it was because this same group had already
learned to read literature using the exercises of self-problematization and
self-transformation developed for the spiritual reading of the holy book.

I should not like to leave the impression, however, that the post-Kantian
hermeneutic of Schiller and Schleiermacher exhausts the aesthetic domain. Their version of the aesthetic is of particular interest here only
because of its genealogical role in the formation of modern literary
theory. In her invaluable study *Die ästhetische Ordnung des Handelns*, Doris
Bachmann-Medick discusses the appearance of a different (though related)
deployment of aesthetics in early modern Germany. Emerging from the
so-called *Popularphilosophen* (nonacademic journalist-intellectuals such as
Feder, Garve, Meiners, and Nicolai) and significantly influenced by the
"anti-enthusiast" ethics and civics of Christian Thomasius, this aesthetic
questioned Kant's insistence on self-governance through reason alone. It
located the shaping of conduct outside pure reason, in empirical psychol-
ogy and in the actual (prudential) circumstances of political and social life.[44]
Unlike the tradition of critical–theoretical aesthetics that would flow from
Schiller through neo-Kantianism and into the work of Benjamin, Marcuse,

and Adorno, "popular-philosophical" aesthethics did not see the work of literature as a contemplative bulwark against the so-called instrumental administration of civil life. On the contrary, it found in literature's more vivid and empirical representation of the circumstances of moral struggle a practical means for investigating and shaping the new styles of comportment demanded by an emergent civil society. This "civil aesthetics" thus appears to be a path not taken—at least not by the critical hermeneutics of "university aesthetics"—but one perhaps with significant lessons for those who are today attempting to develop a less intellectualist and rejectionist aesthetic.

Finally, the Christian hermeneutics of the self can be linked to modern literary theory through its early modern deployment as a counter-politics. The political discourse characteristic of post-Kantian philosophy and aesthetics did not emerge as a positive knowledge of or intervention in the field of government. It appeared instead as a reaction to the radical transformation of that field associated with the development of the early modern territorial–administrative state. This is not to say, as Marxism has long held, that the aesthetic represents a sublimated or ideological expression of a "true" politics rendered impossible by the statist alienation of power or the capitalist division of labor.[45] In fact, that view—with its stationing of the aesthetic on one side of a stalled historical dialectic and its longing for a society that will reconcile the aesthetic and the material—should be regarded an *instance* of post-Kantian counter-political discourse.[46] This discourse did not emerge, however, as the ersatz expression of a historically delayed true politics. Rather, it was elaborated as a positive means of subordinating the empirical politics of the territorial state to a practice of philosophical–aesthetic critique. It was, in fact, the means by which a hostile intellectual caste measured this politics against the spiritual yardsticks of its own ethos—"reason," *Bildung*, aesthetic completeness—and, of course, found it wanting. Moreover, this discourse emerged not from some fragmentation of the moral "life–world"—the splitting of culture and society or of substantive and technical reason—but from the new relations between civil and religious governance that characterized the administrative state.

Without attempting to do any more than gesture toward a field of complex and particular historical developments, let us say that, driven by the early modern tasks of religious peacemaking and territorial state-building, a practice of politics emerged that was autonomous from spiritual ideals and that treated the state as an object of purely worldly knowledge and management. Emblematic of this new ordering of the political field was the reconstruction of the prince's "moral personality" undertaken by Christian Thomasius. Disputing the Lutheran doctrine that the prince should wield the two swords of spiritual and civil discipline, Thomasius asserted that the prince acts under three different capacities ("persons") that must not be confused. As a man, the prince is, like all men, bound by a natural moral law—to love his fellows. As a Christian, he must observe the laws of religion and seek his own salvation through personal piety. As for the "prince as prince," however, his conduct should be governed neither by moral law nor by Christian piety but by something reducible to neither: the ends of the state as a purely worldly historical entity. Chief among these ends is the establishment and maintenance of social peace (i.e., among warring confessions). And the pursuit of this end dictates that the government no longer concern itself with the inner faith and morality of the people (leading to religious tolerance) but only with their "outer" civil conduct.[47] Thomasius's work is thus indicative of a dissociation of the spheres of personal spirituality and social governance, and of the appearance of an intellectual stratum for whom politics was a practical problem rather than a hermeneutic occasion.

It was in and through its struggle against this "atheist-managerial" practice of government that post-Kantian philosophy and aesthetics gave birth to a specific counter-politics.[48] It should come as no surprise to us that this counter-politics centered on the defense of a particular spiritual comportment. As the spiritual discipline of a prestigious comportment and way of life—that of "secularized contemplatives"—post-Kantianism's own historical mode rendered it incapable of comprehending the new plurality of civil personae and ethical standpoints. In this regard, both Thomasius's pluralization of the prince's moral personality and the popular-philosophical use of literature as a kind of handbook for a variety of new civil styles of deportment represent more sober and flexible responses to their respective political circumstances. For its part, however, in reacting to the new plurality from the singularity of an elite practice of life (*Lebensführung*), post-Kantian "critique" condemned itself to representing the painstaking elaboration of new spheres of life and civil styles of deportment as the fragmentation of its own ideal comportment—the philosophically or aesthetically unified moral personality.

This is the historical light in which we must view all those depictions of the inner disintegration of man and society, including Schiller's, which was among the first and remains current: "Once the increase of empirical knowledge, and more exact modes of thought, made sharper divisions between the sciences inevitable, and once the increasingly complex machinery of State necessitated a more rigorous separation of ranks and occupations, then the inner unity of human nature was severed too, and a disastrous conflict set its [harmonious] powers at variance."[49] Far from being what they appear—accounts of the pluralization of the civil persona that accompanied the emergence of the administrative state—such discourses were actually devices for filtering out this reality, the means by which a sidelined spiritual intelligentsia could preserve its worldview, admitting the political only to the extent that it occasioned exercises in hermeneutic self-decipherment and self-transformation. Post-Kantian counter-politics thus took the form of a discourse that stigmatized empirical politics for its lack of moral transparency and that aspired to reunite political administration and spiritual self-determination under the aegis of a single moral personality—the people, the nation, the community, or humanity.

Kant's own discussion of political enlightenment in the *Conflict* presents us with a typical instance. Government, as the external imposition of social discipline, is viewed as a symptom of the people's historical moral and political incompetence. Manifested as the confusion of morality with sensuous well-being, this incompetence is the avenue through which government controls the people, blocking the path to rational self-governance by exploiting their literal belief in biblical rewards and punishments.[50] As we may recall, though, this political incompetence has a supra-political source. It is a projection of the moral anthropology that posits the citizen as an ethical being split between sensuous inclinations and pure ideas. In thus aspiring to make each person self-governing through rational self-reflection, this anthropology ignores the pluralized capacity for civil action and portends the collapse of the hard-won distinction between civil government and spiritual self-governance. Kant's identification of the empirical exercise of power with the occlusion of reason thus parallels his identification of true politics with the hermeneutic recovery of the capacity for action on the basis of rational contemplation. For by developing the self-clarification/-transformation exercise into an eschatological historicism, these teachings identify true politics with the historical cultivation of individuals capable of governing themselves through pure rational insight ("enlightenment"):

> The humiliating distinction between *laity* and *clergy* disappears, and equality arises from true freedom, yet without anarchy, because, though each obeys the (non-statutory) law which he prescribes to himself, he must at the same time regard this law as the will of a World-Ruler revealed to him through reason, a will which by invisible means unites all under one common government into one state—a state previously and inadequately prepared for by the visible church. . . . The basis for the transition to that new order of affairs must lie in the principle that the pure religion of reason is a continually occurring divine (though not empirical) revelation for all men.[51]

What some have called the Enlightenment project—that is, the will to close the gap between governmental administration and personal self-governance by inaugurating the rule of reason—might thus be better seen as the aspiration of an intellectual caste to maintain the prestige of its own ethos against the pluralization of civil comportment.

Again, there are those who would criticize Kant's "political rationalism" in the name of more conciliatory or historical principles—play, feeling, community—which they find better represented in the dialectics of Schiller or Schleiermacher (or Hegel or Marx).[52] And again such criticisms are idle from our standpoint here. In the case of Schiller, who does indeed attribute the division in man's ethical being to the division of labor and the specialization of politics—thereby identifying the reconciliation of intellect and feeling with the formation of a self-governing political community—these ostensibly more "sociological" and "communitarian" doctrines teach only a variant form of post-Kantian counter-politics. For Schiller's truly political community is shaped not by any actual (economic, military, legal, educational, or welfare) problem of governance but by a prescribed exercise in moral problematization: the problem that history poses and solves when, through the dialectical reconciliation of law and inclination, it gives rise to people who require no external political discipline—that is, people who obey the law because they are inclined to. Such people are, of course, simply an aesthetic variation on Kant's ideal political community, in which "each obeys the law which he prescribes to himself." In other words, the political disposition of self-governing people is a phantasmatic counter-political projection of the intellectual's own spiritual comportment.

The indelible sign of this counter-politics lies in its conversion of political realities into hermeneutic occasions. Said's treatment of imperialism as an expression of the "human" attempt to know and control "a radically unstable reality to which words approximate only by will or convention" can now be situated as a modern variant of post-Kantian counter-politics. By representing imperialism as a "closure" of contemplative insight, and by stigmatizing positive knowledge and empirical politics for their "assertive authority," Said's discourse provides us with a typical instance of the manner in which literary theory converts a political situation into an occasion for hermeneutic self-clarification. It is this conversion that allows the theorist's "bravura performances" to capture the misery of the people's historical fragmentation and the promise of their self-decipherment and reunification: "All these hybrid counter-energies, at work in many fields, individuals, and moments provide a community or culture made up of numerous anti-systemic hints and practices for collective human existence . . . that is not based on coercion or domination."[53] Were we to hold this appeal to a self-governing community accountable to any particular governmental problem, such as that faced by the United Nations in dealing with the "anti-systemic hints and practices" of the warring communities in Bosnia, we would find it connected to the actual political situation by only the slenderest of threads: the theorist's moral prestige. For this appeal too is neither more nor less than a counter-political projection of the theorist's own spiritual comportment.

═══

The civil disposition of literary theory is thus manifested not in the objects of its occasional political interpretations but in the comportment of the theorist for whom a political situation occasions an interpretative exercise. Literary criticism is connected to the sphere of government through pedagogical deployment rather than political knowledge. Moreover, it is not just because it is now taught in educational institutions that literary theory and criticism is pedagogical, for it is pedagogical at its intellectual core, being a discipline whose access to its object occurs only through the ethical grooming of the individuals so disciplined. I have written elsewhere about the historical circumstances in which the spiritual exercises of an intellectual elite were deployed, toward the end of the nineteenth century, as a social pedagogy in governmental school systems.[54] Here, it is enough to say that literary education was connected to social governance not through specialized knowledge but via prestigious deportment, for what this peda-

gogy delivered to government was a civil variant of the milieu of hermeneutic spiritual direction. And at the center of this milieu stands a figure
whose pedagogical authority derives from a "harmonious and clarified"
personality and from the hermeneutic exercises administered by such a
figure. The civil disposition of literary studies is thus formed in the seminar rooms of university English departments, and it is to this specialized
milieu that we turn now.

Let us consider two cases, the first being perhaps the earliest instance of
the fully developed academic English seminar—I. A. Richards's practical
criticism seminar assembled at Cambridge in the 1920s. In his published
account of this seminar, Richards describes his method of presenting the
students with various unattributed poems and recording their responses.
For our purposes, this account is remarkable not for its decipherment
of the seminarians' aesthetic sensibilities but for what it tells us about
the pedagogical milieu and relationship in which such decipherment was
routinized. For there—in the enigmatically presented poems, in the peda-
gogically extorted "stock responses" of the students, in the unimpeachable
insights of the teacher–critic to whom their sensibilities were revealed—
we find the indelible marks of an academic hermeneutics of the self (*Schul-
hermeneutik*).

Commenting on his students' rejection of "sentimental" phrases in
"Poem VIII" (Lawrence's *Piano*), for example, Richards remarks: "That the
poet might have a further use for such phrases, beyond that which his
readers made of them, they failed to notice in their uneasy haste to withdraw."[55] This, of course, is an updated version of Schiller's claim that the
apparent lack of form in the work of art "may just as often be evidence
of a lack of form in him who judges it." In short, it is indicative of the
poem's deployment as an instrument for the ethical problematization of
the reader—one designed to turn the reader inward to contemplate the
condition of his "sensibility." By Richards's time, though, this regimen was
no longer the voluntary practice of an aesthetic elite but the compulsory
discipline of a pedagogical cadre.

Like Schiller's, Richards's version of this discipline is contrapuntal. If
"Poem VIII" was used to reveal the students' emotional "inhibition" (as
manifested in their withdrawal from the immediacy of "feeling"), then
"Poem VII" was administered to uncover an inverse failure of sensibility,
"sentimentality": "Most of the admirers were more occupied by the effect

of the poem on their feelings than by the detail of the poem itself."[56] Thus, in their compulsory shifting between the poles of sentimentality and inhibition, didacticism ("doctrinal adhesion") and formalism ("technical presuppositions"), Richards's students were to move toward a "full realisation" of poetic meaning. It would be a mistake, though, to join the theorists of the 1970s and 1980s by identifying this New Critical immediacy of meaning as a pretheoretical "empiricism." For, unlike empirical observation, the "full realisation" of meaning is never to be attained. Instead, it can only be approached, through a series of contrapuntal acts of self-problematization, each one leaving the reader aesthetically off-balance—"too relaxed" or "too tense"—and forcing him to begin the reading again. The central characteristics of New Criticism—the form/content doctrine, the stigmatization of intention (paraphrase) and context (philological description), the practice of an inexhaustible "close reading"—thus derive not from methodological empiricism but from pedagogical deployment of the hermeneutics of the self.

Our second English seminar case derives from the theory boom itself and comes from the classroom of an American professor of literature, Stanley Fish. Like Richards's, Fish's attempt to show how reading occurs entails an "experiment" performed on his students. The similarities do not end there. Fish also presented his students with an unattributed "poem" (in fact a mere list of words) and required them to interpret it, misinforming them that it was a seventeenth-century devotional poem. Finally, Fish too observed his students' performances, deciphered their sensibilities— here, their latent reading conventions—and drew conclusions regarding the nature of literary interpretation and the best way to teach it. In particular, focusing on the class's ability to read the word list as a religious poem, Fish concluded: "Skilled reading is usually thought to be a matter of discerning what is there, but if the example of my students can be generalized, it is a matter of knowing how to *produce* what can thereafter be said to be there. Interpretation is not the art of construing but the art of constructing."[57] Lest it be thought that this would amount to a dangerous relativism or nihilism, however, Fish inverts the expected consequence— arguing that it is just because of the instability of interpreted meaning that we tacitly agree to stabilize it by forming "interpretive communities."[58] Fish's discourse thus organizes an antinomy between reason and authority. On the one hand, it sets off on the radical path of showing that all stable and objective meanings are, in fact, interpretive constructs open to willful transformation via theoretical reflection on their conventions. On the other hand, it is the very instability of meaning that drives interpreters into the community of shared conventions which, if it is to protect us against nihilism, must not be subject to theoretical reflection. Authority thus wears two faces, depending on whether it is construed as blocking access to rational self-decipherment (by ordering the false objectivity of meaning) or as guaranteeing such access (by ordaining the "tacit" conventions according to which an intersubjective community of meaning is formed). What disappears during this meditation on the "Authority of Interpretive Communities" is, of course, the teacher–critic's own authority in the seminar. Moreover, we can identify the point at which pedagogical authority vanishes, namely, when Fish presents the apparent meaning of the text as an interpretive construct whose reality lies elsewhere, in the institutional conventions that "produce" it. For if this pedagogical presentation is (as Fish claims) merely a dramatization of the process of human sense-making, then the teacher's authority is indeed merely the expression of processes inherent to subjectivity. Needless to say, this is far from being the case.

Despite its apparent novelty, Fish's claim that reading is not "a matter of discerning what is there" but "of knowing how to *produce* what can thereafter be said to be there" is, of course, one that we have met before. "In explaining the Bible to the people," we recall Kant saying, "the preacher must be guided, not by what scholarship *draws out* of Scripture by philological studies . . . but by what a moral cast of mind . . . *puts into* it." Moreover, as we also recall, this claim belongs to a specific spiritual discipline—one in which the student is required to doubt his initial (external) perceptions as the means of constituting himself as an object of self-decipherment. Fish's instruction to read the text as a poem, followed by his revelation that it isn't one, can thus be regarded as an exercise for inducing self-doubt (*skepsis*), that is, as a means of compelling his students to cross the seminar's hermeneutic threshold. Finally, we may recall that in Kant this act of self-problematization is followed not by the discovery of a doctrinal truth but by a controlled intellectual oscillation between two opposed doctrines: an orthodoxy that identifies moral redemption with the institutionally ordained meaning of the letter and a heterodoxy that identifies it with the individually intuited spirit. And this dialectical exercise is present in Fish's account too. For his resolution of the dilemma between orthodoxy and nihilism—his notion of individuals achieving "community" by treating their constructed meanings as if they were institutionally ordained—is not a "truth"; it is a deportment of the self with regard to meaning, a way of acceding to the truth, formed only through the exercise. In Fish's case, this prestigious deportment is that of the personage who, having forsaken the bonds of institution through reflection and seen into the arbitrariness of meaning, reinvents community as the guarantor of meaning's stability.

Those who thought they saw in Fish's "reader-response" theory (and its cognates) the signs of a nihilistic relativism could not have been more mistaken. Here the relativizing of meaning takes place only as the opening exercise—the move of hermeneutic self-problematization—in a series designed to induct students into a specialized disciplinary milieu. In this milieu, self-doubt is a task of behavior and the students' responses are acts of self-revelation, confessions made to a teacher whose exemplary reconciliation of reason and authority equips him with the persona of the spiritual guide. Hence, far from representing fundamentally opposed kinds of literary studies, (Fishian) literary theory and (Ricardian) New Criticism can be regarded as optionally equivalent variants of the academic hermeneutics of the self. It is not the "postmodern" splintering of meaning and fracturing of selves that characterizes literary studies today, for this is just an emblem worn by those undergoing a certain civil–spiritual training. What characterizes such studies are the relations of self-examination and supervision, the exercises in self-decipherment and self-realization, that the representations of splintering and division are used to initiate.

If we are to understand the civil consequences of this hermeneutic pedagogy, then, we may have to cease trying to derive them from a hermeneutic investigation of literature and society or aesthetics and politics. In place of such an investigation, which is in fact a symptom of this pedagogy, we might better understand literary theory as an outcome of the civil deployment of the Christian hermeneutics of the self.

≡

To describe modern literary theory as the outcome of the civil deployment of the Christian hermeneutics of the self does not by itself amount to a critique, least of all a critique in the sense of exposing literary theory as an ideological obstacle to a "deeper" process of human becoming. On the contrary, discovering theory's dependence on specific spiritual exercises has allowed us to assert its autonomy as a particular practice of the self and sphere of life. At the same time, we have not, of course, remained within the self-understanding of literary theory. We have discovered that theory is based not on a positive knowledge of texts but on their use as instruments of hermeneutic grooming. In doing so, we have shifted our focus from theoretical disputes over the true nature of literature's hidden operations to the investigation of literary theory as a particular way of acceding to the truth—as the uncovering of literature's hidden operations.

Similarly, in recognizing that literary theory relates to empirical politics not as a positive knowledge or intervention but as a counter-political defense of a particular spiritual deportment, we have effectively reframed the debate around literature and politics. Arguments over which variant of literary theory will best decipher and liberate the divided energies of an ideal political community thereby become idle, while the important question becomes why every variant assumes that politics entails deciphering man's occluded ethical being and dialectically reconciling the fragments of a once and future humanity. The answer, it seems to us, is that literary theory's "political" discourse is actually a means of converting political situations into hermeneutic occasions. Therefore, grasping literary theory's civil disposition entails understanding its historical relation, as a sphere of life, to the governmental management of the territorial state that forms the political envelope for all such spheres. Unfortunately, this relation cannot be understood from within the hermeneutic horizon of literary theory itself, for, as we have seen, the post-Kantian counter-politics inherited by this theory developed in reaction to the governmental pluralization of the moral personality that actually constitutes the domain of civil governance. The condition for this zone of "liberal" tolerance is, in fact, civil government's agnosticism regarding true moral personhood, coupled with its power to constrain any group wishing to impose a particular truth on others. To the extent that it takes itself seriously as the vehicle for humanity's true self-decipherment and self-realization—whether vested in the people, the community, women, ethnic minorities, or postcolonial peoples—literary theory necessarily undergoes a historical regression, rejoining the religious sects and political factions that aspire to "reform" society by uncovering its hidden truth.

Finally, there is, of course, no need for literary theory to take itself this seriously—and, perhaps, few theorists who actually do. The civil role of modern literary studies is determined not by its hermeneutic decipherment of true community but by the historical contingencies through which a spiritual discipline was redeployed as a governmental pedagogy. Literary theory, as we have discovered, relates to social governance via the prestigious deportment of the teacher–theorist. Holding sway in the hermeneutic milieu of the seminar through a civil variant of spiritual guidance, this figure is charged with forming the "teachers of the people" who staff our pastorally organized school systems. Few would dispute that the self-reflective and self-cultivating persona formed in this milieu remains among those that European societies count as valuable. Individuals dedicated wholly to the milieu, however, run the occupational risk of imagining that their group ethos—aesthetic wholeness, reason, *Humanität*, complete development, *Bildung*, the Enlightenment project, community—represents the true form of human being rather than just a prestigious ethical comportment. When it comes to their roles as citizens, then, it is important for literary theorists not to take their work home with them.

Notes

A number of the ideas for this article were developed in the spring 1995 semester during my time as Hinkley Professor in the Department of English at Johns Hopkins University. In addition to thanking my then colleagues for providing me with a welcoming and productive intellectual environment, I would like to acknowledge the work of the members of my seminar—Courtney Berger, Daniel Denecke, Will Harris, Elizabeth Kelleher, Tina Kelleher, Lara Kriegel, Leah Pettway, and Douglas Robertson—many of whose contributions have found their way into this paper. I am also grateful to John Frow, Wayne Hudson, Noel King, Vassilis Lambropoulos, Denise Meredyth, Jeffrey Minson, Meaghan Morris, Mary Poovey, Tim Rowse, and David Saunders for their questioning and commentary.

1   See Max Weber, *Economy and Society: An Outline of Interpretive Sociology*, 2 vols. (New York, 1968), 2: 1047–51.

2   See Peter Brown, *Power and Persuasion in Late Antiquity: Towards a Christian Empire* (Madison, 1992), 35–70.

3   See Gerhard Oestreich, *Neostoicism and the Early Modern State* (Cambridge, 1982), 39–56; and "Die antike Literatur als Vorbild der praktischen Wissenschaften im 16. und 17. Jahrhundert," in *Classical Influences on European Culture A.D. 1500–1700*, ed. R. R. Bolgar (Cambridge, 1971), 315–24; see also Justus Lipsius, *Of Constancie* (New Brunswick, 1939), 87.

4   For basic accounts of the relation between Protestant discipline and print-disseminated literature, see Elizabeth Eisenstein, "The Advent of Printing and the Protestant Revolt: A New Approach to the Disruption of Western Christendom," in *Transition and Revo-*

lution: Problems and Issues of European Renaissance and Reformation History, ed. R. M. Kingdon (Minneapolis, 1974), 231–62; Lawrence Stone, "Literacy and Education in England 1640–1900," *Past and Present* 42 (1969): 76–83; and Isabel Rivers, "Dissenting and Methodist Books of Practical Divinity," in *Books and Their Readers in Eighteenth-Century England*, ed. I. Rivers (Leicester, 1982), 127–64. On the emergence of the novel from this milieu, see J. P. Hunter, *The Reluctant Pilgrim: Defoe's Emblematic Method and the Quest for Form in Robinson Crusoe* (Baltimore, 1966).

5 See John Feather, *The Provincial Book Trade in Eighteenth-Century England* (Cambridge, 1985), 40–43; and Richard Altick, *The English Common Reader* (Chicago, 1957), chap. 5.

6 For some differing accounts of this development, all of which are also symptomatic expressions of it, see Chris Baldick, *The Social Mission of English Criticism, 1848–1932* (Oxford, 1983); John Dixon, *A Schooling in "English"* (Milton Keynes, 1991); Gerald Graff, *Professing Literature: An Institutional History* (Chicago, 1987); and Gauri Viswanathan, *The Masks of Conquest: Literary Study and British Rule in India* (New York, 1989).

7 For further discussion, see Ian Hunter, *Culture and Government: The Emergence of Literary Education* (London, 1988); and "History Lessons for English," *Cultural Studies* 8 (1994): 142–61. Following Foucault, I use "governmental" for any sizeable program of social governance, whether originating in state action, organized religion, or private philanthropy.

8 Terry Eagleton, *Literary Theory: An Introduction* (Oxford, 1983), 210.

9 Jacques Derrida, "Mochlos; or, the Conflict of the Faculties," in *Logomachia: The Conflict of the Faculties*, ed. R. Rand (Lincoln, 1992), 3–34; quotation from 15.

10 For further discussion, see Paul Rabbow, *Seelenführung: Methodik der Exerzitien in der Antike* (Munich, 1954); and Pierre Hadot, *Exercises spirituels et philosophie antique* (Paris, 1981), recently revised and translated by M. Chase as *Philosophy as a Way of Life* (Oxford, 1995).

11 Edward Said, *Culture and Imperialism* (London, 1993), 24; his emphasis here and in subsequent quotations.

12 Ibid., 115, 113–14.

13 Ibid., 33.

14 Ibid.

15 Ibid., 114.

16 Ibid., 33.

17 For a discussion of the Pyrrhonist use of this exercise, see Julia Annas, "Doing without Objective Values: Ancient and Modern Strategies," in *The Norms of Nature: Studies in Hellenistic Ethics*, ed. Malcolm Schofield and Gisela Striker (Cambridge, 1986), 3–30.

18 The illustrative quotations are from Said, *Culture and Imperialism*, 113–16.

19 Ibid., 366–67.

20 Ibid., 378.

21 Ibid., 403.

22 See Michel Foucault, "About the Beginning of the Hermeneutics of the Self: Two Lectures at Dartmouth," *Political Theory* 21 (1993): 198–227. I make no comment on the historical adequacy of Foucault's contrast between pagan mnemonics and Christian hermeneutics, and particularly on the difficult question of whether the terms of com-

parison are pertinent to Neoplatonic (as opposed to Stoic and Epicurean) philosophy. Here I am only clarifying the character of the hermeneutics of the self as a discrete ethical practice, leaving open the question of its relation to particular Greek and Roman philosophical schools.

23 For a detailed description, see Rabbow, *Seelenführung*.

24 See Michel Foucault, "L'Ecriture de soi," *Corps écrit* 5 (1983): 3–23.

25 John Cassian, "Cassian's Conferences," in *A Select Library of Nicene and Post-Nicene Fathers of the Christian Church*, ed. Philip Schaff and Henry Wace (Grand Rapids, 1952), II: 306.

26 See Henning Graff Reventlow, *The Authority of the Bible and the Rise of the Modern World*, trans. James Bowden (Philadelphia, 1985), 147–84.

27 For a parallel argument, see Hans Erich Bödeker, "Die Religiosität der Gebildeten," in *Religionskritik und Religiosität in der deutschen Aufklärung*, ed. K. Gründer and K. H. Rengstorf (Heidelberg, 1989), 145–96.

28 For a historically specific account of the process of confessionalization showing that the political consequences of theological doctrines cannot be determined without investigating their use by particular social and political groups, see Heinz Schilling, "Between the Territorial State and Urban Liberty: Lutheranism and Calvinism in the County of Lippe," in *The German People and the Reformation*, ed. R. Po-chia Hsia (Ithaca, 1988), 263–84. See also R. Po-chia Hsia, *Social Discipline in the Reformation: Central Europe 1550–1750* (London, 1989).

29 R. Emmet McLaughlin has argued that in Germany the universities played this crucial bridging role. He treats the anti-sacramental, inward, and "scripturalist" character of Reformation religion and philosophy as characteristic of the spiritual *Bildung* of the university milieu, later transmitted more broadly via pastoral pedagogy; see "Universities, Scholasticism and the Origins of the German Reformation," *History of Universities* 9 (1990): 1–44. Seen in this historical light, Kant appears to have been representative of a specific spiritual habitus rather than the radical innovator of a novel rational Enlightenment.

30 Immanuel Kant, *The Conflict of the Faculties* (1798), trans. Mary J. Gregor (Lincoln, NE, 1979), 87; his emphases here and in subsequent quotations.

31 Ibid., 63, 61–67.

32 Ibid., 125.

33 Ibid., 121.

34 Immanuel Kant, *Religion within the Limits of Reason Alone* (1793), trans. T. M. Greene and H. H. Hudson (London, 1934), 102. For an account of the bitter conflict between Kantians and historical theologians at the University of Jena in the 1790s, see Bodo Seidel, "Kant und die Zielgerade der Historiotheologie in der Späten Aufklärung," in *Der Aufbruch in den Kantianismus: Der Frükantianismus an der Universität Jena von 1785–1800 und seine Vorgeschichte*, ed. N. Hinske, E. Lange, and H. Schröpfer (Stuttgart–Bad Cannstatt, 1995), 139–70.

35 Kant, *Conflict*, 97; *Religion*, 109.

36 Kant, *Conflict*, 107; see also *Religion*, 110.

37 Friedrich Schiller, *On the Aesthetic Education of Man* (1795), trans. E. M. Wilkinson and L. A. Willoughby (Oxford, 1967), 141.

38 Friedrich Schiller, "Über Anmuth und Würde" (1795), in *Schillers Werke: National-ausgabe*, ed. Benno von Wies (Weimar, 1962), 20: 251–309.

39 Friedrich Schleiermacher, *On Religion: Speeches to Its Cultured Despisers* (1799), trans. Roger Crouter (Cambridge, 1988), 141–61.

40 See, for example, Hans Reiner, *Duty and Inclination: The Fundamentals of Morality Discussed with Special Regard to Kant and Schiller* (The Hague, 1983); and Roger Crouter's introduction to his translation of Schleiermacher's *On Religion*.

41 For an important empirical study of the general shift from the lecture-based teaching of philosophy as a "canon of subjects" to a pedagogy based on hermeneutic seminars devoted to the texts of great philosophers, see Ulrich Johannes Schneider, "The Teaching of Philosophy at German Universities in the Nineteenth Century," *History of Universities* 12 (1993): 197–338.

The circle around Susanna von Klettenberg was representative of Schiller's milieu. Possessing the leisure, education, and means to make her own personality the chief object of her life, this beautiful spirit was at the center of an epistolary network that included the Pietist leader Count Zinzendorf, on one side, and, on the other, Goethe, Lavater, and Schiller. Her major letters and meditations, which mark the point at which Pietist ascetic inwardness crossed over into aesthetic self-cultivation, are collected in *Die schöne Seele: Bekenntnisse, Schriften und Briefe der Susanna Katharina von Klettenberg herausgegeben von Heinrich Funck* (Leipzig, 1912).

42 For further discussion of this transformation, see Bödeker, "Religiosität"; and Volker Kapp, "Der Einfluß der französischen Spiritualität auf das deutsche Geistesleben des 18. Jahrhunderts," in Gründer and Rengstorf, eds., *Religionskritik*, 25–42.

43 Schiller, *Aesthetic Education*, 157.

44 See Doris Bachmann-Medick, *Die ästhetische Ordnung des Handelns: Moralphilosophie und Asthetik in der Popularphilosophie des 18. Jahrhunderts* (Stuttgart, 1989), 18–38.

45 See, for example, Terry Eagleton, *The Ideology of the Aesthetic* (Oxford, 1990); and David Lloyd, "Analogies of the Aesthetic: The Politics of Culture and the Limits of Materialist Aesthetics," *New Formations* 10 (1990): 109–26.

46 I have argued this case in "Aesthetics and Cultural Studies," in *Cultural Studies*, ed. Lawrence Grossberg, Cary Nelson, and Paula Treichler (New York, 1992), 347–66.

47 See Christian Thomasius and E. R. Brenneysen, *Das Recht Evangelischer Fürsten in Theologische Streitigkeiten* (Halle, 1696), 26–29.

48 For a striking and underutilized account of this development, see Reinhart Koselleck, *Critique and Crisis: Enlightenment and the Pathogenesis of Modern Society* (Oxford, 1988).

49 Schiller, *Aesthetic Education*, 33.

50 Kant, *Conflict*, 47–59.

51 Kant, *Religion*, 112–13.

52 For a discussion that works within these terms of reference, see Josef Chytry, *The Aesthetic State: A Quest in Modern German Thought* (Berkeley, 1989). See also the works cited in notes 40 and 45.

53   Said, *Culture and Imperialism*, 406.

54   Hunter, *Culture and Government*; and "History Lessons for English"; see also Ian Hunter, *Rethinking the School* (Sydney and New York, 1994).

55   I. A. Richards, *Practical Criticism: A Study of Literary Judgment* (London, 1929), 109.

56   Ibid., 100.

57   Stanley Fish, *Is There a Text in This Class? The Authority of Interpretive Communities* (Cambridge, MA, 1980), 327.

58   Ibid., 331–32.

Notes on Contributors

REY CHOW, Professor of English and Comparative Literature at UC–Irvine, is the author of *Woman and Chinese Modernity* (1991), *Writing Diaspora* (1993), *Primitive Passions* (1995), and *Ethics after Idealism* (forthcoming from Indiana University Press).

DAVID AMES CURTIS is a translator, editor, writer, and activist whose work has appeared in U.S., European, and Australian books and journals. His book-length translations include works by Cornelius Castoriadis, Pierre Vidal-Naquet, and Dick Howard.

J. PETER EUBEN, Professor and Chair of Politics at UC–Santa Cruz, is the coeditor of *Athenian Political Thought and the Reconstitution of American Democracy* (1994) as well as the author of *The Tragedy of Political Theory* (1990) and *Corrupting Youth: Socratic Political Education and Democratic Politics* (forthcoming from Princeton University Press).

IAN HUNTER is an Australian Research Council Fellow in the Faculty of Humanities, Griffith University. He is the author of several books and articles on the historical formation of ethical deportments, including *Culture and Government: The Emergence of Literary Education* (1988) and "The Regimen of Reason: Kant's Defence of the Philosophy Faculty" (*Oxford Literary Review*, 1995).

PETER JASZI, Washington College of Law, The American University, is the coauthor (with Craig Joyce, William Patry, and Marshall Leaffer) of a standard text on copyright and the coeditor (with Martha Woodmansee) of *The Construction of Authorship* (1994). Currently, he is coediting (with Woodmansee) a Duke University Press series on "Cultures of Authorship."

VICTORIA KAHN is Professor of English and Comparative Literature at UC–Irvine and the author, most recently, of *Machiavellian Rhetoric: From the Counter-Reformation to Milton* (1994).

VASSILIS LAMBROPOULOS, Professor of Modern Greek at The Ohio State University, is the author of *Literature as National Institution: Studies in the Politics of Modern Greek Criticism* (1988) and *The Rise of Eurocentrism: Anatomy of Interpretation* (1993).

CLAUDE LEFORT, currently affiliated with the Centre de Recherches Politiques Raymond Aron, Ecole des Hautes Etudes en Sciences Sociales, is the author of numerous political and philosophical works in French as well as two collections of essays in translation, *Democracy and Political Theory* (1986) and *The Political Forms of Modern Society* (1988).

ADAM ZACHARY NEWTON, Assistant Professor of English, University of Texas–Austin, is the author of the prize-winning *Narrative Ethics* (1995) and the forthcoming *Facing Black and Jew: Re-Imagining American Literary History*. His article "Déjà-vu All Over Again: *Fires in the Mirror, Homicide*, and the Simpson Trial" is forthcoming in *Literary Encounters: African Americans and American Jews*, ed. Carole Kessner (Wayne State University Press).

LEONARD TENNENHOUSE teaches in the Comparative Literature, Modern Culture and Media, and English departments at Brown University. He is the author of *Power on Display: The Politics of Shakespeare's Genres* (1986) and coauthor (with Nancy Armstrong) of *The Imaginary Puritan: Literature, Intellectual Labor, and the Origins of Personal Life* (1992).

RICHARD H. WEISBERG, Floersheimer Professor of Constitutional Law, Cardozo Law School, Yeshiva University, is the author of *The Failure of the Word: The Protagonist as Lawyer in Modern Fiction* (2d ed., 1989), *Poethics* (1992), and *Vichy Law and the Holocaust in France* (1996).

MARTHA WOODMANSEE is Professor of English at Case Western Reserve University. Her works include *The Author, Art, and the Market* (1994) and (with coeditor Peter Jaszi) *The Construction of Authorship* (1994).

The South Atlantic Quarterly

Volume 95
Copyright © 1996 by Duke University Press
Durham, North Carolina

Contents of Volume 95

Allitt, Patrick, English Cricket and Literature 385

Batten, Guinn, "He Could Barely Tell One from the Other": The Borderline Disorders of Paul Muldoon 171

Carlson, Julie A., Forever Young: Master Betty and the Queer Stage of Youth in English Romanticism 575

Chow, Rey, We Endure, Therefore We Are: Survival, Governance, and Zhang Yimou's *To Live* 1039

Christensen, Jerome, The Detection of the Romantic Conspiracy in Britain 603

Cleary, Joe, "Fork-Tongued on the Border Bit": Partition and the Politics of Form in Contemporary Narratives of the Northern Irish Conflict 227

Deloria, Philip, "I Am of the Body": Thoughts on My Grandfather, Culture, and Sports 321

Dodd, Luke, Famine Echoes 97

Euben, J. Peter, When There Are Gray Skies: Aristophanes' *Clouds* and the Political Education of Democratic Citizens 881

Fabian, Ann, Gamblers in the Garden: The Political Consequences of the Fix 501

Fisher, James T., Editor's Note [*Real Sports*] 279

Fisher, James T., "The Great Beader": Pete Axthelm and the Bonds of Tradition 523

Gibbons, Luke, Topographies of Terror: Killarney and the Politics of the Sublime 23

Gleckner, Robert F., Blake's "Dark Visions of Torment" Unfolded: *Innocence* to *Jerusalem* 699

Goldsmith, Steven, Blake's Agitation 753

González Echevarría, Roberto, Literature, Dance, and Baseball in the Last Cuban Fin de Siècle 365

Haag, Pamela, "The 50,000-Watt Sports Bar": Talk Radio and the Ethic of the Fan 453

Hogle, Jerrold E., The Gothic and the "Otherings" of Ascendant Culture: The Original *Phantom of the Opera* 821

Hunter, Ian, Literary Theory in Civil Life 1099

Jaszi, Peter, and Martha Woodmansee, The Ethical Reaches of Authorship 947

Johnston, Dillon, Cross-Currencies in the Culture Market: Arnold, Yeats, Joyce 45

Kahn, Victoria, Political Theology and Reason of State in *Samson Agonistes* 1065

Kellogg, David, Kinsella, Geography, History 145

Kercsmar, Rhonda Ray, Displaced Apocalypse and Eschatological Anxiety in *Frankenstein* 729

Kiberd, Declan, The Periphery and the Center 5

Lambropoulos, Vassilis, Introduction: Approaches to Ethical Politics 849

Lambropoulos, Vassilis, Nomoscopic Analysis 855

Lefort, Claude, Sade: The Boudoir and the City 1009

Mee, Jon, Apocalypse and Ambivalence: The Politics of Millenarianism in the 1790s 671

Newton, Adam Zachary, From Exegesis to Ethics: Recognition and Its Vicissitudes in Saul Bellow and Chester Himes 979

O'Brien, Áine, Marketing and Managing Colonial Spectacle as National History: In the Belly of the Archive 103

Oriard, Michael, Home Teams 471

Parker, Kenneth L., Never on a Sunday: Why Sunday Afternoon Sports Transformed Seventeenth-Century England 339

Pettitt, Lance, G(ay)uinness Is Good for You 205

Pfau, Thomas, "Beyond the Suburbs of the Mind": The Political and Aesthetic Disciplining of the Romantic Body 629

Pfau, Thomas, and Rhonda Ray Kercsmar, Editors' Note [*Rhetorical and Cultural Dissolution in Romanticism*] 571

Rachman, Stephen, It Isn't Easy Being Green 437

Rajan, Tilottama, Coleridge, Wordsworth, and the Textual Abject 797

Rotella, Carlo, Three Views of the Fistic Summits from College Hill 281

Taylor, Lawrence J., "There Are Two Things that People Don't Like to Hear about Themselves": The Anthropology of Ireland and the Irish View of Anthropology 213

Tennenhouse, Leonard, The Case of the Resistant Captive 919

Waters, John Paul, Introduction [*Ireland and Irish Cultural Studies*] 1

Weisberg, Richard H., The Text as Legislator: *Devoir* and the Millennial Stendhal 1029

Wills, Clair, Joyce, Prostitution, and the Colonial City 79

No. 1, Winter, pp. 1–278; No. 2, Spring, pp. 279–569; No. 3, Summer, pp. 571–848; No. 4, Fall, pp. 849–1139.

Theories of History
History of Theories

Early Postmodernism: Foundational Essays
Paul A. Bové, editor

Paul Bové assembles distinguished and influential statements of *boundary 2*'s 1972-1982 era into a basic text in the history of post-modernism. Essays by noted cultural and literary theorists join with Bové's contemporary preface to represent the important and unique moment in recent intellectual history when post-modernism was finding power and place in the literary realm.

304 pages, paper $17.95, library cloth edition $49.95

a *boundary 2* book

Theories and Narratives: Reflections on the Philosophy of History
Alex Callinicos

Theories and Narratives explores the relationship between historical writing and theoretical understanding and seeks to establish the legitimate scope of large-scale theories to grasp historical processes as a whole.

264 pages, paper $16.95, library cloth edition $45.00

Post-Contemporary Interventions

Duke University Press
Box 90660 • Durham, NC
• 27708-0660

qui parle

Twice a year, **qui parle** publishes provocative interdisciplinary articles, covering a range of new outstanding theoretical and critical work in the humanities. Founded in 1986 by an editorial board from the University of California at Berkeley, **qui parle** is dedicated to expanding the dialogues that take place between and among disciplines, and that challenge received notions about reading and scholarship in the university.

Recently published articles include:

8:2 Miran Božovič, "'An Utterly Dark Spot': The Fiction of
      God in Bentham's Panopticon"
      Amos Funkenstein, "Terrorism and Theory"
      Thomas Laqueur, "Masturbation, Credit and the Novel
      During the Long Eighteenth Century"
8:1 Alexander García Düttmann, "On Translatability"
      Jane Gallop, "The Translation of Deconstruction"
      Ann Smock, "On Jean Paulhan's *Récits*"
7:2 John Dolan, "'Today the Mind is Not Part of the
      Weather': Cognitive and Rhetorical Perspectives on
      the Construction of Poetic Metaphor"
      Jerry Herron, "Facing Death: Modernity, Morality,
      Postcards"
7:1 Benedict Anderson, "Replica, Aura, and Late Nationalist
      Imaginings"
      Stathis Gourgouris, "Notes on the Nation's Dreamwork"
      Michael Hardt, "On John Rawls' *Political Liberalism*"

SUBSCRIPTIONS

individual $14 one year $25 two years
institutional $30 one year $60 two years
student $8 one year $16 two years

Inquiries, submissions and subscriptions:
qui parle, The Doreen B. Townsend Center for the Humanities
460 Stephens Hall, University of California
Berkeley, CA 94720-2340
quiparle@garnet.berkeley.edu

Learning Processes with a Deadly Outcome

Alexander Kluge
Translated by Christopher Pavsek

With this translation of *Learning Processes with a Deadly Outcome*, a novella first published in German in 1973, one of Kluge's most important literary works becomes available to an English-speaking audience. Written in a quasi-documentary style, this hybrid work combines science fiction with modernist forms of montage and reportage to describe a future in which Earth has been almost totally destroyed following the catastrophic Black War.

Kluge gives us some of his most bizarre and hilarious characters in this peculiar world in which the remains of the past are mixed with the most advanced elements of the future. The cast includes highly specialized women workers who have adapted to the massive gravitational field of their heavy-metal planets, a commander with lethal foot-fungus, and ex-Nazi space pioneers who, in their lonely exile from the conflagrations on earth, spend their time carving enormous facsimiles of operatic sheet music in the forests of uninhabited planets.

128 pages, 55 b&w photographs, paper $13.95, library cloth edition $36.95

Duke University Press Box 90660 Durham, North Carolina 27708-0660
http://www.duke.edu/web/dupress/

differences

A Journal of Feminist Cultural Studies,
edited by Naomi Schor and Elizabeth Weed, focuses on how concepts and
categories of difference—notably but not exclusively gender—
operate within culture.

More Gender Trouble: Feminism Meets Queer Theory

Introduction: Against Proper Objects
by Judith Butler

Interview: Feminism by Any
Other Name by Rosi Braidotti
with Judith Butler

Interview: Sexual Traffic by Gayle Rubin
with Judith Butler

Extraordinary Homosexuals and the Fear
of Being Ordinary by Biddy Martin

Black (W)holes and the Geometry of
Black Female Sexuality by Evelynn
Hammonds

Camp, Masculinity, Masquerade
by Kim Michasiw

Melancholic Modernity: The
Hom(m)osexual Symptom and the
Homosocial Corpse by Trevor Hope

Passing, Narcissism, Identity, and
Difference by Carole-Anne Tyler

The More Things Change
by Elizabeth Weed

The Labors of Love, Analyzing Perverse
Desire: An Interrogation of Teresa de
Lauretis's The Practice of Love
by Elizabeth Grosz

Responses by Rosi Braidotti, Trevor
Hope, and Teresa de Lauretis

Price: $14.95

Volume 7, Number 3

Baby Killers by Jonathan Crewe

How to Do Things with Fetishism
by E.L. McCallum

(Dis)figuring the Nation: Mother,
Metaphor, Metonymy by Sandhya Sheety

The Hollow Women: Modernism,
The Prostitute, and Commodity
Aesthetics by Laurie Teal

Reconstructions: Prosthetics and the
Rehabilitation of the Male Body in World
War I France by Roxanne Panchasi

Mechanizing the Female: Discourse
and Control in the Industrial Economy
by Katherine Stubbs

Price: $10.00

Subscriptions (3 issues)
Individuals: $32.00
Institutions: $65.00
Surface post outside the USA: $10.00

Single Issues:
Add $3.00 postage and handling
for the first and $1.00 each additional

Journals Division,
Indiana University Press,
601 N. Morton, Bloomington, IN 47404

Phone: 812-855-9449
Fax: 812-855-8507

E-Mail: Journals@Indiana.Edu
http://www.indiana.edu/~iupress

COLONIALISM & CULTURE FROM DUKE

PHANTASMATIC INDOCHINA
French Colonial Ideology in Architecture, Film, and
Literature • Panivong Norindr
240 pages, paper $16.95, library cloth edition $44.95
Asia-Pacific

WHOSE INDIA?
The Independence Struggle in British and Indian
Fiction and History • Teresa Hubel
248 pages, paper $16.95, library cloth edition $46.95

A RULE OF PROPERTY FOR BENGAL
An Essay on the Idea of Permanent Settlement
Ranajit Guha
With a Foreword by Amartya Sen
264 pages, paper $17.95, library cloth edition $49.95

DISPLACEMENT, DIASPORA, AND
GEOGRAPHIES OF IDENTITY
Smadar Lavie and Ted Swedenburg, editors
344 pages, 6 b&w photographs, paper $16.95, library
cloth edition $49.95

DUKE UNIVERSITY PRESS
Box 90660 Durham, North Carolina 27708-0660
http://www.duke.edu/web/dupress/

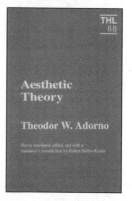